D0931211

Transparency in Global Environmental Governance

© 2014 Massachusetts Institute of Technology

MIT Press books may be purchased at special quantity discounts for business or sales promotional use. For information, please email special_sales@mitpress.mit.edu.

This book was set in Sabon by the MIT Press. Printed and bound in the United States of America.

Library of Congress Cataloging-in-Publication Data

Transparency in global environmental governance : critical perspectives / edited by Aarti Gupta and Michael Mason.
    pages   cm. — (Earth system governance)
Includes bibliographical references and index.
ISBN 978-0-262-02741-0 (hardcover : alk. paper) — ISBN 978-0-262-52618-0 (pbk. : alk. paper)
1. Environmental policy—International cooperation. 2. Transparency in government—International cooperation. 3. Global environmental change—International cooperation.
I. Gupta, Aarti, 1967–
GE170.T77   2014
333.7—dc23
2013043435

10   9   8   7   6   5   4   3   2   1

Contents

Series Foreword

Humans now influence all biological and physical systems of the planet. Almost no species, no land area, and no part of the oceans have remained unaffected by the expansion of the human species. Recent scientific findings suggest that the entire earth system now operates outside the normal state exhibited over the past 500,000 years. Yet at the same time, it is apparent that the institutions, organizations, and mechanisms by which humans govern their relationship with the natural environment and global biogeochemical systems are utterly insufficient—and poorly understood. More fundamental and applied research is needed.

Yet such research is no easy undertaking. It must span the entire globe because only integrated global solutions can ensure a sustainable coevolution of natural and socioeconomic systems. But it must also draw on local experiences and insights. Research on earth system governance must be about places in all their diversity, yet seek to integrate place-based research within a global understanding of the myriad human interactions with the earth system. Eventually, the task is to develop integrated systems of governance, from the local to the global level, that ensure the sustainable development of the coupled socioecological system that the Earth has become.

The series Earth System Governance is designed to address this research challenge. Books in this series will pursue this challenge from a variety of disciplinary perspectives, at different levels of governance, and with a plurality of methods. Yet all will further one common aim: analyzing current systems of earth system governance with a view to increased understanding and possible improvements and reform. Books in this series will be of interest to the academic community but will also inform practitioners and at times contribute to policy debates.

This series is related to the long-term international research program "Earth System Governance Project."

Frank Biermann, VU University Amsterdam and Lund University
Oran R. Young, University of California, Santa Barbara
Earth System Governance Series Editors

Preface

As this book goes to press in late 2013, Edward Snowden, the US National Security Agency "whistleblower," is suspended in limbo in Russia, unable to make his way out; and the geopolitics of surveillance versus transparency (and its consequences for diplomacy, human rights, national sovereignty, and global security) is front-page news everywhere. Debates rage about whether Snowden is a traitor or a hero for revealing that the United States is engaged in covert surveillance of its own citizenry, the citizenry of other countries, and of (friendly and not so friendly) governments worldwide.

In light of these revelations, the need for transparency to disclose what the powerful are doing, and to hold them to account, seems ever more urgent. Yet, even as the practices of surveillance are routinely condemned, its counterpart, transparency, is not necessarily the panacea that it is made out to be. This is so whether transparency is about the practices of surveillance (as with Snowden's revelations) or about national security threats, the practices of war and diplomacy, financial and economic relations, or even (relatively more benignly) about the environmental performance of different powerful actors.

This book explores the claim that transparency is *not* a panacea by addressing the workings of transparency and disclosure in the global environmental and sustainability realm. Although transparency has always been front and center in certain domains of international relations, its power and its promise to effect desired changes in global sustainability governance is only now receiving more attention.

This edited book thus explores the phenomenon of "governance-by-disclosure" in global environmental governance. It has its genesis in a *Forum* article in the journal *Global Environmental Politics (GEP)* in 2008, in which one of us suggested that transparency was a curiously understudied phenomenon in our field, even though it was becoming an increasingly ubiquitous element of global environmental governance arrangements. The article claimed that the existence and nature of a "transparency turn" in global environmental governance merited more scrutiny than it had received to date. The editors of *GEP* proactively solicited two additional *Forum* contributions to engage with this claim. Taken as a whole, this *Forum* debate outlined the contours of an emerging research agenda in this field. For this, our first debt of gratitude goes to the editors of *GEP* at the time, Jennifer Clapp and Matthew Patterson, for helping to stimulate a fruitful initial debate on this topic within the pages of the journal.

It seemed logical to follow this up with a more extended in-depth comparative analysis of the role of transparency in the global environmental domain. This we did through a *GEP* special issue in 2010, which brought together a group of senior and early-career global environmental governance scholars to (re)examine their specific environmental issue areas through a transparency and disclosure lens.

This edited book extends this line of research much further. It undertakes a wide-ranging (comparative) analysis of diverse areas of global environmental governance, in which transparency and information disclosure play a key role. It deploys, as starting hypotheses, some of the central findings of the *GEP* special issue and subjects these to further empirical and comparative analysis. It includes fourteen contributions, including three context-setting conceptual treatments of transparency in governance and ten empirical examples of governance by disclosure. Four of these draw on the earlier *GEP* special issue articles, yet each one has undergone a significant metamorphosis in order to engage with the specific analytical framework advanced in this book. Two of the short *GEP* commentaries are also included in this book, yet now as full-length research contributions. Supplementing these are eight new chapters written exclusively for this book.

In the journey toward this edited book, we have incurred a number of important debts. First, we would like to thank the European Union Cooperation in Science and Technology (COST) Action on "Transformations in Global Environmental Governance" for providing funding support to host two author workshops to present various iterations of our transparency research. The first was held at Wageningen University, the Netherlands, in May 2009, and the second at the London School of Economics and Political Science in September 2011. For serving as discussants in the Wageningen workshop, we thank Frank Biermann, Kristine Kern, Kris van Koppen, Arthur Mol, and Jan van Tatenhove; as well as Hilde Toonen for her enthusiastic organizational support. For the London workshop, we acknowledge useful feedback on book chapters from Reut Snir. We also thank Philipp Pattberg, chair of this EU COST Action, for his leadership of the Action.

We presented earlier iterations of this research at two International Studies Association annual conventions over the last few years, and here we would like to thank Dimitris Stevis (before he came on board as an author), as well as Erika Weinthal and Ronald B. Mitchell for their insightful comments on the research presented.

Finally, as editors, we were indeed very fortunate to have worked with a stellar cast of contributing authors, all of whom responded promptly and efficiently to our various requests, whether to adhere to an overarching book structure, engage with hypotheses, respond to reviewer comments, or participate in author workshops. We thank them for their hard work, commitment, and insightful contributions—it was indeed a pleasure to work together. We would also like to thank Clay Morgan and Miranda Martin of the MIT Press for their very professional and able guidance of this manuscript through the review and publication process, and Deborah M. Cantor-Adams of the MIT Press for production and careful copyediting. Finally, we are very grateful to the three anonymous reviewers for MIT Press who gave generously of their time—their extensive comments have significantly strengthened this book.

We view this book as a first step in advancing an exciting and diverse research agenda on a multifaceted transparency turn in global sustainability governance. As such, we hope that it will stimulate much critical commentary and engagement from the global environmental governance community and beyond, in moving debate on these timely issues forward.

Acronyms

ABS access and benefit sharing

BCH Biosafety Clearing-House

CAO Compliance Advisor/Ombudsman

CBD Convention on Biological Diversity

CDM Clean Development Mechanism

CDP Carbon Disclosure Project

CSE Centre for Science and Environment

CSPOG Civil Society Platform on Oil and Gas

CSR corporate social responsibility

EECCA Eastern Europe, the Caucasus, and Central Asia

EITI Extractive Industries Transparency Initiative

ESG environmental, social, and corporate governance

EU European Union

FAO Food and Agriculture Organization

FCPF Forest Carbon Partnership Facility

FOIA Freedom of Information Act

FSC Forest Stewardship Council

GHEITI Ghana Extractive Industries Transparency Initiative

GHG greenhouse gas

GIFAP International Group of National Associations of Manufacturers of Agrochemical Products

GMO(s) genetically modified organism(s)

GR genetic resources

GRI Global Reporting Initiative

GTZ German Organization for Technical Cooperation (now **GIZ**)

IFC International Finance Corporation

ILCs indigenous and local communities

IPCC Intergovernmental Panel on Climate Change

IPE Institute of Public and Environmental Affairs

IPRs intellectual property rights

ISEAL International Social and Environmental Accreditation and Labelling

LULUCF Land use, land use change, and forestry

MAT mutually agreed terms

MRV measuring, reporting, and verification

MSC Marine Stewardship Council

NGO(s) nongovernmental organization(s)

OECD Organisation for Economic Co-operation and Development

OEI Open Environmental Information

OGI Open Government Information

P&C Principles and Criteria

PAN Pesticide Action Network

PEFC Program for the Endorsement of Forest Certification

PIC prior informed consent

PROPER Program for Pollution Control, Evaluation and Rating

PRTR(s) pollution release and transfer register(s)

PWYP Publish What You Pay

REDD Reducing emissions from deforestation and forest degradation in developing countries

REDD+ Reducing emissions from deforestation and forest degradation in developing countries; and the role of conservation, sustainable management of forests and enhancement of carbon stocks in developing countries

SEE South-Eastern Europe

SHPF severely hazardous pesticide formulations

SRI socially responsible investment

TK traditional knowledge

TRI Toxics Release Inventory

UN United Nations

UNECE United Nations Economic Commission for Europe

UNEP United Nations Environment Programme

UNFCCC United Nations Framework Convention on Climate Change

UN-REDD United Nations REDD Programme

WHO World Health Organization

WIPO World Intellectual Property Organization

WRI World Resources Institute

WTO World Trade Organization

WWF World Wide Fund for Nature

1

A Transparency Turn in Global Environmental Governance

Aarti Gupta and Michael Mason

Publicity is justly commended as a remedy for social and industrial diseases. Sunlight is said to be the best of disinfectants.
Louis Dembitz Brandeis, 1913[1]

A century after Justice Louis Brandeis uttered these prescient words, we live, seemingly, in an era of transparency. Transparency is equated most often with openness and reduced secrecy, garnered through greater availability and increased flows of information (Florini 1998; see also Fenster 2010). Whether to enhance global security, secure human rights, discipline borderless business, or hold to account faceless bureaucrats, transparency is increasingly seen as part of the solution to a complex and diverse array of economic, political, and ethical challenges in our increasingly interconnected world (Finel and Lord 2000; Fung et al. 2007; Soederberg 2001).

Aided and abetted by the rapid diffusion of information-communication technologies, transparency is implicated in many of the most high-profile controversies of our times. These range from the much-publicized 2010 WikiLeaks disclosures of US diplomatic cables and wartime activities; to design of "robust" international monitoring, reporting, and verification systems for global climate mitigation; to calls for transparency to combat opaque business practices implicated in the global financial crisis. In each of these cases, the benefits sought through transparency include empowering the weak, and holding accountable the powerful, by reducing informational asymmetries between authority holders and affected actors (e.g., Grigorescu 2007; Roberts 2004; Stasavage 2003). Transparency is also implicated in the pursuit of substantive regulatory outcomes, such as environmental improvements, stabilized markets, reduced corruption, or enhanced human security (e.g., Weil et al. 2006; Stephan 2002).

Yet can and does transparency live up to its many promises? A growing number of transparency analysts have revealed not only the promise but also the pathologies and limitations associated with the growing uptake of transparency by public and private actors across a range of policy areas (Bannister and Connolly 2011; Fung et al. 2007; Hood and Heald 2006; Lord 2006). For example, a requirement under a domestic freedom of information act to disclose minutes of government proceedings may result in minutes not being formally recorded, thereby increasing secrecy and hindering accountability (Roberts 2006). Debates about the consequences of the wide-ranging WikiLeaks disclosures support the uneasy conclusion that ever-greater openness may not only breed greater secrecy but also have other undesirable impacts, such as exacerbating conflict or mistrust (see also Birchall 2011). In the same vein, opposition to aggressive US governmental investigation of media leaks in 2013 was grounded in the belief that secrecy (in this case, maintaining anonymity of journalistic sources) is sometimes a prerequisite for the very disclosure that can hold the powerful to account.

The relationship between transparency and more accountable, legitimate, and effective governance is thus far from straightforward. The ideal(s) of transparency may be contested or may not be attained in practice. Our objective in this book is to scrutinize these ideals and their rendering in practice across a diverse set of global governance initiatives. We focus, in particular, on the global *environmental* domain, as a paradigmatic case of transparency being embraced as an unmitigated good. In doing so, our point of departure is that transparency is becoming a central component of global environmental discourse and practice. Our aim in this book is to identify the configuration of factors fueling such a posited "transparency turn" in global environmental governance, as well as its breadth and quality and potential transformative effects.

We proceed as follows: we first address definitional issues and specify our focus in this book on "governance by disclosure" as symptomatic of a transparency turn in the global environmental realm. We then draw on various theoretical traditions in (global) environmental politics scholarship to outline a distinctive approach—critical transparency studies—that informs the analyses in this book. The next part draws on this perspective to outline an analytical framework to assess the *uptake, institutionalization,* and *effects* of transparency in global environmental governance. We identify a set of overarching questions and hypotheses with which the empirical chapters engage. We conclude with an overview of contributions and a summary of key findings.

I

Transparency in Broader Context

Conceptualizing Transparency as Governance by Disclosure

In a most general sense, transparency is associated with openness, communication, the opposite of secrecy, and information flows. Yet there are few widely accepted definitions of the term, and it is often conflated in scholarly writings with related notions such as accountability or publicity (on the latter, see Gilbert 2007). Scholarly reactions to this definitional diversity range from lamenting the lack of a shared definition (e.g., Etzioni 2010; Seidman 2011), to unpacking the normative and political underpinnings of specific understandings of transparency (e.g., Birchall 2011), to developing typologies of the concept as a way to clarify its scope and meaning (e.g., Heald 2006; Mitchell 2011).

Our point of departure in this book is that different framings of transparency by different actors in diverse contexts itself merits critical scrutiny and explanation, rather than being a conceptual flaw or practical failure to be remedied (see also Langley 2001). Etymologically, transparency connotes *rendering visible* or seeing through (Michener and Bersch 2011). An association of transparency with visibility leaves aside, however, its relational and normative dimensions, such as *what* is to be made visible, by whom, and for whom; the desired *quality and/or quantity* of transparency; and the (governance) *effects* expected to flow from it. Our aim in this book is to further understanding of such relational and normative aspects of transparency, including how such aspects are differently framed and institutionalized in specific instances, and with what consequences for the processes and outcomes of global environmental governance.

It is important to note at the outset that our study of transparency is both broader and narrower in scope than specific lay usages of the term might suggest. First, transparency tends to be associated in common parlance with *governments disclosing information to interested publics*. We go beyond this narrow understanding of (the scope of) transparency in this book. In line with the changing dynamics of multilevel and multiactor global governance, our point of departure is that transparency is being deployed in a much broader context than that of states being transparent to their domestic publics or even, in a global context, to other states. Our focus here is rather on the *multiple instigators, architects, and recipients* of transparency in global governance, going beyond states to include corporations, civil society groups, international organizations, consumers, and citizens. As Michener and Bersch (2011, 5) have observed, both the demand and supply of transparency is now "multidirectional."

At the same time, given our interest in *governance,* we focus here on a specific manifestation of a transparency turn in global politics: the reliance on targeted *disclosure of information* as a means by which to evaluate and steer behavior, that is, as a means by which to govern. We refer to this phenomenon as *governance by disclosure* (Gupta 2008) by which we understand *public and private governance initiatives that employ targeted disclosure of information as a way to evaluate and/or steer the behavior of selected actors.* We view the proliferation of governance by disclosure initiatives in the global environmental domain as clearly reflective of a transparency turn in this realm. Our focus on governance by disclosure permits a manageable delimitation of the scope of this study, even as it enables a systematic comparison of the uptake and effects of transparency across a range of public and private environmental governance initiatives.

We select the global environmental policy domain for two reasons. The first is that multiple state and nonstate actors are now increasingly embracing transparency as a necessary feature of decision making and regulatory action to address global environmental challenges. Diverse actors champion transparency as a means to enhance efficiency, accountability, and effectiveness of global environmental governance, a phenomenon that we believe deserves a comprehensive theoretical and empirical examination. The normative rationales underpinning a multidirectional embrace of transparency in this realm are also diverse. Thus, private actors may promote transparency as a voluntary means by which to further corporate sustainability goals, and perhaps thereby avoid mandatory regulation. By contrast, public actors and civil society may promote transparency as a way to correct perceived democratic deficits in environmental decision making or ensure informed choice in environmental governance. These multiple (and often opposing) rationales for transparency thus may include extending the reach of the state in order to enhance effectiveness of state-led policy, or scaling back the state in advocating for voluntary private governance. Similarly, transparency may be deployed to further a morally grounded right to know in order to hold government or private actors accountable, or as a means to facilitate individual lifestyle choices and market-based solutions to sustainability (Langley 2001; Mason 2008b).

Notwithstanding the diverse architects of transparency and the diverse rationales to embrace it, a common underlying presumption underpinning governance by disclosure is that transparency matters; yet, a systematic analysis of how, under what conditions, and for whom remains to be done. Despite the increasing importance of transparency in global environmental governance, the concept remains surprisingly little scrutinized in this field (but see Langley 2001 and Mitchell 1998 for important exceptions). This is in contrast to, for example, international financial and economic relations, global security, human rights, and diplomacy, in which transparency studies have a longer and more established trajectory (e.g., Graham 2002; Grigorescu 2007; Lord 2006; Roberts 2004; Stasavage 2003).

This lack of attention to transparency is the second reason we select the global environmental realm as our focus. Even as transparency, as such, has received less attention here, closely related concepts such as information and (scientific) knowledge *have* long enjoyed pride of place in scholarly analyses in global environmental politics from diverse theoretical perspectives (e.g., Gupta 2006; Haas 1989; Litfin 1994; Mitchell et al. 2006). Transparency is intimately related to these fields of inquiry but appears to have fallen between the cracks of their core analytical concerns. This holds as well for analyses of legitimate and democratic global environmental governance that routinely evoke the link to transparency (e.g., Bernstein 2001; Dryzek 1999; Keohane 2006). This link, however, remains more stated than scrutinized (but see Dingwerth 2007).

The recently launched international research program on "Earth System Governance" emphasizes as well a need to examine such posited relationships. Earth system governance is defined in this global research program as "the interrelated ... system of formal and informal rules, rule-making mechanisms and actor-networks at all levels of human society (from local to global) that are set up to steer societies towards preventing, mitigating and adapting to ... environmental change and earth system transformation" (Biermann et al. 2010, p. 279). Accountability (including its relationship to transparency) is identified here as one of the five core analytical challenges of earth system governance research, and one that has been relatively less studied (Biermann and Gupta 2011; Mason 2008a).

We address transparency in global environmental governance in this book by analyzing both state-led and private disclosure initiatives. The rationale to include public and privately fueled disclosure is to reflect on the multidirectional nature and consequences of the transparency turn in the global environmental realm. The environmental issues covered include climate change, deforestation, marine pollution, sustainable use of genetic resources, technological and chemical risk reduction, sustainable natural resource extraction, reduced environmental harm from foreign direct investment, and improved corporate sustainability performance. Such a wide-ranging and comparative analysis of diverse disclosure-based governance in the global environmental realm has not yet been undertaken, making this the first book to do so.

We turn next to the critical transparency studies perspective that informs our analysis of governance by disclosure in this book.

A Critical Transparency Studies Perspective

Multiple writings on transparency in the social sciences yield a range of insights regarding the uptake and effectiveness of transparency-based governance. Transparency has been analyzed at some length in national-level (environmental) policy analyses, where it has received significantly more attention than in a global context. This body of work has extended the frontiers of transparency scholarship under the rubric of what it terms "regulation by revelation" as a third wave of domestic environmental rule making since the late 1990s (Florini 1998). According to this literature, a third wave of disclosure-based regulation has been stimulated by the ineffectiveness and implementation gaps dogging the first (command-and-control) and second (market-based) waves of national environmental policy making (Fung et al. 2007; Graham 2002; Konar and Cohen 1997; Stephan 2002).

In one of the most extensive analyses, Fung and colleagues examine the conditions under which what they call targeted transparency (i.e., disclosure of specific types of information, in contrast to a more general right to know) can be effective. Through detailed comparative analyses of various national-level, and to lesser extent, global transparency policies, they find that effective transparency requires disclosed information to become embedded in the decision-making processes of disclosers *and* recipients. This, they note, is difficult to obtain in practice, ensuring that transparency often falls short of meeting desired aims (see also Weil et al. 2013).

These studies are important precursors to our analysis of governance by disclosure in a global environmental context. They have tended, however, to be more or less aligned with a dominant *liberal institutionalist* perspective on the role of information and power in global environmental governance scholarship. Such a perspective holds that openness, communication, reporting, and information exchange can aid in more effective global environmental governance by correcting for information asymmetries between the powerful and those seeking to hold them to account and/or by facilitating more evidence-based, rational decision making (see, for example, Esty 2003; Mitchell 1998, 2011).

Analyses informed by this approach have highlighted the promise and also the many dysfunctionalities of disclosure-based governance, which may impede its potential to empower, hold governors to account, or further specific regulatory aims. Such dysfunctionalities include disclosure of incomplete or unreliable data; lack of comparability, comprehensibility, or accessibility of disclosed data; and a lack of capacity on the part of recipients to interpret and use disclosed data (Fung et al. 2007; Graham 2002; Weil et al. 2006). Although these are important insights into the hurdles facing governance by disclosure, a liberal institutionalist perspective on transparency tends to attribute lack of effective disclosure to inadequacies of institutional design or bureaucratic capacity, to lack of attainability of "full disclosure" (Fung et al. 2007), or to transparency not having proceeded "far enough, fast enough" (e.g., Florini 2007).

By contrast, our point of departure in this book is that transparency's uptake and effects can be understood only within the broader, often contested, normative and political context within which disclosure is being deployed. We adopt a critical perspective on transparency that analyzes disclosure as a site of political conflict, and hence transparency itself as fundamentally contested political terrain. We label this a *critical transparency studies* perspective, by which we mean approaches that (1) problematize transparency and governance by disclosure, (2) account for the historicity and sociopolitical embedding of transparency and disclosure practices, and (3) acknowledge the unavoidable normativity (value-laden structure) of transparency and disclosure. In developing this perspective, we draw on theoretical groundwork laid by constructivist and critical political economy approaches in global environmental politics scholarship.

Constructivist analyses of science, knowledge, and information have long highlighted the changing authority and accountability relationships around the generation and sharing of (scientific) information in governing environmental challenges. As such, this strand of scholarship is particularly relevant to studies of governance by disclosure. As writings in this vein suggest, current global environmental challenges, such as climate change or safe use of biotechnology, are characterized by fundamental normative conflicts and scientific uncertainties over what is valid knowledge and whose information counts. If so, agreeing on what is "more and better" information, that is, on the scope and quality of information, is inevitably a matter of political conflict (Jasanoff 2004; Litfin 1994; see also Gupta 2006, 2008). As Fischer (2009, 185) notes, environmental information presented as technical is shaped by the situational and sociopolitical contexts of its production, dissemination, and reception.

Furthermore, as science acquires ever-greater prominence as a source of authority in global environmental governance (Gupta et al. 2012), the imperative to *disclose* scientific data and knowledge-generation processes also increases. This implies that political conflicts over valid knowledge shape the contours of governance by disclosure as well.

Drawing on these insights, a critical transparency studies perspective holds that the effects of transparency in the global environmental realm will turn not so much on reducing information asymmetries in order to promote more rational outcomes, but rather on *whose* information counts and is accorded primacy in environmental decision making and governance. It postulates, furthermore, that the very processes of negotiating the scope and practices of disclosure serve to selectively frame, and hence constitute, the object of governance (see, for example, Jasanoff 2004; Lövbrand 2011).

Critical political economy perspectives in global environmental scholarship (e.g., Clapp 2007; Clapp and Helleiner 2012; Levy and Newell 2005; Newell 2008a, 2008b) inform our thinking here as well. Such perspectives build on influential early analyses of the sources and location of power in international politics (Strange 1988, 1996) to more recent studies of the distinct and unequally distributed forms of public and private authority and vulnerabilities that shape global environmental governance (e.g., Fuchs 2005).

Such research emphasizes, for example, the current (unstable) dominance in global environmental governance of what Steven Bernstein (2001) labels liberal environmentalism—an authoritative complex of norms that frames environmental governance challenges according to market liberal values and interests. The institutionalization of liberal environmentalism may legitimize governance practices and further ecological goals insofar as these do not challenge underlying structures of market or political power.

In line with this, a critical transparency perspective holds that transparency's uptake and effects in global environmental governance need to be understood within this broader (unequal) political economic context, one in which private actors, furthermore, are likely to have a major role in shaping and deploying public modes of information disclosure. Insofar as liberal environmentalism has political and policy currency, transparency, if adopted, is likely to have minimal market-restricting effects and may be skewed by state economic development or corporate interests.

Such a perspective allows that transparency may *reproduce* rather than disrupt socially and ecologically harmful concentrations of public and private power. It is of particular relevance to an analysis of transparency in a global context, characterized by North-South disparities in the power and capacity to demand disclosure and to access and use disclosed information. It may help to explain, as well, a potential paradox of the transparency turn in global politics: that the desired quality and quantity of disclosed information (such as its breadth, comparability, comprehensibility, comprehensiveness, or accessibility) may *follow* from rather than *precipitate* changes in the broader normative and political context. Thus, greater levels of "actionable" transparency may be obtainable only *after* broader democratic, participatory, and environmental gains have been secured in a given context (Gupta 2010a).

This leaves open a fundamental question: is transparency epiphenomenal? Even as transparency becomes ubiquitous in global environmental governance, its transformative potential remains uncertain and contingent. From a critical transparency studies perspective, we can identify a continuum of views—ranging from the more skeptical to the more pragmatic—on the transformative potential of transparency, each of which is present, to greater or lesser extent, in the contributions to this book.

From a more skeptical perspective, there is little hope for transparency to transform entrenched structural imbalances of power or unequal life and livelihood options (for a similar view, in the case of global peace and security, see Lord 2006). Such a perspective would characterize transparency as, for example, a red herring of modern political culture (Brown 2002, 1). As Brown argues, one response to a perceived crisis of trust in dominant governance institutions is a demand for greater transparency to foster trust in public and private decision-making processes and outcomes. A widespread assumption is that transparency can build trust, yet transparency as an antidote to a crisis of trust is failing (see also O'Neill 2006). As O'Neill argues, this is because disclosure is not embedded in "the epistemic and ethical norms required for successful communicative acts" (O'Neill 2006, 81). Transparency, from this perspective, mirrors instead the broader meta-normative and political economic conflicts that shape global governance, and hence can only acquire meaning and relevance in such a context (see, for example, in this book, Mason, chapter 4; Gupta, chapter 6; Gupta et al., chapter 8; and Knox-Hayes and Levy, chapter 9). Transparency's transformative potential, particularly if understood as structural change, thus remains severely attenuated.

A more pragmatic perspective emphasizes that, although transparency is no panacea, context-specific incremental gains in empowerment, accountability, and environmental improvements are feasible and attainable (see, for example, in this book, Jansen and Dubois, chapter 5; Orsini et al., chapter 7; Dingwerth and Eichinger, chapter 10; and Auld and Gulbrandsen, chapter 12). In such a perspective, disclosure may be viewed as a default option or as "the only game in town," given the difficulties of negotiating more far-reaching or costly regulatory options in contested issue areas (Haufler 2010). Even as a default option, however, it need not be lacking in empowerment or effectiveness potential (e.g., Van Alstine, chapter 11; and Ehresman and Stevis, chapter 13). Some scholars in this tradition claim as well that transparency can deliver governance gains, but only under relatively demanding conditions that may not obviate the need for other regulatory tools (e.g., Etzioni 2010).

Going further, and most optimistic about transparency's transformative potential, are perspectives that emphasize that transparency's engagement with the institutions and practices of power is more dialectical, that is, shaped by but also able to shape the dominant norms and practices of global governance (e.g., Florini and Jairaj, this book, chapter 3; see also Picciotto 2000). In line with this, Mol (2006, 2008) observes, for example, that information provides a resource for political transformation as a growing constitutive element of environmental governance, which he labels informational governance (see also Mol, this book, chapter 2).

The foregoing discussion reveals that, even from a broadly critical perspective, transparency's transformative potential is differently understood and framed and can range from structural to incremental change. What the transformative effects of transparency might consist of is, then, a context-specific empirical question.

We turn next to our analytical framework to study governance by disclosure, which runs through the cases in this book. In advancing this framework, we suggest that only by assessing a broad range of governance ends—normative, procedural, and substantive—can we capture the difference that transparency makes in particular contexts.

Governance by Disclosure: An Analytical Framework

We bring our critical transparency studies perspective to bear on the central concerns of this book, relating to the nature and implications of a multidirectional transparency turn in global environmental governance. We do so by outlining an analytical framework here that specifies a set of research questions and hypotheses relating to three aspects of governance by disclosure: its uptake, institutionalization, and effects. The empirical chapters then explore in-depth these three aspects.

Uptake of Transparency: Drivers of Disclosure

In line with our aim to historicize and contextualize the role of transparency in global environmental governance, the first element of our analytical framework relates to explaining the *uptake of transparency* in a given issue area. All empirical contributions thus analyze the question: why transparency now? In posing this question, we draw on the existing state of the art in transparency studies to hypothesize about possible *drivers* of transparency's uptake in global governance.

A growing body of literature suggests, first, that a rights-based democratic push for individual liberty, choice, and participation is driving a growing embrace of transparency in global politics (Florini 2008; Graham 2002; Gupta 2008; Mason 2008b). We label this a *democratization* driver, insofar as democratic forms of governance seem to require more open and inclusive forms of collective choice. A democratization driver of transparency is seen to underpin, for example, the spread of right-to-know and freedom-of-information laws in multiple national contexts since at least the 1980s (Florini 2007; see also Florini and Jairaj, this book, chapter 3). This has now evolved into a broader association of transparency with securing multidirectional accountability and a more legitimate and democratic global polity (e.g., Bernstein 2005; Dingwerth 2005; Keohane 2003).

Those positing such relationships assume that disclosure of relevant information is often a necessary step in holding actors to account for their (in)actions according to set environmental standards. A reasonable expectation is that, insofar as information is disclosed by those responsible for decisions that significantly affect the interests of others, such disclosure will facilitate individual and institutional answerability or even change. However, this involves assumptions about the capacity and responsiveness of particular actors and the political systems within which they operate (Fox 2007), including the assumption that democratic institutions foster greater accountability for environmental harm.

An empirical question for this book as a whole is thus the extent to which the democratic rationale for transparency is significant for the environmental governance initiatives studied, and if so, whether it is necessarily *liberal* democratic: we return to this in our conclusion. Although there is a substantial literature on the relationship between democratic decision-making processes and ecological sustainability, much of it informed by theories of deliberative democracy (e.g., Baber and Bartlett 2005; Bäckstrand et al. 2010; Dryzek 2000; Dryzek and Stevenson 2011; Smith 2003), the relationship between democratization and the uptake of transparency remains much less examined.

Included in a democratizing imperative for disclosure is an increasing pressure to *democratize science and expertise* as well, which is of particular relevance in the global environmental realm. As we noted previously, an ever-growing role for science is evident in global environmental governance, insofar as the framing of cause and effect in global environmental challenges is increasingly influenced by expert bodies (Mitchell et al. 2006; Moore et al. 2011). As Ulrich Beck notes in *Risk Society*, it is a paradox of our times that the most politically and scientifically contested environmental and risk governance challenges, those where the authority of science is most likely to be questioned, are also the issue-areas that most *need* scientific input (Beck 1992). This intensifies the need to subject scientific processes of knowledge generation to greater public scrutiny and engagement (see also Jasanoff 2003a, 2003b).

Much writing on the need to democratize science in the environmental realm focuses, as a result, on the institutional and normative challenges of designing participatory processes of knowledge generation and validation (e.g., Leach et al. 2007; Lövbrand et al. 2011). Our interest here rather is in how disclosure of knowledge-generation processes and expert data is implicated in the push to democratize science.

In sum, as a first driver of disclosure, we hypothesize that a multifaceted democratization imperative (including calls to democratize science) is driving the uptake of transparency in global environmental governance.

Tensions arise, however, from the fact that efforts to improve the democratic quality of (global) environmental governance, by embracing information disclosure, often go hand-in-hand with a neoliberal privileging of market-based solutions to global sustainability challenges, and "light touch" regulation of the private sector (Moore et al. 2011; Bernstein 2001). This can, in turn, stimulate an uptake of market-based and voluntary transparency, often as a way to avoid more stringent, mandatory, or costly governance options (on this point, see also Haufler 2010).

In line with this, we posit *marketization* to be a second driver of transparency's uptake in global environmental governance. In contrast to a democratization imperative for disclosure, a neoliberal market-driven uptake of transparency may seek to minimize the scope of (potentially market-restricting) disclosure and exempt corporate actors from stringent disclosure (Florini 2008; Haufler 2010). Alternatively, however, disclosure of (certain types of) information might well be seen as essential to the establishment and functioning of *newly created markets* in environmental goods and services, such as those for carbon or genetic resources. In such cases, transparency might be promoted by powerful actors, such as corporations and policy elites, as desirable and necessary in order to create and facilitate markets, rather than being perceived as a regulatory burden that can restrict markets.

An empirical question we address is thus whether (and what kind of) marketization imperative drives uptake of transparency in global environmental governance. In addressing this, we are also interested in whether a marketization rationale for disclosure facilitates, follows, or restricts markets.

Our discussion yields a general hypothesis (H1) that all empirical chapters engage with, in addressing "why transparency now" for their case: that *democratization and marketization are driving uptake of transparency in global environmental governance*. More broadly, the theoretical and empirical task we set ourselves, individually and collectively, is to analyze how these drivers of disclosure may intersect with each other and the conditions under which one or the other may dominate.

A logical next question is how specific drivers of disclosure shape the manner in which transparency is institutionalized and functions in practice. We turn next to this second element of our analytical framework.

Institutionalizing Transparency: Scope and Modalities

The second component of our analytical framework—and second question addressed by all contributions—relates to how transparency is being *institutionalized* in a given issue area. By institutionalization, we refer to specific configurations of the scope and modalities of disclosure in given instances.

One much-debated aspect of institutionalization relates to the *quantity* of disclosed information. Much scholarly and policy attention in mainstream transparency studies has focused on the desirability of—and challenges facing—complete or "full" disclosure. In the policy realms of international finance, security, and diplomacy, an oft-posed question is whether full disclosure is feasible and/or desirable. Most analyses conclude that complete disclosure in such areas is unattainable and undesirable, given the merits of retaining varying degrees of secrecy, anonymity, or privacy in many instances (e.g., Birchall 2011; Lord 2006).

This raises, however, an intriguing question: is the (global) environmental realm distinct? The imperative to balance transparency with secrecy, privacy, and anonymity may not hold in this policy domain to the extent that it does in others, yet this eventuality has not been systematically analyzed. What specific features of global environmental governance challenges might either impede full disclosure or make its pursuit more or less desirable? Impediments to full disclosure in this realm may relate, among others, to corporate confidentiality concerns or proprietary ownership of environmental information (see, for example, Orsini et al., this book, chapter 7); or to scientific uncertainties and unknowabilities in governing complex (transboundary) environmental challenges. It may also relate to the *materiality* of the environmental resource in question, whereby the physical properties of, for example, carbon, genetic resources, oil, or forests—and their location in wider circuits of material production and consumption—shape the scope of disclosure obtainable in a given context. An empirical task for this book is thus to examine the limits of full disclosure and the merits and demerits of *partial transparency* in global environmental governance, given the geopolitical and material contexts for disclosure.

Turning from quantity to *quality* of disclosed information, much scholarly and policy attention has focused, as well, on desired attributes of disclosed information as central to the success of transparency-based governance. These attributes include disclosed information being (perceived as) accessible, comprehensible, comparable, accurate, or relevant (Dingwerth and Eichinger 2010) and whether it is standardized or nonstandardized.

Such attributes of disclosure may make transparency more or less *actionable*, that is, usable by recipients to further their desired ends (e.g., Fung et al. 2007; Michener and Bersch 2011; see also Dingwerth and Eichinger, this book, chapter 10). Nonactionable transparency can result not only from the scope of disclosure being limited, but also from "drowning in disclosure" when too much (or "irrelevant") information is provided (Gupta 2008, 4). An empirical task for the book is thus also to analyze attributes of disclosure obtained in practice.

In institutionalizing disclosure, an increasingly important development in transparency politics is the rise of information *intermediaries or infrastructures* that seek to validate or increase the utility of disclosed information for specific stakeholders (Etzioni 2010; Fung et al. 2007, Graham 2002, Gupta 2008; Lord 2006). These include auditors and verifiers of disclosed information or civil society groups seeking to render disclosed information more user-friendly (see also Langley 2001 for an early and detailed discussion of this). Such new transparency "powerbrokers" may produce shifts in the loci of authority and expertise in environmental governance that are also important to examine.

In sum, this second component of our analytical framework calls for examining, individually and collectively, the scope, quantity, and attributes of disclosed information and whether and how transparency's intermediaries enhance the actionability of disclosure for diverse actors.

In assessing these dynamics, we propose a second hypothesis (H2) to be examined by contributions to this book: that *institutionalization of transparency decenters state-led regulation and opens up political space for new actors.* This hypothesis derives from a prominent view in transparency analyses that private actors and civil society are crucial agents in institutionalizing disclosure-based governance, particularly in a neoliberal environmental context (e.g., Langley 2001; Mol 2006). As such, it permits detailed comparative analysis of whether transparency-based arrangements, including their scope and modalities, reconfigure public and private authority to govern specific environmental issue areas.

Our analytical concern with shifting sites of authority in governance also stems from writings that emphasize a *changing role for the state* in newer modalities of (global environmental) governance (e.g., Eckersley 2004; Strange 1988, 1996; for a more recent assessment, see Compagnon et al. 2012). For instance, institutionalized disclosure may *qualify* state sovereign authority if it facilitates the generation and dissemination of streams of information beyond the legal and epistemic control of governments. This may result in a shift away from state-led regulation, even as it opens up political space for other actors (on this point, see also Mol, this book, chapter 2).

In hypothesizing a potential decentering of state-led regulation, we do not consider "states" to be a homogenous category. Instead, we are interested in *whose* sovereign authority may be affected through institutionalized disclosure. We assume that this will vary across developed versus developing countries or emerging economies versus so-called failed states (on the changing role of different types of states in global environmental governance, see Compagnon et al. 2012).

Taken as a whole, our aim in postulating this hypothesis is to assess the multidirectional nature of transparency's demand and supply, and the evolving roles of state and non-state actors in institutionalizing disclosure.

We turn next to the third element of our analytical framework, the effectiveness of governance by disclosure.

Effects of Transparency: Normative, Procedural, and Substantive
The third and final component of our analytical framework—and third question addressed by all contributions in this book—relates to the *effects of transparency.* Transparency, as we noted at the outset, is associated with more accountable, democratic, and/or effective governance.

Our third strand of inquiry focuses on whether governance by disclosure furthers these diverse aims. We are interested thus in assessing the *effectiveness* of governance by disclosure.

Assessing effectiveness of (global) environmental policies is a long-standing concern in scholarly research and political practice, with effectiveness most often conceptualized as reduced environmental harm (Mitchell 1998; Young 1999). A prominent typology here is the "output, outcome, impact" distinction in effectiveness research, which seeks to distinguish different aspects and stages of policy effectiveness but retains a dominant ultimate concern with environmental improvements (EEA 2001).

Governance by disclosure, however, seeks to further a broader set of governance ends, requiring an analytical openness to a variety of effects. These go beyond environmental gains to include a right to know and enhanced accountability and inclusiveness of decision-making processes. Such broader effects are captured, at least partially, in another long-standing distinction in effectiveness analysis; that between input and output legitimacy. Scharpf (1997) developed this distinction to assess the legitimacy and effectiveness of European decision-making processes and outcomes. By input legitimacy, he referred to legitimacy conferred on the rule-setting process by virtue of its procedural characteristics (such as how open and inclusive it is). By output legitimacy, he referred to legitimacy garnered through the (perceived) ability of governance processes and outcomes to effectively address the underlying environmental problem. Output legitimacy is thus akin to environmental effectiveness, yet with an important difference: it assesses *perceived* effectiveness among stakeholders rather than actual reductions in environmental harm or improvements in environmental quality. It thus circumvents a key causality challenge facing analyses of environmental effectiveness, that of ascertaining direct and indirect causal pathways between governance measures and environmental improvements (see also Dingwerth 2005, 2007).

We build on these various conceptions of effectiveness in our analytical framework, but adapt them to capture the diversity of governance aims associated with transparency. Specifically, we propose a typology of three categories of effects expected from governance by disclosure: *normative, procedural,* and *substantive* effects. This typology builds on the different ways in which transparency is conceptualized in multidisciplinary writings, including as a norm, a procedural principle, and/or as a mechanism of governance. These diverse ways of conceptualizing transparency give rise, in our view, to an associated set of aims pursued by governance by disclosure. These include a *normative* right to know of information recipients, *procedural* aims of holding the powerful to account and/or securing enhanced choice or voice in environmental governance processes, and *substantive* aims of improving environmental performance or reducing harm.[2]

Such a typology of effectiveness enables us to engage also with a long-standing debate in global environmental governance relating to synergies or trade-offs between legitimacy of global environmental governance processes, secured through enhanced participation or voice in decision making, and effectiveness in delivering desired environmental improvements (e.g., Andresen and Hey 2005; Bäckstrand 2006; Bernstein 2005). Our assessment of procedural and substantive effects of disclosure enables us to assess linkages or trade-offs between these governance ends. We elaborate further on our typology of effects next.

Normative effects   Underlying an embrace of transparency in governance is often the normative belief that those exposed to potential harm have a right to know about damaging environmental behaviors or products (Beierle 2004; Rowan-Robinson et al. 1996). Such a moral right to know is then a first-order normative goal that governance by disclosure may seek to further. Analyzing whether this goal is being met requires analyzing, for example, who is pushing for a right to know, whether such a right is contested, how it is being institutionalized, and how it is functioning. Such an analysis can shed light on the *normative effectiveness* of governance by disclosure—that is, the consensual strength and currency of a right to know in a given governance realm and the extent to which this right is institutionalized and furthered.

In short, the question we collectively address relating to normative effects is *whether transparency informs* (and if so, whom, and under what conditions).

Procedural effects   Going beyond a right to know are a range of important procedural aims associated with transparency. In political theory and legal analysis, transparency is typically linked to *empowerment,* understood as enhanced prospects for more participatory, accountable, and legitimate global governance (e.g., Graham 2002; Keohane 2006; Pattberg and Enechi 2009; Rose-Ackermann and Halpaap 2002; Stasavage 2003; van den Burg 2004). These desired effects of disclosure are closely linked to the democratization driver for uptake of transparency, discussed previously.

In assessing the *procedural effectiveness* of governance by disclosure, we explore here the assumed link between transparency and empowerment, and in so doing, further the research agenda on how empowerment is being conceptualized and realized (or not) in disclosure-based global governance. In order to do so, we assess, for example, links between *transparency and participation* in decision making (e.g., Auld and Gulbrandsen, this book, chapter 12); and *transparency and informed choice* (e.g., Jansen and Dubois, this book, chapter 5; Gupta, this book, chapter 6; and Orsini et al., this book, chapter 7).

In addition, the posited relationship between *transparency and accountability* is also central to procedural effectiveness. In a global governance context, accountability mechanisms are necessarily distinct from electoral accountability or constitutional representation, mechanisms that serve this function in a national context (Keohane 2003, 2006). Ensuring accountability of global environmental processes and outcomes, and of transnational private governance, is much more challenging (Biermann and Gupta 2011; Mason 2008a). Transparency is, however, one of the most oft-evoked mechanisms of securing accountability, even as the specific nature and validity of this posited relationship has been relatively little studied (but for a comprehensive attempt, see Fox 2007).

In discussing the distinct nature of accountability in a global governance context, Keohane (2003, 141) for example distinguishes between internal and external accountability. In internal accountability, the "principal and agent are institutionally linked to each other" whereas in external accountability, those whose lives are affected and hence who would desire to hold to account, are not directly (or institutionally) linked to the one to be held to account. How might transparency play a role in furthering internal and external accountability? Is one prioritized over the other, and what scope and modalities of disclosure are suitable to each? We make a start in this book in addressing such questions (see for example, Auld and Gulbrandsen, chapter 12; Dingwerth and Eichinger, chapter 10; and Knox-Hayes and Levy, chapter 9).

To sum up, the *procedural aims* of disclosure include enhancing participation or informed choice of recipients or permitting them to hold disclosers accountable—in a word, empowering recipients of disclosure. As such, the question we collectively address relating to procedural effects is whether transparency empowers (and if so, whom, and under what conditions).

Substantive effects   Finally, governance by disclosure aims for *substantive* regulatory effects, such as reduced emissions, risk mitigation, and environmental improvements (e.g., Fung et al. 2007; Gouldson 2004; Mitchell 1998; Stephan 2002). A key example is the much-analyzed United States Toxic Release Inventory, where an ultimate goal of disclosure is reduced emissions of toxic pollutants (e.g., Konar and Cohen 1997). In global environmental governance, these substantive regulatory goals converge on the prevention or mitigation of significant transboundary environmental harm or harm to the global commons.

The link between transparency and environmental improvements remains, again, little examined and challenging to assess. This is related to long-acknowledged causality hurdles inherent in such assessments. A lack of attention to substantive effects may also result from a more dominant association of transparency with a procedural turn in global environmental governance, whereby its empowerment potential (and link to informed, accountable, participatory, and legitimate governance) is often privileged over its role in securing substantive environmental gains (e.g., Rose-Ackermann and Halpaap 2002; see also Gupta 2008). Yet the relationship between transparency and environmental improvements is ever-more important to assess, insofar as disclosure might be relied on, more so than previously, as an innovative means by which to secure (transboundary) environmental improvements in a neoliberal, marketized global governance context.

In line with this, the question we collectively address relating to substantive effects is whether transparency improves environmental performance (and if so, under what conditions).

In summary, in assessing effectiveness of governance by disclosure, we distinguish among normative, procedural, and substantive effects, and assess whether transparency informs, empowers, and improves environmental performance. In doing so, we advance a final hypothesis (H3) here that derives from a dominant claim in the transparency literature (e.g., Fung et al. 2007): that *transparency is likely to be effective when its contexts of application resonate with the goals and decision processes of both disclosers and recipients.* However, in line with our critical transparency studies perspective—one alert to prevailing global configurations of political and economic power—we hypothesize that the dominance of liberal environmentalism in global environmental governance skews the effects of governance by disclosure. We propose therefore a *directional version of H3 as well:* that in *liberal environmentalist contexts, disclosure will have minimal market-restricting effects.* In comparatively assessing this hypothesis, we consider whether this is the likely outcome across public *and* private governance by disclosure initiatives.

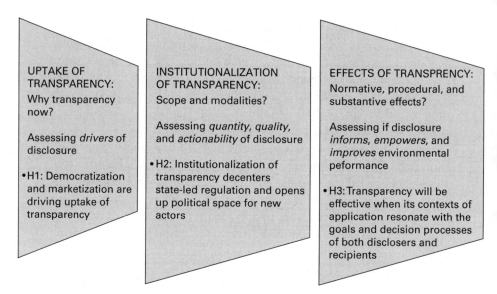

Figure 1.1
Governance by Disclosure: An Analytical Framework

Taken as a whole, an overarching concern in assessing transparency's effectiveness is the extent to which transparency is transformative (understood as the potential of governance by disclosure to inform, empower, and improve environmental quality). We leave as an empirical question the existence and degree of transformation (whether structural or incremental) obtainable in specific contexts.

Figure 1.1 presents an overview of our analytical framework on uptake, institutionalization, and effects of governance by disclosure.

We turn next to the diverse cases of governance by disclosure included in this book and conclude with an overview of contributions.

Governance by Disclosure: The Cases

Informed by our analytical framework, the contributions to this book explore the uptake, institutionalization, and effects of transparency in diverse issue areas of global environmental governance. In selecting the governance by disclosure cases included here, we did not aim for comprehensiveness. Instead, we have been guided by the need to capture (1) the multidirectional demand for governance by disclosure, including from public and private actors and their associated modalities, such as mandatory versus voluntary disclosure; (2) diverse motivations for disclosure, including a democratization and marketization imperative; and (3) breadth and diversity in the environmental issues covered. We focus as a result on five state-led mandatory and five private voluntary disclosure initiatives, which vary in who is pushing for disclosure from whom and why. The environmental issues covered include long-standing challenges (such as combating deforestation or reducing pesticide risks) and newer issues (such as equitable access to and benefit sharing from genetic resources or forest carbon accounting for global climate governance).

The five state-led mandatory disclosure initiatives cover some of the most prominent multilateral environmental treaties that emphasize transparency as central to their governance aims. These include the 1998 Convention on Access to Information, Public Participation in Decision-Making and Access to Justice in Environmental Matters (henceforth Aarhus convention) as a state-led multilateral treaty that has been characterized as an extensive experiment in "environmental democracy" in a regional and transnational context (Wates 2005).

Also included here are two multilateral treaties that rely on the governance mechanism of "prior informed consent" (PIC) to regulate transboundary flows of risk and harm as quintessential examples of governance by disclosure. These include the Rotterdam Convention on the Prior Informed Consent Procedure for Certain Hazardous Chemicals and Pesticides in International Trade (henceforth Rotterdam Convention) and the Cartagena Protocol on Biosafety regulating trade in genetically modified organisms, negotiated under the Convention on Biological Diversity. In both, disclosure of information is a central means by which to empower developing countries to exercise informed choice in making risk-mitigation decisions (with the potential that such disclosure may have market-restricting effects).

Both these treaties build on the earlier Basel Convention on Control of Transboundary Movements of Hazardous Waste and Their Disposal (henceforth Basel Convention). This treaty first introduced the mechanism of informed consent as the basis for governing transfers of hazardous wastes between developed and developing countries, before finally instituting a ban on such transfers (for detailed analyses of the Basel Convention, see Clapp 2001; Krueger 1998; O'Neill 2000). In including the Rotterdam and Cartagena treaties in this book, our aim is to extend the research agenda on disclosure-based risk governance, through analyzing the pros and cons of relying on information disclosure (as opposed to a ban) as the chosen approach in governing global transfers of risky substances.

The final two cases of state-led disclosure cover newly emerging global environmental governance arrangements. Both are motivated, furthermore, and to greater degree than the previous three, by a *marketization* and *market-facilitation* imperative for disclosure. These include, first, the PIC and disclosure of origin negotiations within the Convention on Biological Diversity's Nagoya Protocol on Access to Genetic Resources and the Fair and Equitable Sharing of Benefits Arising from Their Utilization (henceforth Nagoya Protocol). The second analyzes the transparency-based measuring, reporting, and verification systems underpinning one of the newest forest carbon-related climate mitigation mechanisms being negotiated under the United Nations Framework Convention on Climate Change (UNFCCC). This mechanism is designated REDD+ (reducing emissions from deforestation and forest degradation in developing countries; and the role of conservation, sustainable management of forests and enhancement of forest carbon stocks in developing countries).

In these cases of state-led disclosure, there is also important diversity in the categories of states demanding and receiving disclosure. In the case of the Rotterdam Convention and the Cartagena Protocol, those demanding transparency are mostly developing (importing) countries seeking information from industrialized (exporting) countries about risky substances in international trade, in order to prevent or mitigate harm within their borders. Alternatively, in the case of forest carbon accounting for climate mitigation (REDD+), those demanding transparency are developed (donor) countries soliciting forest carbon-related disclosure from developing countries to permit performance-based compensation for environmental improvements. The Nagoya Protocol, in contrast, has a fascinating double-edged state-to-state transparency requirement, whereby distinct types of disclosure are required from developing countries (as a way to facilitate access of developed countries to genetic resources) and from developed countries (as a way to facilitate sharing of benefits with developing countries).

Taken as a whole, the five cases of state-led disclosure initiatives allow assessment of diverse drivers of disclosure, along with variation in the categories of states pushing for and receiving disclosed information (both developed and developing) in both long-established and newly emerging global environmental issue areas.

Turning next to the five private (and mostly voluntary) disclosure initiatives included here, we again cover a diversity of issue areas as well as variation in the actors pushing for and demanding disclosure. The first two cases analyze corporate transparency in global environmental governance through in-depth analyses of the Global Reporting Initiative and the Carbon Disclosure Project. Both these entail (voluntary) disclosure about corporate sustainability performance from corporations to other interested actors (including other corporations, states, civil society, and citizens).

The other cases are public-private disclosure arrangements, with civil society exercising leadership as well. These include the nonstate disclosure-based certification schemes of the Forest Stewardship Council and the Marine Stewardship Council, whereby the imperative driving disclosure is to secure accountability of disclosers, informed choice of recipients, and improved environmental performance. Also included here are two less-analyzed cases in environmental governance. The first is voluntary disclosure in natural resource extraction through comparative assessment of the government-led Extractive Industries Transparency Initiative and the civil society-led Publish What You Pay initiative. The final case assesses disclosure by international organizations, with a focus on the International Finance Corporation's disclosure policies relating to foreign direct investment projects in developing countries.

Table 1.1 provides for an overview of the ten empirical cases covered in this book, including who is required to reveal what information to whom.

Overview of Contributions

This book is organized in four parts. Part I comprises two broad context-setting contributions that supplement this introductory chapter in exploring the nature and dynamics of a transparency turn in global environmental politics. Part II contains the five cases of state-led mandatory governance by disclosure initiative, and part III contains the five cases of private voluntary and international organization disclosure. Part IV presents the concluding chapter, which distills comparative insights from the preceding contributions, and presents overall findings on transparency's uptake, institutionalization, and effects in global environmental governance.

Launching our detailed examination, Arthur P. J. Mol discusses in chapter 2 the rise of what he terms informational governance in an era of globalization. He characterizes the transparency turn in global environmental governance as having entered a reflexive phase, in which secondary transparency, that is, additional layers of transparency provided by interpreters and intermediaries, become key to making primary disclosure actionable. In elaborating on the promise, pitfalls, and perils of governance by disclosure, Mol concludes that transparency has "lost its innocence" as an arbiter of democratic and environmental gains, a conceptual and empirical claim to which we return in the conclusion.

In chapter 3, Ann Florini and Bharath Jairaj present a comparative analysis of diverse *national contexts* shaping uptake, institutionalization, and effects of global transparency arrangements. Their starting

Table 1.1
Governance by Disclosure in Global Environmental Politics

	Disclosure about what: Environmental processes and decisions Environmental performance Environmental quality	
Disclosure from whom to whom:	Mandatory	Voluntary
State to publics	**Aarhus Convention** (disclosure of environmental data, regulatory processes, decisions)	
State to state	**Rotterdam Convention** (disclosure of risk assessments, regulatory decisions for pesticides in trade, export notifications) **Cartagena Protocol** (disclosure of risk assessments, regulatory decisions for transgenic crops in trade, intent to trade) **Nagoya Protocol** (disclosure of access requirements; disclosure of origin of genetic resources for benefit sharing [still being negotiated]) **REDD+** under climate regime (disclosure of actions to reduce forest carbon emissions; disclosure of carbon sequestered in forests; disclosure of safeguard information systems in place)	

	Disclosure about what: Environmental processes and decisions Environmental performance Environmental quality	
Disclosure from whom to whom:	Mandatory	Voluntary
Corporations to corporations (and consumers and publics)		**Carbon Disclosure Project** (disclosure of carbon emis- sions, performance, manage- ment plans) **Global Reporting Initiative** (disclosure of corporate sustainability performance, management plans) **Forest Stewardship Council** (disclosure of certification processes and decisions, sus- tainability assessments) **Marine Stewardship Council** (disclosure of certification processes and decisions, sus- tainability assessments)
Corporations to states (and publics)		**Extractive Industries Trans- parency Initiative** (disclosure of revenue payments and contracts) **Publish What You Pay** (dis- closure of revenue payments and contracts)
International orga- nizations to states (and publics)	**International Finance Corporation** (disclosure of environmental impacts of foreign direct investment in developing countries)	

assumption is that global transparency can acquire meaning only in specific (national and local) contexts. The chapter documents the democratization impulse underpinning a global spread of right-to-know and
freedom-of-information laws and their institutionalization in the specific
national contexts of the United States, India, South Africa, Mexico, Indonesia, and China. Even as democratization is identified as a key imperative
driving uptake of transparency, alternative drivers, such as marketization

and privatization, are also evident in these contexts. The authors conclude that *local context matters* in institutionalizing and securing desired effects of governance by disclosure. These contributions from Mol and Florini and Jairaj provide additional context for the critical transparency perspective and the analytical framework to assess governance by disclosure outlined in this introduction.

As the first of the state-led multilaterally negotiated disclosure cases in part II, Michael Mason analyses, in chapter 4, the environmental rights, including the "right to environmental information," laid down in the 1998 Aarhus Convention. In historicizing the adoption and functioning of Aarhus environmental rights in Europe, Mason demonstrates that an original democratization impulse underpinning environmental disclosure, in this case intended to promote the spread of democracy in Eastern Europe, is being jeopardized by a concurrent market liberal push for open markets and privatization in the region. He shows that the private sector is largely excluded from Aarhus disclosure obligations, ensuring that disclosure has few market-restricting effects in this case.

The critical stance of this chapter on the prospects of transparency to effect transformative change permeates the next four contributions as well. In chapter 5, Kees Jansen and Milou Dubois analyze transparency in global pesticide governance through a focus on the Rotterdam Convention and its informed consent procedure. The authors consider whether the embrace and institutionalization of PIC has empowered developing countries to make informed choices about imports of risky chemicals. They show that, although disclosure has had certain empowering effects, this is so only if empowerment is narrowly understood as enhanced capacities to make decisions. Furthermore, the substantive impact of the Rotterdam Convention is limited by the fact that very few chemicals are currently subject to its PIC procedure, a result of the geopolitical and material contexts within which these decisions are made.

In chapter 6, Aarti Gupta also analyses the uptake and institutionalization of PIC as a disclosure-based risk governance mechanism, this time within the Cartagena Protocol on Biosafety regulating safe trade and use of genetically modified organisms (GMOs). The chapter analyzes whether the scope and practices of disclosure relating to transgenic crops in agricultural trade further a right to know and choice of developing countries to permit or restrict such trade. Through analyzing the limited disclosure obligations imposed on GMO exporting (industrialized) countries by the protocol, Gupta shows that disclosure follows rather than shapes market developments in this case, with caveat emptor (let the buyer beware) prevailing in practice. As a result, it fails to empower the poorest countries most reliant on globally induced disclosure in this case.

In chapter 7, Amandine Orsini, Sebastian Oberthür, and Justyna Pożarowska analyze one of the newest disclosure-based global governance arrangements: the Nagoya Protocol on access to and benefit sharing (ABS) from genetic resources. The chapter documents the double-sided transparency requirements (for access versus benefit sharing) now being negotiated within this protocol. The authors show that the institutionalization of disclosure for *accessing* genetic resources (required from developing, provider countries) is much further advanced in the Nagoya Protocol than that for *benefit sharing* (required from industrialized countries and powerful market actors). This outcome results, they argue, from the institutionalization of a marketized, decentralized, and bilateral contract-based approach to governance by disclosure in this case.

As the final contribution to part II, chapter 8 focuses on the politics of measuring, reporting, and verification (MRV) systems underpinning the REDD+ climate mitigation mechanism now being negotiated within the UNFCCC, which calls for compensating developing countries for reducing carbon emissions from forest-related activities. The authors, Aarti Gupta, Marjanneke J. Vijge, Esther Turnhout, and Till Pistorius, analyze the scope and practices of REDD+ MRV systems, including what these systems seek to make transparent, how, and to what end. This chapter pinpoints the role of transparency as a means to assess and reward environmental performance, in a broader context wherein forest carbon has become a valorizable (global) commodity. In so doing, it questions who is held to account and who is empowered by expert-led, carbon-focused REDD+ MRV systems.

Taken as a whole, these empirical cases of state-led disclosure examine transparency's uptake, institutionalization, and diverse effects. In so doing, they shed light, collectively, on how state and nonstate authority might be reconfigured in such multilateral regimes of transparency, including by considering how private actors might shape such public (mandatory) disclosure regimes, whether by engaging with or remaining absent from them.

Part III then shifts attention to voluntary corporate and civil society–led, as well as international organization disclosure. In chapter 9, Janelle Knox-Hayes and David Levy analyze the rise of corporate disclosure in global environmental governance through a focus on two prominent nonfinancial reporting systems: the Global Reporting Initiative (GRI) and the Carbon Disclosure Project (CDP). The chapter argues that two competing institutional logics underpin the embrace and spread of nonfinancial disclosure: a logic of civil regulation, promoted by civil society actors and intended to secure greater corporate accountability, versus a functionalist corporate logic of sustainability management that highlights the instrumental benefits of disclosure to company managers, investors, and auditors. The chapter reveals how the growing ascendancy of a corporate instrumental logic shapes the quality and modalities of carbon and corporate sustainability disclosure.

In chapter 10, Klaus Dingwerth and Margot Eichinger focus, as well, on the Global Reporting Initiative. They scrutinize the rhetoric, policies, and disclosure practices in the GRI, with a specific focus on the role of intermediaries in making GRI information actionable. The authors show that the GRI's normatively demanding rhetoric on transparency does not permeate the organization's policies and practices. Moreover, disclosed information does not permit comparison across corporate reporting entities. They argue, as a result, that transparency is "tamed" in this case, insofar as it fails to facilitate holding disclosers to account. However, commercial organizations and "for-benefit" groups are now using GRI data to produce corporate sustainability ratings. The authors analyze the enhanced prospects for empowerment vis-à-vis other effects deriving from the "marketization of transparency" by these intermediaries.

Following these cases of corporate voluntary nonfinancial disclosure, the next three chapters in part III explore other sources and modalities of nonstate disclosure. In chapter 11, James Van Alstine focuses on the dynamics of transparency in the extractive industry sector and in global energy governance. He examines the Extractive Industries Transparency Initiative (EITI) and Publish What You Pay campaign (PWYP), both of which target private actors investing in resource-rich developing countries to reveal payments to host governments to exploit oil, gas, and mineral resources. Using the specific case of Ghana, Van Alstine highlights the hybrid (mandatory-voluntary) character and rescaling of sovereignty and authority that shape transparency's effects in this case. These effects are mediated, he argues, by the challenges to disclosure posed by the unique material qualities of oil as compared to other extractive resources.

In chapter 12, Graeme Auld and Lars H. Gulbrandsen analyze the central role of transparency in the non-state-led certification movement. Certification embodies the idea that information disclosure can be a tool for nongovernmental organizations (NGOs), investors, governments, and consumers to support high sustainability performers. Auld and Gulbrandsen assess this claim by comparing the uptake and effects of transparency in the rule-making and auditing processes of the Marine Stewardship Council (MSC) and Forest Stewardship Council (FSC). The authors show that the MSC uses transparency instrumentally, whereas the FSC treats it more as an end in itself. The chapter thus identifies key differences in how transparency contributes to the (perceived) accountability and legitimacy of these two prominent certification programs.

In the final empirical case, Timothy Ehresman and Dimitris Stevis examine, in chapter 13, how the International Finance Corporation (IFC) deploys disclosure as a way to mitigate negative impacts of foreign direct investment projects in developing countries. Their particular concern is to scrutinize the link between transparency and environmental justice. The authors find that IFC disclosure has only modestly served the cause of distributive justice, but hold out the hope that this effect can be strengthened.

Taken as a whole, these empirical cases examine transparency's uptake, institutionalization, and diverse effects in private and public-private disclosure initiatives. In so doing, they collectively shed light on how state and nonstate authority is being reconfigured by such voluntary regimes of transparency, including by assessing how the "shadow of hierarchy" might shape the functioning and effects of private voluntary disclosure.

In the concluding chapter 14, we distil comparative insights from the chapters relating to the core elements of our analytical framework: why transparency now? How is transparency being institutionalized? What effects (normative, procedural, and substantive) is it having? In addressing these questions, we also assess whether the contributions here validate or modify the hypotheses relating to democratization and marketization as drivers of disclosure, if and how disclosure-based governance decenters state-led regulation and opens up political space for other actors, and the conditions under which transparency may be transformative.

Taken as a whole, the book's findings reaffirm that transparency is here to stay, with information disclosure becoming widely embraced and institutionalized in diverse ways in multilateral and transnational governance of environmental harm and sustainability performance. At the same time, our analysis also suggests that claims about the "rise and rise" (Raab 2008, 600) of transparency need to be tempered by acknowledgment of competing trends that restrict both the uptake and scope of actionable disclosure.

This book thus documents the many ways in which the transparency turn in global environmental governance is evident but partial. It also highlights *how* the broader (contested) normative context shapes the embrace of transparency by various actors and its uneven institutionalization across diverse areas of global environmental governance. Transparency's effects, we show here, manifest themselves and acquire meaning in very specific constellations of power, practice, and authority relationships. Although this may be transparency's undoing as a broadly transformative force in governance, it does keep alive the hope for emancipatory politics in specific instances. Our book makes a start in exploring whether, and under what conditions, such emancipatory effects may be realized.

Notes

1. As noted in an article in *Harper's Weekly,* December 20, 1913, by US Supreme Court Justice Louis D. Brandeis (1856–1941). A century hence, this remains one of the most famous quotes about the importance of transparency in public life.

2. This typology of effects builds on the discussion of transparency's effectiveness in Gupta 2010b.

References

Andresen, Steinar, and Ellen Hey. 2005. Effectiveness and Legitimacy of International Environmental Institutions. *International Environmental Agreement: Politics, Law and Economics* 5: 211–226.

Baber, Walter F., and Robert V. Bartlett. 2005. *Deliberative Environmental Politics: Democracy and Ecological Rationality.* Cambridge, MA: MIT Press.

Bäckstrand, Karin. 2006. Multi-stakeholder Partnerships for Sustainable Development: Rethinking Legitimacy, Accountability and Effectiveness. *European Environment* 16 (5): 290–306.

Bäckstrand, Karin, Jamil Khan, Annika Kronsell, and Eva Lövbrand. 2010. *Environmental Politics and Deliberative Democracy: Examining the Promise of New Modes of Governance.* Cheltenham, UK: Edward Elgar.

Bannister, Frank, and Regina Connolly. 2011. The Trouble with Transparency: A Critical View of Openness in e-Government. *Policy and Internet* 3 (1): 158–187.

Beck, Ulrich. 1992. *Risk Society: Towards a New Modernity.* London: Sage.

Beierle, Thomas C. 2004. The Benefits and Costs of Disclosing Information about Risks: What Do We Know about Right-to-Know? *Risk Analysis* 24 (2): 335–346.

Bernstein, Steven. 2001. *The Compromise of Liberal Environmentalism.* New York: Columbia University Press.

Bernstein, Steven. 2005. Legitimacy in Global Environmental Governance. *Journal of International Law and International Relations* 1 (1–2): 139–166.

Biermann, Frank, Michelle M. Betsill, Joyeeta Gupta, Norichika Kanie, Louis Lebel, Diane Liverman, Heike Schroeder, Bernd Siebenhüner, and Ruben Zondervan. 2010. Earth System Governance: A Research Framework. *International Environmental Agreement: Politics, Law and Economics* 10 (4): 277–288.

Biermann, Frank, and Aarti Gupta. 2011. Accountability and Legitimacy in Earth System Governance: A Research Framework. *Ecological Economics* 70 (11): 1856–1864.

Birchall, Clare. 2011. Introduction to "Secrecy and Transparency": The Politics of Opacity and Openness. *Theory, Culture & Society* 28 (7–8): 7–25.

Brown, Nik. 2002. *Transparency—the Very Idea.* Keynote address at the Royal Society for the Arts seminar on Transparency in Public and Corporate Life, London, United Kingdom, September 19.

Clapp, Jennifer. 2001. *Toxic Exports: The Transfer of Hazardous Waste from Rich to Poor Countries.* Ithaca: Cornell University Press.

Clapp, Jennifer. 2007. Illegal GMO Releases and Corporate Responsibility: Questioning the Effectiveness of Voluntary Measures. *Ecological Economics* 66 (2–3): 348–358.

Clapp, Jennifer, and Eric Helleiner. 2012. International Political Economy and the Environment: Back to the Basics? *International Affairs* 88 (3): 485–501.

Compagnon, Daniel, Sander Chan, and Aysem Mert. 2012. The Changing Role of the State. In *Global Environmental Governance Reconsidered*, ed. Frank Biermann and Philipp Pattberg, 237–263. Cambridge, MA: MIT Press.

Dingwerth, Klaus. 2005. The Democratic Legitimacy of Public-Private Rule-Making: What Can We Learn from the World Commission on Dams? *Global Governance* 11 (1): 65–83.

Dingwerth, Klaus. 2007. *The New Transnationalism: Transnational Governance and Democratic Legitimacy.* Basingstoke, UK: Palgrave.

Dingwerth, Klaus, and Margot Eichinger. 2010. Tamed Transparency: How Information Disclosure under the Global Reporting Initiative Fails to Empower. *Global Environmental Politics* 10 (3): 74–96.

Dryzek, John S. 1999. Transnational Democracy. *Journal of Political Philosophy* 7 (1): 30–51.

Dryzek, John S. 2000. *Deliberative Democracy and Beyond: Liberals, Critics, Contestations.* Oxford: Oxford University Press.

Dryzek, John S., and Hadley Stevenson. 2011. Democracy and Global Earth System Governance. *Ecological Economics* 70 (11): 1865–1874.

Eckersley, Robyn. 2004. *The Green State: Rethinking Democracy and Sovereignty.* Cambridge, MA: MIT Press.

EEA (European Environmental Agency). 2001. *Reporting on Environmental Measures: Are We Being Effective?* Environmental Issue Report no 25. Copenhagen: European Environmental Agency.

Esty, Daniel. 2003. *Environmental Protection in the Information Age.* Yale Law School Research Paper Series, paper no. 58. Available at http://papers.ssrn.com/abstract=429580.

Etzioni, Amitai. 2010. Is Transparency the Best Disinfectant? *Journal of Political Philosophy* 18 (4): 389–404.

Fenster, Mark. 2010. Seeing the State: Transparency as Metaphor. *Administrative Law Review* 62 (3): 617–672.

Finel, Bernard I., and Kristin M. Lord, eds. 2000. *Power and Conflict in the Age of Transparency.* New York: Palgrave.

Fischer, Frank. 2009. *Democracy and Expertise.* Oxford: Oxford University Press.

Florini, Ann. 1998. The End of Secrecy. *Foreign Policy* 111: 50–63.

Florini, Ann, ed. 2007. *The Right to Know: Transparency for an Open World.* New York: Columbia University Press.

Florini, Ann. 2008. Making Transparency Work. *Global Environmental Politics* 8 (2): 14–16.

Fox, Jonathan. 2007. The Uncertain Relationship between Transparency and Accountability. *Development in Practice* 17 (4/5): 663–671.

Fuchs, Doris. 2005. Commanding Heights? The Strength and Fragility of Business Power in Global Politics. *Millennium Journal of International Studies* 33 (3): 771–801.

Fung, Archon, Mary Graham, and David Weil. 2007. *Full Disclosure: The Perils and Promise of Transparency.* Cambridge, UK: Cambridge University Press.

Gilbert, Jeremy. 2007. Public Secrets: "Being-with" in an Era of Perpetual Disclosure. *Cultural Studies* 21 (1): 22–44.

Gouldson, Andy. 2004. Risk, Regulation and the Right to Know: Exploring the Impacts of Access to Information on the Governance of Environmental Risk. *Sustainable Development* 12: 136–149.

Graham, Mary. 2002. *Democracy by Disclosure: The Rise of Technopopulism.* Washington, DC: Brookings Institution Press.

Grigorescu, Alexandru. 2007. Transparency of Intergovernmental Organizations: The Roles of Member States, International Bureaucracies and Nongovernmental Organizations. *International Studies Quarterly* 51: 625–648.

Gupta, Aarti. 2006. Problem Framing in Assessment Processes: The Case of Biosafety. In *Global Environmental Assessments: Information and Influence,* ed. Ronald B. Mitchell, William C. Clark, David Cash, and Nancy M. Dickson, 57–86. Cambridge, MA: MIT Press.

Gupta, Aarti. 2008. Transparency under Scrutiny: Information Disclosure in Global Environmental Governance. *Global Environmental Politics* 8 (2): 1–7.

Gupta, Aarti. 2010a. Transparency in Global Environmental Governance: A Coming of Age? *Global Environmental Politics* 10 (3): 1–9.

Gupta, Aarti. 2010b. Transparency to What End? Governing by Disclosure through the Biosafety Clearing-House. *Environment and Planning. C, Government & Policy* 28 (1): 128–144.

Gupta, Aarti, Steinar Andresen, Bernd Siebenhuener, and Frank Biermann. 2012. Science Networks. In *Global Environmental Governance Reconsidered,* ed. Frank Biermann and Philipp Pattberg, 69–93. Cambridge, MA: MIT Press.

Haas, Peter M. 1989. Do Regimes Matter? Epistemic Communities and Mediterranean Pollution Control. *International Organization* 43 (3): 377–403.

Haufler, Virginia. 2010. Disclosure as Governance: The Extractive Industries Transparency Initiative and Resource Management in the Developing World. *Global Environmental Politics* 10 (3): 53–73.

Heald, David. 2006. Varieties of Transparency. In *Transparency: The Key to Better Governance?* ed. Christopher Hood and David Heald, 25–43. Oxford: Oxford University Press.

Hood, Christopher, and David Heald, eds. 2006. *Transparency: The Key to Better Governance?* Oxford: Oxford University Press.

Jasanoff, Sheila. 2003a. (No?) Accounting for Expertise. *Science & Public Policy* 30 (3): 157–162.

Jasanoff, Sheila. 2003b. Technologies of Humility: Citizen Participation in Governing Science. *Minerva* 41: 223–244.

Jasanoff, Sheila, ed. 2004. *States of Knowledge: The Co-Production of Science and Social Order.* London: Routledge.

Keohane, Robert O. 2003. Global Governance and Democratic Accountability. In *Taming Globalization: Frontiers of Governance*, ed. David Held and Mathias Koenig-Archbugi, 130–159. Cambridge, UK: Polity Press.

Keohane, Robert O. 2006. Accountability in World Politics. *Scandinavian Political Studies* 29 (2): 75–87.

Konar, Shameer, and Mark A. Cohen. 1997. Information as Regulation: The Effect of Community Right to Know Laws on Toxic Emissions. *Journal of Environmental Economics and Management* 32: 109–124.

Krueger, Jonathan. 1998. Prior Informed Consent and the Basel Convention: The Hazards of What Isn't Known. *Journal of Environment & Development* 7 (2): 115–137.

Langley, Paul. 2001. Transparency in the Making of Global Environmental Governance. *Global Society* 15 (1): 73–92.

Leach, Melissa, Ian Scoones, and Brian Wynne, eds. 2007. *Science and Citizens: Globalization and the Challenges of Engagement.* London: Zed Books.

Levy, David, and Peter Newell. 2005. *The Business of Global Environmental Governance.* Cambridge, MA: MIT Press.

Litfin, Karen T. 1994. *Ozone Discourses, Science and Politics in Global Environmental Cooperation.* New York: Columbia University Press.

Lord, Kristin M. 2006. *The Perils and Promise of Global Transparency: Why the Information Revolution May Not Lead to Security, Democracy, or Peace.* Albany, NY: SUNY Press.

Lövbrand, Eva. 2011. Co-producing European Climate Science and Policy: A Cautionary Note on the Funding and Making of Useful Knowledge. *Science & Public Policy* 38 (3): 225–236.

Lövbrand, Eva, Roger Pielke, and Silke Beck. 2011. A Democracy Paradox in Studies of Science and Technology. *Science, Technology & Human Values* 36 (4): 474–496.

Mason, Michael. 2008a. The Governance of Transnational Harm: Addressing New Modes of Accountability/Responsibility. *Global Environmental Politics* 8 (3): 8–24.

Mason, Michael. 2008b. Transparency for Whom? Information Disclosure and Power in Global Environmental Governance. *Global Environmental Politics* 8 (2): 8–13.

Michener, Greg, and Katherine Bersch. 2011. *Conceptualizing the Quality of Transparency*. Paper prepared for the Global Conference on Transparency, Rutgers University, Newark, NJ, May 17–20. Available at http://gregmichener.com/ Conceptualizing_the_Quality_of_Transparency--Michener_and_Bersch_for_ Global_Conference_on_Transparency.pdf.

Mitchell, Ronald B. 1998. Sources of Transparency: Information Systems in International Regimes. *International Studies Quarterly* 42: 109–130.

Mitchell, Ronald B. 2011. Transparency for Governance: The Mechanisms and Effectiveness of Disclosure-Based and Education-Based Transparency Policies. *Ecological Economics* 70 (11): 1882–1890.

Mitchell, Ronald B., William C. Clark, David Cash, and Nancy M. Dickson, eds. 2006. *Global Environmental Assessments: Information and Influence*. Cambridge, MA: MIT Press.

Mol, Arthur P. J. 2006. Environmental Governance in the Information Age: The Emergence of Informational Governance. *Environment and Planning. C, Government & Policy* 24 (4): 497–514.

Mol, Arthur P. J. 2008. *Environmental Reform in the Information Age: The Contours of Informational Governance*. Cambridge, UK: Cambridge University Press.

Moore, Kelly, Daniel Lee Kleinman, David Hess, and Scott Frickel. 2011. Science and Neoliberal Globalization: A Political Sociological Approach. *Theory and Society* 40 (5): 505–532.

Newell, Peter. 2008a. The Marketization of Environmental Governance: Manifestations and Implications. In *The Crisis of Global Environmental Governance: Towards a New Political Economy of Sustainability*, ed. Jacob Park, Ken Conca, and Matthias Finger, 77–95. London: Routledge.

Newell, Peter. 2008b. The Political Economy of Global Environmental Governance. *Review of International Studies* 34 (3): 507–529.

O'Neill, Kate. 2000. *Waste Trading among Rich Nations: Building a New Theory of Environmental Regulation*. Cambridge, MA: MIT Press.

O'Neill, Onora. 2006. Transparency and the Ethics of Communication. In *Transparency: The Key to Better Governance?* ed. Christopher Hood and David Heald, 75–90. Oxford: Oxford University Press.

Pattberg, Philipp, and Okechukwu Enechi. 2009. The Business of Transnational Climate Governance: Legitimate, Accountable, and Transparent? *St. Antony's International Review* 5 (1): 76–98.

Picciotto, S. 2000. Democratizing the New Global Public Sphere. Working Paper, Lancaster University. Available at http://www.lancaster.ac.uk/staff/lwasp/dem globpub.pdf.

Raab, Charles. 2008. Review: *Transparency: The Key to Better Governance?* ed. Christopher Hood and David Heald. Oxford: Oxford University Press, 2006. *Public Administration* 86 (2): 591–618.

Roberts, Alasdair. 2004. A Partial Revolution: The Diplomatic Ethos and Transparency in Intergovernmental Organizations. *Public Administration Review* 64 (4): 410–424.

Roberts, Alasdair. 2006. Dashed Expectations: Governmental Adaptation to Transparency Rules. In *Transparency: The Key to Better Governance?* ed. Christopher Hood and David Heald, 107–125. Oxford: Oxford University Press.

Rose-Ackermann, Susan, and Achim A. Halpaap. 2002. Democratic Environmental Governance and the Aarhus Convention: The Political Economy of Procedural Environmental Rights. In *Research in Law and Economics—2001*, ed. Timothy Swanson and Richard Zerbe, 27–64. Amsterdam: Elsevier.

Rowan-Robinson, Jeremy, Andrea Ross, William Walton, and Julie Rothnie. 1996. Public Access to Environmental Information: A Means to What End? *Journal of European Law* 8 (1): 19–42.

Scharpf, Fritz W. 1997. Economic Integration, Democracy and the Welfare State. *Journal of European Public Policy* 4: 18–36.

Seidman, Guy I. 2011. *Lawyers Are from Mars, Political Scientists Are from Venus: Who Gets Transparency Right?* Paper prepared for the Global Conference on Transparency Research, Rutgers University, NJ, May 17–20. http://andromeda.rutgers.edu/~ncsds/spaa/images/stories/documents/Transparency_Research_Conference/Papers/Seidman_Guy.pdf (document now on file with author).

Smith, Graham. 2003. *Deliberative Democracy and the Environment*. London: Routledge.

Soederberg, Susanne. 2001. Grafting Stability onto Globalization? Deconstructing the IMF's Recent Bid for Transparency. *Third World Quarterly* 22 (5): 849–864.

Stasavage, David. 2003. Transparency, Democratic Accountability and the Economic Consequences of Monetary Institutions. *American Journal of Political Science* 47 (3): 389–402.

Stephan, Mark. 2002. Environmental Information Disclosure Programmes: They Work but Why? *Social Science Quarterly* 83 (1): 190–205.

Strange, Susan. 1988. *States and Markets*. London: Pinter.

Strange, Susan. 1996. *The Retreat of the State: The Diffusion of Power in the World Economy*. Cambridge, UK: Cambridge University Press.

van den Burg, Sander. 2004. Informing or Empowering? Disclosure in the United States and the Netherlands. *Local Environment* 9 (4): 367–381.

Wates, Jeremy. 2005. The Aarhus Convention: A Driving Force for Environmental Democracy. *Journal for European Environmental & Planning Law* 1: 2–10.

Weil, David, Archon Fung, Mary Graham, and Elena Fagotto. 2006. The Effectiveness of Regulatory Disclosure Policies. *Journal of Policy Analysis and Management* 25 (1): 155–181.

Weil, David, Mary Graham, and Archon Fung. 2013. Targeting Transparency. *Science* 340 (June 21): 1410–1411.

Young, Oran, ed. 1999. *The Effectiveness of International Environmental Regimes: Causal Connections and Behavioral Mechanisms*. Cambridge, MA: MIT Press.

2

The Lost Innocence of Transparency in Environmental Politics

Arthur P. J. Mol

Transparency is high on the public, political, and research agendas in national and global environmental politics and governance. Roughly defined as the disclosure of information, transparency is particularly prominent in the field of environment, although it is by no means limited to this field. The origins can be located in earlier right-to-know movements, legislation, and practices in the 1960s and 1970s, particularly in the United States and other advanced industrialized democracies. Transparency practices and developments in environmental politics have spread since the 1990s to other countries and localities, among them China (Mol et al. 2011; Zhang et al. 2010), but also to transnational networks and institutions.

With this proliferation, the scientific study of and reflection on transparency has become one of the key subjects of (global) environmental politics research. Transparency in environmental politics is usually analyzed and assessed against two sets of criteria: normative criteria related to democracy, participation, and right to know; and substantive criteria related to better environmental protection (see also Gupta and Mason, this book, chapter 1).

In general, transparency in environmental politics has a positive connotation, not unlike concepts of democracy and participation. These three concepts (transparency, democracy, and participation) are more than incidentally related, although they do not always strengthen each other. Transparency joins democracy and participation in striving for emancipatory environmental politics, by giving prevalence to and making room for bottom-up civil society engagements and countervailing power against markets and states. Markets and states are most often perceived as the institutions responsible for environmental devastation, extraction, and pollution. The assumption is that the more transparency, the better—that is, better for the environment and better for empowering the less powerful.

In contemporary (global) environmental politics, transparency in practice has many shortcomings and practical limitations in terms of, among others, lack of standardization of disclosure (Dingwerth and Eichinger 2010), the uneven scope of mandatory disclosure (Haufler 2010; Mason 2010), a focus on procedures rather than outcomes (Auld and Gulbrandsen 2010), and the (power) inequalities accompanying governance through transparency (Florini 2010; Gupta 2010a). These shortcomings notwithstanding, the common assessment is that we should not conclude that transparency is a red herring and that initiatives to further transparency are doomed to fail. Although many scholars illustrate that current disclosure practices and institutions in (global) environmental politics have numerous shortcomings in their design and operationalization, they often conclude that transparency is, nonetheless, to be welcomed, spread around the globe, and perfected. As a result, most transparency studies in environmental politics call for further inclusion of (powerful) private entities and state institutions in mandatory—rather than voluntary—information disclosure in order to empower victims of extraction and pollution and civil society, and stimulate environmental improvements (e.g., Esty 2004; Florini 2010; Gouldson 2004; Mol 2008).

These assumptions and claims are subject to further scrutiny in this book. As the introduction to this book also points out, the growing popularity of and attention to transparency is not an accidental and fashionable wave, soon to be replaced by another timely topic or development in environmental politics and governance. Transparency in environmental politics is here to stay and to further develop. It will further spread not only because it is widely seen as normatively good but also, and even more so, because it is closely related to a number of wider social developments in globalized modernity: globalization, the information age, and shifting modes of (environmental) governance (Mol 2008). Hence, this alignment with structural developments and a positive outlook ensures that we are, in all likelihood, only at an early stage of a development toward more full-fledged, comprehensive, standardized, geographically spread, and institutionalized transparency.

However, the structural alignment of transparency, with tendencies of globalization, the information age, and shifting modes of (environmental) governance, has changed transparency from a (peripheral) set of practices and strategies of and for powerless pollution fighters into a development that is fully institutionalized in the heart of modern society. With that, transparency is no longer only about democracy, participation, and a right to know by the oppressed but also about power, markets, profits, and surveillance. Although I concur with the generally positive assessment of the past performance of transparency in environmental politics, we cannot naively believe that more transparency in the future will always be better. Instead, we need to ask how, in what ways, for whom, shaped by whom, and with what (side) effects will transparency further develop in future environmental politics? Moreover, how should future transparency arrangements be evaluated? In this contribution, I argue that transparency has lost its innocence in automatically advancing democratic and environmental goals.[1] This calls for a new research agenda that focuses on analyzing diverse settings for transparency arrangements (with respect to, among others, political economy, environmental issues, and diverse states and sectors experimenting with transparency).

I proceed as follows: in the next section, I analyze the uptake of transparency in governance by discussing how transparency developments should be understood as structurally connected to wider developments in environmental politics and society, giving transparency some permanency and power. I then consider the dynamics of institutionalizing transparency and its effects. Specifically, I balance and condition the idea that more transparency is always better by noting (potential and actual) drawbacks and pitfalls of current transparency practices in environmental politics. In concluding, I highlight developments that might shape future transparency practices and institutions, of which the contours already now can be identified. This constitutes a research agenda for transparency in governance that subsequent chapters in this book begin to engage with, in conjunction with the critical theoretical lens and analytical framework for governance by disclosure outlined in the introduction.

The Permanence and Power of Transparency

To understand the growing uptake of transparency, as well as its logic, strengths, and (transformative) power, we have to place it against the backdrop of what I have elsewhere called *informational governance* (Mol 2006, 2008) and what others have referred to as *regulation by information* (Case 2001; Florini 2003; Tietenberg 1998). The concept of informational politics and governance implies that to understand current innovations and changes in environmental governance, we have to concentrate on the centripetal movement of informational processes, informational resources, and informational politics. Production, processing, use, and flow of, as well as access to and control over, information is increasingly becoming vital in contemporary environmental governance practices and institutions.

Information and knowledge are becoming important resources in environmental politics, the sites and spaces of environmental controversy are relocating to information, and the motivations and sources for changing unsustainable behavior are increasingly informational.

This centripetal movement of informational processes in current environmental governance is not just an answer to the shortcomings and failures in conventional command-and-control environmental policies and politics. It should not be seen as yet another environmental policy innovation adopted by policy makers, instead of laws or environmental taxes, to change the behavior of polluters. Rather, it has to be understood against the background of and closely connected to key social processes of the information age (Castells 1996/1997). These include globalization, the changing sovereignty and steering powers of nation-states and the emergence of new modes of governance, the growing uncertainties connected to the disenchantment with science, and the various (sociotechnological) developments related to information and communication technologies and the Internet. Few have yet analyzed in sufficient depth what the information age means for environmental politics and governance (for some early attempts, see Esty 2004; Fung et al. 2007; Mol 2006). It is clear, however, that informational governance—and with that transparency—is structurally embedded in and increasingly institutionalized within wider developments of global modernity. As such, it has some permanency.

The notion of informational governance brings together under one common denominator a number of seemingly scattered developments. These include, among others, the increasing significance and value of reputational capital of companies and the growing power—but also vulnerability—of the legitimatory capital of environmental nongovernmental organizations (NGOs). It also includes the emergence and power of new environmental monitoring arrangements involving multiple actors, the central role of conventional and new (digital) media in environmental politics and controversies, and the power and influence of accountability mechanisms in environmental governance. Although one can study each of these developments separately, it is vital to be aware that such developments are interconnected, and "structurally" embedded in wider social developments and trends.

Thus, the growing attention to and power of transparency in environmental politics can be understood only against this broader context of informational politics and governance. With information becoming more central in governance and politics, transparency is moving from just a normative call for a right to know from peripheral environmental activists toward the center of struggles for environmental quality and sustainability. Access to and control over information, data, and knowledge have become vital in contemporary environmental politics, because environmental controversies and struggles are increasingly located within what can be called the information scape. Transparency relates directly to power, because it aims to democratize information and empower the powerless by providing them with one of the most powerful resources in current times: access to and control over information and knowledge. The Internet further facilitates and enhances the possibilities of countervailing powers to also produce and disseminate information, making these powers less dependent on the conventional media and its gatekeepers. The various contributions to this book provide evidence of the centrality of power in transparency and disclosure practices and institutional arrangements.

Finally, the power of transparency also manifests itself increasingly as "informational capital." Ever since the early days of the environmental movement (in the 1960s and 1970s) environmental activists and victims of pollution have used information as one of their main resources in environmental struggles with the powerful, not least due to a shortfall in economic and political capital and resources. Now that informational capital is becoming increasingly influential in environmental politics, and many environmental controversies are resolved in the information scape, civil society environmentalists have gained a comparative advantage. They have not just informational capital but also the legitimacy and trust to operate powerfully and effectively in the information scape, especially when transparency provisions and institutions limit an information monopoly by economic and state elites. In that sense, transparency adds to the comparative strength and power of civil society actors in the information age. However, with the uptake and growing institutionalization of transparency, other (market and state) actors increasingly aim to capture transparency arrangements for their own goals, challenging the initial advantaged position of civil society in informational resources.

Two examples illustrate the centrality and institutionalization of transparency and disclosure developments in contemporary (global) environmental politics. Regulatory and voluntary carbon markets are currently at the center of global strategies to mitigate climate change. Within this area, the politics of information disclosure, certification and verification, and accountability are crucial. For example, disclosure politics shape, among other things, the verification of additionality and carbon credits, the certification of verification organizations (Mol 2012), and climate risk disclosures by major companies, such as the S&P 500 and through the Carbon Disclosure Project.[2] They also shape the growing role of accounting organizations in the European Emissions Trading System (Lovell and MacKenzie 2011), and the registration and control (and fraud) of EU greenhouse gas emission reductions in national emission registries and the EU Community Independent Transaction Log, to name but a few. Information is thus moving to the very heart of the environmental politics of global carbon markets.

Second, one can also understand the institutionalization of transparency in environmental governance through the dissemination of its practices, institutions, and infrastructures from a handful of developed countries originally to a much wider group of states, localities, and transnational institutions. China is a good example to illustrate this institutionalization process. Known as an "information-poor environment" (Mol 2008, 234ff) with limited freedom with respect to information, more recently China has made significant advances in transparency and disclosure in environmental politics. Since the new millennium, China has institutionalized increasing public access to environmental information. This is evident, among other sources, from the growing numbers of newspaper reports and publications on environmental quality data and risks and the increasing numbers of environmental websites (in all major cities but also NGO sites). It is also evident from ongoing information disclosure experiments with industries, such as the Green Watch program and a national and provincial company-rating program. Additional examples include the development of an environmental auditing system, the establishment of a web-based pollutant emission and transfer register, and the entry into force in 2008 of the Environmental Information Disclosure Decree (as part of the Opening Governmental Information Regulation) (Liu et al. 2010; Mol 2009b; Mol et al. 2011; Zhang et al. 2010). Following their internationalization strategy, Chinese companies are increasingly working with internationally agreed transparency provisions, such as those of the Extractive Industry Transparency Initiative, the Equator Principles, the International Standard Organization, and UN's Global Compact (Mol 2011). At the same time, China is still obstructing other international transparency proposals, such as systems for the monitoring, reporting, and verification of developing country voluntary climate mitigation actions, proposed by industrialized countries in the 2009 climate negotiations in Copenhagen. It is also trying to restrict the digital disclosures and campaigns of environmental and other NGOs, with only partial success (Yang 2009).

The Drawbacks of Transparency

The power of transparency discussed above might hold in ideal typical situations. In practice, however, numerous shortcomings can be identified in transparency legislation, institutional arrangements, "infrastructures," and practices. In order to fulfill their normative and substantial aims, current transparency arrangements are thus in need of further improvement. Starting from the fundamental notion that transparency is good, but that it only needs to be perfected and further advanced, numerous scholars provide suggestions for improving the design and implementation of transparency institutions and practices (e.g., Fung et al. 2007). Hence, there is still a road to travel to further develop and implement mature transparency institutions, which can deliver more environmentally effective and democratic outcomes.

In this section, however, I want to focus on transparency drawbacks that are not only limited to imperfect design and implementation of transparency provisions but rather to developments that endanger the fundamental idea of emancipatory transparency. I outline six (potential and actual) pitfalls facing transparency provisions and requirements. The six transparency drawbacks discussed are not all widely apparent currently and do not yet massively endanger emancipatory transparency practices and institutional arrangements. However, ongoing calls in environmental politics for furthering transparency should make us attentive to the emergence of such fundamental pitfalls. With these six points, it becomes clear that transparency is no longer innocent in and of itself.

Although meant to empower the powerless, transparency in environmental politics can as well empower the powerful and thus become an instrument in furthering inequality. This can work in various ways. The transparency provisions in several public and private international agreements call for quite sophisticated measurements, reporting, auditing, and verification arrangements. Such provisions are easier to fulfill for developed states and larger international market players, whereas poor nations and smaller companies have considerable difficulties (Haufler 2010). Such difficulties are exacerbated if implementation failures of transparency provisions are combined with sanctions or restrictions in market access (such as in labeling and certification schemes) (Auld and Gulbrandsen 2010). Under such conditions, transparency can empower and advantage powerful international actors and strengthen their position in global environmental politics. This is counter to its emancipatory promise. Fulfilling transparency requirements then exacerbates existing inequalities or creates a new dimension in existing power differences.

Second and related, putting transparency at the center of new forms of environmental politics does not yield similar benefits in all circumstances. Transparency will deliver on its potential only under specific conditions: when those meant to use disclosed information have access to and literacy regarding this information and when those whose information is disclosed are vulnerable to accusations of poor environmental performance. Both are not always the case. Minorities in developing countries faced with environmental pollution or resource destruction have to rely on support from western NGOs in order to understand, access, and use disclosed information in any claims against multinational companies operating in their territory. For instance, international NGO networks were necessary to effectively disclose oil pollution in Ogoniland, Nigeria, caused by different multinational oil companies. In addition, not all polluting companies are receptive to the risk of reputational damage. Companies poorly linked to the global economy have a significant degree of inertia against reputational damage (Mol 2009b). Similarly, in a global environmental context, not all countries are concerned about, or responsive to, their poor environmental performance being disclosed. In such circumstances, transparency is of little help, either in empowering recipients or in improving the environment.

Third, rather than a means of empowerment, transparency can also be implicated in further surveillance and control (Braman 2006; Mol 2008, 116). This is closely related to the question asked by, among others, Gupta regarding transparency for and by whom (Gupta 2010b). Usually, we interpret transparency as disclosure of (environmental) information from polluting producers and failing states for civil society actors and pollution victims. However, this is a limited reading of possible architectures and recipients of information disclosure. Now that we are witnessing a consumerist turn in environmental politics (Spaargaren and Mol 2008), and now that producers are also identified as change agents for environmental reform (Mol et al. 2009), transparency may also turn into the disclosure of environmental practices, resource use, and environmental impacts of citizen-consumers for producers. Moreover, both producers and states and citizen-consumers can disclose environmental information for "internal" use. Figure 2.1 specifies variations of information disclosure architectures.

If information about citizen-consumers is disclosed for use by states and producers, should we not interpret such transparency in terms of

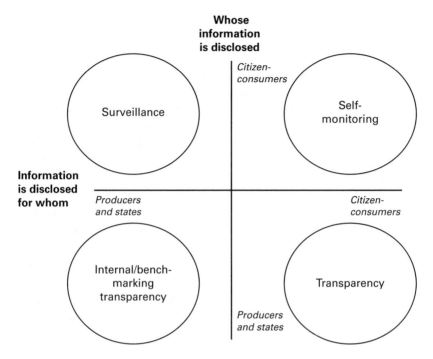

Figure 2.1
Varieties of Transparency

surveillance rather than empowerment of the oppressed? The smart util-ity meters, which can identify detailed personal water- and energy-use patterns, and communicate this information back to utility companies for monitoring and billing purposes, represent a form of transparency. Citizen-consumers are increasingly worried about the surveillance con-sequences of such developments.[3] Monitoring car mobility through (na-tional or European) road-pricing systems raises similar concerns, as does use of price-reduction card systems by large retailers to monitor green shopping behavior. It is also relevant to scrutinize what transparency and disclosure related to Personal Carbon Trading implies for the surveillance and privacy of citizen-consumers (Fawcett and Parag 2010; Spaargaren and Mol 2013). More institutionally, environmental NGOs are increas-ingly required to disclose information on financial donations and spend-ing. None of this is necessarily problematic, but it does raise an important set of new questions about enhanced state and market surveillance relat-ing to these (new) forms of transparency in environmental politics.

Fourth, mature transparency comes together with growing flows of information and claims. Scott Lash has been rather critical about the increasing informationalization, mediatization, and digitalization of every aspect of human life, resulting in what we could call a disinformation age (Lash 2002). In a disinformation age, information is out of control through overloads, misinformation, and disinformation. With the advance of transparency and the popularity of information-based modes of governance, (global) environmental politics can also fall victim to a tsunami of environmental information, to "drowning in disclosure" (Gupta 2008, 4). Especially if we fail to have powerful, legitimate, and widely accepted institutions that can be trusted to distinguish true from false information[4] and that can help us to prioritize valuable above less valuable information, transparency can become the victim of its own success and disempower itself. It goes without saying that there are major interests that will not be unhappy with such outcomes and actively support disinformation, information controversies, and information overloads. Right-wing coalitions of climate skeptics have been rather successful in developing such an informational strategy, in which transparency and disclosure is no longer associated with transformative powers but rather with "stuck-in-the-mud" strategies (Jacques et al. 2008). Especially in situations of information scarcity and secrecy and with "certified" information, transparency seems to work well as a powerful transformative mechanism. If not, disclosure of information can also disempower civil society and paralyze environmental reforms.

Fifth, and directly connected to the former point, transparency will work only when the quality and reliability of information is guarded and guaranteed. Disclosure of unreliable and poor quality information does not yield desired outcomes or empower the powerless (see Dingwerth and Eichinger 2010). For the same reason, calls for quality and reliability of environmental information can turn against stringent environmental protection politics. The US Data Quality Act[5] is a clear case by which the Bush administration (2000–2008) used information quality and reliability arguments to limit transparency as information disclosure. The act requires state agencies to establish stringent procedures to ensure and maximize the quality, objectivity, utility, and integrity of the information they disseminate. Because of this act, the growing regulation *by* information of (environmental) agencies could be counteracted by business and industry via the regulation *of* (environmental) information. Information transparency and dissemination is chilled, because agencies find it too troublesome to fulfill the detailed Data Quality Act guidelines (for the

US Environmental Protection Agency alone, the guidelines run to fifty-five pages) and risk petitions from industry based on the Data Quality Act (Environmental Protection Agency 2010; Mol 2008, 146–150; OMB Watch 2010). This results in a major setback for transparency and informational governance.

Finally, the question emerges whether transparency actually improves environmental performance. Can we indeed relate the often normative and procedural transparency provisions to substantive improvements in environmental performance? Recent scholarship suggests that the relations between procedural provisions of information disclosure on the one hand and substantive environmental improvements on the other are (at best) poor and often difficult to prove (Auld and Gulbrandsen 2010; Fung et al. 2007; Kraft et al. 2011; Mason 2010; Mol 2008). Three explanations are possible for this lack of a clear causal relation. First, lack of a clear relation might reflect the current state of the art in transparency implementation, implying that we have not yet advanced transparency far enough to witness causal environmental improvements. For instance, can it be that only quite advanced transparency will show a correlation (or even causality) with environmental improvements, similar to what Buitenzorgy and Mol (2011) found for the relation between the degree of democracy and environmental improvements? Second, the lack of a clear relation might be connected to problems of establishing causal relations between transparency and environment quality improvement; this would mean that our current methodologies fall short in measuring it. The third possibility is that something more fundamental is at stake and that the hypothetical relation between transparency and environmental quality is incorrect. Future transparency debates will no doubt focus on these issues, and I elaborate on them further in the following section.

The Future of Transparency

As argued so far, transparency is here to stay and will become ever-more important (rather than marginalized) in (global) environmental politics. Hence, we anticipate more calls for, practices of, infrastructures for, and legal provisions on environmental transparency. Transparency politics of the future will deviate from those in the past in four major ways.

Future environmental controversies will contain major *information* controversies. Information is likely to become—much more so than in the past—a major environmental battlefield. With information and transparency moving to the center of environmental politics and controversies, issues of accountability, auditing and verification, the codification of transparency requirements, and scandals around misinformation and disinformation will turn out to be central. Consequently, future transparency will become multilayered. Primary transparency is related to disclosure and openness of environmental information and remains important. In addition, transparency will also focus on the disclosing agencies and institutions, the media "owners" who facilitate or hinder transparency, and the actors verifying, certifying, and auditing environmental information (the new transparency powerbrokers); this we might label *secondary transparency*. Hence, transparency in environmental politics will develop from "simple" transparency to "reflexive" transparency.[6] In the future, transparency will no longer be simply the disclosing of information and the access to this information, but will also involve a complex of reflexive questions around the interests, the legitimacy, and the secondary effects of disclosure and disclosing agencies and institutions. The media, green product certification organizations, NGOs such as Transparency International, and carbon certification organizations have all become subject to transparency and verification demands and procedures themselves. Reflexive transparency is a sign of the lost innocence of "simple" transparency and a deepening of transparency, and as such a progressive step forward; but it is no guarantee of power- and interest-free information disclosure. In his agenda-setting book *The Audit Society* Michael Power has already analyzed some of the consequences that follow from this multilayered transparency, including the need not just to verify information but also the verifying institutions themselves (Power 1999).

Second, and related to the former point, the growing centrality of information in environmental controversies will mean new balances of power and new resource allocation strategies of actors compared to those around "conventional" environmental controversies. Positions of actors, power balances, coalitions, resource dependencies, the rules of the "environmental game," and effective strategies—to name but a few—of environmental controversies in the information scape are fundamentally different from the those around "conventional" environmental controversies. It is not easy to predict who will win and lose in these new constellations. Winners and losers may differ under different settings and conditions (for instance liberal democracies versus nondemocracies, sectors dominated by visible multinationals versus sectors dominated by local small enterprises). However, prediction is also difficult because actors and interest groups constantly react to changing conditions and adapt and change their strategies and coalitions accordingly. I argued previously that environmental NGOs, with their advantage of legitimatory capital, seem well-placed vis-à-vis vulnerable multinational companies that have a reputation to protect. However, developments around the plan to sink the Shell oil platform Brent Spar in 1995 in the Atlantic Ocean have shown us that legitimatory capital of environmental NGOs (in this case Greenpeace) is also vulnerable and easily "melts into thin air." Similarly, table 2.1 shows that—compared to business, governments, and politicians—environmental NGOs and science still have a comparative advantage in terms of institutions whose environmental information is trusted. However, their legimatory capital seems to be shrinking in this respect. The 2009–2010 Climategate controversy had a similar effect on the trustworthiness of climate science, as the Brent Spar had on Greenpeace, forcing climate science to rethink its procedures and strategies (van der Sluijs et al. 2010). Thus, future transparency developments have no easy, automatic, or undisputed winners or definite losers, but do involve major changes in the rules and resources of global environmental politics.

Third, transparency has to date been predominantly related to, fueled by, and based within civil society. Hence, it has strong normative undertones of fueling empowerment, democracy, and participation. With the growing importance of transparency in environmental politics, we can expect transparency to increasingly be part of, and ruled and fueled by, markets and monetarization. Environmental information has never been

Table 2.1
Trustworthy Sources of Environmental Information in the European Union in 1992 to 2011 (in % of respondents) (European Commission 2011)

	1992**	1995	1999	2002	2004	2007	2011
Environmental protection associations	63	63	51	48	42	36	37
Scientists	50	51	37	32	32	36	40
Green political parties	—	—	11	10	13	8	9
European Union	—	—	—	13	12	10	9
National governments*	12	13	9	12	11	9	7
Companies	4	2	2	1	2	2	3

Notes: *In 1992, 1995, and 1999 the category was public authorities. **1992 EU 12; 2007 and 2011 EU 27; the other years EU 15.

isolated from economics and markets, as evident from the funding of environmental monitoring programs; markets for certified green and organic products, processes, and services; or geographical information systems, remote-sensing and other satellite-based information systems that are increasingly in the hands of private companies. Nevertheless, with the expansion and growing importance of transparency in environmental controversies and politics, states and market actors increasingly focus on the economic value and political importance of transparency. We already see an exponential growth of firms and systems that not only sell and market environmental information and certifications but also (try to) market transparency and trust. In the voluntary carbon credit market, carbon credits that are verified through an arrangement including NGOs (such as the Gold Standard and SOCIALCARBON) have not only a higher credibility and trustworthiness but also a significantly higher market price (Bloomberg/Ecosystem Marketplace 2011, 35; see also Newell and Paterson 2010). We also see environmental NGOs monetarizing their reputation, trust, and legitimacy, via financial compensation for their logos and endorsements, as is happening with the Worldwide Fund for Nature (WWF) and its Panda logo. In addition, the sharp boundaries between NGOs and business get blurred, as in various countries NGOs also become market actors and consultancy firms profile themselves as being rooted in civil society (Anshelm and Hansson 2011; Mol 2009a; Sustain-Ability 2003).

This opens up a completely new set of questions on the relationship between markets and transparency, which will become pressing in the near future. How much of the normative undertones will be, can be, and have to be realized in market-based transparency arrangements? Can market-based transparency arrangements be more environmentally effective because they are not "burdened" with the normative undertones of participation and democracy? If yes, in what settings and at what cost? Such questions are also explored in this book in line with the hypothesis advanced in the introduction (Gupta and Mason, chapter 1) relating to democratization and marketization as key drivers fueling uptake of transparency.

Finally, transparency as information disclosure in Organisation for Economic Co-operation and Development [OECD] countries initially entailed place-based and state-organized systems facilitating the right to know about local environmental pollution. However, recent systems are placeless (that is, attached to transnational flows), organized by nonstate actors (although more than incidentally backed by states), and with a focus on environmental improvements (Fung et al. 2007, 169; Mol 2008). The market-driven disclosures in transboundary genetically modified food trade—rather than the transparency provisions in international environmental treaties—provide a clear example of this (Gupta 2010a). We see this also in the Tradable Green Certificates and Guarantees of Origin in the European renewable electricity market (Ragwitz et al. 2009) and even more clearly in the regulatory (especially the Clean Development Mechanism) and voluntary carbon credit markets. Transparency practices and demands with respect to various carbon credit systems and products (including complex futures, repackaged bundles, and multiple-traded carbon credit products) resemble those in financial markets (Mol 2012).

Transparency thus becomes part of transboundary markets, with transparency itself becoming a marketable product. These tendencies in transparency systems very much reflect current conditions of globalization and diversity in modes of governance. Moreover, they fit very well into the rapid developments in transnational environmental politics since the 1990s. At the same time, quite a few (developing and transitional) states have had much less experience with the first layer of "simple" transparency but are directly confronted with new reflexive transparency systems through their inclusion in global (environmental) interactions in polity, markets, and global civil society. Although transparency dissemination and learning across borders does take place, as was noted with the example of China, one can identify the emergence and growing awareness of a global transparency divide. This is not only related to the fact that different layers of disclosure and transparency are better operationalized, institutionalized, and implemented in developed countries. In a globalized economy, transparency and disclosure requirements touch on issues of competitiveness and access of developing and transitional countries to developed country markets. Thus within the International Standards Organization, as well as private certification schemes such as those of the Marine Stewardship Council, the Forest Stewardship Council, and biofuel-related roundtables, we see strong protests from developing countries against transparency and disclosure requirements (Krut and Gleckman 1998; Oosterveer and Mol 2010; Ponte 2008). The closing of global "information disclosure gaps" will be a key challenge for future transparency politics because these will increasingly be placeless and globalized. If we do not succeed in closing this gap, the future of transparency in global environmental politics will definitely look less bright, from empowerment and participation point of views and from an environmental improvement perspective. Transparency requirements will, in such a scenario, strengthen power inequalities and frustrate truly legitimate and effective environmental agreements.

Conclusion

Keeping in mind the key themes of this book, a balanced answer follows on two key transparency challenges in (global) environmental politics.

First, do transparency politics live up to their normative and democratic promises? We seem to have reached a crucial point in time. Looking to the past, the conclusion should be that transparency and disclosure have done more good than harm in terms of democracy, setting favorable conditions for participation, making access to information more equally distributed across different interest groups in society, and disseminating procedures, practices, and experiences toward less-transparent countries. The past of transparency is far from ideal, but more and better transparency, especially in relation to democracy, was more often than not a cause for celebration. However, in assessing current transparency tendencies and looking to the future, this overall positive past assessment does not automatically hold for the coming decade or so.

The growing importance attached to transparency in environmental politics ensures that it is now a central object of power struggles, with uncertain outcomes in terms of democracy. Future transparency will not be linked to civil society alone or focus only on disclosing the practices of polluters and states. Instead, markets and states are likely to "capture" transparency arrangements for their own goals more frequently, which will not necessarily be aligned with the original normative ideals of democracy and participation (e.g., Brown et al. 2009). Transparency is marketized and monopolized to gain power and profits, it is used as a form of public relations in symbolic politics, it functions in disinformation and information overflow campaigns, it is part of state and market surveillance of citizen-consumers, and it can further empower the powerful as much as the powerless. In short, transparency has lost its innocence. This should not surprise us and certainly should not lead us to denounce transparency. Instead, it signals the coming of the age of transparency and its full institutionalization in global modernity and opens up an entirely new research agenda.

The second challenge asks whether disclosure of environmental information leads to a better environment. In assessing new modes of environmental governance (such as information-based governance), a key concern will indeed be related to what might instrumentally be labeled *environmental effectiveness.* Various studies have tried to assess the effectiveness of new governance approaches and modes based on disclosure of information (Esty 2004; Fung et al. 2007, 85–86). Yet it is not possible to arrive at a general conclusion about whether, how, and to what extent effective transparency and disclosure systems protect environmental quality or reduce environmental burdens. We can only assess the environmental success of informational governance in concrete time-space contexts insofar as specific transparency arrangements operate with regard to specific environmental flows and practices. This is, among other areas of focus, one of the tasks undertaken by this book. Although results and assessments remain difficult to interpret and to generalize, conclusions and recommendations regarding specific improvements for particular transparency schemes should be feasible (as we see put forward in some contributions to this book).

Assessing environmental successes of concrete (that is, time-space specific) eco-labeling schemes, monitoring and disclosure practices, auditing and verification institutions, and company-reporting systems can provide insight into how to improve such arrangements, whether and how they should be connected with multilaterally negotiated regulatory regimes, and where the sites of power are located to make a difference. These questions become even more interesting now that transparency is no longer primarily a vehicle of civil society, but is fueled and ruled by markets and states.

Notes

1. This contribution is a significantly expanded and updated version of Mol 2010.

2. S&P 500 are the five hundred largest US companies according the Standard & Poor's; see Doran et al. 2009. The Carbon Disclosure Project (http://www .cdproject.net) reviews GHG emissions of 4,700 of the world largest companies.

3. A smart meter is an advanced meter that identifies consumption in more detail than a conventional meter and communicates that information via a network to the local utility for monitoring and billing purposes. By December 2011, more than 20,200 persons had signed a petition against the use of such meters in the Netherlands as a result of concerns about surveillance (available at http://www .wijvertrouwenslimmemetersniet.nl).

4. This touches on the changing role and position of science and scientists in global modernity (Mol 2008).

5. Section 515(a) of the US Treasury and General Government Appropriations Act for Fiscal Year 2001 (Public Law 106–554). The origin of the act lies in a political dispute over air pollution when the US Environmental Protection Agency

proposed to tighten national ambient air quality standards for fine particulates and opponents felt unable to assess and review some of the supporting scientific data. The industry-sponsored Center for Regulatory Effectiveness was the main lobby group for this act.

6. I draw parallels here with the distinction between simple and reflexive modernity made by, among others, Beck et al. 1994. It partly parallels the idea of layers of transparency put forward by Klintman and Boström 2008, 180.

References

Anshelm, Jonas, and Anders Hansson. 2011. Climate Change and the Convergence between ENGOs and Business: On the Loss of Utopian Energies. *Environmental Values* 20 (1): 75–94.

Auld, Graeme, and Lars H. Gulbrandsen. 2010. Transparency in Nonstate Certification: Consequences for Accountability and Legitimacy. *Global Environmental Politics* 10 (3): 97–119.

Beck, Ulrich, Anthony Giddens, and Scott Lash. 1994. *Reflexive Modernization: Politics, Tradition and Aesthetics in the Modern Social Order*. Cambridge, UK: Polity Press.

Bloomberg/Ecosystem Marketplace. 2011. *Back to the Future: State of the Voluntary Carbon Markets 2011*. New York/Washington, DC: Bloomberg/Ecosystem Marketplace.

Braman, Sandra. 2006. *Change of State: Information, Policy, and Power*. Cambridge, MA: MIT Press.

Brown, Halina S., Martin de Jong, and David L. Levy. 2009. Building Institutions Based on Information Disclosure: Lessons from GRI's Sustainability Reporting. *Journal of Cleaner Production* 17 (6): 571–580.

Buitenzorgy, Meilanie, and Arthur P. J. Mol. 2011. Does Democracy Lead to a Better Environment? Deforestation and the Democratic Transition Peak. *Environmental and Resource Economics* 48 (1): 59–70.

Case, David W. 2001. The Law and Economics of Environmental Information as Regulation. *Environmental Law Reporter* 31: 10773–10789.

Castells, Manuel. 1996/1997. *The Information Age: Economy, Society and Culture* (3 vols.). Oxford: Blackwell.

Dingwerth, Klaus, and Margot Eichinger. 2010. Tamed Transparency: How Information Disclosure under the Global Reporting Initiative Fails to Empower. *Global Environmental Politics* 10 (3): 74–96.

Doran, Kevin L., Elias L. Quinn, and Martha G. Roberts. 2009. *Reclaiming Transparency in a Changing Climate: Trends in Climate Risk Disclosure by the S&P 500 from 1995 to Present*. Boulder, CO: Centre for Energy & Environmental Security.

Environmental Protection Agency. 2010. Environmental Protection Agency Office of Environmental Information. Available at http://www.epa.gov/quality/informa tionguidelines.

Esty, Daniel. 2004. Environmental Protection in the Information Age. *New York University Law Review* 79 (1): 115–211.

European Commission. 2011. *Attitudes of European Citizens towards the Environment*, various editions. Brussels: EC DG Environment. Available at http://ec.europa.eu/environment/working_en.htm.

Fawcett, Tina, and Yael Parag. 2010. An Introduction to Personal Carbon Trading. *Climate Policy* 10: 329–338.

Florini, Ann. 2003. *The Coming Democracy: New Rules for Running a New World*. Washington, DC: Island Press.

Florini, Ann. 2010. The National Context for Transparency-based Global Environmental Governance. *Global Environmental Politics* 10 (3): 120–131.

Fung, Archon, Mary Graham, and David Weil. 2007. *Full Disclosure: The Perils and Promise of Transparency*. New York: Cambridge University Press.

Gouldson, Andy. 2004. Risk, Regulation and the Right to Know: Exploring the Impacts of Access to Information on the Governance of Environmental Risk. *Sustainable Development* 12 (3): 136–149.

Gupta, Aarti. 2008. Transparency under Scrutiny: Information Disclosure in Global Environmental Governance. *Global Environmental Politics* 8 (2): 1–8.

Gupta, Aarti. 2010a. Transparency as Contested Political Terrain: Who Knows What about the Global GMO Trade and Why Does It Matter? *Global Environmental Politics* 10 (3): 32–52.

Gupta, Aarti. 2010b. Transparency to What End? Governing by Disclosure through the Biosafety Clearing-House. *Environment and Planning. C, Government & Policy* 28 (2): 128–144.

Haufler, Virginia. 2010. Disclosure as Governance: The Extractive Industries Transparency Initiative and Resource Management in the Developing World. *Global Environmental Politics* 10 (3): 53–73.

Jacques, Peter, Riley Dunlap, and Mark Freeman. 2008. The Organisation of Denial: Conservative Think Tanks and Environmental Skepticism. *Environmental Politics* 17 (3): 349–385.

Klintman, Mikael, and Magnus Boström. 2008. Transparency through Labeling? Layers of Visibility in Environmental Risk Management. In *Transparency in a New Global Order: Unveiling Organizational Visions*, ed. Christina Garsten and Monica Lindh de Montoya, 178–197. Cheltenham, UK: Edward Elgar.

Kraft, Michael E., Mark Stephan, and Try D. Abel. 2011. *Coming Clean: Information Disclosure and Environmental Performance*. Cambridge, MA: MIT Press.

Krut, Riva, and Harris Gleckman. 1998. *ISO 14001: A Missed Opportunity for Sustainable Global Industrial Development*. London: Earthscan.

Lash, Scott. 2002. *Critique of Information*. London: Sage.

Liu, Xianbing, Qinqin Yu, Tetsuro Fujitsuka, Beibei Liu, Jun Bi, and Tomohiro Shishime. 2010. Functional Mechanisms of Mandatory Corporate Environmental Disclosure: An Empirical Study in China. *Journal of Cleaner Production* 18: 823–832.

Lovell, Heather, and Donald MacKenzie. 2011. Accounting for Carbon: The Role of Accounting Professional Organisations in Governing Climate Change. *Antipode* 43 (3): 704–730.

Mason, Michael. 2010. Information Disclosure and Environmental Rights: The Aarhus Convention. *Global Environmental Politics* 10 (3): 10–31.

Mol, Arthur P. J. 2006. Environmental Governance in the Information Age: The Emergence of Informational Governance. *Environment and Planning. C, Government & Policy* 24 (4): 497–514.

Mol, Arthur P. J. 2008. *Environmental Reform in the Information Age: The Contours of Informational Governance.* Cambridge, UK: Cambridge University Press.

Mol, Arthur P. J. 2009a. Environmental Deinstitutionalization in Russia. *Journal of Environmental Policy and Planning* 11 (3): 223–241.

Mol, Arthur P. J. 2009b. Environmental Governance through Information: China and Vietnam. *Singapore Journal of Tropical Geography* 30 (1): 114–129.

Mol, Arthur P. J. 2010. The Future of Transparency: Power, Pitfalls and Promises. *Global Environmental Politics* 10 (3): 132–143.

Mol, Arthur P. J. 2011. China's Ascent and Africa's Environment. *Global Environmental Change* 21 (3): 785–794.

Mol, Arthur P. J. 2012. Carbon Flows, Financial Markets and the Challenge of Global Environmental Governance. *Environmental Development* 1:10–24.

Mol, Arthur P. J., Guizhen He, and Lei Zhang. 2011. Information Disclosure as Environmental Risk Management: Developments in China. *Journal of Current Chinese Affairs* 40 (3): 163–192.

Mol, Arthur P. J., Gert Spaargaren, and David A. Sonnenfeld, eds. 2009. *The Ecological Modernisation Reader: Environmental Reform in Theory and Practice.* London: Routledge.

Newell, Peter, and Matthew Paterson. 2010. *Climate Capitalism: Global Warming and the Transformation of the Global Economy.* Cambridge, UK: Cambridge University Press.

OMB Watch. 2010. OMB Watch home page. Available at http://www.ombwatch.org.

Oosterveer, Peter, and Arthur P. J. Mol. 2010. Biofuels, Trade and Sustainability: A Review of Perspectives for Developing Countries. *Biofuels, Bioproducts and Biorefining* 4 (1): 66–76.

Ponte, Stefano. 2008. Greener Than Thou: The Political Economy of Fish Ecolabeling and Its Local Manifestations in South Africa. *World Development* 36 (1): 159–175.

Power, Michael. 1999. *The Audit Society: Rituals of Verification.* Oxford: Oxford University Press.

Ragwitz, Mario, González Pablo del Río, and Gustav Resch. 2009. Assessing the Advantages and Drawbacks of Government Trading of Guarantees of Origin for Renewable Electricity in Europe. *Energy Policy* 37 (1): 300–307.

Spaargaren, Gert, and Arthur P. J. Mol. 2008. Greening Global Consumption: Redefining Politics and Authority. *Global Environmental Change* 18 (3): 350–359.

Spaargaren, Gert, and Arthur P. J. Mol. 2013. Carbon Flows, Carbon Markets and Low-Carbon Lifestyles: Reflecting on the Role of Markets in Climate Governance. *Environmental Politics* 22 (1): 174–193.

SustainAbility. 2003. *The 21ˢᵗ Century NGO: In the Market for Change*. London: SustainAbility.

Tietenberg, Tom. 1998. Disclosure Strategies for Pollution Control. *Environmental and Resource Economics* 11 (3/4): 587–602.

van der Sluijs, Jeroen P., Rinie van Est, and Monique Riphagen. 2010. Beyond Consensus: Reflections from a Democratic Perspective on the Interaction between Climate Politics and Science. *Current Opinion in Environmental Sustainability* 2 (5–6): 409–415.

Yang, Guobin. 2009. *The Power of the Internet in China: Citizen Activism Online*. New York: Columbia University Press.

Zhang, Lei, Arthur P. J. Mol, and Guizhen He. 2010. An Implementation Assessment of China's Environmental Information Disclosure Decree. *Journal of Environmental Sciences (China)* 22 (10): 1649–1656.

3

The National Context for Transparency-Based Global Environmental Governance[1]

Ann Florini and Bharath Jairaj

As is true for all of global governance, the rules of global environmental governance may be negotiated transnationally, but in a world of sovereign states they are implemented nationally. Even rules arrived at by transnational private sector self-regulation will play out in national contexts that vary wildly in the degree to which they are hospitable to transparency. In other words, global governance initiatives do not float free of the state system. Absent some degree of transparency-friendly institutions within countries, global transparency systems have little hope of success. The uptake and efficacy of disclosure-based systems depend heavily on the degree to which norms and practices of transparency are institutionalized at the domestic level.

Since the early 1990s, there has been an extraordinary transformation in transparency views and practices in numerous countries around the world. Such changes have occurred in rich countries and poor, democratic and authoritarian (Florini 2007), driven in part by the democratization and marketization trends discussed throughout this book, but also by processes of transnational learning. This growing domestic receptivity to transparency-based governance provides the crucial context for understanding how the transparency transformation is unfolding in global environmental governance and what its potential and limits might be.

Thus, as a complement to the subsequent chapters in this book, which focus on global transparency measures, the focus here is on the extent to which disclosure has been embraced at the national level and why, how it functions in distinct national circumstances, and to what effect. In particular, we aim to provide insights into the largely unexplored terrain of national transparency discourse and practices in some of the world's emerging powers, with special attention to China and India.

Embracing Transparency

At the national level, transparency policies generally emerge first in the form of broad right-to-know or freedom-of-information laws or regulations, often—but not always—accompanying broader processes of democratization. In democracies, these come about based on the fundamental democratic premises that public (government-held) information is by definition the public's information and that governmental accountability requires transparency. In the oft-quoted words of one of the framers of the US Constitution, former US president James Madison:

A popular Government, without popular information, or the means of acquiring it, is but prologue to a farce or a tragedy; or perhaps both. Knowledge will forever govern ignorance; and a people who mean to be their own governors must arm themselves with the power which knowledge gives. (Madison 1822)

Such laws and regulations are important precursors to the more targeted disclosure-based systems of environmental governance that are the focus of subsequent chapters in this book. In the absence of some basic acceptance of right-to-know principles somewhere in the political system, it is implausible that there would be widespread adherence to the more demanding requirements of disclosure-based regulation or governance.

This notwithstanding, more targeted "regulation-by-revelation" rules are also arising as responses to regulatory voids at the national level, paralleling what is happening at the transnational level. Since the 1980s, governments have privatized not only state-owned companies but also the provision of a vast array of what are usually considered public goods (from prisons to electricity to basic education and water).[2] Such processes of privatization and marketization require, but have not always fostered, new national regulatory mechanisms to ensure that public goods continue to be provided and that externalities generated by private businesses are appropriately managed. Thus, just as the globalization of production has created regulatory voids that the global environmental governance initiatives described elsewhere in this book try to address, the increased reliance on the private sector has created regulatory voids at the domestic level as well. Moreover, the globalization of production by multinational corporations has permitted supply chains to penetrate deep into developing countries, including into those with less regulatory capacity than the home countries of these corporations.[3] In addition, the globalization of finance has led to a growing reliance on disclosure systems to attract foreign direct investment (such as the International Monetary Fund fiscal transparency standards).[4] The global transparency initiatives described in this book reflect multiple efforts to bridge governance gaps in the environmental arena. Yet such initiatives remain dependent on national preferences and implementation capacity, a factor often not given due consideration.

Institutionalizing Transparency

Institutionalizing a Right to Know

The rapid growth in national freedom-of-information laws and regulations is impressive.[5] From fewer than a dozen at the beginning of the 1990s, some eighty-six countries now claim some sort of public information disclosure law. Yet buried within this startling growth are significant disparities in intention, scope, and implementation.

The most familiar right-to-know legislation takes the form of the US Freedom of Information Act (FOIA) and similar laws in a handful of developed countries. These generally require some proactive disclosure of government-held information and provide means for citizens to demand specific information from governments. Virtually all have significant "exemptions," that is, arenas of government-held information to which the transparency laws do not apply. These exemptions always include some degree of protection for information of importance for national security.

Since the early 1990s, dozens of countries have adopted laws that in some cases have provisions that are considerably more far-reaching than those of the US FOIA, which applies only to federal government agencies (Florini 2007). Most notably, some of the newer laws apply under certain conditions to information held by nongovernmental actors, including private for-profit firms.

One of these is India. The 2005 Indian Right to Information law, which originated in a grassroots movement in the Indian state of Rajasthan, applies to all levels of government as well as, in some cases, to the private sector. As in the FOIA, this law requires proactive disclosure of government-held information and provides multiple mechanisms for citizens to demand specific information from all wings of government and, under some conditions, from nongovernmental bodies that are substantially financed, directly or indirectly, by government funds. This can include private companies such as privatized public utility companies (Ashraf 2008). Significantly, information seekers are not required to provide any reason for seeking the information or to prove *locus standi*.[6] Almost every government department has to appoint one or more officers to function as "information officers" to receive requests for information from the public and ensure a timely response to such requests. Officers can be penalized in case of delays or failure to provide information.

Since its coming into force, there is some evidence that this act has helped to empower citizens and improve government performance (RTI Assessment and Analysis Group [RaaG] and National Campaign for People's Right to Information [NCPRI] 2009). Anecdotal accounts of how the act has been used indicate a broad range of applications—exposing local corruption, pressuring the government to act on complaints and to address grievances, and providing information that should already have been in the public domain. India's combination of a flourishing NGO sector, free media, and public outrage in response to exposure of wrongdoing provides the necessary ingredients to enable the broad right-to-know rules to have significant impact. Nonetheless, awareness of such rights is greater in urban (compared to rural) areas, and implementation problems include bureaucratic obstructions, huge delays in processing applications, and poor record management (RTI Assessment and Analysis Group [RaaG] and National Campaign for People's Right to Information [NCPRI] 2009). Such challenges are likely to apply to transparency-based governance in many other national contexts.

Another country that has gone further than the US FOIA is South Africa, where broader processes of democratization have clearly motivated the shift to greater reliance on transparency. The 1996 South African Constitution recognizes access to information as a fundamental human right. The right is detailed and elaborated in the Promotion of Access to Information Act (2000) that creates a presumption of disclosure and places the onus on the state to show why it should not disclose particular information. A unique feature of this right is its horizontal application between public and private persons, whether natural or legal persons. In practice, this means that a member of the public may also request information held by a private company, subject to being able to show that the information is necessary for the exercise or protection of a fundamental constitutional right.[7] In all cases, disclosure is mandatory when the public interest overrides the harm that may arise from such disclosure.[8] The 2010 Kenyan Constitution includes similar provisions.[9]

In contrast to India and South Africa, the attitude of the one-party state in China toward transparency is far more instrumentally motivated by a desire to promote efficient market functioning. It allows for some degree of disclosure-based regulation, but does not foster widespread acceptance of norms favoring transparency. That attitude is most apparent in the national Open Government Information (OGI) regulations, which came into effect in May 2008 (Horsley 2007; Zhou 2007; see also Florini et al. 2012). At first glance, the regulations are similar to right-to-know laws around the world, requiring government agencies to proactively disclose information and giving citizens the right to receive government-held information, including environmental information, on request. However, the motivations and drivers of the Chinese regulations reflect the particularities of a government determined to manage an increasingly complex and globalized society that keeps political control firmly in central party hands.

The apparent contradiction of an authoritarian, one-party state pursuing open government requires some explanation (Florini et al. 2012, chapter 5). The OGI regulations are part of a larger effort to tackle corruption and improve the efficiency of governmental service delivery in a rapidly modernizing country. China's OGI regulations can be attributed in large part to elite-driven decisions that continued economic success— the basis of the legitimacy of the one-party system—would require "informationizing" China (to use the standard but awkward English translation of the Chinese term). This includes not only the spread of information technology but also greater governmental openness to make government more effective and responsive to the needs of citizens. However, the regulations do not reflect grassroots demands for information and are intended only to allow the citizenry to monitor government performance, not to have voice in decisions about the ends that government should serve. The general lack of grassroots-level demand for information and the relatively weak (though rapidly evolving) state of civil society organizations in China raises questions about the likely impact of environmental regulation by revelation in this context.

The experiences of India, South Africa, and China reflect patterns seen in scores of countries since the early 1990s, experimenting with new approaches to information disclosure at the national level. The end of the Cold War and the subsequent wave of democratization saw new right-to-know laws sweeping through much of Central and Eastern Europe as well. In such diverse parts of the world as East Asia and Latin America, democratization has also played a similar role. In general, combating corruption and holding public officials accountable are primary goals of right-to-know laws. Their potency in furthering the goals of governmental (and private actor) accountability in the environmental domain is a crucial area requiring further systematic and comparative study.

Institutionalizing Targeted Disclosure

Governments are increasingly turning to disclosure as a form of direct regulation, in what can be termed "regulation by revelation" (Florini 1998). Whereas right-to-know policies aim to inform the public as an end in itself, targeted transparency provides information that aims to influence choices. Disclosure-based regulation at the national level is not new—it has been the basis for regulation of the US stock market for many decades—but it is now an approach of choice for everything from nutritional labeling to airline baggage handling. The basic idea is simple: rather than requiring the targets of regulation to achieve specific behavioral standards, regulators require that those targets provide information about what behavioral standards they are achieving. The public release of that information is intended to push those targets into behaving in more socially desirable ways. The targets for such policies are typically organizations that are "viewed as responsible for some public risk or performance problem (and therefore have unique access to information about it)" (Fung et al. 2007, 41).

Probably the closest parallel to global environmental disclosure-based regulation is seen in global economic regulation. From the 1990s onwards, there has been growing pressure on governments to publicly disclose economically salient data as a means of making economies function more efficiently, countering corruption, and attracting foreign direct investment. Prior to the 1990s, many countries treated basic economic statistics, including such matters as international reserve holdings, as state secrets. However, the globalization of capital and the desire of countries to attract foreign direct investment have resulted in new pressures to make such information publicly available, as investors increasingly demanded such data as a condition of investment. The push for greater release of economic information has received strong support not only from such private sector actors but also from the international financial institutions, particularly the International Monetary Fund, which established new standards for "good practices" in this area (International Monetary Fund 2001, 2004). Countries as diverse as India, China, Mexico, and South Korea are now, to greater or lesser extent, disclosing economically salient information that they previously held secret (International Monetary Fund 2001, 2004, 2006).

The most rigorous work to date on targeted transparency is that of Archon Fung, Mary Graham, and David Weil, who have assessed the conditions under which national disclosure-based regulation has the impacts for which it was designed in diverse sectors such as health, insurance, and the environment (although they looked primarily at US cases) (Fung et al. 2007). They have found that disclosure-based regulation works well under three conditions. First, a potential audience for disclosure exists, one that is making less-than-ideal choices about a matter of public concern because of lack of information. Second, those potential recipients of information could and would change their behavior if they had appropriate information. Third, the changed behavior would cause disclosers, in turn, to act in ways desired by regulators (Weil et al. 2006). When any of these conditions is missing, government may have to do more than require disclosure to bring about desired changes in behavior. And even if all conditions are present, regulatory systems need to carefully design what information is to be provided, to whom, in what format, and when, if disclosure is to have a significant impact on behavior.

Meeting these fundamental design requirements is not easy, particularly if transparency arrangements are placed in the broader political economic context that shapes them (on this point, see Gupta and Mason, this book, chapter 1). In a few relatively simple cases, labels (in the right place and with the right content) can work effectively. In Los Angeles County, as Fung et al. (2007) report, restaurants are required to post their grade for hygiene (from A to C) in their windows. This puts a simple, accurate, relevant, and easily understood piece of information in the hands of potential restaurant-goers exactly when they are deciding where to eat—and the immediate feedback to restaurant owners from increased or decreased sales has helped to improve restaurant hygiene standards throughout the county.

However, such cases are rare. In the environmental field, disclosure-based governance is much more complex and not easily solved by simple labels. Enabling factors, such as prevalence and sophistication of environmental NGOs, receptivity of state and business actors to disclosure mechanisms, nature of the environmental problem, and capacity to design and implement transparency-based arrangements, come into play (Florini 2008; Gupta 2008; Mason 2008; see also the critical transparency perspective outlined in Gupta and Mason, this book, chapter 1).

Dozens of countries now make some use of disclosure-based regulation in the environmental field, in such mechanisms as the US Toxics Release Inventory (TRI), and the related Pollution Release and Transfer Registries now operational in most OECD countries (e.g., Ramkumar and Petkova 2007 offer a positive assessment; Fung et al. 2007 offer a more critical view). The approach represents a third wave of environmental regulation, following difficulties arising from reliance on traditional command-and-control regulatory approaches and limits to the success of the second wave relying on market-based instruments.

The TRI approach began as a response to the 1984 tragedy in Bhopal, India, when an explosion at a Union Carbide factory unleashed a toxic cloud that killed thousands and left thousands more injured. The US Congress responded with the Emergency Planning and Community Right to Know Act in 1986, requiring the private sector to report its releases of certain chemicals to the US Environmental Protection Agency, which then made the data public. NGOs, notably the Environmental Defense Fund, put those data into user-friendly formats that made it possible to mobilize public pressure on firms releasing such chemicals. Those pressures helped to bring about significant reductions in toxic chemical emissions in the United States (Florini 1998). OECD countries have broadly adopted similar regulations, and as we describe in detail in the rest of this section, a number of developing countries have experimented with related approaches. Along with the growing receptivity to transparency at the national level, this growing acceptance of targeted transparency as a regulatory tool may be an important factor in generating support for global environmental disclosure initiatives.

In India, despite significant moves toward institutionalizing a domestic right-to-know law, the government does not yet rely a great deal on disclosure-based regulation as a policy instrument of choice. This is not to say that disclosure-based regulation is absent in India. On the contrary, the Indian Parliament and regulators have used it to regulate, in particular, corporate behavior. In 1988, for example, the Indian Parliament required companies to publish their annual foreign exchange earnings.[10] In 1989, the central government required companies handling hazardous chemicals to submit details of chemicals they were manufacturing or importing.[11] As another example, in 2000, companies seeking to raise capital or debt from the market were required to publish financial, sectoral, and company-related risks to potential investors[12] and more recently, companies selling packaged food have been required to display nutritional information (Chitrodia 2008).

However, it is unlikely that these examples of disclosure-based regulation form part of a coherent policy design. It is more likely that specific disclosure-based regulatory options were chosen based on their appropriateness in response to a particular policy gap. This has resulted in an entire body of disclosure-based regulation in India. It is also relevant to note that Indian civil society has a long tradition of working on transparency and disclosure-based initiatives. For instance, there is a vast network of civil society organizations and groups working in the pro-disclosure realm under the National Campaign for People's Right to Know.[13] From the publication of minimum wage records at the village level[14] to the disclosure of financial assets by Indian Supreme Court judges (Supreme Court Judges Agree ... 2009), civil society has worked with different types of information disclosure.

Another significant effort by an Indian NGO has pursued the approach directly with industry, with some effects on corporate environmental performance and public policy. The Centre for Science and Environment (CSE) launched a Green Ratings Project in the late 1990s, initially covering thirty-one large corporations in the pulp and paper industry. It secured their participation in providing data on environmental performance in part by threatening to rank last a company that failed to disclose data. Thereafter, the CSE expanded its scope to cover other sectors, such as the car industry (Kathuria 2006). One assessment of the experience with the pulp and paper industry component found that it had been effective in improving the industry's environmental performance (Powers et al. 2008). Other NGOs have used disclosure to benchmark Indian companies against international competitors, with positive results. For instance, when Indian environmental NGOs lobbied local chlor-alkali industries to stop using mercury and instead to replace it with membrane technology, it resulted in a 30 percent reduction in energy usage, even though the toxic effects of mercury, rather than energy conservation, was the focus of the campaign.

China too is beginning to experiment extensively with targeted transparency in the environmental domain. Article Eleven of China's Environmental Protection Law requires that "the competent administrative department of environmental protection under the State Council establishes monitoring systems, constitutes monitoring criteria, organizes monitoring networks with related departments, and strengthens management of environmental monitoring. The competent administrative departments of environmental protection under the State Council, provincial and municipal governments shall regularly publicize environmental status reports" (China Environmental Protection Law 2010). Article Ten of the Chinese State Council's Decision on Several Issues Related to Environmental Protection encourages public participation in environmental regulation and defines an important role for the news media in publicizing actions that damage the environment (China State Council's Decision on Several Issues Related to Environmental Protection 2010). Other rules lay the foundation for reporting on "major pollutants, method, content and total volume of emission, information on emission that has surpassed the standards or total emission that has surpassed the prescribed limits; information on the construction and operation of environmental protection facilities; and emergency plans for sudden environmental pollution accidents" (State Environmental Protection Administration of China 2007, 6). A World Bank study suggests that local experimentation with disclosure-based regulation appears to be expanding (World Bank 2005).

The 2008 Open Government Information regulations are providing another legal basis for action to environmental proponents inside and outside of government. The OGI rules require all government agencies to develop their own implementing measures. The first to take up the challenge was the Ministry of Environmental Protection, which issued Measures for Open Environmental Information (for Trial Implementation) (OEI) on May 1, 2008—the very date the OGI regulations took effect.

However, although the existence of disclosure policies is important, implementation remains a challenge. Here, the record is mixed. One recent assessment found considerable variation in local implementation of disclosure policies in China. A few cases stand out. These include release (by the city of Hangzhou in Zhejiang Province and the province of Qinghai) of lists of companies polluting and violating relevant environmental laws, or a requirement for a monthly Corporate Open Day in the city of Zhuzhou in Hunan Province, on which enterprises must reveal production processes, operation status, and environment-related information to the public. Elsewhere, however, localities have been far less responsive to a regulation-by-disclosure approach (Kaiser and Liu 2009).

Multinational corporations operating in China also have a mixed record on disclosure. This was evident from a recent assessment by Greenpeace of pollutants emissions disclosures by twenty-eight of the global top one hundred companies with business operations in China. This assessment found that "only 6 of the 28 companies under investigation have disclosed information on pollutants emissions on their official websites; thirteen companies released information on pollutants emissions in other countries or regions abroad, but not in China" (Greenpeace China 2008, 3).

Environmental NGOs are important actors in promoting and using transparency mechanisms in China. One environmental group, the Institute of Public and Environmental Affairs (IPE) has explicitly set itself up to serve as an intermediary between governmental disclosure requirements and the public. IPE immediately responded to the promulgation of the OEI measures:

Our organization … is refining our water and air pollution database so that we can update our corporate discharge datasheet after the measures come into effect. This new data can make IPE's database more comprehensive, and it will eventually allow users to compare the volume of discharge by listed polluters. Besides making disclosure mandatory for listed polluters, the measures also encourage other companies to voluntarily share pollution data with the public. IPE believes that it will make far more sense to the public if the data disclosed by companies could be published in a consistent and cross-comparable way. To facilitate a more standardized disclosure, IPE has created a discharge data disclosure form, which it has distributed to local and multinational companies. (Jun 2008)[15]

IPE's increasingly sophisticated online databases on air and water pollution have proven to be eminently usable, enabling multinational companies to check whether their local suppliers in China have been complying with pollution standards. Such major multinationals as Walmart and Nike, for example, use the database to examine whether their suppliers are meeting environmental performance standards. Violators are pressed to improve their pollution management procedures, and a third-party auditor and an alliance of environmental NGOs (called Green Choice Audit) verifies claims of corrective action (Florini et al. 2012, chapter five). Starting in 2008, IPE has collaborated with the American-based Natural Resources Defense Council to issue the annual Pollution Information Transparency Index, which ranks over a hundred municipal governments on environmental disclosure. Other international and national NGO uses of the OEI measures include a Greenpeace report in 2010 detailing the dismal environmental disclosure performance of eight Fortune 500 multinational companies and ten Fortune China 100 companies, all of which were listed by Chinese environment agencies as having exceeded pollution discharge standards. The Center for Legal Assistance to Pollution Victims published a citizen manual on how to use the OEI measures and conducted training for local NGOs as well as an assessment of how well seven municipalities complied with the OEI measures.

Across other national contexts, ranging from Korea to Mexico, countries have developed pollutant release and transfer registers (PRTRs), in keeping with the global trend in this direction (Republic of Korea 2009; Mexico Mandates Pollutant Release and Transfer Registry 2004). Agenda 21 and the Rio Declaration in 1992 provided specific references to the establishment of national pollution inventories and the right of the public to access this information. To implement these international decisions, the United Nations Economic Commission for Europe (UNECE) developed the Kiev Protocol on PRTRs, a legally binding document of the Aarhus Convention. PRTRs were seen as a tool for public access to environmental information and thus closely tied to the Aarhus Convention's procedural and substantive goals (on this, see also Mason, this book, chapter 4). However, not all countries have had success in implementing PRTRs. For instance, several central Asian signatories to the Kiev Protocol have struggled to comply with the measurement and disclosure requirements of the PRTR.

In contrast, Mexico's experience with PRTRs is instructive (Pacheco-Vega 2005). The first effort at Mexico's PRTR was via the US-Mexico Free Trade Agreement. This reproduced verbatim the US TRI program, which includes mandatory reporting. Mexico's business community felt this approach would be onerous and lobbied against it. In its second effort, the PRTR (*Registro de Emisiones y Transferencia de Contaminantes*) was designed to include a smaller group of chemicals and a lower threshold for companies to start collecting and reporting the data, voluntarily at first. Over time, the list of chemicals and reporting requirements were ratcheted up, accompanied by simplification of reporting methodologies and capacity building of industries.

Another approach to targeted transparency has been taken by Indonesia's PROPER (Program for Pollution Control, Evaluation and Rating), a PRTR-type program that combines PRTR with a corporate social responsibility policy. PROPER was designed in 1995 as a national environmental reporting initiative, but instead of providing raw data to the public, Indonesian policy makers decided to provide color-coded rating of companies based on their compliance with pollution standards. This included a gold rating for companies demonstrating excellence, green for those exceeding the standards, blue for those who meet the standards, red for companies that have some pollution control methods but are not complying with the standards, and black for the rest. Participation was mandatory for selected polluting firms, but others could participate voluntarily. Anticipating reactions against companies rated black, the initial effort focused on reporting nondisclosure. PROPER went hand-in-hand with legal enforcement, and so if public praise and competitive advantage was the incentive for companies aiming for gold or green, legal action and public pressure were deterrents for those at black, red, and blue. As in the Mexico PRTR experience, PROPER started small (187 factories in 1995) and grew rapidly. Despite a temporary suspension at the time of the Asian financial crisis in 1998, the program has had significant impact in reducing pollution from the covered facilities (Garcia Lopez et al. 2004).

As these descriptions of India, China, Mexico, and Indonesia make clear, the broad trend toward usage of disclosure-based environmental regulation of toxic chemical facilities plays out in quite disparate ways in specific national contexts. The Mexican example reveals that what works in one national context (that of the United States) is not necessarily successful when transplanted elsewhere without due consideration of existing institutional capacity and local systems of governance. The Indonesian case similarly highlights that its creative color-coding approach, as an innovative deployment of targeted transparency, can be effective in regulating environmental performance in that specific context.

This discussion highlights that across diverse national contexts, and in a range of political systems, institutionalized transparency is promoted by, and is opening up political space for, nonstate actors, as hypothesized in the introductory chapter to this book, yet this is not necessarily accompanied by a decentering of state-led regulation.

Effects of Transparency

Global governance by disclosure is intended to help compensate for the large and growing gap between the need to regulate economic activities and the capacity and willingness of national governments to play such a role. Moreover, as noted in the introduction, the effects to be garnered from disclosure-based governance go beyond substantive regulatory aims to include normative and procedural effects. Clearly, however, such effects are more likely to be pursued and secured in some societies than others.

The introduction to this book hypothesizes that democratization and marketization are key factors driving uptake of disclosure at the global level, and these appear to be relevant considerations domestically as well. The Chinese leadership's desire to informationize the Chinese economy drives its approach, which is part of a larger effort to transform China into an economic great power, so political space for engaging China in global environmental initiatives may be limited. However, as we have seen, there are some domestic actors, includes some NGOs and the environment ministry, for whom engagement may be more feasible. India's Right to Information law arose from a grassroots movement of impressive staying power. South Africa's open-ended right to public information and inclusion of a right to private information was embraced as part of the public participation process of the Constitutional Assembly.

More generally, in considering a "democratization" driver, we find two aspects that influence whether transparency approaches are embraced and institutionalized: whether the society and political system is broadly hospitable to the idea of transparency and whether civil society is sufficiently powerful and has the capacity to demand transparency and act on disclosed information. In assessing who is empowered and what substantive gains are secured through disclosure, state (and societal) capacity thus remains essential to consider. States vary greatly in their capacity to understand, design, and implement disclosure-based regulatory or voluntary initiatives. Governance by transparency thus needs to meet quite demanding criteria if the result is to be a significant change of behavior in the desired directions. However, even countries with advanced regulatory capacities have had mixed success in implementing the approach. Societal capacity, in the form of social capital and organizational infrastructure, also varies greatly between countries, with some having much more than others. Furthermore, a lack of capacity among civil society organizations often creates a stumbling block because even when information is placed in the public domain, comprehending it and being able to act on it assumes capacities (human, technical, financial, institutional) that civil society organizations may not possess. In such cases, the efficacy of transparency-based regulatory systems may require attention to civil society capacity building or development of alternative structures. Thus, examining the promise of global transparency initiatives needs to be done in parallel with studies of specific national contexts.

Our analysis highlights as well that the diversity of countries disclosing information represent a wide range of regime types, not just advanced industrialized democracies. Until recently, open government, or more broadly open governance, was a Western and particularly US ideal that was closely associated with economically developed liberal democracies. An extraordinary degree of experimentation with transparency is, however, now underway in diverse contexts. As a result, in addition to this book's hypotheses about the causal influence of democratization (evident in the South Africa and Mexico cases) and market-based approaches to economic development (particularly significant in China), this chapter has also found that a significant driver is the transnational spread of transparency as a standard practice to be emulated.

PRTR is an example of transnational transmission of a new approach to environmental regulation. Indonesia and Mexico's PRTR approaches, which were based on, among others, the institutional capacities within the countries, demonstrate, however, that such transnational transmission works only when modified to take into account local context. Mexico's initial effort, which lacked such modification, failed. Indonesia's decision to replace point source pollution data with color-coded ratings of companies, for instance, was to avoid confusing messages to the Indonesian public from disclosure of raw data. Indonesia chose to make reporting mandatory from the very beginning for a select number of polluting facilities, whereas Mexico started with voluntary reporting, but both started with a few pollutants and expanded over time. Compared to the Kiev (PRTR) Protocol approach of laying down international and regional norms and expecting all EU countries to achieve the disclosure requirements, Mexico and Indonesia designed their PRTR approach within a local context and ratcheted up the effort over time and in scope. By contrast, there are thirty-eight signatories to the Kiev Protocol, but only twenty-eight ratifications,[16] with varying degrees of compliance.

It is important to keep these distinctions in mind in considering how specific environmental disclosure initiatives might work in diverse national contexts. For example, to the extent that private voluntary transparency arrangements aim to attract "green" investors, national capacity to provide reliable economically salient data will be a crucial factor. By contrast, global transparency initiatives that aim to empower citizens to engage in processes of environmental decision making need to examine national approaches to citizens' general right to know and/or targeted disclosure policies in order to evaluate how receptive government officials and businesses operating in specific countries are likely to be to such initiatives. Identifying and responding to the constituencies or users of the disclosed information will thus determine the scope and success of specific disclosure policies.

As globalization and privatization shift ever more information of public concern into the hands of the private sector, questions of who has the right to access what information will also become ever more significant. In the absence of any systematic debate on, much less consensus about, what constitutes a public function that the public has a right to know about (even if a private entity handles the function), we are currently making do with a hodgepodge of voluntary standards and occasional mandatory disclosure requirements. This raises a question central for the study of governance by disclosure: how far beyond governments should mandatory disclosure obligations extend? A few national laws, notably those of India and South Africa, do address the private sector, but most do not. That more systematic debate in the environmental realm, within and across countries, is long overdue.

Conclusion

The preceding discussion might indicate a reasonably rosy future for disclosure-based approaches to environmental governance. In many of the countries explored in this chapter, we find an increasingly favorable legal environment for transparency-based governance. In addition, the experiences of India and China demonstrate a perhaps surprising degree of civil society capacity to demand and use transparency. The efficacy of targeted disclosure approaches to environmental governance depends heavily on the existence of intermediary groups that demand effective implementation, organize the disclosed information in ways that are relevant and comprehensible to the public, and help to channel responses to disclosure. Such groups tend to be civil society organizations, a sector that is notably underdeveloped in China but one that is beginning to grow, particularly in the environmental area (Florini et al. 2012, chapters 4 and 5). Indian civil society already has a strong tradition of working with disclosure, and as a policy approach, it has been tried and found to be reasonably successful. However, as mentioned, this has been more ad hoc rather than by coherent policy design.

Despite factors pushing in the direction of greater disclosure, however, transparency also faces substantial counterpressures in every country. Bringing about a meaningful increase in transparency at the national level always involves a power struggle. Those who are currently enjoying the benefits of obscurity (rent seeking or just avoiding the hassles of accountability) are loath to renounce these privileges. There are also legitimate reasons for secrecy under many circumstances—national security concerns, corporate proprietary data, and individual privacy concerns— which require a careful balancing of the right to know with the public interest in some degree of secrecy. Given the lack of broadly agreed principles in most countries about where the boundaries of disclosure should lie, transparency policies continually evolve with changes in the domestic political climate.

Even when governments or other actors wish to implement disclosure policies, they may find it difficult to do so. Disclosure can be costly and complex, requiring archiving of materials, staff training, changes to bureaucratic procedures, and availability of financial and human resources (Neuman and Calland 2007). Moreover, only information that exists, or has been collected, can be disclosed. Hence, a key challenge to effective disclosure-based systems of (voluntary) regulation is that, in many cases, relevant information is not collected or does not exist, particularly in developing countries that lack substantial traditions of record keeping.

In short, the national contexts for global transparency initiatives present a very mixed picture. Overall, receptivity to disclosure has spread since the 1990s, supply is (reluctantly) improving (despite continued sovereignty issues, practical issues with data and information management, and efforts to preserve rent-seeking privileges), and demand for disclosure is growing (although the efficacy of the demand is constrained by limited civil society capacity). However, transparency is still far from being a universal norm. More than eighty countries now have freedom-of-information laws or regulations—but the majority of the world's roughly two hundred countries lack any such rules. Moreover, even where transparency is nominally embedded in diverse national contexts, rhetoric frequently outstrips reality.

Notes

1. This chapter is a significantly revised and expanded version of Florini (2010). Ann Florini is grateful to Saleena Saleem for excellent research assistance for this chapter.

2. The World Bank provides a database of privatizations exceeding US$1 million through 2008 in developing countries. Available at http://go.worldbank.org/W1ET8RG1Q0.

3. The annual World Investment Report (WIR) of the United Nations Conference on Trade and Development (UNCTAD) provides detailed analysis of the globalization of production. See, for example, UNCTAD 2011.

4. International Monetary Fund, Data Dissemination Standard Bulletin Board. Available at http://dsbb.imf.org.

5. Several NGOs do excellent monitoring and overviews of freedom-of-information laws around the world. See Vleugels (2008). Another leading website for information related to transparency is www.Freedominfo.org.

6. Right to Information Act, 2005, Section 6(2).

7. Section 32, Constitution of the Republic of South Africa, 1996.

8. Sections 46 and 70, Promotion of Access to Information Act, 2000.

9. Article 35, Constitution of Kenya.

10. The Companies Act, 1956 section 217(1).

11. Manufacture, Storage and Import of Hazardous Chemical Rules, 1989.

12. Securities and Exchange Board of India (Disclosure and Investor Protection) Guidelines, 2009.

13. See http://www.righttoinformation.info.

14. See About Us, MKSS India. Available at http://www.mkssindia.org/about-us.

15. The independent Institute for Public and Environmental Affairs Internet based, publicly accessible, and interactive pollutant emission register for China. Available at http://www.ipe.org.cn/En/index.aspx.

16. As of November 23, 2011, as reported at http://www.unece.org/env/pp/prtr.html.

References

Ashraf, Tariq. 2008. Empowering People through Information: A Case Study of India's Right to Information Act. *International Information & Library Review* 40 (3): 148–152.

China Environmental Protection Law. 2010. Available at http://www.china.org.cn/english/environment/34356.htm.

China State Council's Decision on Several Issues Related to Environmental Protection. 2010. Available at http://www.asianlii.org/cn/legis/cen/laws/dotscosicep803/.

Chitrodia, R. B. 2008. Packaged Foods Must List Nutritional Facts. *Times of India*. Oct. 31. Available at http://timesofindia.indiatimes.com/biz/india-business/Packaged-foods-must-list-nutritional-facts/articleshow/3656231.cms.

Florini, Ann. 1998. The End of Secrecy. *Foreign Policy* Summer (111): 50–63.

Florini, Ann, ed. 2007. *The Right to Know: Transparency for an Open World*. New York: Columbia University Press.

Florini, Ann. 2008. Making Transparency Work. *Global Environmental Politics* 8 (2): 14–16.

Florini, Ann. 2010. The National Context for Transparency-based Global Environmental Governance. *Global Environmental Politics* 10 (3):120–131.

Florini, Ann, Hairong Lai, and Yeling Tan. 2012. *China Experiments: From Local Innovations to National Reform*. Washington, DC: Brookings Institution Press.

Fung, Archon, Mary Graham, and David Weil. 2007. *Full Disclosure: The Perils and Promise of Transparency*. New York: Cambridge University Press.

Garcia Lopez, Jorge, Thomas Sterner, and Shakeb Afsah. 2004. *Public Disclosure of Industrial Pollution: The PROPER Approach for Indonesia?* Discussion Paper 04–34, Resources for the Future, Washington, DC.

Greenpeace China. 2008. *An Investigation into Environmental Information Disclosure by Companies, China: Green Peace*. Available at http://www.sustainability-fj.org/seminar/pdf/091120_08.pdf.

Gupta, Aarti. 2008. Transparency under Scrutiny: Information Disclosure in Global Environmental Governance. *Global Environmental Politics* 8 (2): 1–7.

Horsley, Jamie P. 2007. *China Adopts First Nationwide Open Government Information Regulations*. Available at http://www.freedominfo.org/2007/05/china-adopts-first-nationwide-open-government-information-regulations.

International Monetary Fund (IMF). 2001. *Report on the Observance of Standards and Codes (ROSC)—India: Fiscal Transparency*. Available at http://www.imf.org/external/np/rosc/ind/fiscal.htm.

International Monetary Fund (IMF). 2004. *India: Report on Observance of Standards and Codes—Data Module, Response by the Authorities, and Detailed Assessments Using Data Quality Assessment Framework*. IMF Country Report No. 04/96. Available at http://www.imf.org/external/pubs/ft/scr/2004/cr0496.pdf.

International Monetary Fund (IMF). 2006. *People's Republic of China: 2006 Article IV Consultation—Staff Report; Staff Statement; and Public Information No-*

tice on the Executive Board Discussion under Article. IMF Country Report No. 06/394. Available at http://www.imf.org/external/np/rosc/ind/fiscal.htm.

Jun, Ma. 2008. *Your Right to Know: A Historic Moment*. China Dialogue. Available at http://www.chinadialogue.net/article/show/single/en/1962.

Kaiser, Tod, and Rongkun Liu. 2009. *Taking the Pulse: The One-Year Anniversary of China's Open Government Information Measures*. China Environmental Health Project Research Brief, Woodrow Wilson International Center for Scholars. Available at http://www.wilsoncenter.org/topics/docs/ogi_final21.pdf.

Kathuria, Vinish. 2006. *Public Disclosures—Using Information to Reduce Pollution*. Concept Note. Madras School of Economics. Available at http://coe.mse.ac.in/dp/Public%20Disclosure.pdf.

Madison, James. 1822. *James Madison, Letter to W. T. Barry*, August 4. Available at http://press-pubs.uchicago.edu/founders/documents/v1ch18s35.html.

Mason, Michael. 2008. Transparency for Whom? Information Disclosure and Power in Global Environmental Governance. *Global Environmental Politics* 8 (2): 8–13.

Mexico Mandates Pollutant Release and Transfer Registry. 2004. *EIA Track*. June 10. Available at http://www.eiatrack.org/r/480&Is_News=0.

Neuman, Laura, and Richard Calland. 2007. Making the Law Work: The Challenges of Implementation. In *The Right to Know: Transparency for an Open World*, ed. Ann Florini, 185–208. New York: Columbia University Press.

Pacheco-Vega, Raul. 2005. Democracy by Proxy: Environmental NGOs and Policy Change in Mexico. In *Environmental Issues in Latin America and the Caribbean*, ed. Aldemaro Romero and Sarah E. West. Dordrecht, The Netherlands: Springer.

Powers, Nicholas, Allen Blackman, Thomas P. Lyon, and Urvashi Narain. 2008. *Does Disclosure Reduce Pollution? Evidence from India's Green Rating Project*. Discussion Papers DP-08–38. Washington, DC: Resources for the Future. Available at http://www.rff.org/documents/RFF-DP-08-38.pdf.

Ramkumar, Vivek, and Elena Petkova. 2007. Transparency and Environmental Governance. In *The Right to Know: Transparency for an Open World*, ed. Ann Florini, 279–308. New York: Columbia University Press.

Republic of Korea. 2009. *National Report: 18th–19th Session of the Commission on Sustainable Development (CSD)*. Available at http://sustainabledevelopment.un.org/index.php?page=view&type=6&nr=44&menu=172.

RTI Assessment and Analysis Group (RaaG) and National Campaign for People's Right to Information (NCPRI). 2009. *Safeguarding the Right to Information*. Report of the People's RTI Assessment 2008: Executive Summary. Available at http://rti-assessment.org/exe_summ_report.pdf.

State Environmental Protection Administration of China. 2007. *Measures on Open Environmental Information*. Available at http://www.epa.gov/ogc/china/open_environmental.pdf.

Supreme Court Judges Agree to Make Their Assets Public. 2009. *The Hindu*. August 26. Available at http://www.thehindu.com/news/national/article9774.ece.

United Nations Conference on Trade and Development (UNCTAD). 2011. *World Investment Report 2011: Non-Equity Modes of International Production and Development.* Available at http://www.unctad-docs.org/files/UNCTAD -WIR2011-Full-en.pdf.

Vleugels, Roger. 2008. *Overview of All 86 FOIA Countries.* Available at http:// www.statewatch.org/news/2008/sep/foi-overview-86-countries-sep-2008.pdf.

Weil, David, Archon Fung, Mary Graham, and Elena Fagotto. 2006. The Effectiveness of Regulatory Disclosure Policies. *Journal of Policy Analysis and Management* 25 (1): 155–181.

World Bank. 2005. *Disclosing Emissions Information Helps Check Pollution in Asia.* Available at http://econ.worldbank.org/WBSITE/EXTERNAL/EXTDEC/ EXTRESEARCH/0,,contentMDK:20865079~pagePK:64165401~piPK:6416502 6~theSitePK:469382,00.html.

Zhou, Hanhua. 2007. Open Government in China: Practice and Problems. In *The Right to Know: Transparency for an Open World*, ed. Ann Florini, 92–115. New York: Columbia University Press.

II

State-Led Multilaterally Negotiated Transparency

4

So Far but No Further? Transparency and Disclosure in the Aarhus Convention

Michael Mason

Insofar as the transparency turn in global environmental politics includes multilateral agreements, one treaty stands out as seminal—the Convention on Access to Information, Public Participation in Decision-Making and Access to Justice in Environmental Matters (henceforth Aarhus Convention 1998).[1] The Aarhus Convention, negotiated under the auspices of the United Nations Economic Commission for Europe (UNECE), contains a striking invocation of human environmental rights. Its article 1 affirms the "right of every person of present and future generations to live in an environment adequate to his or her health or well-being" as justification for its recognition, in environmental matters, of rights to information access, public participation, and access to justice.

These Aarhus procedural rights bring corresponding duties to states. Thus, for citizen access to information, there are information disclosure obligations for public authorities. Similarly, for citizen rights of access to decision making and justice in environmental matters, the convention sets out associated duties. The effective realization of these procedural rights becomes a condition for realizing the substantive right to an adequate level of environmental quality. This claim about the necessary conjoining of procedural and substantive environmental rights is also found in the preamble to the Protocol on Pollutant Release and Transfer Registers (Kiev Protocol 2003), adopted at a meeting of the parties to the Aarhus Convention.[2] In force since October 2009, the Kiev Protocol is the first legally binding international instrument facilitating access to pollution registers.

UNECE has lauded "Aarhus environmental rights" for increasing citizen access to environmental information across Europe and helping to secure more transparent and accountable regulatory processes. As will be shown, the agreement has indeed introduced innovative mechanisms for empowering public participation in national and international decision making and affording legal standing to affected publics and nongovernmental organizations (NGOs). This in part reflects the efforts of environmental NGOs in lobbying UNECE regarding decision-making entitlements for civil society actors—lobbying that found fertile ground in the 1990s in the context of external democracy promotion within Eastern Europe. Transparency, expressed as information disclosure, was seen as a necessary expression of, and condition for, democratic governance. In this chapter, which revises and updates an earlier article on the Aarhus Convention (Mason 2010), I examine the nature and scope of its information disclosure obligations. Combining elements of constructivism and critical political economy, the theoretical concern is with the historical emergence, institutionalization, and effects of the information disclosure norms prescribed by the convention.

The close association of Aarhus transparency with democracy promotion suggests confirmation of the first hypothesis set out chapter 1—that the extensive adoption of transparency in global environmental governance is largely driven by democratization and marketization trends, although this finding does not capture the relationship between the two drivers in this case. In the next section, I argue that the marketization driver has been more significant in shaping Aarhus information disclosure, because the UNECE's promotion of political modernization in Central and Eastern Europe has deferred in practice to market liberal norms of governance dictated by multilateral economic actors.

After setting out this historical context for the adoption of the Aarhus Convention, I then survey the institutionalization of its information rights. Drawing on materials from the treaty secretariat and parties to the convention, as well as relevant nonstate actors (notably public communications to the Aarhus Convention compliance committee), I examine the second hypothesis, presented in chapter 1, that the institutionalization of transparency decenters or qualifies state-led regulation and also opens up political space for new actors. For the Aarhus Convention, these tendencies relate, first, to the extent to which state sovereign actors implement and comply with treaty obligations and, second, to the governance scope for civil society actors in realizing and validating information disclosure. An analysis of the implementation record of the parties to the convention reveals a mixed picture of compliance with information disclosure obligations, with civil society actors playing a major role in scrutinizing and challenging states over their implementation practice.

Finally, I investigate the normative, procedural, and substantive effects of Aarhus governance by disclosure. The third hypothesis examined in this book is that transparency is more likely to be effective under contexts resonant with the goals and decision processes of disclosers and recipients. The Aarhus Convention advances disclosure obligations that are general enough to fit divergent political systems and administrative cultures, and at the same time holds enough legal specificity to steer behavior. I identify major normative, procedural, and substantive effects arising from the application of these obligations: I argue that they reflect a structural imbalance in the articulation of Aarhus rights between social welfare and market liberal perspectives, and that the dominance of the latter has eroded the efficacy of the convention's information disclosure obligations. This seems to corroborate the "loss of innocence" thesis posited by Mol in chapter 2, though given that market liberal ideas framed the convention from its inception, Aarhus transparency was never innocent.

Embracing Transparency

The genealogy of the Aarhus Convention is closely bound up with the widening diplomatic work of UNECE over several decades. Although ostensibly a forum for pan-European economic integration, UNECE has developed a body of international environmental law covering transboundary aspects of air pollution, environmental impact assessment, industrial accidents, and the protection and use of shared watercourses. During the East-West détente process of the mid- to late 1970s, it was the selection of transboundary air pollution as a negotiation issue for mutual gain that favored UNECE as an institutional setting for environmental rule making (Wettestad 2000, 95). Following the collapse of communist rule in Eastern Europe, the UNECE co-initiated an "Environment for Europe" initiative in 1991 to promote pan-European environmental cooperation. Environment for Europe discussions served as the immediate backdrop for the two years of negotiations that produced the Aarhus Convention, and it was at the fourth ministerial conference (in Aarhus, Denmark, in June 1998) under this process that the convention was adopted.

According to UNECE, the Aarhus Convention was based in part on its experience of implementing previous environmental agreements, including the application of information-disclosure provisions (Economic Commission for Europe 2000, 25). In an effort to codify these various entitlements, in 1995 UNECE produced *Guidelines on Access to Environmental Information and Public Participation in Environmental Decision-Making*. The geopolitical context of regime change and independence in former Warsaw Pact countries gave an unprecedented opportunity for the commission to set a regional governance agenda that, in the creation of new legal instruments, fused democratic entitlements with environmental protection norms. Between 1990 and 1995, sixteen newly independent Central and Eastern European states joined UNECE and, at least symbolically, were keen to embrace democratic values. In October 1995, at the third ministerial conference under the Environment for Europe umbrella, the participating environment ministers endorsed the UNECE guidelines and, in the Sofia Ministerial Declaration, called for all countries in the region to ensure that they had an effective legal framework to secure public access to environmental information and public participation in environmental decision making.

Thus, the pan-European development of environmental information disclosure by UNECE cannot be divorced from its democracy promotion efforts in Central and Eastern Europe. Indeed, Secretary-General Kofi Annan labeled the Aarhus Convention the most ambitious venture in "environmental democracy" undertaken by the United Nations (Economic Commission for Europe 2000, v). From 1989 onward, the European Commission and the United States funded major governmental and nongovernmental capacity-building programs in the former communist countries, which included the creation in Budapest of a Regional Environmental Center for Central and Eastern Europe. In this context of external democracy promotion, the development of the Aarhus Convention was notable for the active role of transition countries in shaping its provisions, given that these states were already adopting new environmental information and participation laws with an explicit human rights component (Jancar-Webster 1998; Stec 2005). It is not surprising, therefore, that article 1 of the convention champions a substantive environmental right—the equal entitlement of all persons, across generations, to a decent level of environmental quality. This represents a strong conception of *social welfare*, which is compatible, in principle, with socialist and social democratic norms from a range of European political traditions. It implies regulatory constraints on private investment and trade decisions generating significant environmental harm.

However, the substantive commitment to environmental justice in article 1 was soon at odds with the aggressive free-market restructuring facilitated for the new democracies by multilateral development banks (e.g., European Bank for Reconstruction and Development) and private investment actors. The UNECE mandate for facilitating European economic development—interpreted in the preamble to the Aarhus Convention as "sustainable development"—deferred in practice to this *market-liberal* model of economic development. Thus, the commission's commitment to information disclosure as supportive of its core commitment to East-West cooperation mirrored Western economic liberalization and privatization objectives for transition countries, which were set as conditionalities for European Union and World Trade Organization (WTO) membership. Within this dominant norm complex of neoliberalism, information disclosure by governmental and private actors is market correcting rather than market forcing: it is seen as reducing the incidence of environmental externalities by rectifying information deficits and asymmetries. In other words, it is appropriate for states to facilitate information disclosure as a public good to promote market efficiencies, but in the service of, rather than as a challenge to, profit-motivated imperatives for economic growth (Tietenberg 1998; Dasgupta et al. 2001).

It is necessary to recognize, therefore, the *historicity of the governance by disclosure* formulated by UNECE for the Aarhus Convention. Although democratization served as the main driver for the multilateral embrace of environmental information disclosure, there were ideological divisions over the aims and scope of this disclosure from the outset. In the first place, UNECE embraced the transformative potential of governance by disclosure as part of a new social contract between the citizens of the new democracies and their first elected governments. As detailed in the following, this is evident in the development of convention obligations that embodied far-reaching public entitlements to information access. The causal assumption that information can empower members of the public is explicitly made in the ninth and tenth preambular paragraphs of the convention, where improved access to information—conjoined with public participation—is claimed to enhance public awareness and understanding, the communication to decision makers of matters of public concerns, and greater accountability of public authorities. Many parties to the convention, in their implementation reports, support the view that information disclosure is enabling for their citizens (Economic Commission for Europe 2008c, 21–22).

Second, and at variance with the convention commitment to public empowerment, is the deference to market liberal norms that exempt private entities from democratic accountability. In keeping with market liberal notions of regulation, the Aarhus Convention restricts its direct obligations to public authorities. Although "public authority" is understood in an expansive sense as all governmental authorities and natural or legal persons with public administrative functions and other environmental responsibilities, functions, and public service providers (article 2), this definition clearly circumscribes its class of duty holders. Privately owned entities fall within the immediate scope of the convention only insofar as they perform public functions deemed to be environment-related, such as the provision of energy or water services.

The discretion allowed here has invited inconsistencies among parties. The UK government, for example, has exempted private water and sewage companies from Aarhus obligations by applying a restrictive definition, whereas Ireland has defined public authorities more broadly (Economic Commission for Europe 2011b, 11–12; Ryall 2011, 58–59). Significantly, when UNECE considers the role of the private sector in the implementation guide to the Aarhus Convention, it is in relation to nonmandatory notions of "corporate citizenship" and stakeholder engagement. Business and industry is one of the "major groups" identified by the Rio Declaration and Agenda 21 at the 1992 UN Conference on Environment and Development (Economic Commission for Europe 2000, 19–20). The claim that direct environmental information disclosure for private operators can effectively be tackled by voluntary means (e.g., eco-labeling and eco-auditing schemes) is stated explicitly in article 5(6) of the convention, which relates to the public dissemination of information held by private entities.

To summarize, the uptake of Aarhus information disclosure confirms the first hypothesis presented in chapter 1—that *the adoption of transparency in global environmental governance is largely driven by democratization and marketization trends*—although this finding, by itself, does not capture the dynamic tension between the two drivers. Although political modernization was particularly important to the uptake of the convention, especially in the new European democracies, its information disclosure provisions were significantly inflected and compromised by market liberal norms of governance. The restrictive influence of the marketization driver becomes more evident as we turn now to the institutionalization of Aarhus information disclosure.

Institutionalizing Transparency

The Access-to-Information Pillar

The Aarhus Convention articulates a rights-based framework of governance by disclosure, focusing on the procedural rights of citizens, with access to information supportive of access to decision making and access to justice in environmental matters. As the first pillar, access to information thus becomes an indispensable prerequisite for the other environmental rights in the convention (Hayward 2005, 178). Aarhus information disclosure combines obligations on convention parties with novel public entitlements. To what extent, then, does it confirm the hypothesis posited in chapter 1 that *the institutionalization of transparency decenters state-led regulation and opens up governance space for new actors?*

In the context of an international treaty, the first part of this hypothesis denotes how shared decision-making rules qualify sovereign state authority. Articles 4 and 5 of the convention cover, respectively, the means by which environmental information is requested from public authorities and the obligations on parties to ensure that such authorities actively disseminate environmental information from a variety of sources. Both articles include the provision that obligations are enacted "within the framework of national legislation," which allows parties significant discretion in disclosing information, including conditions for refusing information requests (e.g., for reasons of national defense and security, commercial confidentiality, and personal data protection). However, parties are obliged to interpret grounds for refusal in a restrictive way "taking into account the public interest served by disclosure and taking into account whether the information requested relates to emissions into the environment" (article 4(2)). In contrast to the passive (request-based) disclosure obligations on public authorities contained in article 4, article 5 covers the forms and categories of environmental information that public authorities are actively required to collect and disseminate. The priority accorded to public access to such information places the onus on these authorities to order and publish relevant environmental information, including national state-of-the-environment reports, legislation and policy documents, environment-related policy information, and information on pollution releases and transfers.

Furthermore, article 5 provided a legal basis for the Aarhus parties to develop the Kiev Protocol, with the goal of enhancing public access to information through the establishment of coherent, integrated, nationwide pollutant release and transfer registers. Parties are obliged to ensure effective public access to the information contained in national registers, which follow a harmonized reporting scheme that is mandatory, annual, multimedia, facility-specific, and pollutant- or waste-specific. In an important distinction, the Kiev Protocol is open to all states, so its governance by disclosure ambit transcends membership of UNECE. The other new legal instrument proposed to parties of the convention is an amendment adopted at the second meeting of the parties in Almaty, Kazakhstan, May 2005. The amendment, which is not yet in force, adds a provision to the convention (article 6 bis) requiring each party to "provide for early

and effective information and public participation prior to making decisions on whether to permit the deliberate release into the environment
and placing on the market of genetically modified organisms." This clause
is designed to render more precise a reference to genetically modified organisms in article 6(11) of the convention, which was deliberately left
vague in recognition of the political conflicts underway at the time in
negotiating what became the Cartagena Protocol on Biosafety under the
Convention on Biological Diversity (see also Gupta, this book, chapter 6).

The comprehensive scope of Aarhus transparency rights and obligations represents a major international commitment to governance by disclosure and thus the willingness of convention parties to forego at least
some freedom of unilateral movement in this realm. In principle, extensive
areas of public decision making are covered by the access-to-information
pillar, although the following discussion on implementation practices suggests the resistance of at least some parties to a generous interpretation of
the Aarhus obligations on information disclosure.

The second facet of institutionalization of Aarhus transparency—new
governance entitlements for civil society actors—owes, in the first instance,
a semantic debt to another UNECE agreement, the 1991 Convention on
Environmental Impact Assessment in a Transboundary Context (Espoo
Convention 1991). The Aarhus Convention imports the broad notion of
the public as "one or more natural or legal persons" from this agreement,
and adds to this associations, organizations, or groups in accordance with
national legislation or practice.[3] It also has a separate formulation of "the
public concerned," encompassing those persons likely to be affected by, or
having an interest in, relevant environmental decision making, including
environmental NGOs (article 2(5)). These expansive notions of the public
are politically significant, because Aarhus entitlements address persons
regardless of nationality, residence, or citizenship (article 3(9)). At least in
principle, then, information disclosure (and other Aarhus) obligations on
public authorities are extensive and without discrimination.

Public entitlements under the Aarhus Convention also extend to its
compliance mechanism, representing a major innovation in judicial oversight (Krämer 2012, 98). Article 15 of the convention expressly allows
"appropriate public involvement," which may include "the option of consideration of communications from members of the public related to this
Convention." The first meeting of the parties to the Aarhus Convention in
October 2002 in Lucca, Italy further elaborated and adopted these entitlements. They now include the right of members of the public to nominate
candidates to the compliance committee, as well as the right to submit

allegations of noncompliance by any party and thereafter be entitled to participate in the discussions of the committee (Economic Commission for Europe 2004a). At the Lucca meeting, the United States (attending as a UNECE member state but not an Aarhus Convention signatory) criticized the novel scope of these public oversight rights as contrary to established multilateral treaty practice. Nevertheless, they are extensively used (as noted in the following). Similar public oversight rights are also included in the compliance committee mechanism established in April 2010 under the Kiev Protocol. I now turn to the implementation record on Aarhus information disclosure to gauge the role in practice of state commitment and compliance challenges from civil society actors.

Implementation and Compliance Experience

The Aarhus Convention entered into force on October 30, 2001. As of April 2013, there were forty-six parties to the convention, thirty-two parties to the Kiev Protocol, and twenty-seven parties to the amendment on genetically modified organisms. Decision I/8, adopted at the first meeting conference of the parties, requires parties to the convention to report on their implementation activities before the relevant meeting of the parties. Three reporting cycles had been completed by the fourth meeting of the parties in Chisinau, Republic of Moldova, June 29–July 1, 2011. For each reporting cycle, the Aarhus Convention secretariat is charged with producing a synthesis report on implementation but is limited by its mandate and resource constraints in verifying the content of the reports—a common problem associated with the reliance on self-reporting in the implementation of multilateral environmental agreements (Treves et al. 2009).

In generating these reports, the Aarhus Convention secretariat has categorized countries into three regional groupings on the basis of implementation capacity. First, the parties from Eastern Europe, the Caucasus, and Central Asia (EECCA) face common implementation issues because of their shared experience as post-Soviet states transitioning to democratic governance. These parties are credited by the secretariat with having made the most progress with the access-to-information pillar in the convention, in part enabled by significant capacity building for implementation financed since 1999 by the Organization for Security and Co-operation in Europe. The organization has supported the creation of Aarhus Centers and Public Environmental Information Centers—for awareness raising, training, and communications activities—in Albania, Armenia, Azerbaijan, Belarus, Georgia, Kyrgyzstan, and Tajikistan (Organization for Security and Co-operation in Europe 2008).

In the second regional grouping—the European Union (EU) countries and Norway—implementation of information-access provisions is more advanced, given prevailing legislation and mature democratic systems. Furthermore, European Community ratification of the Aarhus Convention means that it is binding on community authorities and on member states, harmonizing the implementation of the convention across the European Union. Thus, Regulation (EC) No. 1367/2006 applying the Aarhus Convention to community institutions and bodies was adopted in September 2006. The European Commission subsequently published directives designed to align community legislation with each of the three Aarhus pillars, with Directive 2003/4/EC on public access to environmental information adopted in January 2003, repealing a 1990 directive on environmental information access (Commission of the European Communities 2008, 4).[4]

The third regional grouping—South-Eastern Europe (SEE)—covers three parties (Albania, Bulgaria, and the former Yugoslav Republic of Macedonia) deemed by the Aarhus Convention secretariat to share implementation challenges arising from their experience of regional insecurity in the western Balkans and their participation in Stabilization and Association Agreements with the European Union. Indeed, the European Commission sponsors a Regional Environmental Reconstruction Programme for South Eastern Europe, which supports capacity-building for Aarhus Convention implementation (Regional Environmental Reconstruction Programme for South Eastern Europe 2007).

The synthesis reports on implementation produced by the convention secretariat have noted that parties appear to have fewest problems in implementing information disclosure obligations compared to the other two pillars of the convention. For the provisions on access to information on request (article 4), all submitted national implementation reports show relevant legislation in place. However, for EECCA and SEE parties, the secretariat has identified recurring implementation obstacles. These include legislative gaps and discrepancies compared to convention clauses, ambiguities over the meaning of "environmental information," and lack of explanation from public authorities when refusing information requests. Different legal approaches to implementing article 4 are also found in EU countries and Norway, but within a more established culture of openness. The most significant variation—and one that goes beyond Aarhus right-to-information provisions—is the right of the public in Norway to access information directly from private enterprises rather than only from public authorities (Economic Commission for Europe 2008c, 10–11; 2011b, 16).

The reported experience of parties in implementing the Aarhus obligations on the collection and dissemination of environmental information (article 5) attests to extensive legal development, though many EECCA and SEE parties point to procedural uncertainties and resource constraints as negatively affecting active information disclosure. By contrast, most EU countries and Norway have reported no major obstacles to the implementation of Aarhus provisions on information collection and dissemination. Indeed, the convention secretariat applauded progress by these parties in developing electronic tools for information disclosure and in setting up pollutant release and transfer registers consistent with their ratification of the Kiev Protocol (Economic Commission for Europe 2008c, 11–13; 2011b, 15–17).

Nevertheless, public communications to the Aarhus Convention Compliance Committee reveal a more mixed picture—at least in terms of alleged breaches of information disclosure obligations of the convention. By the end of 2011, the compliance committee had received only one submission from a party to the convention with regard to compliance by another party, but had received sixty-three communications on compliance from the public.[5] Over half of the public submissions concern issues of public participation, which has led the compliance committee to register concerns about the implementation of the second pillar of the convention. As table 4.1 indicates, in the period 2004–2011 there were twenty-one public communications alleging noncompliance of parties with the information-disclosure provisions of the Aarhus Convention.

Table 4.1 shows that public communications to the compliance committee about information disclosure have focused on article 4—the convention provision on access to information. Interestingly, of the twelve cases in which the committee had adopted findings by the end of 2012, ten were rulings of noncompliance. All but two of these cases of noncompliance featured article 4(1)—requiring public authorities to respond effectively to requests for information. Most noncomplaint countries were from the EECA regional grouping: under the convention's soft compliance regime, these countries have been granted extensions and assistance in bringing relevant legislation or practices into compliance: only Ukraine, taking seven years to realign information access provision, induced the compliance committee to raise the prospect of a diplomatic caution from convention parties. Spain has twice been ruled to be noncompliant with convention obligations on access to environmental information, highlighting deficiencies in its domestic transposition of the

Table 4.1
Public Communications to the Aarhus Convention Compliance Committee (2004–2011) citing Information Disclosure Provisions of the Convention (Articles 4 and 5)*

Party Concerned	Articles Cited	Received(m.d.yr)	Status [NC = noncompliance]
Kazakhstan	4(1), 4(2)	02.07.2004	Findings adopted: NC—4(1) and 4(2)
Ukraine	4(1)	05.06.2004	Findings adopted: NC—4(1) and 4(2)
Armenia	4(1), 4(2)	09.20.2004	Findings adopted: NC—4(1) and 4(2)
Armenia	Articles 4, 5	09.22.2004	Not admissible
Poland	Article 4	07.04.2005	Not admissible
European Commission	4(1), 5(3)	08.14.2007	Findings adopted
Spain	4(8)	05.13.2008	Findings adopted: NC—4(8)
Denmark	4(1), 5(1)	09.07.2008	No decision
Poland	Article 4	10.20.2008	No decision
Moldova	4(1), 4(4)	11.03.2008	Findings adopted: NC—4(1) and 4(4)
Spain	Articles 4, 5	12.10.2008	Not admissible
Spain	4(1), 4(2)	03.02.2009	Findings adopted: NC—4(1) and 4(2)
Belarus	4(1)	03.14.2009	Findings adopted: NC—4(1)
United Kingdom	4, 5(1)	05.07.2009	Findings adopted
Belarus	4(1)	12.10.2009	Findings adopted: NC—4(1)
Austria	4(2), 4(7)	03.13.2010	Findings adopted: NC—4(2) and 4(7)
Romania	4(1), 4(4), 4(6)	09.02.2010	No decision
United Kingdom	Article 4	09.01.2010	Closed (UK judicial review)
United Kingdom	Articles 4, 5	11.26.2010	Findings adopted: NC—4(1)
European Union	Article 5	10.15.2010	Not admissible
United Kingdom	Article 4	12.03.2010	Suspended (European Court of Justice case)

Note: *References in these public communications to any other convention articles are excluded here.

convention. Compliance discussions at the fifth meeting of the parties in 2011 did not identify any serious shortcomings in the implementation of the information-access pillar of the convention. The parties decided, nonetheless, to create a task force that was charged, among other duties, with identifying capacity-building needs, barriers, and solutions with respect to public access to environmental information (Economic Commission for Europe 2011a, 5–7).

The implementation practice of the Aarhus Convention offers partial support to the second hypothesis, presented in chapter 1, that the institutionalization of transparency decenters state-led regulation and opens up political space for new actors. There is no clear confirmation of the first part of the hypothesis, because the constraints on sovereign authority posed by Aarhus rules on transparency are significantly offset by the discretionary space afforded to parties in interpreting these rules. There are firmer grounds to accept the second part of the hypothesis, because, under the convention, civil society actors have held states answerable for their compliance with Aarhus obligations, including those pertaining to information disclosure.

Effects of Transparency

Drawing on transparency scholarship, the first two chapters of this book put forward the hypothesis that transparency is more likely to be effective under contexts resonant with the goals and decision processes of disclosures and recipients. A directional version of this hypothesis—posited in chapter 1 and addressing the dominance of market liberal ideas in global environmental governance—is that *the adoption of transparency in liberal environmental contexts will have minimal market-restricting effects.* This is not to suggest an absence of "positive" transparency outcomes, but rather that transparency effects will tend to reinforce understandings of public and private authority consistent with market liberalism. In line with the categorization of effects elaborated in chapter 1 of this book, I distinguish next among key normative, procedural, and substantive effects of Aarhus governance by disclosure.

The Normative Selectivity of Aarhus Rights

As noted, the Aarhus Convention articulates a rights-based approach to governance by disclosure forged in the crucible of democracy promotion for Central and Eastern Europe. Notwithstanding its embrace of "environmental democracy," this worldview of political modernization was largely framed by Western European and US models of market liberalism. As evident in Aarhus implementation practice, the normative selectivity of this governance project is most telling regarding the exclusion of private actors from mandatory information disclosure duties.

To recall, Aarhus obligations fall directly on convention parties and constituent public authorities, with privately owned entities having Aarhus responsibilities only insofar as they perform public functions deemed to be environment-related. Convention provisions on information disclosure addressing the environmental impact of private operators (article 5(6)) and products (article 5(8)) are framed in a nonmandatory, aspirational fashion. To be sure, the obligation on parties to establish pollutant release and transfer registers (article 5(9)), as developed in the Kiev Protocol, is regarded as an important convention mechanism for increasing corporate accountability (Economic Commission for Europe 2004b, 4). Although the protocol has entered into force, there are few signs within convention practice of a "hardening" of information disclosure duties on private entities. For example, the United Kingdom has resisted claims by NGOs that privatized water companies have "public authority" functions subject to Aarhus Convention duties. In its reviews of implementation practice, the Aarhus Convention secretariat has noted an extensive preference among parties for voluntary eco-labeling and environmental auditing by the private sector, with mandatory disclosure of product information generally limited to specific sectors, for example, European energy efficiency requirements for household appliances and vehicles (Economic Commission for Europe 2008c, 13; 2011b, 15–16). Moreover, at the third meeting of the parties, during negotiations on the 2009–2014 strategic plan for the convention, the European Union vetoed a proposal by Norway to grant public actors the right to access information directly from industry. This proposal had been inspired by community right-to-know entitlements enshrined in the Norwegian constitution and Environmental Information Act 2003 (Economic Commission for Europe 2008b, 19; European ECO Forum 2008).

Excluding private enterprises from mandatory information disclosure duties is of course consistent with a market liberal model of corporate social responsibility in which information disclosure depends on the voluntary consent of the operator (Gunningham 2007; Garsten and Lindh de Montoya 2008). Pollution release and transfer registers create indirect obligations on operators. Although typically structured, as under the Kiev Protocol, to promote free, user-friendly access to standardized pollution- and facility-specific information, they defer to commercial control over the generation of raw data. The right to confidentiality of commercial information is a justifiable basis under the Aarhus Convention for public authorities to refuse requests for environmental information (article 4(4)(d)). This exemption is tempered in principle by a public interest in information disclosure, but this has not been borne out by implementation practice. Of particular relevance here is the tendency of EU institutions to shield corporate actors from Aarhus responsibilities. For example, the European ombudsman censured the European Commission in March 2010 for citing commercial confidentiality as a reason to block NGO access to copies of communications with a German carmaker over proposed reductions in vehicle emissions (European Ombudsman 2010). Similarly, the European Union has diluted a public entitlement, under the access-to-justice pillar of the convention (article 9(3)), to allow access to legal mechanisms for facilitating the direct liability of private parties and public authorities for noncompliance with environmental law (including information disclosure). In Regulation (EC) No. 1367/2006, applying the convention to community institutions and bodies, the European Union omits the reference to private parties in its legal codification of this article, thereby blunting its regulatory potential (Ryland 2008, 530–531). This reinforces a market liberal perspective on regulatory authority, one in which private operators are shielded from administrative and judicial challenges issuing from civil society actors.

Procedural Flexibility: National Discretion and Implementation Gaps
In several provisions of the Aarhus Convention—including the specification of obligations by parties for each of the three pillars—there are references to prescribed action "within the framework of/in accordance with national legislation." The convention secretariat has interpreted this to mean that parties are allowed "flexibility" in deciding how to implement selected Aarhus obligations.[6] This discretionary space seems sensible in view of the varying legal systems and governance capacities of parties across the UNECE region. Nonetheless, early commentators on the convention already anticipated difficulties arising from the ambiguity of these phrases, including for the access-to-information pillar (Lee and Abbot 2003, 93). Implementation experience indicates that the discretion allowed to parties regarding Aarhus information provisions has been most problematic for EECCA parties, some of whom have struggled to accommodate the right to information within administrative cultures with an institutional memory of secret and closed decision making. As Stec notes, "access to information, the right to disseminate information,

and the control of information are still contentious issues in many countries with a common legacy of strict information control" (2005, 14). Of course, part of the administrative challenge facing public authorities in EECCA (and SEE) countries is to respect the political legitimacy of civil society actors as Aarhus rights holders. For EECCA parties facing public charges of noncompliance under the convention, most submissions to the convention compliance committee were made by domestic NGOs.

Even for Western European democracies and the European Union, however, it has been claimed that the interpretive discretion allowed to parties by the convention has diluted the force of its obligations. The compliance committee has criticized the excessive time taken by some parties to meet public requests for environmental information, for example, declaring the seven years that Danish authorities took over one information request as "not compatible with the Convention" (Economic Commission for Europe 2012, 1). There are particular concerns that rights to information and participation are sometimes treated more narrowly in implementing legislation than in the letter or spirit of the convention. For example, EU Directive 2003/35/EC—transposing Aarhus public participation provisions to EU member states—restricts the right to participate in environmental decision making to those affected by or with an interest in the decision, rather than to any member of the public (Verschuuren 2005, 38–39). This has implications for information access, because the public participation provisions of the convention have corresponding information-disclosure entitlements. Aarhus-enabled public rights to information and participation seem to be most at risk of truncation for decision making with transboundary environmental effects. Although the convention recognizes that Aarhus rights have effect regardless of nationality (article 3(9)), state practice has not been to grant decision-making rights to foreign publics. The activities of European investment and export credit agencies expose most vividly the implementation gap here, because Aarhus rights to information and participation extend in principle to those abroad affected by the environmental effects of projects financed by such agencies. Yet in practice, these foreign publics typically have no access to information on investment and credit decisions affecting their lives and livelihoods (Economic Commission for Europe 2009, 9; Zwier 2007, 228–229).

Discretion to each party "within the framework of its national legislation" is also expressed in article 9(1) of the Aarhus Convention concerning access to justice for those persons who consider that their requests for information under article 4 were not effectively met. Self-reporting by parties on their implementation of article 9(1) reveals a wide range of administrative and/or judicial proceedings and bodies for review of appeals related to requests for information (Economic Commission for Europe 2008c, 18–19; 2011b, 22–24). The routing of appeals through divergent legal vehicles justifies the flexibility of implementation allowed by the convention, although this makes it difficult to assess the equality of treatment of applicants across the parties. Although the convention compliance committee has received only a few public communications regarding article 9(1), there have been, since 2010, a significant number of complaints relating to the wider range of access to justice obligations covered by article 9. Most of these public communications reveal a perception that the discretion afforded to Aarhus parties has allowed them to restrict public access to justice, whether through narrow interpretations of standing (Czech Republic, Armenia), inadequate access to review procedures over alleged contraventions of national environmental law (Austria, European Union), and prohibitively expensive procedures (Denmark, United Kingdom). There are also ongoing concerns about the European Commission's adoption of an unduly restrictive interpretation of article 9 to limit its Aarhus obligations on access to justice in environmental matters (Justice and the Environment 2010; Poncelet 2012). Indeed, the EU General Court ruled in June 2012 that the European Commission was violating the Aarhus Convention in applying narrow grounds for public challenges to administrative acts and omissions contravening relevant environmental law.[7]

The Retreat from Substantive Rights

Implementation reports submitted by parties to the Aarhus Convention secretariat reveal little reflection on the effectiveness of the convention in protecting or promoting substantive environmental rights. In other words, there has been no systematic scrutiny of a key assumption informing its adoption: that information disclosure by parties to the convention will lead to environmental improvements. The right to an adequate environment contained in article 1 lacks specification in treaty practice; and this indeterminacy reflects more than the procedural thrust of the convention, for it is surely in the interests of the parties to identify substantive benefits promoted by increased transparency, participation, and access to justice in environmental matters. Instead, the indeterminacy reveals, above all, the liberal rights–based paradigm dominating convention design and implementation.

In the first place, it expresses a *liberal political aversion* to prescribe a particular set of life choices by empowering a substantive environmental right. A declaration made by the UK government on adopting the Aarhus Convention expresses this, treating the human right to a healthy environment as no more than an aspiration, and according legal recognition only to the procedural rights created by the convention. Even for those Aarhus parties who legally recognize this substantive right, there is extensive uncertainty about its connection to convention's procedural rights. In the structuring of their national implementation reports, parties are requested to follow a template provided by the convention secretariat: this includes the request to report on how their implementation of the Aarhus Convention contributes to the protection of the right to live in an environment adequate to human health and well-being. Of the thirty-seven implementation reports received by the convention secretariat in the second (2008) round of reporting, thirteen contain no response to this request, and the majority of the rest feature substantive right statements that are cursory and/or vague. Interestingly, the recurring claim in those reports that construct a more significant response is that Aarhus procedural rights contribute to fulfilling the substantive right by empowering civil society (Azerbaijan, Georgia, Slovenia, Ukraine), especially when that substantive right has national constitutional protection (Belgium, Finland, Germany, Kazakhstan).

Second, the absence of substantive environmental standards in the convention is also a *practical obstacle* impinging on its commitment to human rights, because it arguably reduces the scope for public deliberation on the appropriateness of environmental decision making according to competing social values (Bell 2004, 103–104; Jones 2008). Information disclosure and public participation risk becoming more a means for legitimizing rather than interrogating governance institutions and for benchmarking public authorities against procedural checklists rather than substantive environmental standards. Advances in information and communications technologies, which allow citizens to use complex information in a politically transformative way, may however increase the scope for citizens and civil society groups to explore the conditions needed to realize environmental health and well-being for current and future generations. Article 5(3) of the Aarhus Convention requires parties to ensure that environmental information progressively becomes available in electronic databases that are publicly accessible, and most parties are now using electronic communications tools (Economic Commission for Europe 2008c, 12). Thus, it is becoming more feasible for these parties to advance "targeted transparency" in which the holders of Aarhus rights are able to make reasoned judgments about specific policy choices (Fung at el. 2007, 39–46). Such moves would complement rather than supplant the general information disclosure provisions of the convention but by themselves will not thicken its substantive effects.

Conclusion

Marking a decade since its entry into force, on July 1, 2011, the fourth meeting of the parties to the Aarhus Convention adopted the Chisinau Declaration to reaffirm their commitment to the convention as a touch-stone for environmental democracy, promoting public access to information, decision making, and justice in environmental matters. This optimism as to the transformative potential of Aarhus rights resulted in a decision by the parties to encourage global accession to the convention (Economic Commission for Europe 2011a, 26–27). At least for the access-to-information pillar, the assumption is that transparency and disclosure are transferable norms of democratic governance. I have argued here, however, that the information rights given force by the convention articulate a selective liberal framing that limits their application and transformative force. The preoccupation with procedural entitlements fits comfortably with existing liberal expressions of civil and political rights in the domestic law of western UNECE states, even as the bold declaration in the treaty of a universal human right to an environment adequate for health and well-being anticipates a more ambitious conception of social justice. In implementation practice, the de facto bracketing of the Aarhus substantive right dissipates the tension between these two perspectives.

The historicity of Aarhus governance by disclosure is central to understanding the limits to transparency set by this marginalization. This is characterized, above all, by a geopolitical context featuring the spread of market liberalism and representative democracy to Eastern Europe, as well as the embrace of neoliberalism by leading Western governments. The key driver of Aarhus transparency was democratization, fed by popular demands for openness and inclusivity in decision making on environmental matters but one inflected by a deepening marketization of European economies. As noted, this ideological current has affected the treatment in the convention of private entities, which (in contrast with public authorities) are shielded from direct information-disclosure duties concerning environmental information. Other chapters in this book indicate that a structured preference for voluntary disclosure from private actors is typical of new transparency regimes in global environmental governance (e.g., Dingwerth and Eichinger, this book, chapter 10; Van Alstine, this book, chapter 11). The reporting requirements placed by the Kiev Protocol on private owners and operators of polluting facilities suggest that it is possible under the convention to go further in promoting corporate accountability for environmental harm, though these remain indirect obligations mediated by treaty parties.

The foregoing discussion of the implementation of Aarhus information rights offers some support to the hypothesis that the institutionalization of transparency decenters state-led regulation and opens up political space for new actors. On the first part of the hypothesis, sovereign powers are indeed steered in favor of transparency by multilateral obligations, although the discretionary space afforded to parties in interpreting rules has diluted the force of Aarhus information disclosure. More confidence accompanies confirmation of the second part of the thesis in the sense that civil society actors have acquired a major governance role, over and above their information-access rights, in holding states to account for their compliance with Aarhus obligations. The Aarhus Convention has achieved significant gains in the transparency of public authorities. However, the review of its normative, procedural, and substantive effects confirms the hypothesis that transparency adopted in liberal environmental contexts will tend to have minimal market-restricting effects. A number of factors significantly compromise the transformative potential of Aarhus rules on information disclosure. These include the exclusion of private actors from mandatory disclosure requirements, the low regulatory ambition of parties (evident in their restrictive interpretations of Aarhus rights), and the symbolic treatment of the article 1 environmental right, suggesting that Aarhus procedural rights require no substantive outcomes vis-à-vis the activities of public and private actors. The convention has not breached centers of private authority responsible for major environmental harm: it could, and should, go further.

Notes

1. Aarhus Convention 1998 (adopted June 25, 1998; in force October 30, 2001).
2. Kiev Protocol 2003 (adopted May 21, 2003; in force October 8, 2009).
3. Espoo Convention 1991, art. 1(x); Aarhus Convention 1998, art. 2(4).
4. Although a directive (2003/35/EC) has also been adopted in relation to the public participation pillar of the Aarhus Convention, a proposed directive on ac-

cess to justice (COM(2003) 624) failed to get sufficient support from member states.

5. See http://www.unece.org/env/pp/pubcom.htm for information on all public communications to the Aarhus Convention Compliance Committee.

6. For the access-to-information pillar, the phrase "within the framework of national legislation" appears in articles 4(1) and 5(2). See Economic Commission for Europe (2000, 30–31).

7. Judgment of the General Court of the European Union of June 14, 2012, Case T-338/08. Available at http://curia.europa.eu/juris/liste.jsf?num=T-338/08.

References

Aarhus Convention. 1998. *Convention on Access to Information, Public Participation in Decision-Making and Access to Justice in Environmental Matters.* Available at http://www.unece.org/env/pp/treatytext.html.

Bell, Derek R. 2004. Sustainability through Democratization? The Aarhus Convention and the Future of Environmental Decision Making in Europe. In *Europe, Globalization and Sustainable Development*, ed. John Barry, Brian Baxter, and Richard Dunphy, 94–113. London: Routledge.

Commission of the European Communities. 2008. *Aarhus Convention Implementation Report: European Community, SEC (2008) 556.* Brussels: Commission of the European Community.

Dasgupta, Susmita, Benoit Laplante, and Nlandu Mamingi. 2001. Pollution and Capital Markets in Developing Countries. *Journal of Environmental Economics and Management* 42 (3): 310–335.

Economic Commission for Europe (ECE). 2000. *The Aarhus Convention: An Implementation Guide.* Geneva: United Nations Economic Commission for Europe.

Economic Commission for Europe (ECE). 2004a. *Decision I/7: Review of Compliance, ECE/MP.PP/2/Add.8.* New York: United Nations.

Economic Commission for Europe (ECE). 2004b. *Report of the First Meeting of the Parties: Addendum: Lucca Declaration, ECE/MP.PP/2/Add.1.* New York: United Nations.

Economic Commission for Europe (ECE). 2008a. *Report by the Compliance Committee, ECE/MP.PP/2008/5.* New York: United Nations.

Economic Commission for Europe (ECE). 2008b. *Report of the Third Meeting of the Parties, ECE/MP.PP/2008/2.* New York: United Nations.

Economic Commission for Europe (ECE). 2008c. *Synthesis Report on the Status of Implementation of the Convention, ECE/MP.PP/2008/4.* New York: United Nations.

Economic Commission for Europe (ECE). 2009. *Findings of the Compliance Committee with Regard to Communication ACCC/C/2007/21.* New York: United Nations.

Economic Commission for Europe (ECE). 2011a. *Report of the Fourth Session of the Meeting of the Parties, ECE/MP.PP/2011/2/Add.1.* New York: United Nations.

Economic Commission for Europe (ECE). 2011b. *Synthesis Report on the Status of Implementation of the Convention, ECE/MP.PP/2011/7.* New York: United Nations.

Economic Commission for Europe (ECE). 2012. *Report by the Compliance Committee on its Thirty-Seventh Meeting, ECE/MP.PP/C.1/2012/5.* New York: United Nations.

European ECO Forum. 2008. *Environmental Citizens' Groups Score Victory on Public Participation.* European ECO Forum. Press Release, Riga, June13. Available at http://www.eco-forum.org/documents/061308-PR-MOPfinalday.doc.

European Ombudsman. 2010. *Special Report from the European Ombudsman to the European Parliament concerning Lack of Cooperation by the European Commission in Complaint 676/2008/RT.* Strasbourg: European Ombudsman.

Fung, Archon, Mary Graham, and David Weil. 2007. *Full Disclosure: The Perils and Promise of Transparency.* New York: Cambridge University Press.

Garsten, Christina, and Monica Lindh de Montoya. 2008. The Naked Corporation: Visualization, Veiling and the Ethico-Politics of Organizational Transparency. In *Transparency in a New Global Order: Unveiling Organizational Visions,* ed. Christina Garsten and Monica Lindh de Montoya, 79–93. Cheltenham, UK: Edward Elgar.

Gunningham, Neil. 2007. Corporate Environmental Responsibility: Law and the Limits of Voluntarism. In *The New Corporate Accountability: Corporate Social Responsibility and the Law,* ed. Doreen McBarnet, Aurora Voiculescu, and Tom Campbell, 476–500. Cambridge, UK: Cambridge University Press.

Hayward, Tim. 2005. *Constitutional Environmental Rights.* Oxford: Oxford University Press.

Jancar-Webster, Barbara. 1998. Environmental Movement and Social Change in the Transition Countries. In *Dilemmas of Transition: The Environment, Democracy and Economic Reform in East Central Europe,* ed. Susan Baker and Petr Jehlièka, 69–92. London: Frank Cass.

Jones, Deiniol. 2008. Solidarity and Public Participation: The Role of the Aarhus Convention in Containing Environmentally Induced Social Conflict. *Global Change, Peace & Security* 20 (2): 151–168.

Justice and the Environment. 2010. *Access to Justice in Environmental Matters under the Aarhus Convention.* Brno, Czech Republic: Justice and the Environment.

Kiev Protocol. 2003. *Protocol on Pollutant Release and Transfer Registers.* Available at http://www.unece.org/env/pp/prtr/docs/PRTR_Protocol_e.pdf.

Krämer, Ludwig. 2012. Transnational Access to Environmental Information. *Transnational Environmental Law* 1 (1): 95–104.

Lee, Maria, and Carolyn Abbot. 2003. The Usual Suspects? Public Participation under the Aarhus Convention. *Modern Law Review* 66 (1): 80–108.

Mason, Michael. 2010. Information Disclosure and Environmental Rights: The Aarhus Convention. *Global Environmental Politics* 10 (3): 10–31.

Organization for Security and Co-operation in Europe. 2008. *Independent Evaluation of Aarhus Centres and Public Environmental Information Centres*. Vienna: OSCE Secretariat.

Poncelet, Charles. 2012. Access to Justice in Environmental Matters—Does the European Union Comply with Its Obligations? *Journal of Environmental Law* 24 (2): 287–309.

Regional Environmental Reconstruction Programme for South Eastern Europe. 2007. *Report of the Tenth REReP Task Force Meeting*. Szentendre, Hungary: REReP Secretariat. Available at http://www.rec.org/REC/Programs/REREP/docs/10th_meeting/meeting_report.pdf.

Ryall, Áine. 2011. Access to Environmental Information in Ireland: Implementation Challenges. *Journal of Environmental Law* 23 (1): 45–71.

Ryland, Diane. 2008. Horizontal Instruments and Miscellaneous Issues. In *Yearbook of European Environmental Law*. vol. 8. ed. T. F. M. Etty and H. Somsen, 524–578. Oxford: Oxford University Press.

Stec, Stephen. 2005. "Aarhus Environmental Rights" in Eastern Europe. In *Yearbook of European Environmental Law*. vol. 5. ed. T. F. M. Etty and H. Somsen, 1–22. Oxford: Oxford University Press.

Tietenberg, Tom. 1998. Disclosure Strategies for Pollution Control. *Environmental and Resource Economics* 11 (3–4): 587–602.

Treves, Tullio, Attila Tanzi, Laura Pineschi, Cesare Pitea, Chiara Ragni, and Francesca Romanin Jacur, eds. 2009. *Non-Compliance Procedures and Mechanisms and the Effectiveness of International Environmental Agreements*. Cambridge, UK: Cambridge University Press.

Verschuuren, Jonathan. 2005. Public Participation Regarding the Elaboration and Approval of Projects in the EU after the Aarhus Convention. In *Yearbook of European Environmental Law*. vol. 4. ed. T. F. M. Etty and H. Somsen, 29–48. Oxford: Oxford University Press.

Wettestad, Jørgen. 2000. The ECE Convention on Long-Range Transboundary Air Pollution: From Common Cuts to Critical Loads. In *Science and Politics in International Environmental Regimes*, ed. Steinar Andresen et al., 95–121. Manchester, UK: Manchester University Press.

Zwier, Wienke. 2007. Export Credit Agencies and the Environment: Implications of the Aarhus Convention for Export Credit Agency Accountability. In *Yearbook of European Environmental Law*. vol. 7. ed. T. F. M. Etty and H. Somsen, 204–233. Oxford: Oxford University Press.

5

Global Pesticide Governance by Disclosure: Prior Informed Consent and the Rotterdam Convention

Kees Jansen and Milou Dubois

Accounts of human suffering and environmental contamination in developing countries because of pesticide use often propose closing the knowledge gap between industrialized (pesticide-exporting) countries and developing (pesticide-importing) countries as a solution (Hough 1998). In such narratives, improved provision of information on pesticide risks and pesticide trade will enable developing countries to design and implement appropriate measures to control pesticide risks. This is the basic premise underlying the major global governance framework that addresses global pesticide flows, the Rotterdam Convention on the Prior Informed Consent Procedure for Certain Hazardous Chemicals and Pesticides in International Trade (hereinafter "the convention"). Transparency, in the form of governance by disclosure through prior informed consent (PIC), is the key pillar of the emerging global system of pesticide regulation. The PIC procedure stipulates that industry in exporting countries is allowed only to export listed chemicals after receiving consent of the importing country. The Rotterdam Convention calls for the sharing of information between states about hazardous chemicals entering international trade and about the regulatory actions taken in participating countries (Rotterdam Convention 2008). A basic concern of the convention is the differential capacity of countries to assess and manage potential risks posed by hazardous chemicals and pesticides (pesticides, the focus of this chapter, form the largest group of chemicals dealt with in the convention). In particular, the convention intends to support developing countries to make sound regulatory decisions.

Transparency, the opposite of secrecy, means deliberately revealing one's actions instead of hiding them (Florini 1998) and has, in this sense, a positive connotation. Recent research, however, has questioned the transparency turn in environmental governance and commented on the overvaluation of what transparency can achieve (Etzioni 2010). Scholars of transparency policies no longer assume a priori that the mechanism of transparency necessarily leads to accountable, legitimate, inclusive, and effective governance (Fung et al. 2007; Gupta 2008, 2010b). The debate has focused on two assumptions that underlie transparency initiatives (Gupta 2008). First, instead of mandating outcomes, priority is given to the establishment of procedures, which are seen as progressive, potentially emancipatory, and opening up the possibility for decision making by the participants themselves. The second assumption is that governance by disclosure can empower through the provision of information. Gupta questions these assumptions, arguing that because of different values behind its provision and interpretation, information itself is subject to conflict. In this critical theoretical reading, information about, for example, pesticide risks cannot be seen as a neutral force that will solve normative or political conflicts. Nor will access to information necessarily change power relations and improve the position of developing countries. Instead, contextual power relationships shape the effects of transparency. For example, transparency may increase inequality when poor nations cannot fulfill their transparency requirements or when recipients (in our case governments) are not able to understand disclosed information (Mol 2010). The perils of an undue emphasis on process in governance by disclosure include that "getting the process right" may divert resources from substantive outcomes, that procedures are left vague and open, and that those with power may undermine desired objectives by providing so much information that receiving parties are not able to process it ("drowning in disclosure," Gupta 2008, 4).

This chapter addresses some of the key questions raised by critical transparency studies for the Rotterdam Convention: we explore the extent to which the convention informs, empowers, and/or improves environmental performance or helps mitigate risk (Gupta 2010b). We will contextualize the convention by discussing Gupta and Mason's argument (this book, chapter 1) that the uptake of transparency is driven by democratization (responding to calls for open and more inclusive forms of collective choice) and marketization (the use of market-based and voluntary transparency in order to minimize market-restricting effects). Here, we will argue that without these drivers, the convention would not exist in its current form, but that other aspects, in particular the nature (or materiality) of the pesticide issue and classical notions of sovereignty, have also had a key impact and cannot be sidelined theoretically as secondary factors.

In developing our argument, we adapt Tyfield's characterization of different approaches to science policy, which also play a role in the formulation of risk management strategies (Tyfield 2012). First, a techno-statist Keynesian governance approach emphasizes that science delivers the facts about pesticide risks and provides the public good of risk information, which governments then use to regulate the complexities and uncertainties of a technological society (in this approach state, market, and society are distinctive spheres). Second, in a neoliberal approach, market actors best deliver risk information, and governance of risk preferably follows market principles (power is passed from professional technocratic elites to consumers who, it is argued, should have a free, though informed, choice about what pesticide they want to use). Third, a deliberative democracy approach to managing technological risk, making explicit tacit normative framings, prescribes risk management based on public participation and a democratized techno-science. Our hypothesis is that the first approach—the techno-statist Keynesian governance of risk—is the key driver for our case of governance by disclosure. This challenges the theoretical prioritization of marketization and democratization as drivers. If our hypothesis turns out to be plausible, it will also have consequences for the proposition that the institutionalization of transparency decenters state-led regulation (Gupta and Mason, this book, chapter 1; see also Mol, this book, chapter 2).

The discussion about "transparency" in relation to governance tends to focus on information disclosure from governments to citizens (e.g., Fox 2007; Fung 2013). To stay true to the state-to-state disclosure focus of the Rotterdam Convention, and in line with the focus of this book, we prefer to use the term governance by disclosure. To date, the Rotterdam Convention is a relatively less-researched intergovernmental agreement. Most of the literature on the convention deals with its genesis or its legal basis (e.g., Langlet 2009; Selin 2010) but a discussion of its current role and wider implications as an example of governance by disclosure has yet to begin. Our analysis is based on available convention documents and databases, scholarly literature, and communications (interviews and e-mail exchanges) with five key actors (a former representative of an advocacy group, a designated national authority, a member of the chemical review committee, a pesticide company, and the convention secretariat) in 2011.

We proceed as follows: the next section describes the emergence of PIC in governing trade in hazardous chemicals, particularly the evolution from a right to know to informed consent. We then discuss institutionalization of the Rotterdam Convention's disclosure obligations and the implementation challenges as perceived by involved actors. Subsequently, we analyze the effects of this governance-by-disclosure regime by assessing whether it informs, empowers, and/or improves environmental conditions. The conclusion highlights the techno-statist nature of the convention and its disclosure-based governance approach.

Embracing Transparency

Since Rachel Carson's *Silent Spring* drew attention to the hazards of increased pesticide use, a vast literature has analyzed the divergent impacts of such use in developed and developing countries, with many more victims in the latter (e.g., Boardman 1986; Castillo et al. 1989; Pesticides Trust 1989; Ríos-González et al. 2013; Rosenthal 2004; Toleubayev et al. 2011; Van den Bosch 1980; Wargo 1998; Wesseling et al. 1997). Scholars and activists have long pointed to the weak capacity in developing countries to regulate pesticide use and trade (Hough 1998), and have called for bans on hazardous pesticides (Jansen 2008). In particular, exports of pesticides that are banned or restricted in an exporting country arouse public indignation. The "circle of poison" argument (positing that hazardous pesticides exported from the North to the South come back as residues in food exports to the North, for example, Galt 2008; Weir and Schapiro 1981) has also supported calls for stricter regulation of trade in pesticides. International action triggered by these concerns started to systematize, standardize, and distribute information about pesticides, rooted in a right-to-know principle.

The United Nations (UN) system became a key player in organizing pesticide-related information in databases and designing models of how governments could use this information in governing the safe trade and use of pesticides. The World Health Organization (WHO), for example, developed a simple classification of hazardousness of pesticides, based on acute toxicity, which has become the worldwide standard for labeling pesticide products. The United Nations Environment Programme (UNEP) created the International Register of Potentially Toxic Chemicals in 1976 (now UNEP chemicals), which provided information on hazard assessments, the main uses, production and consumption of chemicals, and possible legal mechanisms and recommendations to control the risks of chemicals. Furthermore, the UNEP, the UN, and the WHO issued the United Nations Consolidated List of Products with information on regulatory actions taken by governments related to chemicals in 1983

(Winqvist 1999). In 1987, UNEP introduced the London Guidelines for the Exchange of Information on Chemicals in International Trade, which aimed at the exchange of information on economic, scientific, legal, and technical aspects of chemicals (Kummer 1999; Winqvist 1999). All these information-gathering efforts predominantly focused on *what* questions (for example, what are the characteristics of these chemicals? what are the risks for human health and environments?). By contrast, the UN Food and Agriculture Organization (FAO) started to collect other types of information and organized the collected information around *how* questions, such as, how to design best practices for handling and using pesticides? In doing so, the FAO competed with the WHO to take the lead in the pesticide issue (Hough 1998).

Although the FAO launched its first pesticide programs in the late 1950s, it took more than twenty-five years to formulate substantial guidelines on pesticide management (FAO 1990; Pesticides Trust 1989). Dinham (1991) argues that the agrochemical industry–lobbying group GIFAP (French acronym for the International Group of National Associations of Manufacturers of Agrochemical Products; now CropLife International) influenced FAO's policies for a long time as they worked together in a joint Bureau (Paarlberg 1993). This direct link was broken in 1970 under pressure from NGOs and other groups within the FAO. However, the FAO and the pesticide industry shared many of the same objectives, such as the harmonization of methods and procedures for the registration and control of pesticides. The FAO's work in the pesticide issue started to have consequences for the pesticide industry with the introduction of the Code of Conduct on the Distribution and Use of Pesticides (hereinafter "the code") in 1985. This code contains detailed guidelines on best practices regarding, among other things, the distribution of pesticides. It asks the agrochemical industry to test all products before they are exported, to submit this information to importing parties, to package and label exported products properly, and to ensure that subsidiary bodies employ the same standards as the parent company on producing and manufacturing pesticides. These FAO guidelines regarding information exchange anticipated the Rotterdam Convention and demanded that exporting countries send notifications to importing countries on the nature of the shipped pesticides and inform them about regulatory restrictions on the use of a pesticide in their own territory. The FAO, often in collaboration with other development agencies, worked extensively to get the code implemented in developing countries (Jansen 2003, 2008).

A controversial issue in the UNEP London Guidelines and the FAO code was the proposed inclusion therein of a PIC procedure, which would have connected trade regulation to the information provided on risks. In both cases, a provision on PIC was deleted from the draft text before final approval. PIC was included in seven of the eight drafts of the FAO code but removed at the final stage, according to Hough (1998; see also Hough 2003), a result of pressure from the agrochemical industry as well as the United States, the United Kingdom, and Germany.

The exclusion of a PIC procedure stimulated NGOs and activists, including Oxfam, Novib, and the Pesticide Action Network (PAN), to launch a concerted campaign to incorporate PIC in such codes. These groups mobilized country representatives of developing countries in the Group of 77 to push for such an inclusion. Eventually this led to UNEP pledging in 1987 to incorporate PIC in the London Guidelines in its next session in 1989. Similarly, the FAO passed a resolution to add PIC to the code at its next conference in 1989. In 1989, PIC was included in the London Guidelines and the code (FAO 1990). FAO took the lead on pesticides, and UNEP was the lead agency for other chemicals through its International Register of Potentially Toxic Chemicals (Murray 1994). The FAO-UNEP joint group of experts on PIC was established to guide and develop the process (Dinham 1993a). In 1992, a joint program on the PIC procedure was implemented (Murray and Logan 2004). The PIC procedure as designed in the FAO's code was a voluntary guideline.

The industry organization GIFAP initially opposed inclusion of PIC in the code but changed its position and accepted a voluntary PIC in the 1990s (CropLife International 2004; Hough 1998). Hough (1998, 2003) explains this change as resulting from a fear of more stringent and potentially mandatory alternatives. For example, a US bill that proposed pesticide export controls, introduced in 1991–1992, was considered a bigger threat than import controls. Initially, GIFAP argued against this bill by underlining possible contradictions with the FAO code (Hough 1998, 2003). Gradually, GIFAP came around to the view that being seen as responsible and concerned could serve the interests of their members (Dinham 1991). Another reason could be that the research-based pesticide companies dominating GIFAP wanted to fence off competition from generic pesticide producers by accepting higher levels of risk regulation and elimination of older, off-patent pesticides (Clapp 2003).

Advocacy groups such as PAN also shifted position by recognizing that they needed the support of the agrochemical industry to ensure that no chemicals were exported without importer consent (Dinham 1993b).

They supported a voluntary PIC procedure as a first step, though kept pushing for a binding PIC procedure. The opening for a mandatory agreement came with the United Nations Conference on Environment and Development Earth Summit in 1992 (Hough 2000), which stated that the full participation of states in the PIC procedure should be ensured by 2000 (chapter 19 of Agenda 21). A UNEP-FAO Intergovernmental Negotiating Committee thus started in 1996 to draft a mandatory convention that would incorporate a PIC procedure for the pesticide trade. About one hundred governments and some NGOs participated in the negotiations.

The system of information exchange institutionalized by the Rotterdam Convention is not only based on the voluntary PIC procedure in the FAO code. A less-documented force behind the Rotterdam Convention was the work of the European Union to agree on a PIC within the community. Already in 1983, the European Parliament adopted a resolution to amend legislation on pesticides and other chemicals, making export subject to an explicit request by the importing country (Langlet 2003). Regulations adopted in 1988 and 1992 further developed the "principle of informed choice."[1] Hence, when the negotiations for the international convention started, a legally binding form of export notification and PIC was already functioning within the European Union and the community had an interest in establishing a rather stringent international regime (Langlet 2003). Heyvaert (2009) discusses the multiple incentives for the European Union to shape international chemical governance according to its own systems already in place. The Rotterdam Convention resembles important elements of EU regulation,[2] and although the latter is more progressive because a larger number of chemicals are subject to PIC, it also applies to nonparties, and it imposes an absolute export ban on some chemicals (Langlet 2003).

Kummer (1999) describes the major points of discussion during the negotiations of the convention. First, a US-led group succeeded in narrowing the negotiating mandate by limiting the convention solely to the PIC procedure as it was being applied voluntarily to date, against the wishes of a EU-led group that preferred to extend the convention to the management of chemicals more generally. Second, different positions emerged as to how broad the inclusion of chemicals should be: for example, whether only acutely hazardous formulations or also those with chronic effects should be included. A third contentious issue was the number of countries and regions with regulatory actions needed to trigger the process of including chemicals in the PIC procedure. Fourth, much discussion took place regarding the modalities of notification, packaging, and labeling.

Fifth, the relation between the convention and other international agreements, in particular the World Trade Organization (WTO), remained contested: the US-led group stressed that priority should be given to the WTO agreements, whereas the EU-led group strongly opposed this. On this point, countries reached agreement only in the last session. Sixth, different views existed on funding developing countries to implement the convention and its corresponding financial mechanisms. Proposals reflecting the requests by developing countries for financial mechanisms were removed from the draft text. Because of the final compromises over these issues, the convention is narrower in scope than the voluntary mechanism of the FAO code.[3]

The convention was adopted in 1998 and entered into force in 2004 (as of April 2012, 148 parties had ratified it). It uses familiar instruments such as the conferences of parties (which decides about amendments and adding chemicals to annex III, the list of chemicals to which the PIC procedure applies),[4] designated national authorities, and a secretariat (jointly managed by the UNEP and the FAO). A chemical-review committee consisting of government-designated experts reviews the information on specific pesticides and participates in the preparation of "decision guidance documents" and recommendations, used by the conference of parties to make decisions on the addition of chemicals to annex III and by parties to prepare import responses for the pesticides included in the PIC procedure. The convention is only binding for parties to the convention and thus has no direct impact on nonparties.[5]

Institutionalizing Transparency

Organizing Information Disclosure
The Rotterdam Convention organizes information exchange on chemicals and pesticides around two provisions. The first one is a PIC procedure that applies to the chemicals listed in annex III of the convention. Parties are obliged to prepare an import response for the listed chemicals (stipulating whether or not or under what conditions consent is given to import a chemical).[6] Exporting parties are required to respect these decisions and not to export chemicals without consent.

The procedure to evaluate a chemical for inclusion in annex III can start only after receipt of notifications of a final (domestic) regulatory action for a particular chemical taken by parties. Two notifications from two different so-called geographically based PIC regions are required (article 5.5) to qualify a banned or severely restricted chemical for the

PIC procedure.[7] The seven PIC regions are Africa, Asia, Europe, Latin America and the Caribbean, Near East, North America, and South Pacific (COP 2004). Because the addition of pesticides to annex III depends on consensus in the COP, one party can block placing a pesticide on the list (McDorman 2004).

Because the convention aims to address the needs of developing countries, it has created a special, less burdensome procedure for severely hazardous pesticide formulations (SHPF) that pose high risks under the conditions of use in developing countries. This category of chemicals requires only one notification from a developing country. This trajectory institutionalizes differences between parties of the convention.

The second provision of information exchange concerns the collection and distribution of information on final regulatory actions taken by parties to ban or severely restrict chemicals. It also includes proposals from developing countries on severely hazardous pesticide formulations causing problems under conditions of use.[8] This provision broadens the disclosure of information on risks and regulatory actions and goes beyond the PIC procedure, which is limited to the chemicals listed in annex III, because it makes information available on all chemicals restricted or banned by other parties.

The convention has created a complex system of information flows. First, the secretariat communicates each inclusion of a chemical in annex III, together with information on the pesticide (via the decision guidance documents), to all parties. Second, the secretariat communicates all import responses to all parties and makes them publicly available on their website and in circulated documents. Third, parties must inform their chemical-exporting industry about these import responses. Fourth, parties must prepare export notifications (when an industry in their country intends to export a banned or severely restricted chemical that is not listed in annex III) and the importing countries are supposed to respond with an acknowledgment.[9] Fifth, article 13 outlines which information should accompany exported chemicals.[10]

Unresolved Implementation Issues

Involved actors point to several challenges that the regime faces in institutionalizing governance by disclosure and improving implementation of the convention. The first concerns the slow institutionalization and implementation of PIC itself. Since the convention entered into force, only four pesticides have been listed as qualifying for the PIC procedure, one at the fourth conference of the parties to the convention in 2008 and the other three at the fifth conference of the parties to the convention in June 2011.[11] Moreover, the secretariat speaks of "a lack of notifications and proposals of chemicals to be listed in annex III."[12] The current rule of at least two notifications from two different regions strongly affects the working of the convention. According to a former PAN representative,[13] a division of Europe into two PIC regions, using the argument of substantially different climatic conditions, would lead to the required number of notifications for many chemicals already notified by Europe.[14] In this context, ratification of the convention by the United States (who signed it in 1998) could be another pathway to secure the second notification needed to include these chemicals in the PIC procedure. A related problem is that many notifications, in particular those by developing countries, lack scientific quality[15] and are, therefore, dismissed by the chemical review committee.[16] Furthermore, few developing countries use their right to propose chemicals for inclusion as an SHPF, even though such proposals require little data.[17]

The second challenge concerns parties' failure to take and transmit import responses for each chemical listed in annex III, which parties have to transmit to the secretariat. The average response rate (that is, parties who submitted one or more import responses) is 73 percent (as of June 2011). Import responses are distributed unevenly among regions (table 5.1) and pose a particular problem in Africa (e.g., Daudu 2008).[18] Hence, although convention principles have become an intrinsic part of decision-making routines in, for example, the European Union, this is less the case in many developing countries.

Though the convention is supposed to ease decision making relating to hazardous chemicals for countries with little regulatory capacity, the implementation of the convention already requires certain regulatory knowledge and capacity, which is not always present. The convention requires the amendment or adoption of national legislative or administrative measures; establishing national databases and registers that include safety information for chemicals; providing the public with sufficient information on chemical handling, accident management and safer alternatives for the pesticides listed in annex III; and cooperation at global, regional, and subregional levels directly or through competent international organizations. Importing parties also have to implement measures to make timely import decisions, make domestic production and import from nonparties subject to the same conditions as set out in the import decision, propose SHPFs for listing, develop notifications, and acknowledge export notifications.

Table 5.1
Import Responses by Parties

PIC Region	Parties That Have Submitted One or More Import Response	Parties That Have Submitted No Import Responses	Average Import Response Rate per Region (percent)
Africa	34	6	56
Asia	16	1	73
Europe	34	3	86
Latin America and the Caribbean	24	0	80
Near East	10	0	75
North America	1	0	100
Southwest Pacific	4	2	55

Source: Authors' communication with the Secretariat of the convention (May 2011)

Poorer developing countries cannot fulfill all these governance-by-disclosure requirements. The logical outcome is a general call for more capacity building. Within the structure of the convention, training is given and e-learning tools have been prepared in order to increase capacity in this area. The key bottleneck, however, is the lack of resources to implement a comprehensive capacity-building program. At the various conferences of parties, groups of developing countries use every opportunity to press for funding for training programs (e.g., ENB 2011), but to date developed countries have accepted only a voluntary special trust fund to strengthen national capabilities and have resisted other forms of funding, partly because of fear of setting a precedent for other treaties (Selin 2010).

The final challenge is how to address noncompliance, which goes largely unreported, and it is unclear how regularly it occurs. The conference of parties has been working on this issue ever since its first meeting, without reaching any agreement. For example, the fourth conference discussed whether the mechanism should take a facilitative and supportive approach or a punitive one, whereby the former would include financial and technical assistance to parties to motivate them to comply with the convention (COP 2008). Similar to other issues, the negotiations in the Rotterdam Convention are influenced by how the discussion about compliance in the Basel Convention (transboundary movement of hazardous waste) and Stockholm Convention (persistent organic pollutants) evolves

(Kohler 2006; Selin 2010). In the so-called synergies process, the three conventions collaborate to strengthen their implementation.

The Marketization of Disclosure

How much is the emergence and institutionalization of the convention's disclosure-based governance approach driven by techno-statist versus neoliberal imperatives? We consider this here by assessing the extent to which the convention and its disclosure obligations are market following rather than market transforming (see Gupta and Mason, this book, chapter 1). Unlike some other transparency initiatives discussed in this book, the convention itself does not depend on market mechanisms for its implementation. However, its goal is regulating trade, whereby the convention recognizes that trade and environmental policies should be mutually supportive.[19] There is, thus, no explicit intention to restrict trade.

The Rotterdam Convention requires implementation via national laws that are legally binding for industry. The convention will probably affect trade of the chemicals listed in annex III; currently a large number of "no-consent" import notifications restrict imports. Hence, the PIC procedure does not simply follow market developments but instead shapes them. Of course, this applies only to specific chemicals. The convention and its PIC procedure does not restructure the market writ large nor adjusts trade obligations more generally. This may partly explain why, after their initial opposition, large pesticide corporations supported PIC. Although this governance-by-disclosure initiative is congruent with and sometimes uses neoliberal discourses, it also creates a continuous friction with the idea of market-driven decision making because of the underlying techno-statist approach that poses limits to market transactions.

Effects of Transparency

What follows is a discussion of the typology of effects—normative (informing), procedural (empowering), and substantive (improving)— examined by other contributors to this book. The convention text does not limit itself to any one of these three desired effects and is, in fact, an effort to connect them. Hence, in the world of this convention, the analytical distinctions among informing, empowering, and improving is not clear-cut.

Normative Effects: Transparency as Right to Know

About the question, whether this governance-by-disclosure initiative furthers a right to know and hence informs, we can be short. Yes, it does, insofar as it organizes information exchange between governments. The importance of having access to regulatory actions of other countries is not to be underestimated. In previous research on pesticide regulation in Central America (Jansen 2003, 2008), government officials regularly asked about bans of pesticides in exporting countries, of which they only had heard rumors. Nowadays, they have easy access to this information through the convention.

Procedural Effects: Empowerment and Sovereignty

Transparency and empowerment   An assessment of whether the convention leads to empowerment of information recipients (in this case, developing countries) depends on how we understand the concept of empowerment. Here, we make an analytical distinction among four modes of thinking about power, as summarized by Wolf (1999).[20] In the first mode, *empowerment* is equated with capacity building, which means that power is conceptualized as an attribute of a person, or in this case, government, that is, as a potency or capability. As we have seen, the capacity to make informed decisions through the convention is still weak in developing countries, but one could argue that empowerment according to this mode is taking place and likely to increase. As a second form of empowerment, the increased ability of ego to impose its will on an alter ego, the effects of the convention can be considered as empowering, because developing countries will be better able—pushed by the convention—to make exporting countries comply with their import decisions and preferences. A third (stronger) meaning of empowerment, that is, increased control of a setting, can hardly be considered an outcome of the convention: developing countries are not redefining trade and trade rules in chemicals, and there is no reason to think that developing countries have become more powerful vis-à-vis others in decision-making processes within convention structures, the PIC procedure notwithstanding. A fourth form of empowerment refers to the power to organize and operate the governance settings oneself. Historical accounts of the convention (e.g., Langlet 2009) show that developing countries have not been the driving forces behind the convention's design or operationalization. Interviewees even point out that some developing countries were not in favor of the convention initially. Accepting the successive announcements of increasing participation of developing countries on the convention website as increasing commitment, we can conclude that commitment to the convention *follows* rather than orchestrates the implementation process.

In short, only by using a narrow interpretation of empowerment (the first mode as increased capacity), rooted in a nonrelational concept of power, can one conclude that the Rotterdam Convention and its information disclosure obligations lead to the empowerment of information recipients. If a more comprehensive definition of empowerment is used, which includes the relations between developed and developing countries and the power to structure the field of action of others, we can conclude that there has been very little empowerment through transparency and disclosure in this case.

Transparency and sovereignty   We turn next to how the convention relates to democratization (or the rights-based democratic push for individual liberty, choice, and participation, particularly vis-à-vis citizens or civil society) and state sovereignty. The Rotterdam Convention is a case in which governance by disclosure strengthens rather than weakens state sovereignty. The aim of the convention is to help states decide about and control imports of risky substances into their jurisdiction. The critical importance of risk mitigation and reduced environmental harm, and the state-to-state character of information flows, implies that issues of accountability, legitimation, and democracy (particularly vis-à-vis citizens or civil society) are relatively less central here compared to some other transparency initiatives (Biermann and Gupta 2011; Mitchell 2011). Instead, the right to know of governments, democratic or not, is the central issue. This transparency initiative thus has stronger roots in a techno-statist Keynesian governance approach to regulating technology risks rather than in a deliberative democracy approach to risk governance. Based on this case study, we reject, therefore, the hypothesis posited in chapter 1 (Gupta and Mason) of this book that transparency decenters state-led regulation. In the case of governance by disclosure between states, transparency may *strengthen* state-led regulation.

This does not mean that civil society advocacy has been unimportant in the shaping of this case of governance by disclosure. International activism on pesticides focused much attention on getting the PIC procedure in place. The interviewed NGO representative stated that getting the PIC procedure functioning was a priority,[21] being in fact the raison d'être of the Pesticide Action Network. The pesticide activists were willing and able to adopt a long-term strategy toward procedural change (Pesticides Trust 1989; see also Dinham 1991, 1993a, 1993b, 1996, 2004). The transparency literature (e.g., Gupta 2008, see also Dingwerth and Eichinger, chapter 10, this book) sometimes argues that successful governance by disclosure requires intermediary groups. However, for the Rotterdam Convention to function in the future, that seems to be less the case. The possibility of shaming by intermediaries or environmental groups hardly plays a role in the PIC mechanism. This does not mean that NGOs cannot contribute; they are observers at meetings just like the industry, and they sometimes provide inputs into the discussions. However, this form of governance by disclosure, once in place, no longer depends on them.

Substantive Effects: Disclosure-Based Governance and Bans
A crucial issue in the transparency debate is the possible trade-offs between procedural and substantive improvements, and whether the procedural turn or "getting the process" right is not more than a distraction, diverting time and resources from substantive outcomes (Gupta 2008). Improvement has a double meaning in Rotterdam Convention: to improve the regulatory capacity of developing countries and countries in economic transition and to improve environmental and human health. Interviewees tended to be concerned about both types of improvements. We argue that despite its modest impact to date and the limitedness of its scope, the procedural turn induced by the convention strengthens the capacity of states to manage risks in the long term. The convention is making small contributions to improving the risk infrastructure of developing countries and has improved access to information about regulatory decisions and supporting scientific evidence. The implementation challenges previously discussed can be addressed within the framework of the convention. Why nonetheless is the impact limited? We discuss two reasons: first, the number and nature of chemicals listed in annex III, and second, the extent to which a PIC procedure can adequately address the spectrum of governance challenges posed by pesticide use. We conclude with assessing the link between PIC and a trade ban on hazardous pesticides.

Pesticides subject to PIC   Many of the listed chemicals in annex III are outdated pesticides that are not widely used or traded. There are thus few objections to their inclusion (Langlet 2009). Of the forty chemicals listed in annex III, the European Union exported only eight (including chemicals that received more than five export notifications in the European Union in the period 2003–2011; EDEXIM 2011b). When notifications concern chemicals still widely used and thus with larger trade interests, exporting countries object more strongly to their inclusion. The two major, almost iconic, examples to date are chrysotile asbestos and endosulfan, for which the Rotterdam Convention chemical review committee has drafted a decision guidance document. Because decisions of the conference of parties require consensus, countries with export interests can block listing of such important chemicals relatively easily. A group led by India, for example, has opposed the listing of endosulfan in the convention, and a group led by Canada, the largest producer, has opposed the listing of chrysotile asbestos (Bitonti 2009) and has played a leading role in keeping this chemical from being subject to the PIC procedure .[22] Endosulfan was finally approved for inclusion in annex III by the conference of parties to the convention in 2011. The opposition may have been dropped because the Stockholm Convention on Persistent Organic Pollutants included endosulfan in the list of chemicals that have to be eliminated in May 2011. The Stockholm Convention is more far-reaching in its immediate effects on trade than is the Rotterdam Convention, given that the latter's focus is on informing about, rather than banning, a substance (but see the detailed discussion of this below).

One key test for the Rotterdam Convention's substantive impact in the long term is thus whether the list with chemicals subject to the PIC procedure will grow over time. It is too early to conclude that the recent inclusion of endosulfan in 2011 is a turning point, but it may signal future inclusion of more widely used chemicals with a high economic value. This recent inclusion shows that chemicals that are part of the current package of popular pesticides in developing countries can also become subject to stricter regulatory control. The next litmus test is the discussion about the widely used herbicide paraquat at the sixth conference of the parties to the convention.

PIC and the spectrum of governance challenges   In addition to the limited number of pesticides currently listed in annex III, another hurdle to substantive impacts is that the convention addresses only a small component of the whole pesticide chain of production, trade, and use, namely, the moment of export and import. It does not tackle problems related to, for example, pesticide handling during use. In general, developing country governments do not adequately address the unsafe use of pesticides in developing country conditions (Jansen 2008; Karlsson 2007). The sound science and best practice principles that underlie global governance treaties such as the Rotterdam Convention are often at odds with the conditions that lead to unsound practices in farmers' fields.

The ban as regulatory instrument   The observation that poor farmers in developing countries are unable to use hazardous pesticides safely (due to, among others, illiteracy, lack of resources to buy personal protection equipment, and tropical circumstances that make it very difficult to use such equipment) has long motivated many activists to call for bans and other forms of restrictive regulation. Governance by disclosure and PIC are often seen as an alternative to such a ban. Gupta, for example, considers PIC as a compromise between two alternative policy options, which are, respectively, "an outright ban on trade as a way to avoid harm, versus a *caveat emptor* or 'let the buyer beware' approach where the onus to know about and avoid harm rests solely with a buyer" (Gupta 2010a, 33). A nonbanning narrative certainly underpins the Rotterdam Convention. It is often remarked that the convention is not designed to ban chemicals or pesticides but to provide information on the risks of chemicals so that countries can make informed decisions on their import (Murray and Logan 2004). For example, the two first speakers at the fourth conference of parties to the convention in 2008 opened with statements that the convention is not about banning chemicals (ENB 2008). Persons involved in the convention do not hesitate to stress that "it has to be kept in mind that listing a chemical in annex III does not mean that the chemical is banned, but requires parties to exchange all necessary information on this chemical in order to make informed decisions related to its import."[23]

It is in this context that the shift by advocacy groups from their initial activist position to prohibit exports of banned pesticides to an embrace of PIC has been important. From the perspective of the Pesticide Action Network, the choice was either to ban the export of hazardous pesticides or to let importing countries decide whether they wanted to import them or not.[24] PAN was concerned that the first option could result in a shift of the production of these pesticides to countries with less strict export regulations. Furthermore, the second option was more consistent with the principle that developing countries should have the right to decide what to import rather than have the North decide what to export.

The relevant question now is whether the idea of PIC as an alternative to the ban, confidently expressed in nonbanning narratives, really means that the ban as regulatory instrument has disappeared from global pesticide regulation. We do not think so; there are several reasons why the ban can be considered a fundamental part of contemporary pesticide governance, probably more than ever, even though PIC is generally seen as an alternative to an outright ban. A pesticide qualifies for inclusion in the PIC list (annex III) when at least two countries from two different PIC regions have *banned* a pesticide or *severely restricted* its use as a final regulatory action. In fact, the convention provides for the first time a globally recognized definition of a ban.[25] According to a former PAN representative,[26] the convention's definition of "banned chemical" dispelled confusion resulting from different interpretations by NGOs and industry of previous listings of chemicals as banned by UNEP. A remarkable, though yet little discussed, implication of the convention's definition is that withdrawal of a chemical from the regulatory process by industry may (under certain conditions) be seen as a ban of a chemical. This is quite a novel interpretation.

In practice, some developing countries seem to take the listing of a chemical in annex III itself as an indication of a ban (which is logical, given that most of the listed chemicals have been banned in at least some countries). The industry contests this type of decision making: "Unfortunately some parties use the Annex of the Rotterdam Convention as a black list and wrote legislation to ban all listed chemicals without making independent decisions as sovereign states based on the provided information."[27] The interviewed designated national authority simultaneously confirmed and denounced this practice, as did the industry representative, though for a different reason: he was afraid that some governments might block the listing of a particular chemical precisely because they perceive the listing as a ban rather than just a step toward better information exchange.

Although the specter of a ban may have pushed actors to seek compromise around PIC, this does not mean that it is an alternative to the ban. Despite the dominance of a nonbanning discourse, the ban has become a core practice of and a central condition for pesticide risk governance and regulatory practice. The ban as regulatory action is a substantial element of decision making as per the PIC mechanism. Therefore, the notion of a ban relates in complex ways to governance by disclosure (as exemplified in this case by PIC), rather than being in opposition to it.

Conclusion

The Rotterdam Convention does not seem to be one of those transparency systems that are "tacked together in times of crisis" (Fung et al. 2007, 106). Instead, it has taken several decades to arrive at a more-or-less functioning, though modest, governance-by-disclosure regime in this case. The PIC system seems to deliver the public benefits that policy makers aimed for. We conclude that more information regarding regulatory decisions on banning and restricting the use of pesticides, together with scientific evidence of harm, has become available. The convention

combines procedural and substantive elements because it fosters informing and improving capacity and environmental conditions. We have also
argued that, in a limited form, the convention shapes trade rather than being trade or market following, though it has to accept that trade interests
lobby at the level of individual countries. In terms of empowerment, the
results are more ambiguous. If one views empowerment as bringing about
shifts in unequal power relations, little has been achieved by transparency
in this transformative sense. If one views empowerment as the improved
ability to take informed decisions, then some advances can be reported.

Rather than an exercise in deliberative democracy, the convention and
its uptake of transparency is being driven by a techno-statist approach. The
case also illustrates that not all transparency initiatives can be explained
by reference to the marketization driver. The history of the negotiations
and institutionalization of the convention's PIC procedure shows that it is
based on, and results in, the strengthening of sovereignty instead of a decentering of state-led regulation. It increases the legitimacy and the capacity of state regulators in developing countries to control the trade and use
of hazardous chemicals, and manage risks. Science, in the form of government appointed experts, is seen as independent from market actors and the
key source of authority to interpret risk information. Indeed, representatives of advocacy groups, the scientific community, as well as government
officials consider techno-statist risk regulation, based on improved access
to information, as the most appropriate way to reduce pesticide risks.

What is remarkable in this case is the long trajectory needed to shape
a PIC mechanism. As the regime evolves, it remains to be seen whether
all parties will be willing to accept potentially more onerous disclosure
"costs" in the future. For now, many countries are not even able to make
the obligatory import decisions about the PIC-listed chemicals. Furthermore, to date, only a small group of chemicals is included within the purview of the convention, but now that the PIC mechanism is in place, more
may be added. This next step will take time. The convention's history
shows that the key issue for reflexive transparency is not so much a "loss
of innocence" but rather letting go of a naive belief that these multilateral
and complex processes will yield revolutionary changes in the short term.

Notes

1. Regulation (EEC) No. 1734/88 and No. 2455/92. The strongest opponents
were the United Kingdom, Germany, and France, who preferred voluntary arrangements with the industry.

2. In turn, after the adoption of the convention, the EC developed new regulation to bring it fully in line with the convention (see for more details Langlet 2003, 2009).

3. After the adoption of the binding convention, the FAO removed PIC from its voluntary code (FAO 2003).

4. The conferences of parties are open to other parties (article 18.7). The UN, its specialized agencies, and the International Atomic Energy Agency, as well as states that are not party, industry representatives, and NGOs, may attend the meetings as observers.

5. However, when the importing party decides not to consent to the import of a chemical, it has to prohibit the import from any other source, including nonparties.

6. When a party decides not to consent to import, this should apply to imports from nonparties as well, and if the substance is domestically produced, such production should also stop.

7. A severely restricted chemical is a chemical for which a "final regulatory action" in a member country prohibits almost all uses in one or more categories. A banned chemical is a chemical for which a final regulatory action prohibits all uses in one or more categories.

8. Article 14 of the convention sets out the information to be shared between the parties, regardless if the chemical is exported or not. This includes technical, scientific, economic, and legal information on SHPFs, banned and severely restricted chemicals, as well as information on regulatory actions taken domestically. Confidential information can be protected but information requirements of the convention cannot be confidential.

9. The mechanism of export notifications does not apply to chemicals listed in annex III (to which the PIC procedure applies). In contrast to the PIC procedure, the export notification procedure does not require consent of the importing party before export; here the responsibility for taking measures lies with the importing party.

10. For example, for chemicals listed in annex III and banned or severely restricted chemicals in the party's own territory, information on risks and hazards for the environment and human health should be indicated on a safety data sheet in an internationally recognized format.

11. At the time of writing, the agenda for the sixth conference of the parties to the convention listed another six chemicals for evaluation, including the controversial chemical paraquat.

12. Author e-mail communication with the convention secretariat, Geneva, June 2011.

13. Author interview with a former Pesticide Action Network representative, London, June 2011.

14. The European Community has listed (as of September 5, 2011) sixty-two chemicals qualifying for PIC notification, including pesticides that inflict many casualties in developing countries, such as carbofuran, methamidophos, methyl-parathion, and paraquat (EDEXIM 2011a). Inclusion of any of these sixty-two

pesticides in the convention's assessment process depends on a notification from at least one other region.

15. Author interview with a chemical review committee expert, May 2011.

16. For example, notifications from Malawi, Iran, Malaysia, Sweden (CRC 2010), Syrian Arabic Republic, and Japan (CRC 2011) were declined.

17. The secretariat remarks that a proposal still requires field monitoring, data collection, and validation.

18. As of April 30, 2012, thirteen parties have failed to provide any import responses: Botswana, Djibouti, Equatorial Guinea, Lesotho, Maldives, Marshall Islands, Montenegro, Namibia, Russian Federation, Saint Vincent and the Grenadines, Somalia, Tonga, and Ukraine.

19. During the negotiations in the mid-1990s, the United States argued that the convention should not affect rights and obligations flowing from WTO agreements, whereas the European Union opposed this view (Kummer 1999). A sufficiently vague formulation in the preamble was agreed on to create consensus, stating that "nothing in this convention shall be interpreted as implying in any way a change in the rights and obligations of a Party under any existing international agreement."

20. For an interesting discussion of power that covers the same elements as Wolf, but makes a slightly different distinction, see Fuchs (2005).

21. Author interview with a former representative of the Pesticide Action Network, London, June 2011.

22. As of April 2013, asbestos has appeared again on the agenda of the convention (at the sixth conference of the parties to the convention). The Canadian government has declared that it will no longer oppose the inclusion of asbestos in annex III. This is a result of a shift in the Quebec government in 2012, with the newly elected Parti Québécois ending government support for the Quebec asbestos industry (Ruff 2012).

23. Author e-mail communication with secretariat of the convention, Geneva, June 2011.

24. Author interview with a former representative of Pesticide Action Network, London, June 2011.

25. "'Banned chemical' means a chemical all uses of which within one or more categories have been prohibited by final regulatory action, in order to protect human health or the environment. It includes a chemical that has been refused approval for first-time use or has been withdrawn by industry either from the domestic market or from further consideration in the domestic approval process and where there is *clear* evidence that such action has been taken in order to protect human health or the environment" (Article 2.b; italics added). This is almost the same the definition as in Regulation (EC) No 304/2003; the only difference is the extra word *clear*. The convention does not explain what *clear* means.

26. Author interview with a former Pesticide Action Network representative, London, June 2011.

27. Author e-mail communication with a large pesticide corporation representative, July 2011.

References

Biermann, Frank, and Aarti Gupta. 2011. Accountability and Legitimacy in Earth System Governance: A Research Framework. *Ecological Economics* 70 (11): 1856–1864.

Bitonti, Christopher P. H. 2009. Exporting Ignorance: Canada's Opposition to the Regulation of the International Chrysotile Asbestos Trade under the Rotterdam Convention. *Asper Review of International Business and Trade Law* 9: 171–199.

Boardman, Robert. 1986. *Pesticides in World Agriculture: The Politics of International Regulation*. Basingstoke, UK: Macmillan.

Castillo, L., C. Wesseling, H. Aguilar, C. Castillo, and P. de Vos. 1989. Uso e impacto de los plaguicidas en tres países centroamericanos. *Estudios Sociales Centroamericanos* 49: 119–139.

Clapp, Jennifer. 2003. Transnational Corporate Interests and Global Environmental Governance: Negotiating Rules for Agricultural Biotechnology and Chemicals. *Environmental Politics* 12 (4): 1–23.

COP (Conference of the Parties). 2004. *Report of the Conference of the Parties to the Rotterdam Convention on the Prior Informed Consent Procedure for Certain Hazardous Chemicals and Pesticides in International Trade on the Work of Its First Meeting*. Geneva: Rotterdam Convention.

COP. 2008. *Report of the Conference of the Parties to the Rotterdam Convention on the Prior Informed Consent Procedure for Certain Hazardous Chemicals and Pesticides in International Trade on the Work of Its Fourth Meeting*. Rome: Rotterdam Convention.

CRC. 2010. *Report of the Chemical Review Committee on the Work of Its Sixth Meeting*. Geneva: Rotterdam Convention.

CRC. 2011. *Report of the Chemical Review Committee on the Work of Its Seventh Meeting*. Geneva: Rotterdam Convention.

CropLife International. 2004. *Prior Informed Consent (PIC)*. Position paper. Brussels: CropLife.

Daudu, Olurotimi Williams. 2008. *National Implementation of and Compliance with the Rotterdam Convention: A Perspective from African Countries*. PhD Dissertation, University of Calgary.

Dinham, Barbara. 1991. FAO and Pesticides: Promotion or Proscription? *Ecologists* 21 (2): 61–65.

Dinham, Barbara. 1993a. Controlling Hazardous Trade: The Potential of Prior Informed Consent. *Pesticide News* 21:10–11.

Dinham, Barbara. 1993b. *The Pesticide Hazard: A Global Health and Environmental Audit*. London: Zed Books.

Dinham, Barbara. 1996. The Success of a Voluntary Code in Reducing Pesticide Hazards in Developing Countries. In *Green Globe Yearbook of International Cooperation on Environment and Development 1996*, ed. H. O. Bergesen, G. Georg

Parmann, and Ø. B. Thommessen. Oxford: Fridtjof Nansen Institute and Oxford University Press.

Dinham, Barbara. 2004. Can New Global Initiatives Reduce Pesticide Hazards? *Pesticides News* 65: 6–8.

EDEXIM. 2011a. *List of Chemicals Subject to Export Notification Procedure.* Available at http://www.edexim.jrc.it.

EDEXIM. 2011b. *Number of Yearly Export Notifications per Chemical.* Available at http://www.edexim.jrc.it.

ENB. 2008. Summary of the Fourth Meeting of the Conference of the Parties to the Rotterdam Convention: October 27–31, 2008. *Earth Negotiations Bulletin* 15 (168): 1–12.

ENB. 2011. Summary of the Fifth Meeting of the Rotterdam Convention on Prior Informed Consent: June 20–24, 2011. *Earth Negotiations Bulletin* 15 (188): 1–14.

Etzioni, Amitai. 2010. Is Transparency the Best Disinfectant? *Journal of Political Philosophy* 18 (4): 389–404.

FAO (Food and Agriculture Organization of the United Nations). 1990. *International Code of Conduct on the Distribution and Use of Pesticides* (Amended to Include Prior Informed Consent in Article 9 as Adopted by the 25th Session of the FAO Conference in November 1989). Rome: FAO.

FAO. 2003. *International Code of Conduct on the Distribution and Use of Pesticides* (Revised Version, adopted by the 123rd Session of the FAO Council in November 2002). Rome: FAO.

Florini, Ann. 1998. The End of Secrecy. *Foreign Policy* 111: 50–63.

Fox, Jonathan. 2007. The Uncertain Relationship between Transparency and Accountability. *Development in Practice* 17 (4–5): 663–671.

Fuchs, Doris. 2005. Commanding Heights? The Strength and Fragility of Business Power in Global Politics. *Millennium Journal of International Studies* 33 (3): 771–801.

Fung, Archon. 2013. Infotopia: Unleashing the Democratic Power of Transparency. *Politics & Society* 41 (2): 183–212.

Fung, Archon, Mary Graham, and David Weil. 2007. *Full Disclosure: The Perils and Promise of Transparency.* Cambridge, UK: Cambridge University Press.

Galt, Ryan. 2008. Beyond the Circle of Poison: Significant Shifts in the Global Pesticide Complex, 1976–2008. *Global Environmental Change* 18 (4): 786–799.

Gupta, Aarti. 2008. Transparency under Scrutiny: Information Disclosure in Global Environmental Governance. *Global Environmental Politics* 8 (2): 1–7.

Gupta, Aarti. 2010a. Transparency as Contested Political Terrain: Who Knows What about the Global GMO Trade and Why Does It Matter? *Global Environmental Politics* 10 (3): 32–52.

Gupta, Aarti. 2010b. Transparency in Global Environmental Governance: A Coming of Age? *Global Environmental Politics* 10 (3): 1–9.

Heyvaert, Veerle. 2009. Globalizing Regulation: Reaching beyond the Border of Chemical Safety. *Journal of Law and Society* 36 (1): 110–128.

Hough, Peter. 1998. *The Global Politics of Pesticides: Forging Consensus from Conflicting Interests.* London: Earthscan.

Hough, Peter. 2000. Institutions for Controlling the Global Trade in Hazardous Chemicals: The 1998 Rotterdam Convention. *Global Environmental Change* 10 (2): 161–164.

Hough, Peter. 2003. Poisons in the System: The Global Regulation of Hazardous Pesticides. *Global Environmental Politics* 3 (2): 11–24.

Jansen, Kees. 2003. Crisis Discourses and Technology Regulation in a Weak State: Responses to a Pesticide Disaster in Honduras. *Development and Change* 34 (1): 45–66.

Jansen, Kees. 2008. The Unspeakable Ban: The Translation of Global Pesticide Governance into Honduran National Regulation. *World Development* 36 (4): 575–589.

Karlsson, Sylvia I. 2007. Strategies for Reducing Risks with Agricultural Pesticides in Developing Countries. *International Journal of Social Economics* 34 (1/2): 103–126.

Kohler, Pia M. 2006. Science, PIC and POPs: Negotiating the Membership of Chemical Review Committees under the Stockholm and Rotterdam Conventions. *RECIEL Review of European Community and International Environmental Law* 15 (3): 293–303.

Kummer, Katharina. 1999. Prior Informed Consent for Chemicals in International Trade: The 1998 Rotterdam Convention. *RECIEL Review of European Community and International Environmental Law* 8 (3): 323–330.

Langlet, David. 2003. Prior Informed Consent for Hazardous Chemicals Trade—implementation in EC Law. *European Environmental Law Review* 12 (11): 292–308.

Langlet, David. 2009. *Prior Informed Consent for Hazardous Trade: Regulating Trade in Hazardous Goods at the Intersection of Sovereignty, Free Trade and Environmental Protection.* Alphen aan de Rijn, the Netherlands: Wolters Kluwer.

McDorman, Ted L. 2004. The Rotterdam Convention on the Prior Informed Consent Procedure for Certain Hazardous Chemicals and Pesticides in International Trade: Some Legal Notes. *RECIEL Review of European Community and International Environmental Law* 13 (2): 187–200.

Mitchell, Ronald B. 2011. Transparency for Governance: The Mechanisms and Effectiveness of Disclosure-based and Education-based Transparency Policies. *Ecological Economics* 70 (11): 1882–1890.

Mol, Arthur P. J. 2010. The Future of Transparency: Power, Pitfalls and Promises. *Global Environmental Politics* 10 (3): 132–143.

Murray, William J. 1994. Organization and Targets of the Prior Informed Consent Notification Scheme. Part I. Development and Implementation. *Annali dell'Istituto Superiore di Sanita* 30 (4): 383–386.

Murray, William, and Sheila Logan. 2004. The Rotterdam Convention: Why Is It Here and What Is It Trying to Achieve? *UNEP Industry and Environment* 27 (2–3): 9–11.

Paarlberg, Robert L. 1993. Managing Pesticide Use in Developing Countries. In *Institutions of the Earth: Sources of Effective International Environmental Protection*, ed. Peter M. Haas, Robert O. Keohane, and Mark A. Levy. Cambridge, MA: MIT Press.

Pesticides Trust. 1989. *The FAO Code: Missing Ingredients; Prior Informed Consent in the International Code of Conduct on the Distribution and Use of Pesticides*. London: The Pesticides Trust.

Ríos-González, Adriana, Kees Jansen, and Héctor Javier Sánchez-Pérez. 2013. Pesticide Risk Perceptions and the Differences between Farmers and Extensionists: Towards a Knowledge-in-Context Model. *Environmental Research* 124: 43–53.

Rosenthal, Erika. 2004. The DBCP Pesticide Cases: Seeking Access to Justice to Make Agribusiness Accountable in the Global Economy. In *Agribusiness and Society: Corporate Responses to Environmentalism, Market Opportunities and Public Regulation*, ed. K. Jansen and S. Vellema. London: Zed Books.

Rotterdam Convention. 2008. Rotterdam Convention on the Prior Informed Consent Procedure for Certain Hazardous Chemicals and Pesticides in International Trade (revised in 2008).

Ruff, Kathleen. 2012. Quebec and Canadian Governments End Their Historic Support of the Asbestos Industry. *International Journal of Occupational and Environmental Health* 18 (4): 263–267.

Selin, Henrik. 2010. *Global Governance of Hazardous Chemicals: Challenges of Multilevel Management*. Cambridge, MA: MIT Press.

Toleubayev, Kazbek, Kees Jansen, and Arnold Van Huis. 2011. From Integrated Pest Management to Indiscriminate Pesticide Use in Kazakhstan. *Journal of Sustainable Agriculture* 35 (4): 350–375.

Tyfield, David. 2012. A Cultural Political Economy of Research and Innovation in an Age of Crisis. *Minerva* 50 (2): 149–167.

Van den Bosch, Robert. 1980. *The Pesticide Conspiracy*. Garden City: Anchor Press.

Wargo, John. 1998. *Our Children's Toxic Legacy: How Science and Law Fail to Protect Us from Pesticides*. New Haven, CT: Yale University Press.

Weir, David, and Mark Schapiro. 1981. *Circle of Poison: Pesticides and People in a Hungry World*. San Francisco: Food First Books.

Wesseling, Catharina, Rob McConnell, Timo Partanen, and Christer Hogstedt. 1997. Agricultural Pesticide Use in Developing Countries: Health Effects and Research Needs. *International Journal of Health Services* 27 (2): 273–308.

Winqvist, Tina. 1999. *Trade in Domestically Prohibited Goods*. Winnipeg: International Institute for Sustainable Development.

Wolf, Eric R. 1999. *Envisioning Power: Ideologies of Dominance and Crisis*. Berkeley: University of California Press.

6

Risk Governance through Transparency: Information Disclosure and the Global Trade in Transgenic Crops

Aarti Gupta

Transparency is often linked to a democratizing impulse in governance. Yet whether this relationship holds in practice is uncertain and understudied. Transparency is widely assumed to empower those at its receiving end by enabling recipients of information to hold the powerful to account and/or by facilitating informed choices or effective participation in governance processes (e.g., Florini 2008; Fung et al. 2007; Graham 2002; Keohane 2006; Mitchell 1998).

Yet, as argued in the introduction (Gupta and Mason, this book, chapter 1), there are other (competing) normative rationales that underpin a transparency turn in global environmental governance. These include a marketization impulse for the uptake and institutionalization of transparency, one that views information disclosure as integral to regulating and/or facilitating the functioning of global markets. The democratization versus marketization drivers of transparency can work in complementary or contradictory ways, yet their interactions remain relatively little understood.

In this chapter, I analyze transparency as contested political terrain, wherein negotiations over the norms, practices, and objectives of global environmental and risk governance take place.[1] A central concern is whether transparency itself can be transformative of such norms and practices. I focus on the uptake, institutionalization, and (transformative) effects of transparency in global biosafety governance. Ensuring biosafety or safe trade in genetically modified organisms (GMOs) is a controversial global risk governance challenge, one in which the very existence of risk and harm remains contested. Analyzing the workings of transparency in this normatively and scientifically contested area contributes fruitfully to the comparative research agenda of this book.

I focus here on the information disclosure obligations in the Cartagena Protocol on Biosafety, negotiated under the Convention on Biological

Diversity (henceforth Cartagena Protocol). The Cartagena Protocol seeks to govern the safe transboundary transfer and use of GMOs by calling for the "advance informed agreement" of an importing country prior to such transfers (CP 2000). Transparency is thus at the heart of this global biosafety regime, insofar as information disclosure (about GMO risks, risk mitigation practices, and biosafety regulations) is intended to be the basis on which importing countries give or withhold their consent to potentially risky GMO transfers and on which they base risk-avoidance measures.

As I show in this chapter, such aims of disclosure-based governance are by no means shared in this highly contested issue domain (see also Wolf 2000). Although a democratization impulse is evident in the push to *empower* recipients to be informed about and avoid GMO risks, this impulse is being sidelined by the scope and manner of transparency's institutionalization in this case: in particular by the limited scope of agreed disclosure and by the resource-intensive transparency infrastructures required to render limited disclosure actionable. These outcomes result, I argue, from a recasting of transparency as a means toward *market facilitation* by those advocating globally for improved market access for GMOs (i.e., GMO producers and exporters). The result, I conclude, is that disclosure's effects in this case are more market *following* than market *forcing*.

I proceed as follows: section 2 elaborates on the rationales for uptake of transparency in global GMO governance. Section 3 analyzes the scope and practices of institutionalized disclosure in the Cartagena Protocol, and assesses the hypothesis, also advanced in the introduction, that institutionalization of transparency as a governance mechanism decenters state-led regulation and opens up political space for other actors. Section 4 then explores the normative, procedural, and substantive effects of the protocol's (limited) embrace of transparency. I base the analysis on occasional participant observation of Cartagena Protocol negotiations since 2000 and on primary and secondary sources.

Embracing Transparency

The concept of "advance informed agreement" in the Cartagena Protocol derives from the longer established notion of prior informed consent, used in the international realm to govern trade in risky substances such as hazardous wastes and restricted chemicals (Gupta 2000; Rajan 1997). It has long been demanded in a global environmental context by developing countries as a mechanism to prevent the dumping of risky substances within their borders without their knowledge or consent (see also Jansen and Dubois, this book, chapter 5).

In line with the typology of normative, procedural, and substantive effects outlined in chapter 1, advance informed agreement is also premised on a normative right of importing countries to be *informed* about potential risks and a procedural right to exercise *choice* about accepting such risks in order to further the substantive aim of *risk reduction* relating to the GMO trade. As such, advance informed agreement represents a compromise between two options at opposite ends of a policy spectrum: an outright *ban* on risky trade as a way to avoid harm or a caveat emptor (let the buyer beware) acceptance of the status quo, whereby the onus to know about and avoid harm rests solely with a buyer (Mehri 1988).

Yet the objectives to be achieved through advance informed agreement remain contested, as conflicts over the scope of the disclosure obligations that lie at its heart make clear. These conflicts are shaped by the broader political economic context shaping global GMO trade (on the global political economy of biotechnology, see Falkner 2007a, 2007b; Glover and Newell 2004; Pollack and Shaffer 2009; Scoones 2008). In discussing embrace of transparency in this case, I sketch first the broad agricultural trade relationships within which global biosafety disclosure is being negotiated and then outline evolving disclosure obligations.

Negotiating Transparency: The Globalized Context for Disclosure

Disclosure relating to GMOs traded globally for use as food, feed, or for processing (agricultural commodities) has been one of the central axes of conflict within the Cartagena Protocol negotiations (for detailed histories, see Bail et al. 2002; Gupta 2000). Of the most heavily traded agricultural commodity crops, four have a growing number of GMO varieties (soybean, maize, canola, and cotton) (James 2012). Of these, the first three are widely used for animal feed, food, and in a vast array of processed foods. Agricultural commodities account for the vast majority of globally traded GMOs and the economic stakes are high, given that disclosure has important implications for this multibillion-dollar global trade (e.g., Kimani and Gruère 2010; Oliveira et al. 2012). Genetically modified varieties of other important commodity crops such as wheat and rice are also in different stages of testing and commercialization (James 2012).

Although many countries are importers of agricultural commodities, the export of genetically modified varieties of such commodities is (still) limited to relatively few countries. These include the United States (with roughly 50 percent of all genetically modified crop production and trade),

Canada, Australia, Argentina, Brazil, and China (Falck-Zepeda 2006; see also Newell 2009). Key importers of bulk agricultural commodities include the European Union (EU), Japan, Mexico, China, South Africa, and many other countries in the global South. The main axis of conflict in the Cartagena Protocol negotiations is thus between the GMO exporter and importer perspectives.

Transparency obligations are being negotiated by constantly evolving coalitions of GMO-exporting and -importing countries in this realm, which cut across a traditional North-South divide in global environmental governance. For one, two global economic powerhouses fall on either side of this axis of conflict, with the European Union, often allied with Japan and a majority of developing countries, consistently articulating the GMO-importer perspective; and the United States and allies such as Canada, Australia, Argentina, and Uruguay consistently articulating the GMO-exporter perspective. Unlike in some other cases of governance by disclosure, therefore, when the "powerful" may be required to disclose to the "less powerful," here a transatlantic divide of power shapes the norms and practices of disclosure.

The European Union and a coalition of the poorest developing countries have long demanded comprehensive disclosure about presence of, and risks posed by, various genetically modified varieties of crops in the bulk agricultural commodity trade as a way to inform and empower recipients to make context-specific risk-mitigation choices, including imposing trade restrictions if necessary. By contrast, exporting countries, led by the United States in coalition with Australia, Canada, and Argentina, have consistently sought to limit globally agreed disclosure obligations so as not to impede GMO trade. In this view, standardized forms of disclosure about certain aspects of the GMO trade (if unavoidable) should enable a harmonized, evidence-based, and efficient decision-making process that can facilitate trade. These contested visions of what global biosafety governance should deliver have shaped the uptake, institutionalization, and impacts of disclosure in this context. Added to this are the evolving positions of emerging economies and other OECD countries, such as Brazil, China, South Africa, New Zealand, and Mexico, which are either both exporting and importing countries (China, South Africa) or are concerned about impact of GMO trade on their non-GMO agricultural exports (New Zealand)[2] or about trade relationships with GMO exporters (Mexico).[3]

Another key dynamic reinforces the impact on disclosure of these shifting global agricultural trade relationships: whether countries have ratified the Cartagena Protocol and hence are parties to it. Strikingly, most GMO-exporting countries (including the United States, Canada, Argentina, and Australia) have not ratified the Cartagena Protocol, and most of those articulating GMO-importer perspectives (including the European Union and most developing countries) have. Furthermore, countries with competing and shifting interests (whether exporter or importer), such as Brazil, Mexico, New Zealand, China, and South Africa, have also ratified and hence are parties to the protocol. This is a double-edged sword because it gives these countries the opportunity to shape disclosure obligations, yet to do so with an eye to how they are advantaged or disadvantaged by the fact that most of their main agricultural trade competitors and/or trade partners remain outside this global regime.

As one illustration, Brazil wears three hats in this global context: developing country, party to the protocol, and agricultural exporter. This requires a balancing act to support *and* moderate other developing countries' demands for stringent disclosure to ensure that Brazil can itself comply with disclosure obligations as an exporter and not be at a competitive disadvantage vis-à-vis (other) exporting nonparties who are not legally obliged to comply (e.g., Oliveira et al. 2012).

These shifting identities and coalitions within a broader political economic agricultural trade context have resulted in a discernible shift *away* from the original democratizing impulse for disclosure as a way to inform and empower GMO-recipient countries to make considered decisions about novel risks. Instead, a marketization imperative is now also driving institutionalization of disclosure in this case. I turn next to how these two drivers interact in shaping the concrete disclosure obligations mandated by the protocol.

Agreeing on Transparency: Democratization versus Marketization

Following contentious negotiations among GMO-exporter and -importer coalitions, the 2000 Cartagena Protocol agreed on a two-stage disclosure obligation relating to the global GMO commodity trade. The first step calls on GMO-producing countries to disclose *domestic approvals* of specific genetically modified varieties of food crops to an online Biosafety Clearing-House (BCH) within fifteen days of the approval being granted.[4] The second step calls for GMO exporting countries to disclose information about genetically modified varieties contained in bulk agricultural commodity shipments. I focus here on this latter step, given that it is one of the most contested elements of this global regime and is at the heart of its disclosure requirements.

Here, the Cartagena Protocol calls for agricultural commodity ship-ments containing GMO varieties to be accompanied by a declaration that they "may contain" GMOs. The coalition of GMO-producing countries, led by the United States, vigorously opposed any demands for more spe-cific and detailed disclosure requirements, such as a statement that ship-ments "contain" GMOs and specifying which ones, as demanded by the European Union and developing countries. Such disclosure would have required mandatory segregation of genetically from nongenetically modi-fied varieties, as well as segregation between different genetically modified varieties of the same crop in a given shipment, all of which are currently comingled (Elbehri 2007). As a victory for GMO-exporting countries in protocol negotiations in 2000, the "may contain" disclosure obligation does not push markets toward such segregation and its potentially trade-restrictive effects.

Following many more years of acrimonious negotiations among (shift-ing) coalitions of GMO-exporting and -importing countries, a number of additional disclosure requirements were agreed to in 2006. These call for agricultural commodity shipments that contain *identity-preserved GMOs* to declare that they "contain" GMOs. All others, for whom no identity preservation systems exist, still require only a "may contain" declaration (CBD 2006). Further negotiations to strengthen these obligations are now postponed until the end of 2014. Until such time, exporting countries can also use an existing commercial invoice to disclose information, as pushed for by these countries, rather than a stand-alone document, de-sired by importers, which would draw special attention to GMO presence in an agricultural commodity shipment (CBD 2006, 1, 4).

Additional disclosure requirements for shipments still labeled "may contain" include a list of GMO varieties that may be in a shipment, in-cluding their scientific, common, and/or commercial names, as well as a unique identifier code (a numeric code associated with each genetic transformation), if known. Unique identifiers, developed by the OECD, have been promoted by the European Union to facilitate tracking and testing for presence of specific GMO events in individual shipments. Fi-nally, the 2006 agreement specifies that "the expression 'may contain' does not require listing of living modified organisms of species other than those that constitute the shipment" (CBD 2006, paragraph 6). Thus a maize shipment would not require listing of genetically modified soybean varieties that might be inadvertently present. This caveat sidesteps thorny discussions relating to *adventitious* presence of GMOs in trade (that is, unavoidable presence of trace quantities of GMO varieties other than those known/intended to be in a shipment).

I turn next to analyzing the institutionalization of the protocol's disclosure obligations and whose normative, procedural, and substantive goals they further.

Institutionalizing Transparency

This section analyzes how the "may contain" and other protocol disclosure obligations are being institutionalized. In doing so, I engage with the hypothesis advanced in chapter 1 that institutionalization of transparency fosters a decentering of state-led regulation and qualifies state sovereignty, even as it opens up political space for new actors. I consider the first part of this hypothesis in analyzing the implementation burden on states relating to protocol disclosure obligations, particularly through analyzing whether information disclosers' practices *have to change* in order to comply with disclosure obligations. I next consider the second part of the hypothesis, relating to the opening up of political space for other actors. I do so by analyzing whether the "intermediaries and infrastructures of transparency" that now dominate global biosafety governance encourage greater engagement of nonstate actors and/or serve to transfer governance authority to them, and with what consequences.

Implementing Transparency: Decentering State-Led Regulation?

Disclosure stating that bulk agricultural commodity shipments "may contain" GMO varieties, as well as a list of which ones *may* be in a shipment and their common and scientific names, certainly goes beyond no such information being provided (the status quo in the absence of the Cartagena Protocol). This notwithstanding, such a disclosure obligation is imprecise, requiring only that any bulk shipment of a commodity (for example, a shipment of maize) state that it "may contain" *any* of the genetically modified varieties of maize that happen to be commercially available within the country at that moment in time. It does not require disclosure of specific genetically modified varieties that *are* present.

Such specificity, as noted previously, would require segregation of genetically modified from nongenetically modified varieties, and between distinct modified varieties, which does not yet occur in most exporting countries. As such, a "may contain" disclosure requirement simultaneously reveals too much and too little information. Even as it provides a long list of potential GMO varieties that *could be* in a shipment, no information is revealed about which varieties are actually present. This highlights a challenge of relying on transparency as a tool of governance: that it can be subverted in practice via "drowning in disclosure" (Gupta 2008, 4). This entails the provision of too much information, where the relevant is buried in the irrelevant and hard to find, if provided at all (see also CFO 2007 on "drowning in data" in financial transparency).

Second, a "may contain" disclosure obligation reveals information that already exists and is known to exporters. Essentially, any bulk shipment with genetically modified crop varieties requires such a declaration if it is shipped from a country with no segregation between genetically and nongenetically modified varieties in place, a characterization that applies to most GMO-exporting countries. As a result, no new information is generated, decreasing the likelihood that disclosure has behavior-altering consequences (at least for disclosers).

This lack of need for new information is reinforced by the caveat in the protocol's 2006 decision that, in listing GMOs that *may* be present in a shipment, only the same species need to be listed. Here, again, the burden of testing for and disclosing possible adventitious presence of GMOs of other species—information that is not presently known to exporters—is avoided.

In sum, a disclosure requirement that bulk shipments of commodities have to be accompanied by a declaration that they "may contain" GMOs is vague and reveals what is already known to disclosers. Equally important, it does not shift the burden of responsibility to test for the presence of specific GMOs to exporting countries, a key goal pursued by importing countries (on this, see also Jansen and Dubois, this book, chapter 5). Finally, the means of disclosure agreed here—an existing commercial invoice rather than a stand-alone document—is the least burdensome for exporters, entailing little change in existing practices and being the least market-restrictive means of complying with disclosure requirements.

In conclusion, then, the manner in which disclosure is being institutionalized in this global regime ensures that *no established practices have to change* in order for exporting countries to meet GMO disclosure obligations. It avoids a push toward mandatory segregation of modified and nonmodified varieties, and the concurrent need to test for the presence of specific varieties in the commodity chain, and places no onus on exporting countries to do so (Gruère and Rosegrant 2008). Instead, comingling remains as the main practice, a process whereby grain from multiple sources is mixed at different points, with changing ratios of genetically modified to nonmodified varieties in any given shipment (USDA 2008).

From an importing-country perspective, however, the imprecise "may contain" declaration does not reveal relevant and usable information that would help countries to be informed about the GMO varieties entering a country (on desired attributes of disclosure, see also Dingwerth and Eichinger, this book, chapter 10). Nor does it facilitate meeting the related procedural and substantive domestic GMO governance aims of importing countries, such as furthering consumer choice, labeling, traceability, and food safety, all of which—to varying degrees—may require this greater specificity.

Largely the same conclusion holds for the additional disclosure obligation, agreed with much fanfare in 2006, to state (for those genetically modified organisms for which identity-preserved varieties exist) that they "contain" GMOs. At first glance, this appears to be a significant advance over the "may contain" obligation, with potentially market-forcing effects. A quick assessment reveals, however, that identity preservation, as a concept and a practice, is more commonly associated with *nongenetically modified varieties* of those crops for which genetically modified varieties exist.

The idea of identity preservation is to ensure that a high-value crop (usually non-GM, more rarely GM) is not contaminated with other GM or non-GM varieties (Ceres undated; Elbehri 2007; Sahai undated). The practice thus far is that identity preserving a non-GMO variety of a heavily traded crop with GM varieties (such as soybean) makes economic sense for exporting countries who wish to supply markets that desire non-GM soybean (either for use in organic agriculture or because of other domestic imperatives). Brazil is a classic example, whereby identity preservation may be undertaken to supply guaranteed non-GM soya varieties to the EU or Japanese market (Oliveira et al. 2012).

The protocol disclosure requirement, however, states that the "contain" obligation is to apply to *identity-preserved GMO varieties*. There are, however, few of these to date, particularly in the first generation of GMO crops and particularly in countries such as the United States, where genetically and nongenetically modified varieties are considered substantially equivalent, logically suggesting no reason to identity preserve. Only those modified varieties that have special nutritionally altered characteristics (such as vitamin A–enhanced "golden rice"—not yet commercialized or traded) or other product characteristics (such as altered oil content or quality, for example, high oleic soybean) would, from a market perspective, be worthwhile or necessary to identity preserve (Elbehri 2007, 2).

As a result, if they do exist, such shipments are already marked as containing the GMO variety in question and their production is often undertaken under contract between producers and end users (Elbehri 2007, 2). In these cases, the burden of testing and segregation for identity-preserved crops is shouldered (willingly) by exporters for market-access reasons, given higher price premiums that such crops command.[5] If so, this component of disclosure is also *market following* (as is the "may contain" obligation), rather than being *market forcing*.

Notwithstanding their limited nature, are disclosure obligations being complied with by exporting countries? A first point to note here is that, because many GMO-exporting countries are not parties to the protocol, they are not legally obliged to comply. They can only be compelled to do so if an importing country incorporates into its domestic laws the disclosure obligations mandated by the protocol. Notwithstanding this, however, given the non-onerous nature of the protocol's disclosure obligations, it is likely that most nonparty exporting countries are willing and able to declare that shipments "may contain" GMOs (although unwilling to permit more stringent disclosure obligations, even if they are nonparties and hence not legally obliged to comply).

Even assuming such full compliance, however, the current minimal globally mandated disclosure in this realm reveals little that is useful to recipients and has few material consequences for disclosers. If so, caveat emptor prevails, with *market developments shaping how fast and how far disclosure proceeds,* rather than disclosure pushing market developments or restricting (exporting) state GMO governance authority. The onus of responsibility remains, furthermore, on importing countries to ferret out detailed and specific information about traded GMOs.

Related to this, the focus in global biosafety governance is now shifting to the negotiation and establishment of elaborate sampling, detection, testing, and verification guidelines and systems. These are seen as essential to generating additional (specific) information and/or monitoring incoming shipments of agricultural commodities with genetically modified varieties. I turn to the implications of this development next.

Infrastructures of Transparency: Political Space for Other Actors?

Given the current scope of disclosure in this global regime, essentially revolving around a "may contain" obligation, the practices of governance by disclosure have now decisively shifted to establishing infrastructures of sampling, testing, detection, and verification of GMOs in the bulk commodity trade. Such "infrastructures of transparency" appear necessary to augment the limited information currently disclosed and verify the accuracy of disclosed information (and such an imperative exists no matter how much information is disclosed).[6] The question then arises whether these systems and practices of sampling, testing, and verification might be sites of empowerment and shifting authority, not only from GMO-exporting to-importing countries but also from states to nonstate actors.

In recent years, an entire infrastructure of sampling, testing, and verification for GMO transfers is indeed emerging globally (CBD 2008). For each of these components, complex, contested, and uncertain issues arise (Kalaitzandonakes 2004). For example, *detection* of GM content in food, feed, and in processed products looks set to become a key site where battles of knowing and disclosing are likely to be fought—notwithstanding the image it evokes of an esoteric and technically complex activity conducted by neutral scientists toiling in obscure scientific laboratories. The politically contested nature of such testing and verification systems is evident from an emerging transatlantic divide here: two detection methods dominate current GM testing, with one favored by the United States and the other by the European Union. The method preferred by the United States, protein testing, is relatively easy, cheap, and quick but imprecise; the method preferred by the European Union, DNA testing, is technically complex, expensive, and time-consuming but yields more precise results (CBD 2008, 11; Holst-Jensen undated). Which of these is endorsed as an appropriate (or adequate) method of detection is a key political issue, given varying costs and consequences for exporters and importers in the agricultural commodity trade.

Also contested is what and whose "truths" are revealed by sampling, testing, and detection, that is, the reliability of information obtained via testing. In discussing costs and challenges associated with GMO testing and the consequences for agricultural trade, Kalaitzandonakes (2006, 24) notes that, because GMO testing is

a statistical process, repeated sampling and testing of the very same cargo [can] regularly produce different results. There are several sources of variance in test results, including differences in testing and sampling methods as well as testing error. Testing methods can vary appreciably across labs [...] conflicting test results could occur even if identical lab testing protocols are used, unless the same sample is tested. Depending on the concentration and distribution of a particular LMO [living modified organism] in a particular lot and how it was sampled, it could be difficult, if not impossible, to duplicate any set of test results. Finally, some assay [sampling] error (e.g., false positive or false negative test results) will always exist.

With variations in test results and the specter of false positives and false negatives hanging over such results, there can be significant economic consequences for all involved with a testing and verification regime, depending on how liability for error is distributed. If so, whose testing regimen is "sound" and whose knowledge is reliable are key sites of conflict, which science alone cannot resolve.

Debates within the Cartagena Protocol thus have also focused on *standardization* of various elements of such infrastructures of transparency, such as standardized sampling techniques, detection methods, and testing protocols (CBD 2008). This also appears to be a looming battleground in biosafety governance, as evident from the fact that the objectives pursued by standardization vary greatly.

For GMO exporters, the goal is to avoid proliferating national standards and develop minimum agreed-on global standards such that potential liability claims or economic harm resulting from diverging national practices or varying (unstandardized) test results is reduced. For GMO importers, such as the European Union with its stringent regional labeling, thresholds, and traceability requirements, the goal is to pursue global standards that reflect its own preferred methods and approaches. An effort in the global food safety standard–setting body, the Codex Alimentarius Commission, to achieve agreement on standardized testing and thresholds for transgenic food has been stalled for a while (Gruère 2006; see also Smythe 2009), with similar debates now emerging in the context of the protocol as well.

If such infrastructures of transparency are complex, expensive, prone to error, and a challenge to institutionalize globally for the genetically modified varieties currently being traded, the challenges increase in complexity as ever-more modified varieties enter the market. Furthermore, these contain not one or two genetic modification "events" but rather multiple "stacked events" (James 2008), each of which may require separate testing protocol and procedures (CBD 2008). This discussion highlights a crucial aspect relating to infrastructures and intermediaries of transparency: how these new and emerging loci of authority will function and who they will empower (see also Langley 2001).

Clearly, detection techniques can also be a powerful tool for civil society and others seeking information, as evident from *Starlink* and other controversies surrounding release of illegal GMO varieties and their international diffusion over the years. StarLink was a genetically modified variety of maize approved in 1998 in the United States for use as animal feed, but which entered the domestic food chain and was also detected (by anti-GMO watchdog groups) in international commodity shipments. In such cases, civil society efforts rather than state-run systems of oversight detected unauthorized GMOs in bulk shipments (Clapp 2007). A key implication is that availability of simple detection techniques, developed to support governance by disclosure and perhaps disseminated via the protocol (through capacity building), may well force further disclosure and voluntarily change market practices, given the possibility that easily detected illegal presence of GMOs may fuel liability claims and lost market access.

However, to detect presence of illegal and unapproved GMOs, information about *what to test for* is still necessary. Certain types of disclosure are thus required for a testing infrastructure itself to function, and for other political actors to hold disclosers (in this case, GMO-producing states and exporters) to account. Such disclosure includes reference materials and testing protocols for each GMO variety, information that testers need in order to know what to test for.

Such information, however, is often seen as proprietary and not widely available (CBD 2008). As a CBD synthesis report notes, "detection of unauthorized or unknown GMOs [is often not possible] due to lack of molecular knowledge of their genetic contents" (CBD 2008, 15; see also Nielsen 2013). This highlights that the empowerment potential of these infrastructures of transparency remains up for grabs and is linked to market-driven imperatives, such as protection of confidential information that often results in partial transparency (see also Mason, this book, chapter 4). Thus, the potential for such infrastructures of transparency to open up political space for other actors (also to hold disclosers to account) is present, but often circumscribed by market-facilitating considerations.

In addition to confidential information, a concern with liability also has complex effects on disclosure's empowerment potential. Liability discussions have been extremely contentious in Cartagena Protocol negotiations (Bled 2009; CBD 2009; Jungcurt and Schabus 2010), not only because of concerns over ecological or health-related damages resulting from GMO use but also because liability rules alter the incentive structures for disclosure and its testing and verification.

For example, once liability regimes are in place, less precise tests might no longer be an option, given the risk of being held liable for inaccurate information. But on whom the onus for greater accuracy will rest remains unclear and contested. The burden for testing might be shifted onto exporting parties (the intent of those pushing for stringent liability in this context), or rather, remain on those who *currently* need to comply with protocol obligations and ensure accuracy of their own stringent GMO-labeling laws (mainly importing countries who are parties to the protocol). These intricate links between disclosure and liability are increasingly coming to the fore and have consequences for the extent to which disclosure constrains state sovereignty or opens up political space for other actors.[7]

From this discussion, two summarizing observations can be made. First, the growing need for sampling, testing, and verification infrastructures, in this domain as in many others, signals a "technicalization" of political conflict and creation of new epistemic authorities, in which particular forms of expertise are privileged over others (Gupta 2004; Jasanoff 1987). These new loci of authority will reshape existing power relationships, yet in what ways and how is still unclear (on information intermediaries as new sites of authority, see also Dingwerth and Eichinger, this book, chapter 10). This will be dependent on who has the capacity and need to establish such infrastructures as well as the power to shape associated practices and what Power calls "rituals of verification" (Power 1997a).

As Power notes, a key struggle is over competing claims to expertise. This is especially the case, he suggests, when "the nature of the market and the competences to operate in it are ill-defined and immature. In such circumstances, even the driest and most procedural elaboration [...] is not simply neutrally descriptive, it is part of a wider normative discourse which constructs and presents the field in ways which make it receptive to the claims of certain forms of expertise rather than another" (Power 1997b, 124).

This applies to the newly emerging "market" for GMO sampling, detection, testing, and verification infrastructures and practices as well (see also Gupta et al., this book, chapter 8; and Knox-Hayes and Levy, this book, chapter 9, for the same dynamic in carbon markets). The relevance and functioning of governance by disclosure is shaped by these infrastructures of testing and verification and their architects, suggesting a new locus of conflict and power in this realm.

Second, the discussion suggests that relying on transparency as a central governance mechanism has more relevance for some actors and countries than others. Establishing infrastructures of transparency is, for example, more feasible for the European Union, Japan, New Zealand, Mexico, or South Africa, where extensive efforts are underway (CBD 2008; Mayet undated). It poses a far greater challenge for developing countries, particularly in Africa. These countries thus prefer instead to expand the scope of disclosed information in order to shift the onus of responsibility for monitoring and testing onto exporting countries (ENB 2008).

A clarion call for capacity building is also increasingly heard from all within this global governance context. Yet, as the discussion implies, the capacity to ensure biosafety and develop institutions and practices of sampling, testing, and verification (and whose capacity is to be built by whom) cannot be separated from political struggles over *whose* practices are considered reliable, accurate, and trustworthy (for an analysis of capacity building in biosafety, see Gupta 2010b).

I turn next to assessing further the impacts on different actors and the ends furthered by the uptake and institutionalization of disclosure in this case.

Effects of Transparency

In assessing the effects of transparency, I consider in this section the implications of current disclosure obligations and practices for GMO-importing countries in particular, as shaped by their varying domestic governance goals. More specifically, I analyze who (among importing countries) most *needs* protocol-induced disclosure to meet their biosafety governance aims.

Normative and Procedural Effects: Furthering Whose Right to Know and Choose?

Within the category of importing countries, there are wide variations in existence and stringency of domestic biosafety laws with which global disclosure processes interact. Key differences include whether domestic GMO laws exist, and if they do, what they call for. They might require only biosafety risk assessments or also labeling of food with GMO ingredients. Labeling laws might have varying threshold levels that trigger labeling, which may require more or less precise information about GMO content. Most expansively, some laws may call for traceability of GMOs from farm to fork (e.g., Falck-Zepeda 2006; Gruère 2006).

Countries with the most stringent domestic biosafety regulations in place, such as the European Union, require detailed information disclosure as well as guaranteed traceability from exporting countries in order to implement domestic regulations (Pollack and Shaffer 2009). Yet these countries are precisely the ones who least need such disclosure to be globally induced via the protocol, because exporting countries have to automatically comply with such importing-country regulations. This holds for all countries with domestic laws that require labeling of transgenic food or food containing genetically modified ingredients, which includes Brazil, China, New Zealand, Mexico, and Japan (Falck-Zepeda 2006; Gruère 2006).

It is in countries with no domestic regulatory frameworks, mostly developing countries in Africa or elsewhere, or those where such frameworks are only now being developed, that globally induced disclosure through the protocol (and its scope) is of greatest relevance. This is because it is the only available avenue through which to impose disclosure on exporting countries. For these countries, the main goal is one of a right to know (as much as feasible), rather than implementing stringent domestic labeling or traceability laws, particularly given the low prospects for achieving domestic segregation and coexistence of GM and non-GM agricultural systems (on this point, see also Sahai undated).

These countries have thus pushed for protocol-induced disclosure to shift the burden to exporting countries to sufficiently inform importing countries of impending GMO transfers. As I have argued, however, a "may contain" disclosure requirement does not accomplish this, with the emphasis in global biosafety governance now shifting to sampling, testing, and verification guidelines and systems in order to generate additional information or put (limited) disclosed information to use. As such, an institutionalized importing country right to know and choose, to be secured through disclosure of relevant and sufficient information, remains limited in practice.

Substantive Effects of Disclosure

This raises the question whether governance by disclosure (and its associated testing, segregation, identity preservation, and coexistence approach to biosafety governance) is even a suitable choice in this area, and for whom. If it does not inform and empower importing countries to make informed choices, the potential for governance by disclosure to deliver substantive environmental improvements or risk mitigation is then also truncated. In recognition of this, many developing countries have chosen to impose bans or moratoria on entry of GMOs, rather than relying on the global disclosure-based risk governance regime to help them meet domestic GMO governance goals. Arguably, imposing a ban is simpler and quicker than developing comprehensive domestic biosafety laws and an easy way to shift the burden to exporters to comply with such a ban, while removing the need to set up elaborate infrastructures of testing and verification to detect presence of specific GMOs in incoming shipments.

Countries with a ban on imports of GMOs (in food aid or as unprocessed grain) include Algeria, Angola, Lesotho, Malawi, Mozambique, Namibia, Nigeria, Sudan, Swaziland, Zambia, and Zimbabwe (Falck-Zepeda 2006, 1206). It is also striking—but supports the argument here—that many bans are recent, notwithstanding the Cartagena Protocol and its disclosure obligations. Here, too, however, a safety imperative clashes with a trade and marketization context for biosafety decisions, because some of these countries are pressurized, by the United States or others, to lift such bans, particularly for provision of food aid (Clapp 2012).

Yet, as also noted in the literature, an alternative imperative (beyond risk mitigation) for such countries to institute bans is to guarantee continued access to the European Union and other markets for non-genetically modified agricultural exports, which may be threatened by inadvertent comingling with genetically modified varieties (see also Clapp 2006). Because, as industry advocates have long argued, comingling is a technical and political reality in the current marketplace and segregation very costly, it follows that segregation as a way to secure markets for nongenetically modified crops is not a feasible option for poorer countries.[8]

The analysis thus far makes clear that disclosure, as institutionalized by the protocol, has differing relevance for different importing countries, highlighting that "transparency for whom" remains a central issue in assessing the normative, procedural and substantive impacts of governance by disclosure (see also Mason 2008). The analysis suggests that globally induced disclosure is most needed by those with the least capacity to develop domestic regulations and hence to inform themselves via such a route. For these countries, a key imperative is to globalize "a right to be told" rather than simply a "right to know" (because with the latter alone, the burden of testing and verification may not be shifted to those disclosing information).

Yet this demand encounters the strictures of a globalized political economy of GMO trade, often leading to the "bounded autonomy" of developing countries to forge their own policy directions in this contested policy realm (Newell 2007; see also on the global political economy of biotechnology more generally, Clapp 2006; Clapp and Fuchs 2009; Kleinman and Kinchy 2007; Newell 2007).

Conclusion

In concluding, I return to the question of transparency's transformative potential and the prospects for governance by disclosure to meet normative, procedural, and substantive ends. As the analysis in this chapter indicates, the Cartagena Protocol's disclosure obligations pertaining to the agricultural commodity trade allow a dictum of caveat emptor (let the buyer beware) to prevail, rather than sufficiently institutionalizing an importing country right to know and choose. Furthermore, in the absence of supportive domestic regulations, the protocol-induced limited disclosure still leaves the onus on importing countries to detect, verify, and render usable disclosed information through use of complex infrastructures of monitoring, detecting, and sampling.

Debates in the global context have now shifted, inter alia, to standardization of sampling criteria, appropriate detection methods, and availability of testing protocols. These debates reflect divergent EU-US perspectives on detection and testing as a key means to either facilitate trade (United States) or meet stringent domestic labeling and traceability laws (European Union). Disclosure in the Cartagena Protocol, particularly relating to the GMO commodity trade, thus constitutes another global arena in which these transatlantic conflicts play out. The implications of this for constraining or enhancing state sovereignty vary along GMO-exporting versus -importing country fault lines. The analysis suggests that the European Union's push for market-forcing disclosure is counteracted in this context by the push for more market-following disclosure by the United States and exporting countries. This notwithstanding, the European Union can ensure that the United States complies with its stringent regional GMO regulations. Those without their own stringent domestic GMO regulations have attempted but failed to achieve a similar outcome through globally induced disclosure.

For the poorest developing countries, the imperative for disclosure remains to shift the burden of providing information and soliciting consent with regard to incoming GMO varieties to exporting countries. Failing this, some have instituted moratoria or bans, partly because of the technical complexity and significant costs of alternative routes, such as stringent labeling and traceability and related efforts to realize coexistence of conventional, GM, and organic agriculture.[9]

Where, then, does this leave governance by disclosure and its transformative potential? In analyzing how disclosure is working (and where it is failing), my argument here is not that the Cartagena Protocol is irrelevant. Indeed, it has had a range of desired effects, including awareness raising, as well as empowering domestic constituencies supportive of biosafety concerns and the precautionary principle to have more voice in GMO debates (Falkner and Gupta 2009; Kleinman and Kinchy 2007). Its potential to bolster biosafety over trade considerations by providing a counter to global trade regime rules has also been extensively analyzed (Gupta 2013; Pollack and Shaffer 2009).

As it currently stands, however, its disclosure obligations benefit least those who need them the most. In contrast to disclosure to further the normative demand of the poorest countries to be informed about GMO transfers, it is these countries that are left by the wayside in the complex discussions about detection levels and thresholds that now dominate this global governance regime and that result from the marketization drive underpinning disclosure's scope and practices in this case.

This has implications for the transformative potential of transparency. Chapter 1 of this book hypothesized that transparency will have desired effects and thus be transformative when its contexts of application resonate with the goals and decision processes of both disclosers and recipients. Insofar as disclosers and recipients benefit from particular configurations of partial transparency, such disclosure may well be "effective" in generating "win-win" solutions. In a contested issue area such as GMO governance, however, this is emphatically not the case, given the distinct empowerment versus marketization goals pursued by demanders versus providers of disclosure in this context. What we see is the dominance of market liberal approaches to transparency, resulting in disclosure that is market following rather than market forcing.

That said, however, a striking veil of unknowability continues to hang over future normative and political developments in global GMO governance. Given the anticipatory nature of this governance challenge, it is not clear how markets for genetically and nongenetically modified crops will develop, which crops will be approved and win acceptance (or not) in key markets, how norms of risk and choice will evolve, and who will be empowered by emerging systems of testing, sampling, and verification.

Added to this is a new GMO governance dynamic being generated by global debates about "climate smart agriculture," which look set to bring back into the limelight longstanding debates about the promise versus the perils of relying on GMOs in food production. At stake is the role for modern biotechnology in intensifying food production on already existing agricultural lands as a way to minimize the adverse climate change impacts of agriculturally induced land use change. By bringing in a completely new set of actors and interests around climate change, these developments may bolster a democratizing impetus for governance by disclosure in this case. Alternatively, it may make actionable transparency even harder to institutionalize, particularly for the most disenfranchised groups and countries.

Notes

1. This chapter is a revamped and updated version of Gupta 2010a.

2. New Zealand's concern is impact on non-GMO agricultural exports if stringent disclosure requirements are adopted for GMO trade, because adventitious (unintended, technically avoidable) presence of GMOs in non-GMO shipments might require these shipments to be labeled as well (Peters 2006).

3. Mexico (as a GMO-importing country) has been a key interlocutor in this global context for its NAFTA (and GMO-exporting country) trading partners, the United States and Canada, given that both are not parties to the protocol and hence cannot formally participate in the negotiations.

4. I do not discuss this first step further here. In a detailed analysis of BCH disclosure elsewhere, I argue that information currently disclosed to the BCH may promote exporting-country goals of efficient decisions and market access rather than importing-country goals of informed choice. It may thus be market facilitating rather than market forcing (Gupta 2010b).

5. The protocol does not specify *who* decides whether an identity preservation system exists for a GM variety and thus if the "contains" disclosure requirement applies. This decision (and this knowledge) in all likelihood then resides with the exporter, reinforcing that de facto a "may contain" declaration holds for most traded GMOs.

6. Importantly, this need for testing now extends to producers of non-GM foods, including organic agriculture, to prevent contamination with GM crops (Ceres undated).

7. This includes links between domestic liability regimes and global disclosure negotiations.

8. For analysis of how "biotechnology for the poor" rhetoric can affect biosafety frameworks in developing countries, see Jansen and Gupta (2009).

9. Poor countries are not the only ones resorting to bans. The European Union imposed a de facto moratorium on GM imports from 1998 to 2004 until its stringent regulations were in place (Gruère 2006).

References

Bail, Christoph, Robert Falkner, and Helen Marquard, eds. 2002. *The Cartagena Protocol on Biosafety: Reconciling Trade in Biotechnology with Environment and Development?* London: Royal Institute of International Affairs (RIIA)/Earthscan.

Bled, Amandine. 2009. *Privatizing Anticipatory Governance? The Biotechnology Industry Global Compact Initiative for Liability and Redress under the Cartagena Protocol.* Paper presented at International Studies Association, New York.

Convention on Biological Diversity (CBD). 2006. *Handling, Transport, Packaging and Identification of Living Modified Organisms: Paragraph 2(a) of Article 18.* Decision of the Third Meeting of the Parties to the Cartagena Protocol. MOP BS-III/10.

Convention on Biological Diversity (CBD). 2008. *Handling, Transport, Packaging and Identification of Living Modified Organisms. Synthesis of Information on Experience Gained with the Use of Sampling of Living Modified Organisms and Detection Techniques and on the Need for and Modalities of Developing Criteria for Acceptability of, and Harmonizing, Sampling and Detection Techniques (Paragraph 2(a) of Article 18)*. UNEP/CBD/BS/COP-MOP/4/9, April 7.

Convention on Biological Diversity (CBD). 2009. *Report of the Group of the Friends of the Co-Chairs on Liability and Redress in the Context of the Cartagena Protocol on Biosafety on the Work of Its First Meeting*. UNEP/CBD/BS/GF-L&R/1/4.

Ceres. Undated. *Detecting Genetically Modified Organisms: Confronting the Limits of Testing to Resolve a Biotech Food Fight*. Summary of Ceres Roundtable, sponsored by Virginia Tech's Center for Food and Nutrition Policy/Pew Initiative on Food and Biotechnology. Available at http://www.pewtrusts.org/uploaded Files/wwwpewtrustsorg/Summaries_-_reports_and_pubs/proceedings2.pdf.

CFO. 2007. Drowning in Data. *CFO Magazine*, July 1. Available at http://www .cfo.com/article.cfm/9390637.

Clapp, Jennifer. 2006. Unplanned Exposure to Genetically Modified Organisms: Divergent Responses in the Global South. *Journal of Environment & Development* 15 (1): 3–21.

Clapp, Jennifer. 2007. Illegal GMO Releases and Corporate Responsibility: Questioning the Effectiveness of Voluntary Measures. *Ecological Economics* 66 (2–3): 348–358.

Clapp, Jennifer. 2012. *Hunger in the Balance: The New Politics of International Food Aid*. Ithaca, NY: Cornell University Press.

Clapp, Jennifer, and Doris Fuchs, eds. 2009. *Corporate Power in Global Agrifood Governance*. Cambridge, MA: MIT Press.

CP (Cartagena Protocol). 2000. *Cartagena Protocol on Biosafety* Adopted 2000 under the Convention on Biological Diversity. Available at http://www.cbd.int/doc/legal/cartagena-protocol-en.pdf.

Elbehri, Aziz. 2007. *The Changing Face of the U.S. Grain System: Differentiation and Identity Preservation Trends*. Economic Research Report (ERR) Number 35, United States Department of Agricultural Economic Research Service, February, Washington DC.

ENB (Earth Negotiation Bulletin). 2008. *Summary of the Fourth Meeting of the Parties to the Cartagena Protocol on Biosafety*, May 12–16. Available at http://www.iisd.ca/download/pdf/enb09441e.pdf.

Falck-Zepeda, Jose. 2006. Co-existence, Genetically Modified Biotechnologies and Biosafety: Implications for Developing Countries. *American Journal of Agricultural Economics* 88 (5): 1200–1208.

Falkner, Robert, ed. 2007a. *The International Politics of Genetically Modified Food: Diplomacy, Trade and Law*. New York: Palgrave Macmillan.

Falkner, Robert. 2007b. The Political Economy of "Normative Power" in Europe: EU Environmental Leadership in International Biotechnology Regulation. *Journal of European Public Policy* 14 (4): 507–526.

Falkner, Robert, and Aarti Gupta. 2009. Limits of Regulatory Convergence: Globalization and GMO Politics in the South. *International Environmental Agreement: Politics, Law and Economics* 9 (2): 113–133.

Florini, Ann. 2008. Making Transparency Work. *Global Environmental Politics* 8 (2): 14–16.

Fung, Archon, Mary Graham, and David Weil. 2007. *Full Disclosure: The Perils and Promise of Transparency.* New York: Cambridge University Press.

Glover, Dominic, and Peter Newell. 2004. Business and Biotechnology: Regulation and the Politics of Influence. In *Agribusiness and Society: Corporate Responses to Environmentalism, Market Opportunities and Public Regulation,* ed. Kees Jansen and Sietze Vellema, 200–231. London: Zed Books.

Graham, Mary. 2002. *Democracy by Disclosure? The Rise of Technopulism.* Washington, DC: Brookings Institution Press.

Gruère, Guillaume P. 2006. *An Analysis of Trade Related International Regulations of Genetically Modified Food and Their Effects on Developing Countries.* International Food Policy Research Institute (IFPRI), Discussion Paper 147. Washington, DC: IFPRI.

Gruère, Guillaume P., and Mark W. Rosegrant. 2008. Assessing the Implementation Effects of the Biosafety Protocol's Proposed Stringent Information Requirements for Genetically Modified Commodities in Countries of the Asia Pacific Economic Cooperation. *Review of Agricultural Economics* 30 (2): 214–232.

Gupta, Aarti. 2000. Governing Trade in Genetically Modified Organisms: The Cartagena Protocol on Biosafety. *Environment* 42 (4): 23–33.

Gupta, Aarti. 2004. When Global Is Local: Negotiating Safe Use of Biotechnology. In *Earthly Politics: Local and Global in Environmental Governance,* ed. Sheila Jasanoff and Marybeth Long-Martello, 127–148. Cambridge, MA: MIT Press.

Gupta, Aarti. 2008. Transparency under Scrutiny: Information Disclosure in Global Environmental Governance. *Global Environmental Politics* 8 (2): 1–7.

Gupta, Aarti. 2010a. Transparency as Contested Political Terrain: Who Knows What about the Global GMO Trade and Why Does It Matter? *Global Environmental Politics* 10 (3): 32–52.

Gupta, Aarti. 2010b. Transparency to What End? Governing by Disclosure through the Biosafety Clearing-House. *Environment and Planning. C, Government & Policy* 28 (2): 128–144.

Gupta, Aarti. 2013. Biosafety and Biotechnology. In *Handbook of Climate and Environmental Policy,* ed. Robert Falkner, 89–106. Oxford, UK: Wiley-Blackwell.

Holst-Jensen, Arne. Undated. *What Is the Future of GMO Detection? A Freely Speaking Scientist's Opinion.* Available at http://www.coextra.eu/researchlive/reportage765.html.

James, Clive. 2008. *Global Status of Commercialized Biotech/GM Crops: 2008.* Brief 39, Executive Summary, ISAAA.

James, Clive. 2012. *Global Status of Commercialized Biotech/GM Crops: 2012.* Brief 44, Executive Summary, ISAAA. Available at http://www.isaaa.org/resources

/publications/briefs/44/executivesummary/pdf/Brief%2044%20-%20Executive %20Summary%20-%20English.pdf.

Jansen, Kees, and Aarti Gupta. 2009. Anticipating the Future: "Biotechnology for the Poor" as Unrealized Promise? *Futures* 41 (7): 436–445.

Jasanoff, Sheila. 1987. Contested Boundaries in Policy-Relevant Science. *Social Studies of Science* 17 (2): 195–230.

Jungcurt, Stefan, and Nicole Schabus. 2010. Liability and Redress in the Context of the Cartagena Protocol on Biosafety. *Review of European Community & International Environmental Law* 19 (2): 197–206.

Kalaitzandonakes, Nicholas. 2004. *The Potential Impacts of the Biosafety Protocol on Agricultural Commodity Trade.* IPC Technology Issue Brief, December.

Kalaitzandonakes, Nicholas. 2006. Cartagena Protocol: A New Trade Barrier? *Regulation* 29 (2): 18–25.

Keohane, Robert O. 2006. Accountability in World Politics. *Scandinavian Political Studies* 29 (2): 75–87.

Kimani, Virginia, and Guillaume Gruère. 2010. Implications of Import Regulations and Information Requirements under the Cartagena Protocol on Biosafety for GMO Commodities in Kenya. *AgBioForum* 13 (1): 222–241.

Kleinman, Daniel Lee, and Abby Kinchy. 2007. Against the Neoliberal Steamroller? The Biosafety Protocol and the Social Regulation of Agricultural Biotechnology. *Agriculture and Human Values* 24 (2): 195–206.

Langley, Paul. 2001. Transparency in the Making of Global Environmental Governance. *Global Society* 15 (1): 73–92.

Mason, Michael. 2008. Transparency for Whom? Information Disclosure and Power in Global Environmental Governance. *Global Environmental Politics* 8 (2): 8–13.

Mayet, Mariam. Undated. *South Africa's Segregation and Traceability System.* African Center for Biosafety, Gauteng, South Africa.

Mehri, Cyrus. 1988. Prior Informed Consent: An Emerging Compromise for Hazardous Exports. *Cornell International Law Journal* 21: 365–389.

Mitchell, Ronald B. 1998. Sources of Transparency: Information Systems in International Regimes. *International Studies Quarterly* 42 (1): 109–130.

Newell, Peter. 2007. Corporate Power and "Bounded Autonomy" in the Global Politics of Biotechnology. In *The International Politics of Genetically Modified Food: Diplomacy, Trade and Law,* ed. Robert Falkner, 67–84. Basingstoke, UK: Palgrave Macmillan.

Newell, Peter. 2009. Technology, Food, Power: Governing GMOs in Argentina. In *Corporate Power in Global Agrifood Governance,* ed. Jennifer Clapp and Doris Fuchs, 253–283. Cambridge, MA: MIT Press.

Nielsen, Kaare M. 2013. Biosafety Data as Confidential Business Information. *PLoS Biology* 11 (3): doi e1001499.

Oliveira, Andrea Leda R., J. M. Silveira, and A. M. Alvim. 2012. Cartagena Protocol, Biosafety and Grain Segregation: The Effects on the Soybean Logistics in Brazil. *Journal of Agricultural Research and Development* 2 (1): 17–30.

Peters, Winston. 2006. *Outcome of Cartagena Biosafety Protocol Meeting Exceeds New Zealand's Expectations.* Ministry of Foreign Affairs, New Zealand. Press Release, March 20. Available at http://www.scoop.co.nz/stories/PA0603/S00337.htm.

Pollack, Mark, and Gregory C. Shaffer. 2009. *When Cooperation Fails: The International Law and Politics of Genetically Modified Foods.* Oxford: Oxford University Press.

Power, Michael. 1997a. *The Audit Society: Rituals of Verification.* Oxford: Oxford University Press.

Power, Michael. 1997b. Expertise and the Construction of Relevance: Accountants and Environmental Audit. *Accounting, Organizations and Society* 22 (2): 123–146.

Rajan, Mukund Govind. 1997. *Global Environmental Politics: India and the North-South Politics of Global Environmental Issues.* Delhi: Oxford University Press.

Sahai, Suman. Undated. *Can GM and non-GM Crops Be Segregated in India: Is Co-existence Possible?* Gene Campaign, India. Available at http://www.cbd.int/doc/external/cop-09/gc-coexist-en.pdf.

Scoones, Ian. 2008. Mobilizing against GM Crops in India, South Africa and Brazil. *Journal of Agrarian Change* 8 (2–3): 315–344.

Smythe, Elizabeth. 2009. Whose Interests? Transparency and Accountability in the Global Governance of Food: Agribusiness, the Codex Alimentarius, and the World Trade Organization. *In Corporate Power in Global Agrifood Governance,* ed. Jennifer Clapp and Doris Fuchs, 93–123. Cambridge, MA: MIT Press.

United States Department of Agriculture (USDA). 2008. Global Traceability and Labeling Requirements for Agricultural Biotechnology-Derived Products: Impacts and Implications for the United States. *Biotechnology Law Report* 27 (5): 496–498.

Wolf, Amanda. 2000. Informed Consent: A Negotiated Formula for Trade in Risky Organisms and Chemicals. *International Negotiation* 5 (3): 485–521.

7

Transparency in the Governance of Access and Benefit Sharing from Genetic Resources

Amandine Orsini, Sebastian Oberthür, and Justyna Pożarowska

Transparency is a central element in the international governance of genetic resources (GR) under the Convention on Biological Diversity (CBD). GR is material coming from plants, animals, or microorganisms that can be used for commercial applications, among others. Before being commercialized, genetic resources are often transformed by means of bio-technology. The core of the governance of GR under the CBD is known as "access and benefit sharing" (ABS), itself an implication of the CBD's recognition of states' "sovereign right to exploit their resources pursuant to their own environmental policies" (CBD, article 3). As a consequence of this sovereign right, potential GR users are required to receive permission by providers in order to be able to access GR on the latter's territory. In exchange, the GR providers should receive their fair and equitable share of the benefits arising from the use of these GR, as stipulated in the CBD, which establishes fair and equitable benefit sharing as one of its three core objectives in its article 1 (next to the conservation of biological diversity and the sustainable use of its components).

Underlying the ABS mechanism was the idea that the valorization and commercialization of GR, mostly through biotechnology, could create an international market for GR, which would enhance interest in the conservation of biological diversity and the sustainable use of its components (Brand et al. 2008). Given the rise of biotechnology, the benefits arising from the use of GR could be considerable. Genetic resources have been used in bioinventions that have received protection through intellectual property rights (IPRs) such as patents. Depending on the methodology used and the scope of the products considered, the value of the market for products based on GR has been estimated to account for US$220–800 billion annually in the 2000s (Deke 2008, 120).

Transparency of the conditions for getting access to GR and the benefits subsequently generated from their use is central to the effective functioning of the overall system. This double-sided transparency is thus at the core of the ABS regime under the CBD, culminating in adoption of the Nagoya Protocol on Access to Genetic Resources and the Fair and Equitable Sharing of Benefits Arising from their Utilization to the CBD in 2010 (henceforth Nagoya Protocol).[1]

Traditional knowledge (TK) related to GR forms an important part of the issue area and the overall debate. In many if not most cases, the value and use of GR are linked to associated TK, that is, the know-how, skills, innovations, and practices of indigenous and local communities (ILCs). Such TK frequently allows identification of useful GR and its added value—although this is often not acknowledged.[2] At the same time, ILCs that hold TK contribute to the conservation and sustainable use of biological diversity, as also acknowledged by the CBD, including in its articles 8(j) and 10(c). Article 8(j) of the CBD therefore commits parties to respect, preserve, and maintain TK and to "encourage the equitable sharing of the benefits arising from the utilization of such knowledge." Our following discussion therefore relates to GR and associated TK, and unless otherwise specified, a reference to GR includes the TK associated with their use.

Another important feature of international ABS governance is that it has been structured by a North-South conflict, although significant differences within both groups of countries, and especially as regards emerging economies, should not be neglected. On the one side, developing countries belong to the most biodiversity-rich countries with dominant GR-TK provider interests, which have led them to insist on the benefit-sharing side of the equation, including through changes to the IPR system. Among developing countries, there are important differences with regard to capabilities for the valorization and marketization of GR by means of biotechnology and the implementation of domestic infrastructures of ABS governance. Developed countries, on the other side, have dominated biotechnological development so far and have thus been particularly interested in ensuring access to GR, while staving off attempts to enhance benefit sharing with providers and interference with the IPR system (Brand et al. 2008). The share of countries in biotechnological patent applications, displayed in table 7.1, indicates the major GR-user countries and resultant diverging interests of developing and developed countries.

It should be noted that the CBD is not the only forum for international ABS governance but is rather at the center of a complex of relevant international institutions. Nearly a dozen other global institutions contribute to ABS governance in different ways. These include the World Trade

Organization (WTO), the UN Convention on the Law of the Sea, the World Intellectual Property Organization (WIPO), the Antarctic Treaty System, the International Treaty on Plant Genetic Resources for Food and Agriculture of the Food and Agriculture Organization (FAO), the World Health Organization and others. The CBD and its 2010 Nagoya Protocol are central to this complex because they are the only global institutions to address all aspects of ABS governance (Oberthür and Pożarowska 2013). However, other institutions are also important. The WTO and WIPO are particularly relevant to the debate on transparency because of their role in patent regulation.

Against this backdrop, this chapter explores the evolution of global ABS governance under the CBD from the perspective of transparency, taking into account the 2010 Nagoya Protocol. In line with the overall framework of this book, we discuss, first, the emergence and framing of transparency in this area of governance. We argue that transparency, which was not initially envisioned as a policy solution, has increasingly moved to center stage in the debate on ABS governance under the CBD, which especially builds on bilateral contracts between providers and users. This move results, not least, from a growing marketization of GR and increasing awareness (through, for example, NGO campaigns) of the lack of information about GR uses. Subsequently, we outline the main elements and instruments of the transparency infrastructure elaborated, and given legal force, in the Nagoya Protocol, including the bilateral, contract-based approach to ABS governance therein. We then discuss the (in)effectiveness of governance by disclosure thus far, as well as prospects

Table 7.1
Biotechnology Patent Applications: Patent Cooperation Treaty 2006.

Country/Region	%	Country/Region	%
United States	41.5	China	1.9
EU-27	27.4	India	0.9
Japan	11.9	Russian Federation	0.8
Canada	3.2	Brazil	0.3
South Korea	3.0	South Africa	0.1
Australia	2.1	Other	6.9
		TOTAL	100

Source: OECD 2011.

for improvement, especially through the Nagoya Protocol. The overall CBD system has performed weakly since the 1990s. Even after negotiation of the Nagoya Protocol, there remains a lasting imbalance between relatively advanced standards and practices for transparency for access and more problematic and imperfect standards for transparency for benefit sharing, which disadvantages least-developed countries and results in calls for capacity-building efforts. The conclusions summarize the results of the analysis.

Embracing Transparency

In considering the dynamics underpinning an uptake of transparency in ABS governance in this section, we engage also with the first hypothesis advanced in the introduction to this volume: that democratization and marketization are driving the uptake of transparency in global environmental governance. The foundations of ABS governance can be traced to the 1992 CBD agreement, which established the role of transparency herein, especially through the "nationalization" of GR. At this time, ABS was framed as a matter of fairness, property, and redistribution around the broader normative context of justice. Previously, GR were mostly freely accessed under the common heritage principle. Not least because of related IPRs such as patents, they generated significant profit that was generally appropriated by GR users (mainly from developed countries) without significant sharing of these benefits with the GR providers (principally developing countries). On the one hand, as mentioned previously, the CBD established, in its article 1, ABS as one of its three objectives, thus calling for a redistribution of a fair part of the commercial value of GR to the providers (and protectors)—mainly to national governments and ILCs (Rosendal 2006, 431–432). On the other hand, the convention also firmly established the sovereign rights of states over their natural resources in its preamble and articles 3 and 15.1. The heart of the ABS regime therefore became constructed as a bilateral exchange between individual providers and users of GR (rather than as a multilateral exchange system, as we also discuss subsequently).

Transparency of ABS was not a major focus during the CBD negotiations themselves, because developing countries were concerned mainly about sovereignty over natural resources, finance, and technology transfer (Svarstad 1994, 47). Their securing of sovereign rights over GR provided the basis for their request for financial redistribution and compensation. NGOs present at the time noted that the dominant discussion was related to "the idea to link the access to biodiversity to some sort of compensation to the holders, either financially or in terms of technology or end-products" (Arts 1998, 192). Yet, provisions on ABS were included mainly in the convention because of insistence by developing countries as the main providers of GR and TK. In particular, members of the Amazon Cooperation Treaty (Bolivia, Brazil, Colombia, Equator, Guyana, Peru, Surinam, and Venezuela) drafted CBD article 15. These countries had re-iterated their sovereign rights over their natural resources in 1992—in the so-called Manaus Declaration—to establish that users had to comply with their national legislation in order to receive access. In the CBD ne-gotiations, they pushed to exchange access to GR for reciprocal benefits, such as, for example, receipt of developed countries' technologies.[3] For them, ABS was still a central part of the negotiations (Rosendal 2000). By contrast, it was not central to developed country governments, who felt that biosafety (i.e., the safe handling, transfer, and use of genetically modified organisms) was a much more central concern (Hopgood 1998, 134; see also Gupta, this book, chapter 6).

Given the uncertain and variable value of GR, concrete benefit-sharing arrangements necessarily had to be established and agreed case by case. Consequently, the CBD determined, in its articles 15.4 and 15.7, that ABS shall be on "mutually agreed terms" (MAT)—a concept introduced in the 1983 International Undertaking on Plant Genetic Resources for Food and Agriculture (articles 5 and 7.2) of the FAO. Accordingly, as for the exchange of plant GR under the International Undertaking, the terms of ABS needed to be agreed on mutually by providers and users. Further-more, the concept of prior informed consent (PIC) by the providers of GR was enshrined in article 15.5 of the CBD. In practice, PIC can be defined as "a set of administrative procedures for deciding on whether to grant access to genetic resources on defined terms" (Pisupati 2007, 15; see also Jansen and Dubois, this book, chapter 5; Gupta, this book, chapter 6). The concept has its roots in international regulation of transboundary movements of chemicals and hazardous wastes, including the 1989 Basel Convention on the Control of Transboundary Movements of Hazard-ous Wastes and Their Disposal. Whereas PIC was first introduced as a requirement for the import of hazardous substances or materials, in the case of GR it is required for the access to (and export of) GR.

Expectations about these arrangements were fostered by marketiza-tion dynamics, including several apparently promising examples of com-mercial exchanges of GR known as bioprospecting agreements. The most well-known of these was the INBio/Merck agreement signed in 1991 in

Costa Rica. Merck, the leading global pharmaceutical company at that time, agreed to pay US$1 million, including US$135,000 of laboratory equipment, and to train local scientists, in exchange for access to Costa Rican GR. It also agreed to redistribute up to 3 percent of the royalties obtained from any commercialized product derived from the accessed GR to the Costa Rican institute INBio, the main public institute responsible for nature conservation, in collaboration with the Costa Rican Ministry of Natural Resources. Such a contract-based approach to ABS appeared to be a promising way to ensure that GR providers (mainly developing countries) could finally benefit from GR users' profits and invest in domestic biodiversity conservation programs (Rodriguez 1993, 138).

In such a bilateral system, there was a twofold demand for transparency: on the one side, potential users, mainly from developed countries, required information on how to receive PIC for accessing GR in provider countries, including requirements for benefit sharing to be reflected in MAT (if such requirements existed). Provider countries and their stakeholders (including ILCs), needed, on the other hand, information on GR used in user countries as well as the benefits generated in order to identify whether PIC and MAT requirements had been complied with and to enforce MAT. Whereas transparency received little attention in CBD negotiations, the resulting bilateral, contract-based approach to ABS governance nevertheless framed the demand for and the ensuing debate about transparency.

The importance of transparency also gained recognition as the optimism about bioprospecting agreements made way for more sobering assessments of their potential. In the Merck/INBio case, NGOs such as Friends of the Earth and the Tropical Rainforest Coalition expressed concerns about Merck's intentions because the corporation had a total research and development budget that exceeded the Costa Rican national income (Rodriguez 1993, 137). Critics requested information on the exact content of the agreement, in which the most specific provisions were protected by industrial confidentiality (Rodriguez 1993, 138). NGOs and ILCs also revealed that Merck exploited TK in the search for interesting natural compounds, without rewarding such knowledge: the indigenous population that was employed to collect plants and biological samples was paid as a basic work force, despite the dangers involved and their actual participation as biodiversity specialists. Moreover, the very idea of selling public natural resources to a private company was questioned. Such resources could have been valorized in other ways that might have been identified in national consultations, if only they had taken place

(Rodriguez 1993, 137–138; see also Miller 2006). Further scandals about unclear bioprospecting agreements occurred. States were negotiating these contracts with restrained disclosure (in particular due to commercial confidentiality and nonmandatory obligations), and civil society and ILCs were often left out of the debate. Consultation on the commercial exploitation of national GR was lacking and the TK used to facilitate research and development remained uncompensated. Moreover, local communities living dependent on the resources in question were excluded (Burrows 2005).

Therefore, the uptake of transparency as a governance tool was directly linked to the marketization of GR on the one side and to concerns over biopiracy on the other, providing support for the hypothesis advanced in the introduction that uptake of transparency is being fueled by a marketization, commodification, and valuation dynamic to global environmental governance. With transparency moving center stage in global ABS governance, we can describe what ensued as a battle between developed countries advocating "transparency for access" and developing countries demanding "transparency for benefit sharing." On the one side, the GR users claimed that it was difficult to ensure PIC and MAT because of uncertainties regarding national legislation and the procedures they were expected to follow. They advocated a contract-based transparency mechanism that respected market liberalism (free trade in GR) and intellectual property rights, including the possibility to patent GR- and TK-based innovations. In such contract-based transparency, the content of contracts often reflected power asymmetries between users and providers that favored the users.

On the other side, the GR providers requested transparency about the GR being accessed and used, the intentions of the users (including any change of intentions), and the benefits generated and to be shared. Developing countries wanted such information to be available to provider countries and to a much lesser extent to ILCs. One of the main proposals was to have a mandatory requirement to disclose the origin of any GR or TK used and other relevant information in patent applications, as discussed further in the following section. On these grounds, by 1995 developing countries, ILCs, and NGOs denounced any kind of international use of natural GR that did not respect the PIC and MAT requirements as "biopiracy" (Bled 2010, 583). The bioprospecting-biopiracy controversy placed transparency in the center of the battleground for ABS.

In addition, several developing countries developed their own national ABS legislation from the mid-1990s. Following the INBio/Merck controversy, Costa Rica, for example, conducted consultations in 1996 and established a national commission in 1998 (Comisión Nacional para la Gestión de la Biodiversidad), including indigenous peoples' organizations to devise access procedures. Moreover, the Costa Rican law required that 10 percent of the research and development budget as well as 50 percent of the royalties earned for any GR-based products had to be redistributed to the providers (the exact beneficiaries being designated by the commission) (Miller 2006). Brazil adopted similar national legislation in 2000, following a biopiracy controversy with the multinational corporation Novartis. Overall, some forty developing countries, including major biodiversity-rich countries such as India, South Africa, and Brazil, established national ABS legislation by 2007 (CBD 2007b). However, such national action by provider countries could not effectively control transnational flows and use of GR by biotechnological industry and other users.

The double-sided request for ABS transparency was addressed to some extent in the so-called Bonn Guidelines on Access to Genetic Resources and Fair and Equitable Sharing of the Benefits Arising out of Their Utilization adopted by the parties to the CBD in 2002 (CBD 2002). The voluntary guidelines first elaborated the contract-based approach to marketization and valorization of GR outlined in the CBD (Brand et al. 2008, 93–95), promoted international standardization of ABS contracts, addressed the rights of providers and users, and supported transparency. The guidelines elaborated on "transparency for access" by inviting parties to designate national focal points with the task to inform, through the CBD's clearing-house mechanism, potential users about procedures for PIC and MAT. Competent national authorities, to be established, were responsible for granting access and giving directions on negotiating ABS contracts, including establishment of PIC and MAT. Legal certainty and clarity were highlighted as basic principles for PIC and MAT, resulting in a call for any restriction on access to be transparent (CBD 2002, paras. 13, 14, 26, and 42). On the side of "transparency for benefit sharing," however, the possibility of noting the country of origin of GR or TK in IPR applications was only mentioned (CBD 2002, para. 16; see also para. 53). Overall, there was a greater emphasis on "transparency for access" than on "transparency for benefit sharing," and the contract-based approach pursued by the guidelines was the one favored by developed countries.

In practice, however, the Bonn Guidelines did not solve the ABS battle over transparency for a number of reasons. The guidelines were voluntary and, as such, did not satisfy developing countries as key providers. They did not redress the problem that, given the rather "soft" CBD provisions on ABS, parties have no firm obligations to introduce the proposed provisions (for example, there is no compliance mechanism). Countries remained free to regulate ABS within the scope of their national legislation. As a result, many CBD parties, in particular developed countries, did not establish national measures to address ABS at all. Other parties adopted very different approaches, some of which were seen as inefficient or not providing satisfactory guarantees for fair benefit sharing (CBD 2007a, 2007b).

In this context, transparency increasingly moved front and center in global ABS governance and became inextricably linked to calls for substantive regulation. On the access side, transparency with respect to PIC and MAT had to be established by individual states: what would be the procedures for granting PIC, and what kind of terms would be accepted as mutually agreed? On the benefit-sharing side, there was a need to establish measures for cases of noncompliance by users (enforcement or sanctions). Thus, transparency increasingly became a major ingredient in a broader regulatory mixture structured and shaped by the CBD approach of bilateral, contract-based exchange relations.

Further efforts to elaborate, strengthen, and complement the CBD approach (and the Bonn Guidelines) were necessary, leading to the adoption of the Nagoya Protocol in October 2010. The protocol was pushed for by developing provider countries, who created the coalition of "Megadiverse Countries" in 2002 (comprising Bolivia, Brazil, China, Colombia, Costa Rica, Equator, India, Indonesia, Kenya, Malaysia, Mexico, Peru, Philippines, South Africa, and Venezuela). These countries succeeded in receiving a mandate at the Johannesburg World Summit on Sustainable Development in September 2002 to negotiate an international regime on ABS under the CBD.[4] On their side, developed countries increasingly recognized their interest in securing access to GR as a basis for important industries (see, for example, Holm-Müller et al. 2005 for Germany). They also recognized that they might also themselves be or become GR providers in the future. A central component of the ensuing negotiations again revolved around securing a balance between "transparency for access" and "transparency for benefit sharing."

An important characteristic of this battle between the two sides of transparency has been that the marketization of GR fueling disclosure has involved public and private actors on the two opposing sides of the exchange relation. On the provider side, granting of access—resulting from recognition of "sovereign rights"—typically involves public actors such as "competent national authorities" following publicly defined governmental procedures, which may include subnational political entities such as ILCs. The user side, by contrast, primarily features private market actors (biotechnological companies, research institutions). Transparency of GR use thus does not primarily require adaptation of government behavior and procedures, but rather regulation of economic actors and their "private" behavior in the context of market economies (partially considered confidential). This dynamic has also contributed to transparency for access being privileged in ABS governance, given that the behavior of public actors may be more easily addressed through public international law and regulation, in comparison to putting a "burden" on private actors and their market activities.

The following section analyzes the further elaboration and institutionalization of transparency within ABS governance under the CBD, as it has evolved within the Nagoya Protocol.

Institutionalizing Transparency

We analyze the main elements of global ABS governance under the CBD relating to transparency here in two steps. We first address elements relating to transparency for access, followed by those for benefit sharing. In so doing, we also engage with the second hypothesis advanced in the introduction to this book (Gupta and Mason, chapter 1), that an institutionalization of transparency may decenter state-led regulation and open up political space for new actors. We pay particular attention to what the Nagoya Protocol has contributed in this respect.

Institutionalizing Transparency for Access

PIC and MAT are at the core of the ABS governance system under the CBD. They are constitutive of the decentralized, contract-based marketization approach on which this governance system is based. According to the CBD, the Bonn Guidelines, and the Nagoya Protocol, access to GR is subject to PIC of the contracting party providing such resources, unless otherwise determined by that party (CBD, article 15.5; CBD 2002, part IV letter C section II; Nagoya Protocol, article 6). The CBD requirement to establish MAT, enshrined in articles 15.4 and 15.7 of the convention, is closely intertwined with the issue of PIC because the establishment of MAT is usually a requirement for granting PIC. MAT are contractual arrangements containing detailed terms and conditions for access agreed on by the provider and the user (Pisupati 2007). The exchange of GR is thus to occur on the basis of PIC and MAT.

The main contribution of the Nagoya Protocol to the preexisting system of PIC and MAT is to further elaborate mandatory "international access standards," building on core elements already contained in the nonbinding 2002 Bonn Guidelines. The Nagoya Protocol's additional requirements thus primarily aim at enhancing "transparency for access," which should facilitate legal access to GR by users in compliance with substantive PIC and MAT requirements of the provider country. First, as reflected in article 6.3 of the protocol, these access standards provide for enhanced transparency with regard to the conditions and procedures to be followed for receiving PIC. Accordingly, the developing country or provider parties to the protocol, who wish to require PIC, have to take a number of measures. These include providing for legal certainty, clarity, and transparency of domestic ABS legislation. Also required are fair and nonarbitrary rules and procedures on access, information on how to apply for PIC (available from national focal points), a clear and transparent written decision by a competent national authority, and the issuance of a permit (or equivalent) as evidence for the granting of PIC and the establishment of MAT. Further requirements regarding the information a permit should contain are laid down in article 17.4 of the protocol. In accordance with articles 5.2, 5.5, 6.2, and 7, access to GR and TK that is held by ILCs is also subject to PIC by these communities and requires the establishment of MAT.

The national-level institutional infrastructure imported into the Nagoya Protocol from the Bonn Guidelines also primarily seems to strengthen transparency for access. This national-level infrastructure includes "national focal points" and "competent national authorities." According to article 13.1 of the Nagoya Protocol, the primary task of national focal points is to furnish information on PIC and MAT to applicants seeking access to GR and TK. Focal points are also expected to provide information on competent national authorities, relevant ILCs, and stakeholders. As specified in article 13.2 of the protocol, competent national authorities are responsible for granting access or issuing a permit as evidence that access requirements have been met (which after registration in the ABS Clearing-House becomes an internationally recognized certificate of compliance; as discussed subsequently). They are also responsible for advising users (and others) on applicable procedures and requirements for obtaining PIC and entering into MAT, a task that seems to somewhat overlap with that of national focal points. Countries may allocate the functions of the national focal points and the competent national authority to one single entity (article 13.3). Whereas each party to the protocol is obliged to designate a national focal point and one or more competent national authorities, the aforementioned task descriptions make it clear that both institutions primarily serve GR users and aim to enhance transparency for access.[5]

Institutionalizing Transparency for Benefit Sharing

MAT provides a link between providers and users that aims to ensure benefit sharing, and as such is also a means to advance transparency for benefit sharing. The annex to the protocol containing a nonexclusive, essentially illustrative list of potential monetary and nonmonetary benefits to be used in MAT, as well as the encouragement to develop sectoral and cross-sectoral model contractual clauses for MAT included in article 19, may be considered to strengthen transparency for benefit sharing. However, the soft character of these provisions contrasts sharply with the hard requirement for provider countries requiring PIC, included in the international access standards listed in article 6 of the protocol, to establish clear rules and procedures "in writing" for requiring and establishing MAT. These rules and procedures may include a dispute settlement clause, terms on benefit sharing (including in relation to IPRs), terms on possible subsequent third-party use, and terms on changes of intent of GR use.

In contextualizing the "user measures" through which the Nagoya Protocol has enhanced "transparency for benefit sharing," it is important to note that the long-standing central request of developing provider countries—to make disclosure of certain relevant information a mandatory requirement for the patenting of GR- and TK-based innovations internationally—has not become part of the system. The request of developing countries referred to the disclosure of four elements: (1) the origin or source[6] of the GR acquired by a user, (2) PIC (if obtained or not), (3) MAT (if established or not), and (4) benefit sharing (if occurred or not and in what form). This information enables checking if access to GR was legitimate and occurred based on fair benefit sharing. Since the 1990s, developing countries have requested that disclosure of the aforementioned information become mandatory in patent applications and a precondition for granting a patent.[7] This is seen as having the potential to significantly strengthen the implementation of fair and equitable benefit sharing. If adopted, however, this would significantly condition IPR protection for biotechnological innovations. It would also conflict with minimum requirements for patentability laid down in the WTO Agreement on

Trade-Related Aspects of Intellectual Property Rights. As such, developed countries have opposed these proposed disclosure requirements (referred to as "disclosure of origin"). Moreover, they have refused to discuss disclosure at the CBD, considering WIPO or the WTO to be the more appropriate fora (Bled 2010, 573; Medaglia 2009).

As a result, information disclosure requirements have so far become part of global ABS governance in a rather soft form (and unrelated to patents). Whereas disclosure was "encouraged" by the 2002 Bonn Guidelines, the Nagoya Protocol, in its article 17, goes further by obliging its parties to require users to provide information related to PIC, to the source of the GR, to the establishment of MAT, and/or to the use of GR (as appropriate) to so-called checkpoints. According to article 17.1(a) of the Nagoya Protocol, each party shall designate one or more such checkpoints that are to collect or receive, as appropriate, the aforementioned information. Checkpoints should provide this information to relevant national authorities, to the party providing PIC, and to the ABS Clearing-House, without prejudice, however, to the protection of confidential information. The question of which entities may serve as checkpoints was deliberately left open (with developing countries arguing for these to be patent offices; see Buck and Hamilton 2011, 53; Nijar 2011).

Another element of transparency for benefit sharing was the establishment of an "internationally recognized certificate of compliance." The idea of a "certificate of origin" was introduced in the 1990s. Such a certificate could serve as a passport that would allow for the monitoring and verification of the different stages of GR flows (collection, transfer to user countries, research, development, commercialization) (CBD 2006). By confirming that the user met the access requirements of the provider country, the certificate could facilitate GR flows by increasing transparency, building trust, and fostering cooperation among users and providers. Eventually, the idea found its way into the Nagoya Protocol. As soon as a provider country notifies the ABS Clearing-House of the issuance of a permit for access (as mentioned previously), this permit constitutes an "internationally recognized certificate of compliance" (Nagoya Protocol, article 17.2). Article 17.4 provides certain minimum requirements for the information to be included in the certificate (and thus also in the preceding permit).

Overall, it remains questionable whether the Nagoya compromise on the issue of "disclosure of origin" can ensure transparency for benefit sharing. Although the disclosure of relevant information is to be mandatory, there is no immediate incentive for GR users to comply with such a requirement. Providing such incentives and enforcing such a requirement is largely left to the discretion of each individual party (see also Buck and Hamilton 2011, 53–54).[8] The internationally recognized certificate of compliance remains facilitative and nonmandatory under the protocol because it is not legally required for the use of GR. Finally, it is noteworthy that the aforementioned advances of Nagoya apply to GR but not to TK.

Beyond the issue of the "disclosure of origin," information on how to enforce the terms of the contract, that is, the MAT, becomes particularly important in an ABS system based on bilateral contracts. The CBD itself had been rather silent on this aspect, and the Bonn Guidelines only mentioned the possibility of "cooperation between Contracting Parties to address alleged infringements" of ABS agreements (CBD 2002, para. 16(d) (iv)). The Nagoya Protocol advanced this aspect to some extent. First of all, each party (in its role as a user) has to take measures providing that GR or TK used within its jurisdiction have been accessed in accordance with PIC and that MAT have been established, as required by the domestic ABS legislation of the provider country. It also has to take measures to address situations of noncompliance (articles 15 and 16). Therefore, all parties will have to put into place some sort of ABS legislation or administrative or policy measures. Moreover, each party has to provide an opportunity to seek recourse under its legal system in cases of disputes arising from MAT (article 18.2). Each party also has to take measures regarding "access to justice" and "the utilization of mechanisms regarding mutual recognition and enforcement of foreign judgments and arbitral awards" (article 18.3).

Finally, at the international level, the ABS Clearing-House established by article 14 of the protocol facilitates international information exchange and furthers "transparency for access" and "transparency for benefit sharing." Each party shall make key information about ABS available to the Clearing-House, including information on legislative, administrative, and policy measures on ABS; national focal points and competent national authorities; and access permits (which thereby become internationally recognized certificates of compliance). Checkpoints are also required to furnish information on the use of GR to the Clearing-House (article 17.1(a)). The conference of the parties to the protocol is mandated to develop the Clearing-House mechanism further.

Overall, the transparency provisions aim to bring states back into ABS governance. As such, our case does not support the hypothesis advanced in the introduction that an institutionalization of transparency decenters state-led regulation. However, the bilateral, contract-based approach chosen also provides states with great flexibility when implementing ABS provisions by favoring national measures over international ones. Whereas improvements are noticeable after the adoption of the Nagoya Protocol, such flexibility leads to mixed results in terms of efficiency, in particular due to national imbalances regarding capacities for implementation.

Effects of Transparency

In line with the typology of effects proposed in the introduction to this book, this section analyzes the normative, procedural and substantive effects of transparency in global ABS governance, in two steps. We first assess the performance and effects of the framework prior to the Nagoya Protocol, before looking into the likely changes brought about by the protocol.

Pre-Nagoya Normative and Procedural Effects: Partial Transparency

Prior to the Nagoya Protocol, we can identify a general lack of transparency in ABS governance, leading to limited normative and procedural effects. Transparency for access clearly remained deficient. In many (provider) developing countries, ABS regulations did not exist at all. As of 2012, the database on the CBD website still counted fewer than forty developing countries with relevant measures in place.[9] Where regulations existed, they displayed a wide divergence of approaches as well as a lack of clarity and legal certainty. This limited the ability of potential GR users to actually access GR. Transparency for benefit sharing was even more lacking, with little information being generated that would empower providers to seek and enforce fair benefit sharing. Only a few countries, and none of the main user countries, had introduced limited mandatory disclosure requirements. Legislation or measures that had been introduced were in several cases found to be ineffective or not providing satisfactory guarantees for fair and equitable benefit sharing. In general, it was very hard or even impossible to systematically identify whether GR (including TK) that was used had been accessed legally and on what terms, and whether any MAT that had been concluded were actually complied with. Provider countries thus lacked information about the use of GR (lack of normative effectiveness), which undermined their ability to pursue and enforce fair benefit sharing (procedural effectiveness).[10] As such, disclosure of so-called biopiracy—that is, access and use of GR without PIC and MAT in accordance with the requirements of the provider country—had to rely especially on NGO activities and information gathering (Bled 2010; Burrows 2005).

Overall, the system of ABS governance, prior to the Nagoya Protocol, hardly worked. It made little progress toward changing the pre-CBD status quo and ensuring fair and equitable benefit sharing. As such, it failed to empower GR providers, especially ILCs, because they had very limited opportunities to systematically identify cases of biopiracy and enforce PIC and MAT requirements. In terms of normative (in)effectiveness, then, there was a general lack of information on the quantity of GR accessed legally and illegally, making it difficult to assess the situation comprehensively. At the same time, there was no firm data on whether the lack of transparency of access and access requirements (including a lack of legal certainty) hindered actual access to GR on the ground.

Under these circumstances, the normative framework of the CBD at least indirectly empowered some nongovernmental actors, expressly engaged in ABS issues, often benefiting from northern governments' financial support, to problematize and scandalize "biopiracy." The ABS regime under the CBD provided for clarity on the prerequisites of access to GR, namely, the establishment of PIC and MAT, including fair benefit sharing. These international requirements provided a basis and legitimation for selected NGOs to use available information on the use of GR to scandalize particular cases of the use of GR without appropriate benefit-sharing arrangements (Robinson 2010). The creation or at least facilitation of this scandalization potential may be understood as an indirect procedural effect of the CBD system pre-Nagoya enabling the (self-)empowerment of certain NGOs (in the absence of more direct and effective means of governance). The resulting scandalization in turn contributed to an increasing realization by GR users that a sustainable compromise might also be in their interest by providing for greater legal certainty.

Post-Nagoya Normative and Procedural Effects: Imbalanced Transparency
Even though the Nagoya Protocol aims to enhance transparency for access and benefit sharing, it does not remove existing key barriers to transparency for benefit sharing, in particular for least-developed, low-income developing countries.

If the protocol is implemented as agreed, "transparency for access" will increase significantly, especially in developing provider countries (in those that have and those that do not yet have legislation and institutions in place). In this context, the onus is on provider countries that wish to require PIC (and MAT) to establish transparent national legislative and institutional frameworks, as required by the protocol. The protocol thus enhances the users' right to know and be informed about access requirements (normative effects) and, consequently, their right to participate in access procedures (procedural effects). Implementation of transparency for access requirements is likely, however, to present considerable challenges, especially for countries that still have to establish national legislative frameworks, in particular for the less- and least-developed countries among them.

With regard to transparency for benefit sharing, the Nagoya Protocol has also made significant progress. The full implementation of the protocol's relevant requirements regarding access to justice and redressing noncompliance, for example, would significantly enhance the informational basis (normative effects) and the chances to engage and achieve enforcement (procedural effects). However, even if (user) countries fully implement these requirements, important barriers will remain and are likely to severely limit, in particular, the protocol's procedural effects. To begin with, it will remain difficult to identify the use of GR (because there is no obligation or mechanism that would ensure that information on the use of GR would become comprehensively available or be collected in practice). Furthermore, and perhaps more important, enforcement of PIC and MAT requirements relies largely on the providers taking legal action in foreign jurisdictions in case of noncompliance by actual users. The empowerment of providers finds its limits in the knowledge and information of the relevant national legal systems as well as the capacity that is required to enforce compliance. As a result, significant capacity building and assistance to developing countries will be required to ensure that they can take advantage of the increased potential for realizing benefit sharing under the Nagoya Protocol (Medaglia et al. 2011; Oberthür et al. 2011).[11] More generally, arrangements relating to transparency for benefit sharing under the Nagoya Protocol are incomplete, if not questionable.

This brings to the fore, however, that differences in governmental capacities regarding ABS ensure that the powerful gain most from the system, as designed. In the overall assessment of who benefits most from transparency, as designed in the Nagoya Protocol, it is useful to distinguish three groups of countries. First, developed countries are further empowered by transparency of access conditions to the extent that developing provider countries implement the international access standards of the Nagoya Protocol. At the same time, developed user countries are also required to facilitate legal action by providers, thus empowering the latter to enforce PIC and MAT requirements under their jurisdiction. Second, advanced developing countries and emerging economies with relatively advanced domestic legal ABS frameworks (including Brazil, India, Malaysia, Mexico, South Africa, and Thailand) may be more easily able to adapt their national systems, also having significant capacity to make use of enforcement opportunities in developed countries. Third, less- and least-developed countries without appropriate domestic ABS legislation in place are likely to face considerable challenges in establishing their own legal frameworks and, on this basis, exploiting the empowering potential that the new enforcement opportunities in other (developed) countries present. Developed and advanced developing countries, in practice, may be able to benefit from enhanced transparency and the empowerment that flows from it, whereas the situation of less- and least-developed countries may change little without targeted capacity building and assistance (Medaglia et al. 2011; Oberthür et al. 2011). Enhanced transparency provisions thus require a functioning infrastructure to become effective in practice, which may not be easy to establish (see also Dingwerth and Eichinger, this book, chapter 10; Gupta, this book, chapter 6). Because users and providers designed transparency provisions of the protocol, they aim to further procedural and normative effectiveness of double-sided transparency. Notwithstanding this, protocol implementation is likely to favor states with significant capacities in GR management.

ABS Governance by Disclosure: Substantive Effects
The substantive, environmental effects of global ABS governance by disclosure are even more questionable. Regulating ABS under the CBD as a multilateral environmental agreement had the rationale that appropriate benefit sharing with the owners and custodians of GR would provide an incentive for them to conserve biological diversity and ecosystems as the pool of GR (Rosendal 2000, chapters 4 and 5). The Nagoya Protocol incorporates this logic in two places. First, article 1 establishes "contributing to the conservation of biological diversity and the sustainable use of its components" as part of the objectives of global ABS governance. Furthermore, article 9 stipulates that "parties shall encourage users and providers to direct benefits arising from the utilization of genetic resources towards the conservation of biological diversity and the sustainable use of its components." In terms of transparency, however, no mechanisms exist that furnish information about the actual use of benefits, and the overall effect of ABS governance arrangements in terms of these environmental objectives (let alone ensuring the effective channeling of benefits for that purpose).[12] Under these circumstances, and without further action on this

aspect, the environmental benefits even of an improved system of ABS governance with greater transparency for benefit sharing are unlikely to be significant.

Conclusion

The decentralized, bilateral, contract-based approach to global ABS governance enshrined in the CBD and the corresponding GR marketization dynamic have moved transparency to center stage in structuring politics in this policy field (see also Knox-Hayes and Levy, this book, chapter 9). Flowing from the recognition of the sovereign rights of countries to their natural resources, a battleground between GR users (developed countries) primarily interested in transparency of access conditions and GR providers (developing countries) primarily interested in transparency of GR use and benefit sharing (supported by NGOs and civil society protests) was constituted during the course of the 1990s. Ever since, defining the right balance between "transparency for access" and "transparency for benefit sharing" has remained at the center of global ABS politics under the CBD.

Underlying the preferred regulatory approach has been states' willingness to steer a liberal market logic for the marketization of GR as a means toward equity, empowerment and environmentally desirable outcomes (see also Gupta et al., this book, chapter 8). Rather than developing a multilateral governance approach and regulating benefit sharing internationally, the CBD and the Nagoya Protocol aim at controlling the bilateral exchange relations between providers and users of GR. It has defined and established some cornerstones on which the exchange relation can build, including PIC, MAT, and "internationally recognized certificates of compliance" as well as corresponding institutional infrastructures (national focal points, competent national authorities, checkpoints, and the international ABS Clearing-House). It has failed to establish other elements under consideration, most important, a mandatory requirement to disclose the origin of any GR used and related information in patent applications, which would have interfered with a core ingredient of modern market economies, intellectual property rights, with significance far beyond the area of GR.

In this context, the crux of the matter—determining and ensuring the "fair and equitable" sharing of the benefits and thus the pricing of GR—has been largely left to individual providers and users on the basis of, and shaped by, legislation and measures by national governments. Transparency is central to this marketization and to enabling fairness in it and thus has become a major battleground. Transparency regarding use of resources generated through benefit sharing is also important in terms of the eventual environmental objectives of biodiversity conservation, but this has unfortunately been neglected in the shadow of the fight to balance transparency relating to access versus benefit sharing. The environmental benefits of ABS governance thus remain uncertain, at best.

The result has been a lasting imbalance in favor of transparency for access that especially disadvantages the least-developed countries. The 2010 Nagoya Protocol provides for enhanced transparency of access conditions as well as of use and enforcement conditions. However, it does not undo the preexisting imbalance between the two sides that stems from lower levels of transparency of the behavior of "private" GR users and a greater difficulty to get a regulatory grip on them. As a result, the actual use of GR—mainly in developed countries—remains intrinsically less transparent, even if enhanced by as-yet uncertain controls of "checkpoints." In addition, especially capacity-scarce countries such as least-developed countries are likely to face two kinds of constraints. First, they will find it difficult to fulfill the precondition for benefitting from enhanced transparency for benefit sharing, namely, establishing their own administrative, legal, and procedural systems for access. Second, they will also face difficulties in obtaining knowledge about foreign legal systems and in taking part in legal procedures in foreign jurisdictions that would be required in order to enforce their benefit sharing rules vis-à-vis foreign users. Although the Nagoya Protocol empowers them in principle, they may not be able to exploit this potential in practice.

We end pointing to two possibilities for advancing international ABS governance that partially transcend the existing system. First, introducing a mandatory requirement to disclose the origin of any GR used and related information in patent applications continues to have a significant potential to enhance the balance between transparency for access and benefit sharing. Discussions on such a disclosure requirement continue within the WTO and WIPO. Second, multilateral, common-pool approaches to ABS governance constitute a possible alternative to the bilateral, contract-based approach under the CBD and its Nagoya Protocol. They do exist in limited pockets of the overall issue area in the form of the FAO's International Treaty on Plant Genetic Resources for Food and Agriculture of 2001 and the WHO's nonbinding Pandemic Influenza Preparedness Framework for the Sharing of Influenza Viruses and Access to Vaccines and Other Benefits adopted in 2011. In both cases, ABS with regard to the respective GR is being internationally administered in specialized arrangements. The Nagoya Protocol, in its article 4.4, explicitly allows for such specialized arrangements (as long as they are in line with its own objectives). A number of relevant processes provide the opportunity to expand specialized multilateral ABS governance, including for the High Seas, Antarctica, for other GR for food and agriculture and for ex-situ collections (Oberthür et al. 2011). Although such arrangements have their own challenges and may thus not be a panacea, they are not bedeviled by the problems of an intrinsic imbalance of transparency for access and benefit sharing.

Notes

1. As of November 2013, the Nagoya Protocol has not yet entered into force.

2. CBD 2009, especially 7–8; on the importance of TK and its relationship with intellectual property see also von Lewinski 2008; Ullrich 2005.

3. Interview with Colombian delegate, July 9, 2007.

4. See paragraph 44(o) of the Johannesburg Plan of Implementation. Available at http://www.un.org/esa/sustdev/documents/WSSD_POI_PD/English/WSSD_Plan Impl.pdf.

5. The task of competent national authorities to advise on how to implement and enforce ABS agreements was lost on the way from the Bonn Guidelines to the Nagoya Protocol: compare CBD 2002, para. 14(d), with article 13.2 of the protocol.

6. The "origin" refers to where the GR originated in the first place (i.e., before it was placed in, for example, a collection), whereas the "source" refers to the immediate, last provider (which may be an intermediate organization).

7. Alternative, softer concepts of "mandatoriness" that have entered the debate foresee the possibility of fines for the nonprovision of the information (although patents would still be granted).

8. Some countries, especially provider countries, have implemented a requirement to disclose the origin of GR in patent applications domestically in various forms: CBD 2007b, 18–20; Medaglia et al. 2011.

9. See http://www.cbd.int/abs/measures.

10. On the pre-Nagoya implementation of ABS in provider and user countries, see, in particular, CBD 2007a, 2007b; Tvedt and Young 2007.

11. The Nagoya Protocol foresees cooperation on capacity building in its article 22.

12. It deserves mentioning, though, that some countries (e.g., Brazil) have domestically passed legislation to channel benefits toward the conservation of biological diversity; see, for example, CBD 2007b, 10; Medaglia et al. 2011; Oberthür et al. 2011.

References

Arts, Bas. 1998. *The Political Influence of Global NGOs*. Utrecht: International Books.

Bled, Amandine J. 2010. Technological Choices in International Environmental Negotiations: An Actor-Network Analysis. *Business & Society* 49 (4): 570–590.

Brand, Ulrich, Christoph Görg, Joachim Hirsch, and Markus Wissen. 2008. *Conflicts in Environmental Regulation and the Internationalisation of the State. Contested Terrains*. London: Routledge.

Buck, Matthias, and Clare Hamilton. 2011. The Nagoya Protocol on Access to Genetic Resources and the Fair and Equitable Sharing of Benefits Arising from their Utilization to the Convention on Biological Diversity. *Review of European Community & International Environmental Law* 20 (1): 47–61.

Burrows, Beth, ed. 2005. *The Catch: Perspectives in Benefit Sharing*. Washington, DC: The Edmonds Institute.

CBD (Convention on Biological Diversity). 2002. *Bonn Guidelines on Access to Genetic Resources and Fair and Equitable Sharing of the Benefits Arising out of Their Utilization*. Montreal: Secretariat of the Convention on Biological Diversity.

CBD. 2006. *Consideration of an Internationally Recognized Certificate of Origin/Source/Legal Provenance*. Convention on Biological Diversity, UN doc. UNEP/CBD/GTE-ABS/1/2, November 28.

CBD. 2007a. *Analysis of Gaps in Existing National, Regional and International Legal and Other Instruments Relating to Access and Benefit-sharing*. Convention on Biological Diversity, UN doc. UNEP/CBD/WG-ABS/5/3, September 13.

CBD. 2007b. *Overview of Recent Developments at National and Regional Levels Relating to Access and Benefit-sharing*. Convention on Biological Diversity, UN doc. UNEP/CBD/WG-ABS/5/4, August 30.

CBD. 2009. *Report of the Meeting of the Group of Technical and Legal Experts on Traditional Knowledge Associated with Genetic Resources in the Context of the International Regime on Access and Benefit-Sharing*. Convention on Biological Diversity, UN Doc. UNEP/CBD/WG-ABS/8/2, July 15.

Deke, Oliver. 2008. *Environmental Policy Instruments for Conserving Global Biodiversity*. Berlin: Springer.

Holm-Müller, Karin, Carmen Richerzhagen, and Sabine Taüber. 2005. *Users of Genetic Resources in Germany. Awareness, Participation and Positions Regarding the Convention on Biological Diversity*. Berlin: Bfn (Federal Agency for Nature Conservation).

Hopgood, Stephen. 1998. *American Foreign Environmental Policy and the Power of the State*. Oxford: Oxford University Press.

Medaglia, Jorge Cabrera. 2009. *Study on the Relationship between an International Regime on Access and Benefit-sharing and Other International Instruments and Forums That Govern the Use of Genetic Resources: The World Trade Organization (WTO); the World Intellectual Property Rights Organization (WIPO); and* the International Union for the Protection of New Varieties of Plants (UPOV). UN doc. UNEP/CBD/WG-ABS/7/INF/3/Part.2, March 3.

Medaglia, Jorge Cabrera, Frederic Perron-Welch, and Olivier Rukundo. 2011. *Overview of National and Regional Measures on Access to Genetic Resources and Benefit Sharing: Challenges and Opportunities in Implementing the Nagoya Protocol*, December. Montreal: Centre for International Sustainable Development Law.

Miller, Michael J. 2006. Biodiversity Policy Making in Costa Rica: Pursuing Indigenous and Peasant Rights. *Journal of Environment & Development* 15 (4): 359–381.

Nijar, Gurdial Singh. 2011. *The Nagoya Protocol on Access and Benefit Sharing of Genetic Resources: Analysis and Implementation Options for Developing Countries*. Kuala Lumpur: Centre of Excellence for Biodiversity Law.

Oberthür, Sebastian, Christiane Gerstetter, Christine Lucha, Katriona McGlade, Justyna Pożarowska, and Florian Rabitz. 2011. *Intellectual Property Rights on Genetic Resources and the Fight against Poverty*. Brussels: European Parliament, Directorate-General for External Policies of the Union.

Oberthür, Sebastian, and Justyna Pożarowska. 2013. The Impact of the Nagoya Protocol on the Evolving Institutional Complex of Global ABS Governance. In *Global Governance of Genetic Resources: Access and Benefit-Sharing after the Nagoya Protocol*, ed. Sebastian Oberthür and G. Kristin Rosendal, 178–195. Abingdon, UK: Routledge.

OECD. 2011. *Key Biotech Indicators, Share of Countries in Biotechnology Patents Filed under PCT, 2007–09*. Available at www.oecd.org/dataoecd/41/46/48719943 .xls.

Pisupati, Balakrishna. 2007. *UNU-IAS Pocket Guide—Access to Genetic Resources, Benefit Sharing and Bioprospecting*. Yokohama, Japan: United Nations University Institute of Advanced Studies.

Robinson, Daniel. 2010. *Confronting Biopiracy: Challenges, Cases and International Debates*. London: Earthscan.

Rodriguez, Silvia. 1993. *Conservation, Contradiction and Sovereignty Erosion: The Costa Rican State and the Natural Protected Areas (1970–1992)*. PhD Thesis in Philosophy. Madison: University of Wisconsin.

Rosendal, Kristin G. 2000. *The Convention on Biological Diversity and Developing Countries*. Dordrecht, the Netherlands: Kluwer.

Rosendal, Kristin G. 2006. Balancing Access and Benefit Sharing and Legal Protection of Innovations from Bioprospecting: Impacts on Conservation of Biodiversity. *Journal of Environment & Development* 15: 428–447.

Svarstad, Hanne. 1994. National Sovereignty and Genetic Resources. In *Biodiplomacy: Genetic Resources and International Relations*, ed. Vicente Sánchez and Calestous Juma, 45–65. Nairobi: ACTS Press.

Tvedt, Morten W., and Tomme R. Young. 2007. *Beyond Access: Exploring Implementation of the Fair and Equitable Sharing Commitment in the CBD*. Gland, Switzerland: IUCN.

Ullrich, Hanns. 2005. *Traditional Knowledge, Biodiversity, Benefit-Sharing and the Patent System: Romantics v. Economics.* EUI Working Paper LAW No. 2005/07. Available at http://dx.doi.org/10.2139/ssrn.838107.

von Lewinski, Silke. 2008. *Indigenous Heritage and Intellectual Property: Genetic Resources, Traditional Knowledge, and Folklore.* Alphen aan den Rijn, the Netherlands: Kluwer Law International.

8

Making REDD+ Transparent: The Politics of Measuring, Reporting, and Verification Systems

Aarti Gupta, Marjanneke J. Vijge, Esther Turnhout, and Till Pistorius

Reducing emissions from deforestation and forest degradation in developing countries (REDD) is currently one of the most debated climate mitigation options within the United Nations Framework Convention on Climate Change (UNFCCC) negotiations. REDD is intended to be a performance-based financing mechanism, whereby industrialized countries compensate developing countries for reducing forest-related carbon emissions. The mechanism is now labeled REDD+ (reducing emissions from deforestation and forest degradation in developing countries; and the role of conservation, sustainable management of forests, and enhancement of forest carbon stocks in developing countries). Many see great potential in REDD+ to simultaneously deal with climate change *and* loss of the world's forests. It is hoped that REDD+ will deliver cost-effective climate mitigation through reduced carbon emissions and carbon sequestration, as well as co-benefits such as biodiversity conservation (Pistorius et al. 2011; Seymour 2012) and improved livelihoods of forest communities (Cowie et al. 2007). Yet whether REDD+ can satisfy these high expectations remains contested (Visseren-Hamakers et al. 2012).

A much-debated element of these discussions centers on the measuring, reporting, and verification (MRV) systems necessary to ascertain whether and how much forest carbon is being sequestered, and also whether and what co-benefits are being generated and for whom. In this chapter, we focus on the *politics* of REDD+ MRV systems. We view the centrality of measuring, reporting, and verification in REDD+ as aligned with the growing uptake of transparency and governance by disclosure in the global environmental domain. As noted in the introduction to this book, transparency is seen as an important means to hold the powerful to account, empower recipients of information, and thereby also improve environmental performance (Gupta and Mason, chapter 1). Yet a central question in this regard is who is being held to account by whom, and why. This becomes relevant to assess because REDD+ MRV systems are also implicated in the ascendency of neoliberal environmental governance, which emphasizes creation of new markets, efficiencies, and performance-based compensation as key to securing desired environmental aims (Duffy and Moore 2010; Pistorius et al. 2012; see also Knox-Hayes and Levy, this book, chapter 9; Orsini et al., this book, chapter 7).

In much scholarly literature, as well as in the rhetoric and practice of international institutions involved with REDD+, the design and functioning of MRV systems is framed largely as a technical and administrative challenge, requiring accurate and verifiable data, access to technology, and capacity building (Böttcher et al. 2009; GOFC-GOLD 2010; Hiepe and Kanamaru 2008). Yet *what* should be measured, reported, and verified, *how*, and *by whom* are fundamentally political questions, insofar as REDD+ will be constituted in large part by what is measured and valorized.

In this chapter, we analyze the uptake, institutionalization, and impacts of transparency through focusing on debates and developments around REDD+ MRV systems. In analyzing transparency about what, we focus on the *scope* of REDD+ MRV systems, that is, the extent to which they focus on forest carbon alone or also include noncarbon or so-called co-benefits. A proposition we consider is that REDD+ MRV systems may promote a "carbonization" of multilevel forest governance if they promote valorization of forests for their carbon content alone, rather than for the multiple benefits that forests provide.

In addressing *transparency how* and *by whom,* that is, the modalities of REDD+ MRV systems, we analyze whether such systems privilege certain types of scientific expertise and data-generation techniques over others or whether they envision drawing on a diverse array of expertise and assessment techniques (from remote sensing to community-based monitoring) and sources of data. Assessing transparency how and by whom leads us to a second proposition: that REDD+ MRV systems may promote what we refer to as a "technicalization" of multilevel forest governance, if decisions about MRV practices are deferred largely to the scientific realm to be decided by experts. Such technicalization may also entail the empowerment of certain experts over others and representations of "the forest" in ways that render it measurable, monitorable, and hence also more amenable to centralized control (Scott 1998).

In assessing these propositions, we proceed as follows. In line with the conceptual framework of this book, section 2 discusses the rationales for the embrace of transparency in REDD+ by assessing the centrality and role of MRV systems in this new climate governance innovation. Section 3 discusses the institutionalization of transparency by analyzing the scope and modalities, that is, the what, how, and by whom of REDD+ MRV systems. Section 4 considers the prospects for empowerment and environmental gains through REDD+ transparency.

The analysis is based on primary and secondary sources and occasional participant observation by the UNFCCC REDD+ negotiations since 2006.

Embracing Transparency

As hypothesized in chapter 1 (Gupta and Mason, this book), the uptake of transparency in specific issue areas plays out within a broader global context shaped by a democratic imperative to redress governance deficits such as a lack of accountability, but also by a neoliberal privileging of market-based solutions to environmental challenges. We analyze here how these twin dynamics of democratization and marketization underpin a demand for REDD+ transparency.

REDD+ arguably fits within a broader trend in global environmental governance to promote increased efficiency through a combination of commodification of the environment, marketization, globalization, and new public management (e.g., Hood 1991, see also Turnhout and Boonman-Berson 2011). The growing reliance on "payment for ecosystem services" in nature and biodiversity conservation reflects an increasing dominance of economic conceptions of the environment, often accompanied by a shift in governance responsibility from the public to the private sector (Bekessy and Wintle 2008; Bernstein 2001). Examples include national systems of wetland banking (Robertson 2006) and payment schemes for tourism in which representative species such as elephants are expected "to pay" for their own conservation by providing recreational services for tourists (Duffy and Moore 2010; Neves 2010).

In REDD+, forests are similarly conceptualized as providing the ecosystem service of carbon sinks, one that can be measured, valorized, compensated, and/or marketed (Diaz et al. 2011; Mackenzie 2008; Pistorius et al. 2012). In contrast to other neoliberal marketized contexts, however, the focus here is not necessarily on private, voluntary arrangements. Instead, states are centrally implicated in REDD+ transparency, with the contours of REDD+ and its MRV systems now being negotiated within the multilateral regime of the UNFCCC and various types of disclosure required from REDD+ recipient countries. Thus, REDD+ as an experiment in payment for ecosystem services unfolds in an unequal geopolitical context, whereby distribution of, access to, and control over the ecosystem service in question varies, as does the capacity to valorize and be compensated for it.

MRV systems for REDD+ are centrally implicated in this process, given the need for information to ascertain results as a basis for compensation. As such, REDD+ MRV systems also reflect a rapidly growing role for *scientific expertise* in environmental governance. As noted, environmental governance increasingly focuses on performance and efficiency (Mol 1999; Turnhout 2009). Yet assessing performance and efficiency requires information about outputs, costs, and effects. Transparency—in the form of measuring, reporting, and verification—is thus a crucial condition for payment for ecosystem services to work, and expert-led knowledge production is often a key component herein.

In contrast to other aspects of neoliberal approaches to environmental governance (such as privatization, marketization, or the dominance of efficiency), transparency, however, is not often criticized (Gupta 2008; Power 1999). Yet transparency can have empowering and disempowering consequences, depending on who is engaged in monitoring and measuring, reporting and verification, and for what purposes. Monitoring can be a powerful tool, if deployed by civil society or others, to bring to light unsustainable or corrupt (forest) practices and thereby force accountability of powerful actors (Fuller 2006; Transparency and Accountability Initiative 2010). Yet it can also have disempowering consequences if it allows those in power to "see like a state," that is, to enhance control over and appropriate valuable resources through data gathering and surveillance (Scott 1998; see also Luke 1995 and Turnhout 2009).

How REDD+ MRV systems will work, and to whose benefit, is thus contested political terrain. This is particularly so because the outcome of monitoring, measuring, reporting, and verification may be to harmonize or homogenize as a prerequisite to exercising (centralized) control. As Fogel (2004, 111), for example, notes "the notion that 'standardized' carbon units can be produced through standardized sequestration projects [...] is an expression of an instrumental 'global gaze.'" Such a global, or in the case of REDD+, national, gaze requires the development of complex monitoring systems or "infrastructures of transparency" that may be costly and resource intensive to establish (Gupta 2010; on infrastructures of transparency, see also Orsini et al., this book, chapter 7; and Dingwerth and Eichinger, this book, chapter 10).

In a global climate–monitoring context, Bäckstrand and Lövbrand note, for example, that "satellite supervision of the Earth's vegetation cover, advanced computer modeling of atmospheric and oceanographic processes, a global grid of meteorological stations and carbon flux towers [all] exemplify the resource-intensive infrastructure used by expert groups to study, monitor and predict the trajectories of human induced climate change" (Bäckstrand and Lövbrand 2006, 54). In the REDD+ context, calls for powerful satellite systems on a global scale, operated by "independent" international expert bodies to generate "real-time information" and early warning systems about tropical forest loss, are increasingly heard (Lynch et al. 2013).

Yet such systems are not detached from the exigencies of politics, insofar as they raise questions about what is to be seen by whom and to what end, with implications for shifting sovereign authority over resource governance choices and outcomes. Added to this, the view that expert knowledge generation is an apolitical, neutral activity aimed at discovering objective realities or facts of nature has been criticized for its failure to acknowledge the nature of scientific practice as well as the dynamics between knowledge production and use (on the latter, see for example, Gieryn 1995; Latour 1999). Such critiques highlight, for example, the extent to which scientific experts constitute the things that they study or measure (Fogel 2004; Gupta 2004; Jasanoff 2004; Law 2009; Mackenzie 2004; Turnhout and Boonman-Berson 2011).

For REDD+, forest carbon monitoring is to occur largely in a national context, with varying degrees of flexibility and discretion permitted with regard to scope, techniques, and data sources (Herold et al. 2012; Romijn et al. 2012). Furthermore, whether REDD+ compensation will be organized through markets or international fund transfers remains undecided in global policy. Regardless, the imperative for transparency in this case (more so than many others in this book) is to serve as the basis for compensating environmental performance. Thus, rather than a democratization impulse (understood as a push for more open and inclusive governance), transparency is fueled more by the impetus to valorize, commodify, and create new markets in environmental goods and services.

This raises a variety of questions, including what environmental gains (carbon-related or also noncarbon forest services) are to be measured, valorized, and/or compensated with the aid of REDD+ MRV systems, and who is empowered by the generation and provision of such information.

Will REDD+ MRV systems empower global and/or national elites of scientists, policy makers, and carbon market actors at the expense of affected groups such as local forest-dependent communities? What might REDD+ MRV systems *render visible or leave obscure,* and with what implications for environmental gains? We turn to these questions next.

Institutionalizing Transparency

We analyze here the scope and modalities (the what, how, and by whom) of REDD+ MRV systems, as these are now being debated in a global multilateral context. In so doing, we explore the second hypothesis, put forward in the introduction to this book, that governance by disclosure decenters state-led regulation and opens up political space for other actors. In one sense, the first part of this hypothesis does not apply to this case, given that REDD+ MRV systems are envisioned to be national-level, state-based systems, and hence states are central to their establishment and institutionalization. Nonetheless, REDD+ recipient countries have very different capacities to develop and institutionalize such systems. Thus, what the scope of these systems will be, and who will be involved with or have the capacity to generate required information, has consequences for who (i.e., which states) will be empowered and/or cede authority, and the extent to which these systems will open up political space for other actors, whether local communities, experts, or private market actors.

In assessing these dynamics, we discuss in the following, first, the debates and developments relating to *scope* (the what) of REDD+ MRV systems, specifically the multiple political and technical challenges inherent in attempts to monitor, measure, and thereby valorize forest carbon and other forest ecosystem services. Next, we discuss modalities of REDD+ MRV (the how and by whom) by assessing whose knowledge and what techniques are being privileged in debating the contours of these systems.

Institutionalizing Scope of MRV Systems: Disclosure about What?

When REDD was first introduced into the UNFCCC negotiations in 2005, the conference of the parties to the UNFCCC mandated its Subsidiary Body for Scientific and Technological Advice to develop a sound methodological approach to development of MRV systems (Pistorius et al. 2012). The assumed scope of REDD+ MRV at the time was to assess avoided deforestation (and forest degradation), rather than the sustainable management of forests and conservation and enhancement of forest carbon stocks (the + activities added later to REDD).

With the earlier, more limited scope, the MRV challenge turned on assessing land use changes relating to avoided deforestation, with the presumption that this was largely achievable via available remote-sensing techniques and satellite data (Böttcher et al. 2009). Policy makers acknowledged, however, that assessing carbon stock changes associated with forest degradation was much more complex.

Since 2007, the scope of REDD has expanded to include essentially all forest-related activities. This makes it necessary to not only *monitor* changes in deforested areas using proxy values but also to *measure* actual carbon stock changes in different forest types and different carbon pools (living and dead biomass and soil carbon), both in degraded areas and in areas where no change of land use has occurred. This has greatly expanded the scope of MRV systems required for REDD+ forest carbon accounting.

In line with this expanding scope, the international scholarly and political debate over REDD+ MRV systems has intensified, with a focus on developing "adequate scientific methods" for measuring, reporting, and verification of forest carbon emissions (UNFCCC 2008, 42). Many international initiatives, including the World Bank's Forest Carbon Partnership Facility (FCPF) and the United Nations REDD (UN-REDD) Programme, are helping developing countries to get "ready for REDD+," including through capacity building for development of REDD+ MRV systems (Herold and Skutsch 2009). As suggested by a UNFCCC technical paper, the "estimation and reporting of emissions and removals of greenhouse gases (GHGs)" should be guided by five principles, including "transparency, consistency, comparability, completeness, and accuracy" (UNFCCC 2009, 6). This builds on the Intergovernmental Panel on Climate Change (IPCC) good practice guidelines for countries to report on forest carbon emissions relating to land use, land use change, and forestry (LULUCF) in their overall greenhouse gas emission budgets (IPCC 2003).

The outstanding issue remains, however, what constitutes, inter alia, "completeness" and "accuracy" and according to whom. The IPCC good practice guidelines are framed as technical requirements and the rhetoric of intergovernmental organizations is to emphasize that investments in capacity building will permit the development of adequate MRV systems in developing countries that can meet such criteria. Extensive policy and scholarly discussions now turn on the challenges of determining baselines (referred to as reference [emission] levels) and appropriate techniques for monitoring changes in forest cover, as well as measuring carbon density and identifying credible data sources on which to base forest carbon accounting (e.g., Asner 2009; Herold et al. 2012; Olander et al. 2008).

Tellingly, a UNFCCC background paper notes that "due to the complexity of the processes involved and the lack of information, expert opinions, independent assessments or model estimations are commonly used as information sources to produce forest carbon data" (UNFCCC 2009, 13, referring to Holmgren et al. 2007). Insofar as uncertainties persist and experts disagree on carbon accounting methods, what constitutes "good practice" in MRV systems is thus flexible and open to interpretation (Lövbrand 2004). Whose interpretation prevails thus has consequences for implementation and the effects produced by such systems.

The IPCC guidelines explicitly recognize the need for flexibility in determining good practice in accounting, given the very different contexts and preconditions prevailing in different REDD+ countries. In recognition of this, it identifies three different tiers of acceptable data sources in calculating so-called emission factors (that is, forest carbon stock changes) needed to calculate forest carbon emissions. IPCC tier 1–level reporting permits use of (aggregate) default data. As per IPCC tier 2–level reporting, emission factors are to be calculated based on country-specific data. Finally, IPCC tier 3 is the most stringent in calling for emission factors to be based on "models and inventory measurement systems tailored to address national circumstances, repeated over time, and driven by high-resolution activity data disaggregated at sub-national to fine grid scales" (Herold et al. 2012, 3; see also IPCC 2003).

Only IPCC tier 3–level reporting actually entails measurements, whereby then a calculation of scientific uncertainties is also feasible. Although this reflects needed flexibility in what constitutes good practice, it is striking that few industrialized countries have the technical means and infrastructure to generate tier 3–level data, and most developing countries do not. As one illustration, even Germany, with its long tradition of generating forest inventory data, is currently unable to report in "tier 3 quality" on all relevant forest carbon pools, as the latest German national inventory report submitted to the UNFCCC reveals (UBA 2010). Here, the calculation of dead wood carbon pools relies on different data sets, and carbon stored in soil (estimated to constitute approximately 50 percent of the total forest carbon pool) is calculated using tier 1 data. The required calculation of uncertainties in tier 3–level reporting also reveals how very large uncertainty ranges are derived from "practical approaches" that "do not take into account every possible error source" and "neglect correlations" (UBA 2010, 445).

Thus, even in a developed country context, where the LULUCF sector is a relatively small fraction of the national greenhouse gas emission budget, it is difficult to measure (rather than model or estimate) carbon stock changes. Such measurement is a much greater challenge in most developing countries, where the contribution of LULUCF to national greenhouse gas budgets is also likely to be higher.

In developed *and* developing country contexts, given lack of data, it is also challenging to account for the impact of severe biotic (e.g., pests) or abiotic (e.g., fires, storms) calamities on forest carbon pools. Notwithstanding this, there is a global policy debate underway regarding the need to distinguish *human* from *natural* disturbances to forests (e.g., Lövbrand 2004), given the relevance of this distinction for REDD+ performance-based compensation. Such distinctions further exacerbate the challenges of forest carbon accounting. Another expansion in scope of MRV systems now being contemplated is whether to account for carbon stored in *harvested* wood products, as a form of postharvest carbon sequestration. Again, this would rely on estimations and models rather than measurement, but nonetheless pose various sociotechnical challenges (Fox et al. 2010).

The extensive and ever-growing needs of forest carbon accounting implies that the term *measuring* (the "M" of MRV) might well be misleading, given that the expanded set of MRV challenges facing REDD+ can be addressed only through monitoring. Such monitoring relies, furthermore, on long intervals between observations, the use of default values, and the omitting of relevant carbon pools if data are unavailable or cannot be obtained at "reasonable" costs. In addition, the need to supplement historical data on deforestation and forest cover change, with projections of future trends, including the (social, political, and economic) drivers of deforestation, in calculating baselines against which REDD+ country performance is to be assessed, adds to scientific and social uncertainties and accounting challenges (e.g., Herold et al. 2012; Lövbrand 2004).

With the exception of larger emerging economies, such as China, India, Brazil, Mexico, and Argentina, there are considerable gaps in the capacities of most developing countries to even monitor (much less measure) land use and carbon stock changes (Romijn et al. 2012). Multilateral REDD+ readiness support programs of UN-REDD and the World Bank seek to build such capacities to permit countries to participate in REDD+, yet in large intact forest landscapes, such as the Amazon or the Congo Basin, implementing ground-truthing inventories to complement remote-sensing data remains largely out of reach. The costs associated with establishing such systems, even if they are technically feasible now or in the near future, will be easier to bear for some than others. A recent comparative study argues, for example, that monitoring costs associated with REDD+ may have a significant impact on distribution of REDD+ benefits (Plugge et al. 2012).

The preceding discussion highlights that the data generated and the scope of REDD+ MRV systems are necessarily politically negotiated and context driven, rather than being neutral technical means by which to objectively document (comparable) REDD+ performance. This is also evident, for example, from a survey of experts and policy makers from developed and developing countries, on issues such as baselines and credible sources of data for REDD+ MRV systems. Huettner et al. (2009) show that developed versus developing countries, but also policy makers versus technical experts, have different notions of what the parameters for forest carbon monitoring systems should be and who should decide. For example, (southern) policy makers rated a requirement for "national sovereignty over data" for REDD+ MRV systems as much more important than technical experts. Southern policy makers also expressed a preference for baseline measurement methods to have "compatibility with the United Nations Food and Agriculture Organization (FAO) data sets and UNFCCC forest definitions" (Huettner et al. 2009, 6), with policy makers prioritizing this much more than technical experts. Technical experts view FAO data, for example, with suspicion, given that it is submitted by countries with little to no independent verification. Similarly, policy makers support but experts question the UNFCCC definition of forests, because it is broad and open to multiple interpretations (e.g., Putz and Redford 2010; see also Seymour 2012).

Going beyond the challenges of accounting for *forest carbon* in REDD+ MRV systems, the debate has now also moved to the need for and challenges of including *co-benefits and safeguards* in the scope of REDD+ MRV systems. This discussion is now underway in the UNFCCC context and in related global institutional arenas, such as UN-REDD and the World Bank's FCPF. The notion of "safeguards" within the UNFCCC encompasses a set of minimum standards intended to avoid unintended side effects of REDD+ activities, such as negative social impacts on forest-dependent communities or adverse environmental consequences such as biodiversity loss. Safeguards were introduced into the UNFCCC negotiations in 2009 in recognition of the fact that the ever-broadening scope of REDD+ activities could pose significant risks to biodiversity and needs of local forest-dependent communities (Phelps et al. 2012). Going beyond safeguarding against potential negative impacts of REDD+, the concept of co-benefits is concerned with how REDD+ may also have positive consequences for the other environmental and social services that forests provide.

Until recently, however, there have been few attempts to identify monitoring options for co-benefits and safeguards (Hiepe and Kanamaru 2008). This appears to be changing, with the need for "REDD+ safeguard monitoring" now also being discussed within the UNFCCC (Stickler et al. 2009, 2813; see also Pistorius et al. 2011). The UNFCCC's Cancun Agreement in 2010 and subsequent decisions require countries to discuss options for broadening monitoring requirements beyond greenhouse gas emissions to include "a summary of information on how ... safeguards ... are being addressed and respected throughout the implementation of the activities" (UNFCCC 2011a, 2). The Cancun decision that REDD+ countries should establish "information systems for safeguards" focuses, however, only on "how the safeguards are addressed and respected," rather than on whether co-benefits are being realized. This means that such safeguard information systems aim merely for an inventory of formal project statements, and not for the monitoring and measurement of biodiversity and livelihood issues to produce information on actual achievement of co-benefits.

Whether this should be included within REDD+ MRV systems is a contested issue, given that inclusion of such aspects would increase the monitoring burden on developing countries beyond what is currently required from UNFCCC annex I (industrialized) countries. These discussions have raised concerns about infringement of sovereignty of developing countries, if safeguard monitoring is globally mandated through REDD+ MRV systems, rather than being determined through national policy processes in REDD+ recipient countries. A related contested issue is whether REDD+ compensation payments are to be linked to safeguards *monitoring* as opposed to simply documenting existence of "safeguard information systems" and/or whether MRV systems should simply be carbon focused.

Building on the preceding discussion of scope (i.e., the what) of REDD+ MRV systems, we turn next to the how and by whom of REDD+ MRV, that is, to modalities of REDD+ MRV systems and the envisioned involvement of various actors in it.

Institutionalizing Modalities of MRV Systems: How and By Whom?

With regard to the means by which to generate forest carbon and non-carbon information, current debates around REDD+ MRV systems emphasize reliance on globally agreed high-tech and sophisticated methods, more so than local, on-the-ground techniques or monitoring by local communities. Yet there is now a growing consensus that local community-based inventories will be essential for forest carbon monitoring and monitoring for social and environmental co-benefits (Fry 2011; Herold and Skutsch 2011; Stickler et al. 2009).

In considering the prospects to include local-level monitoring in national expert-led MRV systems, prior experience with afforestation and reforestation projects under the Kyoto Protocol's Clean Development Mechanism (CDM) is instructive here. At the international level, experience with CDM projects has suggested a low level of confidence among global and national policy elites in locally produced data, compared to data gathered by technical experts relying on sophisticated methodologies (e.g., Fry 2011). The focus of (international) capacity building for REDD+ MRV systems has similarly been on remote-sensing and satellite-based methods to generate forest carbon (stock) estimates.

The REDD web platform on the UNFCCC website, for example, has a section on methodologies for REDD+ MRV systems that contains elaborate discussions of remote sensing, but not much information on ground-based forest inventories (UNFCCC 2011b). Although this could be because there is already more familiarity and experience with forest inventories in developing countries as compared to remote-sensing techniques, the use of ground inventories in estimating changes to forest carbon stocks remains essential and complex. If so, the implications of promoting sophisticated and remotely deployed methodologies for assessing REDD+ performance are important to examine. The experience with CDM suggests that the globally adopted "overly rigid standards-based approach" (Fry 2011, 185) of CDM afforestation and reforestation projects, with stringent monitoring requirements, complex regulations, and high transaction costs, renders it difficult for local communities to be involved with monitoring (Fry 2011, see also Bose et al. 2012).

Clearly, monitoring tools and practices can also have empowering consequences for local communities. Evidence from forest governance experiences in a variety of regional contexts, also predating REDD+, reveals that indigenous communities have successfully used ground-truthing and remote-sensing techniques to map their customary land rights and thereby "press their claims on behalf of nature and cultural survival" (Gupta et al. 2012, 729). A growing literature now documents how local communities might deploy such systems of transparency to further social and environmental gains (Litfin 1997; see also for recent detailed discussions, Dickson and Kapos 2012; Larrazábal et al. 2012; Visseren-Hamakers et al. 2012). This implies that whether REDD+ MRV systems open up political space for nonstate actors remains contingent and flows from context-specific modes of institutionalization.

In sum, this section has shown that the expanding scope and complexity of globally required, national-level REDD+ MRV systems might well impinge on state sovereign authority, insofar as some states might be less able to develop such systems and hence participate fully in this multilaterally negotiated payment for ecosystem services scheme. Such systems might simultaneously open up space for nonstate actors to engage, whether as a way to reinforce or contest such shifts in state authority. We elaborate further on such effects in the following discussion of the prospects for REDD+ MRV systems to reinforce a "technicalization" and "carbonization" trend in multilevel forest governance, with consequences for who is empowered and what environmental gains are secured.

Effects of Transparency

Drawing on the preceding discussion, we consider here the effects of transparency (via REDD+ MRV systems) in line with the normative, procedural, and substantive typology of effects outlined in the introduction (Gupta and Mason, this book, chapter 1). In doing so, we engage with the final hypothesis advanced therein, which posits that transparency is likely to be effective in contexts resonant with the goals and decision processes of both disclosers and recipients.

REDD+ MRV Systems: Who Is Empowered?
Our preceding discussion highlights that debates over the scope and modalities of REDD+ MRV systems are, ultimately, debates over how to frame the object of governance, in this case the role of forest-related activities in mitigating climate change. The scope and practices of MRV systems are critical to determining whether changing forest-related practices can be harnessed to combat climate change, but also to conserve biodiversity and enhance local livelihoods.

Given the high stakes, it is inevitable that globally negotiated performance assessment systems, such as REDD+ MRV, will encounter the strictures and concerns of state sovereignty *and* local forest-related accountability politics (Niederberger and Kimble 2011; Transparency and Accountability Initiative 2010). This is especially so if they implicate public research institutes, global science networks, a diverse array of countries with multiple and competing priorities, and globalized carbon market actors, as do REDD+ MRV systems.

On the key question of empowerment through transparency, then, debates around internationally mandated measuring, reporting, and verification of (voluntarily assumed) climate mitigation actions of developing countries, going beyond REDD+, has been one of the most contentious issues in UNFCCC discussions. Conflict over MRV of climate mitigation actions being taken by countries came to the fore in the 2009 UNFCCC negotiations in Copenhagen. China, in particular, opposed an international review and verification process for its voluntarily assumed national climate mitigation actions, viewing this as an infringement of sovereignty (Niederberger and Kimble 2011).

With regard to REDD+ MRV systems, the conferences of the parties to the UNFCCC agreed in 2010 that these should be "available and suitable for review as agreed by the conference of the parties" (UNFCCC 2010). However, what such an international review process entails has not been agreed on, because it requires agreeing on *who will assess* whether REDD+ standards are being met and what the consequences are if standards are not met. Thus, a globally organized "independent review" of REDD+ MRV outcomes is a high-level political conflict over potential infringements of national sovereignty (Herold and Skutsch 2011, 2). This is evident as well from the collapse of REDD+ negotiations in the UNFCCC meeting in Doha in December 2012 because of unresolvable disagreements between industrialized countries (led by Norway) and developing countries (led by Brazil) over the need for a "robust" international *verification* procedure for forest emission reductions as a basis for performance-based REDD+ payments (Conservation International undated). The *political* significance of the scope and modalities of REDD+ MRV systems is underscored by this outcome, notwithstanding framing of such matters as "technical," also within the UNFCCC context.

The disagreement also highlights that although some states, including China, India, and Brazil, can contest or block perceived infringements on national sovereignty by determining the scope of their own REDD+ MRV systems or contesting the need for international verification, others are less able to do so. One outcome can be their exclusion from participating in REDD+ in the face of stringent international monitoring, reporting, and verification requirements. As McAlpine et al. (2010, 339) argue, international MRV standards can lead to a "disproportionate representation of some countries [in the REDD+ mechanism] at the expense of others," because not all countries have the capacity to put into place MRV systems that comply with globally negotiated standards and/or successfully contest these standards as an infringement of sovereignty.

If so, as noted previously, transparency-based arrangements can reinforce inequalities in state authority to participate in and shape multilevel governance outcomes. One can conclude then that the effects of REDD+ MRV systems, as currently envisioned, might be to empower those countries with developed capacities for MRV and exclude others (and/or their affected publics) who may lack the capacity to participate in or shape MRV requirements to suit their own circumstances. Thus, such systems of transparency might be "effective" insofar as they are aligned with the goals and priorities of some key REDD+ donor and recipient countries, but not all.

With regard to whether other (nonstate) actors are empowered by REDD+ MRV systems, the struggle between the sovereign state and a mobilized, vocal, active, transnationally connected, and locally embedded civil society that seeks to shape institutional arrangements for REDD+ is now well underway (for detailed discussions, see Gupta et al. 2012; Larrazábal et al. 2012; Visseren-Hamakers et al. 2012). As a result, REDD+ and its MRV systems constitute a still unstable climate governance project, with the jury out on how such systems will develop and who will be empowered in diverse national and local contexts.

Clearly, in the everyday realities of forest management and local livelihood needs, REDD+ MRV systems will perform in unpredictable ways. Notwithstanding this, the priority given in current policy debates to national-level *expert-led* MRV systems, with limited scope and resources for community involvement, might well fuel a technicalization of forest governance in specific instances. Again, such a technicalization of forest governance might well be aligned with the goals of certain REDD+ donor and recipient countries, and hence yield "effective" results-based compensation outcomes for them, but with adverse consequences for others, particularly local communities, who might be left out from negotiating and participating in these arrangements.

REDD+ MRV Systems: Fueling Environmental Improvements?

In addition to empowerment, a related set of questions raised by our analysis turns on the environmental gains sought from transparency. Here, the *materiality* of the resource being governed (forest carbon) comes to the fore. The complexities and uncertainties surrounding the monitoring and measuring of forest carbon, and the challenges of making forest carbon *commensurate* (i.e., equivalent for exchange purposes) with other forms of carbon, are centrally implicated in the prospects of governance by disclosure to fuel desired environmental improvements (such as climate mitigation and biodiversity conservation) in this case (Boyd 2010). In particular, given that co-benefits and the social consequences of potential

REDD+ arrangements are harder to measure and valorize than forest carbon, they are likely to remain outside the scope of MRV systems.

Although an important discussion about safeguards has begun globally under the UNFCCC, the relationship to evolving MRV systems is tentative, and the discussion itself remains contentious because of potential restrictions on sovereignty. Thus, a *carbonization* of multilevel forest governance, whereby forests as sources and sinks of carbon are prioritized over the co-benefits they yield, remains a possibility. When such carbonization is congruent with the goals of specific disclosers and recipients (REDD+ donor and recipient countries), it might well yield results-based compensation and transfers in specific instances, yet this may be to the detriment of valuing noncarbon forest ecosystem services.

Conclusion

This chapter has analyzed what REDD+ MRV systems intend to make visible and for whose benefit. Through focusing on debates and developments around the scope and modalities of REDD+ MRV systems (the what, how, and by whom of such systems), we have suggested that their design and functioning is not merely a (neutral) technical administrative challenge, requiring sufficient resources and capacity and adequate and accurate expertise, as framed in mainstream policy-making circles. Instead, these are fundamentally political processes, whereby the scope and methods of measuring, reporting, and verifying are subject to contestation and fraught with uncertainties and specific enabling assumptions.

Although often cast as technical, these are political processes insofar as they determine who is empowered or disempowered by the pursuit of transparency. We have also argued that an environmental valuation and commodification impetus for disclosure is privileged in this realm. As such, the possibility remains that expert-driven MRV systems, inspired by a neoliberal attempt to valorize and commodify carbon, may promote a *technicalization* of forest governance. This may empower actor groups favored by *epistemic* (forest experts) and *market-based* identities (suppliers and consumers of "verifiable" ecosystem goods and services) over affected actor groups falling outside these categories (forest-dependent communities with unrecognized local knowledge and communal property rights holders). With regard to environmental improvements, a preoccupation with forest carbon in REDD+ MRV systems may well result in marginalizing co-benefits and hence *carbonizing* forest governance.

In conclusion, our analysis suggests that transparency-based governance arrangements serve to constitute and represent the forest in ways that render it measurable. As such, REDD+ MRV systems merit further social science scrutiny, particularly in light of the (contested) neoliberal and technocratic thrust to global environmental governance within which they are now being negotiated and advanced.

References

Asner, Gregory P. 2009. Tropical Forest Carbon Assessment: Integrating Satellite and Airborne Mapping Approaches. *Environmental Research Letters* 4 (3): 1–11.

Bäckstrand, Karin, and Eva Lövbrand. 2006. Planting Trees to Mitigate Climate Change: Contested Discourses of Ecological Modernization, Green Governmentality and Civic Environmentalism. *Global Environmental Politics* 6 (1): 50–75.

Bekessy, Sarah A., and Brendan A. Wintle. 2008. Using Carbon Investment to Grow the Biodiversity Bank. *Conservation Biology* 22 (3): 510–513.

Bernstein, Steven. 2001. *The Compromise of Liberal Environmentalism*. New York: Columbia University Press.

Bose, Purabi, Bas Arts, and Han van Dijk. 2012. Forest Governmentality: A Geneology of Subject Making of Forest Dependent "Scheduled Tribes" in India. *Land Use Policy* 29 (3): 664–673.

Böttcher, Hannes, Katja Eisbrenner, Steffen Fritz, Georg Kindermann, Florian Kraxner, Ian McCallum, and Michael Obersteiner. 2009. An Assessment of Monitoring Requirements and Costs of "Reduced Emissions from Deforestation and Degradation." *Carbon Balance and Management* 4 (1): 1–8.

Boyd, William. 2010. Ways of Seeing in Environmental Law: How Deforestation Became An Object of Climate Governance. *Ecology Law Quarterly* 37: 843–916.

Conservation International (CI). Undated. *Outcome of Doha Climate Negotiations*. Conservation International. Available at http://www.conservation.org/Documents/CI_analysis_Doha_Outcomes_2012_26Nov-8Dec.pdf.

Cowie, Annette, Uwe A. Schneider, and Luca Montanarella. 2007. Potential Synergies between Existing Multilateral Environmental Agreements in the Implementation of Land Use, Land-use Change and Forestry Activities. *Environmental Science & Policy* 10 (4): 335–352.

Diaz, David, Katherine Hamilton, and Evan Johnson. 2011. *State of the Forest Carbon Markets 2011: From Canopy to Currency*. Ecosystem Marketplace. Available at http://www.forest-trends.org/documents/files/doc_2963.pdf.

Dickson, Barney, and Valerie Kapos. 2012. Biodiversity Monitoring for REDD+. *Current Opinion in Environmental Sustainability* 4: 717–725.

Duffy, Rosaleen, and Lorraine Moore. 2010. Neoliberalising Nature? Elephant-Back Tourism in Thailand and Botswana. *Antipode* 42 (3): 742–766.

Fogel, Cathleen. 2004. The Local, the Global and the Kyoto Protocol. In *Earthly Politics: Local and Global in Environmental Governance*, ed. Sheila Jasanoff and Marybeth Long Martello, 103–127. Cambridge, MA: MIT Press.

Fox, Julian C., Mark L. Williams, Tony Milne, and Rodney J. Keenan. 2010. *Protocols for Field Sampling of Forest Carbon Pools for Monitoring, Reporting and Verification of REDD.* International Geoscience and Remote Sensing Symposium. Proceedings, July 25–30, Honolulu, Hawaii. Available at http://ieeexplore.ieee.org/xpl/freeabs_all.jsp?arnumber=5652830&abstractAccess=no&userType=inst.

Fry, Ben P. 2011. Community Forest Monitoring in REDD+: The "M" in MRV? *Environmental Science & Policy* 14 (2): 181–187.

Fuller, Douglas O. 2006. Tropical Forest Monitoring and Remote Sensing: A New Era of Transparency in Forest Governance? *Singapore Journal of Tropical Geography* 27 (1): 15–29.

Gieryn, Thomas F. 1995. Boundaries of Science. In *Handbook of Science and Technology Studies*, ed. Sheila Jasanoff, Gerald E. Markle, James C. Petersen, and Trevor Pinch. Thousand Oaks, CA: Sage.

GOFC-GOLD. 2010. *A Sourcebook of Methods and Procedures for Monitoring and Reporting Anthropogenic Greenhouse Gas Emissions and Removals Caused by Deforestation, Gains and Losses of Carbon Stocks in Forests Remaining Forests, and Forestation.* GOFC-GOLD Report for COP16–1. Alberta, Canada: GOFC-GOLD Project Office.

Gupta, Aarti. 2004. When Global Is Local: Negotiating Safe Use of Biotechnology. In *Earthly Politics: Local and Global in Environmental Governance*, ed. Sheila Jasanoff and Marybeth Long Martello, 127–148. Cambridge, MA: MIT Press.

Gupta, Aarti. 2008. Transparency under Scrutiny: Information Disclosure in Global Environmental Governance. *Global Environmental Politics* 8 (2): 1–7.

Gupta, Aarti. 2010. Transparency in Global Environmental Governance: A Coming of Age? *Global Environmental Politics* 10 (3): 1–9.

Gupta, Aarti, Eva Lövbrand, Esther Turnhout, and Marjanneke J. Vijge. 2012. In Pursuit of Carbon Accountability: The Politics of REDD+ Measuring, Reporting and Verification Systems. *Current Opinion in Environmental Sustainability* 4 (6): 726–731.

Herold, Martin, and Margaret Skutsch. 2009. Measurement, Reporting and Verification for REDD+: Objectives, Capacities and Institutions. In *Realising REDD+: National Strategies and Policy Options*, ed. Arild Angelsen, 85–100. Bogor, Indonesia: CIFOR.

Herold, Martin, and Margaret Skutsch. 2011. Monitoring, Reporting and Verification for National REDD+ Programmes: Two Proposals. *Environmental Research Letters* 6 (1): 1–10.

Herold, Martin, Louis Verchot, Arild Angelsen, Danae Maniatis, and Simone Bauch. 2012. A Step-wise Framework for Setting REDD+ Forest Reference Emission Levels and Forest Reference Levels. *CIFOR Infobrief 52*, April.

Hiepe, Claudia, and Hideki Kanamaru. 2008. Review of Literature on Monitoring to Support REDD. *UN-REDD Programme MRV Working Paper 3.* Available at http://www.unredd.net/index.php?option=com_docman&task=doc_download&gid=942&Itemid=53.

Holmgren P., L.-G. Marklund, M. Saket, and M. L. Wilkie. 2007. Forest Monitoring and Assessment for Climate Change Reporting: Partnerships, Capacity Building and Delivery. Forest Resources Assessment Working Paper 142. Rome: FAO.

Hood, Christopher. 1991. A Public Management for All Seasons? *Public Administration* 69 (1): 3–19.

Huettner, Michael, Rik Leemans, Kasper Kok, and Johannes Ebeling. 2009. A Comparison of Baseline Methodologies for "Reducing Emissions from Deforestation and Degradation." *Carbon Balance and Management* 4 (4): 1–12.

IPCC. 2003. *International Panel on Climate Change (IPCC) Report on Good Practice Guidance for Land Use, Land-Use Change and Forestry, Geneva.* Available at http://www.ipcc-nggip.iges.or.jp/public/gpglulucf/gpglulucf_contents.html.

Jasanoff, Sheila, ed. 2004. *States of Knowledge: The Co-Production of Science and Social Order.* London: Routledge.

Latour, Bruno. 1999. *Pandora's Hope.* Cambridge, MA: Harvard University Press.

Law, John. 2009. Seeing Like a Survey. *Cultural Sociology* 3 (2): 239–256.

Larrazábal, Alejandra, Michael K. McCall, Tuyeni H. Mwampambal, and Margaret Skutsch. 2012. The Community Role for Carbon Monitoring in REDD+. *Current Opinion in Environmental Sustainability* 4 (6): 707–716.

Litfin, Karen T. 1997. The Gendered Eye in the Sky: A Feminist Perspective on Earth Observation Satellites. *Frontiers—A Journal of Women Studies* 18: 26–47.

Lövbrand, Eva. 2004. Bridging Political Expectations and Scientific Limitations in Climate Risk Management: On the Uncertain Effects of International Carbon Sink Policies. *Climatic Change* 67 (2–3): 449–460.

Luke, Timothy W. 1995. On Environmentality: Geo-Power and Eco-Knowledge in the Discourses of Contemporary Environmentalism. *Cultural Critique* 31: 57–81.

Lynch, Jim, Mark Maslin, Heiko Balzter, and Martin Sweeting. 2013. Choose Satellites to Monitor Deforestation. *Nature* 496: 293–294.

Mackenzie, Donald. 2004. The Big, Bad Wolf and the Rational Market: Portfolio Insurance, the 1987 Crash and the Performativity of Economics. *Economy and Society* 33 (3): 303–334.

Mackenzie, Donald. 2008. Making Things the Same: Gases, Emission Rights and the Politics of Carbon Markets. *Accounting, Organizations and Society* 34 (3–4): 440–455.

McAlpine, Clive A., Justin G. Ryan, Leonie Seabrook, Sebastian Thomas, Paul J. Dargusch, Jozef I. Syktus, Roger A. Pielke Sr., Andrés E. Etter, Philip M. Fearnside, and William F. Laurance. 2010. More Than CO2: A Broader Paradigm for Managing Climate Change and Variability to Avoid Ecosystem Collapse. *Current Opinion in Environmental Sustainability* 2 (5–6): 334–346.

Mol, Arthur P. J. 1999. Ecological Modernization and the Environmental Transition of Europe: Between National Variations and Common Denominators. *Journal of Environmental Policy and Planning* 1 (2): 167–181.

Neves, Katja. 2010. Cashing in on Cetourism: A Critical Engagement with Dominant E-NGO Discourses on Whaling, Cetacean Conservation, and Whale Watching. *Antipode* 42 (3): 719–741.

Niederberger, Anne A., and Melinda Kimble. 2011. MRV under the UN Climate Regime: Paper Tiger or Catalyst for Continual Improvement? *Greenhouse Gas Measurement and Management* 1 (1): 47–54.

Olander, Lydia P., Holly K. Gibbs, Marc Steininger, Jennifer J. Swenson, and Brian C. Murray. 2008. Reference Scenarios for Deforestation and Forest Degradation in Support of REDD: A Review of Data and Methods. *Environmental Research Letters* 3 (2): 1–11.

Phelps, Jacob, Dan A. Friess, and Edward L. Webb. 2012. Win-Win REDD+ Approaches Belie Carbon-Biodiversity Trade-offs. *Biological Conservation* 154: 53–60.

Pistorius, Till, Harald Schaich, Georg Winkel, Tobias Plieninger, Claudia Bieling, Werner Konold, and Karl-Reinhard Volz. 2012. Lessons for REDDplus: A Comparative Analysis of the German Discourse on Forest Functions and the Global Ecosystem Services Debate. *Forest Policy and Economics* 18: 4–12.

Pistorius, Till, Christine Schmitt, Dinah Benick, Steffen Entenmann, and Sabine Reinecke. 2011. Greening REDD+—Challenges and Opportunities for Integrating Biodiversity Safeguards at and across Policy Levels. *Allgemeine Forst- und Jagdzeitung* 182 (5/6): 82–98.

Plugge, Daniel, Thomas Baldauf, and Michael Köhl. 2012. The Global Climate Change Mitigation Strategy REDD: Monitoring Costs and Uncertainties Jeopardize Economic Benefits. *Climatic Change* 119 (2): 1–13.

Power, Michael. 1999. *The Audit Society: Rituals of Verification.* Oxford: Oxford University Press.

Putz, Francis E., and Kent H. Redford. 2010. The Importance of Defining Forest: Tropical Forest Degradation, Deforestation, Long-term Phase Shifts and Further Transitions. *Biotropica* 42 (1): 10–20.

Robertson, Morgan M. 2006. The Nature That Capital Can See: Science, State and Market in the Commodification of Ecosystem Services. *Environment and Planning. D, Society & Space* 24 (3): 367–378.

Romijn, Erika, Martin Herold, Lammert Kooistra, Daniel Murdiyarso, and Louis Verchot. 2012. Assessing Capacities of Non-Annex I Countries for National Forest Monitoring in the Context of REDD+. *Environmental Science & Policy* 19–20: 33–48.

Scott, James. 1998. *Seeing Like a State: How Certain Schemes to Improve the Human Condition Have Failed.* New Haven, CT: Yale University Press.

Seymour, Frances. 2012. *REDD Reckoning: A Review of Research on a Rapidly Moving Target.* CIFOR, CABI review article. Available at www.cabi.org/cabreviews/FullTextPDF/2012/20123176557.pdf.

Stickler, Claudia M., Daniel C. Nepstad, Michael T. Coe, David G. McGrath, Hermann O. Rodrigues, Wayne S. Walker, Britaldo Soares-Filho, and Eric A. Davidson. 2009. The Potential Ecological Costs and Co-benefits of REDD: A Critical Review and Case Study from the Amazon Region. *Global Change Biology* 15 (12): 2803–2824.

Transparency and Accountability Initiative. 2010. *Climate Change: New Frontiers in Transparency and Accountability.* London: Open Society Foundation, Cambridge House, UK. Available at http://www.transparency-initiative.org/wp-content/uploads/2011/05/climate_change_final1.pdf.

Turnhout, Esther. 2009. The Effectiveness of Boundary Objects: The Case of Ecological Indicators. *Science & Public Policy* 36 (5): 403–412.

Turnhout, Esther, and Susan Boonman-Berson. 2011. Databases, Scaling Practices and the Globalization of Biodiversity. *Ecology and Society* 16 (1): 35.

UBA (UmweltBundesamt). 2010. *National Inventory Report for the German Greenhouse Gas Inventory 1990–2008, Dessau.* Available at http://www.umwelt daten.de/publikationen/fpdf-l/3958.pdf.

UNFCCC. 2008. *Item 5 of the Provisional Agenda Reducing Emissions from Deforestation in Developing Countries: Approaches to Stimulate Action. Views on Outstanding Methodological Issues Related to Policy Approaches and Positive Incentives to Reduce Emissions from Deforestation and Forest Degradation in Developing Countries.* Submissions from Parties. Subsidiary Body for Scientific and Technological Advice, Twenty-Eighth Session, June 4–13, Bonn.

UNFCCC. 2009. *Cost of Implementing Methodologies and Monitoring Systems Relating to Estimates of Emissions from Deforestation and Forest Degradation, the Assessment of Carbon Stocks and Greenhouse Gas Emissions from Changes in Forest Cover, and the Enhancement of Forest Carbon Stocks.* Technical Paper, FCCC/TP/2009/1, May 31.

UNFCCC. 2010. *Report of the Conference of the Parties on Its Fifteenth Session. Addendum. Part Two: Action Taken by the Conference of the Parties at its Fifteenth Session.* FCCC/CP/2009/11/Add.1, Copenhagen, December 7–19.

UNFCCC. 2011a. *Agenda Item 4: Methodological Guidance for Activities Relating to Reducing Emissions from Deforestation and Forest Degradation and the Role of Conservation, Sustainable Management of Forests and Enhancement of Forest Carbon Stocks in Developing Countries.* FCCC/SBSTA/2011/L.25/Add.1. Subsidiary Body for Scientific and Technological Advice, Thirty-Fifth Session, Durban, November 28–December 3.

UNFCCC. 2011b. [UNFCCC website]. REDD Web Platform. Methodologies and Tools. Available at http://unfccc.int/methods_science/redd/methodologies/items/4538.php.

Visseren-Hamakers, Ingrid, Aarti Gupta, Martin Herold, Marielos Pena-Claros, and Marjanneke J. Vijge. 2012. Will REDD+ Work? The Need for Interdisciplinary Research to Address Key Challenges. *Current Opinion in Environmental Sustainability* 4 (6): 590–596.

III
Public-Private and Private Transparency

9

The Political Economy of Governance by Disclosure: Carbon Disclosure and Nonfinancial Reporting as Contested Fields of Governance

Janelle Knox-Hayes and David Levy

In this chapter, we analyze corporate disclosure as a mechanism of governance, with a focus on two reporting initiatives, the Carbon Disclosure Project (CDP) and the Global Reporting Initiative (GRI). The CDP is a nonprofit UK-based organization that encourages companies to disclose information about their greenhouse gas (GHG) emissions, climate-related risks and opportunities, and carbon management programs and procedures. The core CDP strategy has been to recruit institutional investors, who in turn pressurize companies in which they invest to embrace carbon disclosure. This strategy leverages disclosure to investors to pursue a broader agenda to reduce corporate GHG emissions through civil accountability. By 2009, CDP had signed up 475 investors with a total $55 trillion under management. Although CDP was conceived as a private, voluntary system, an implicit goal was to create the political space for regulatory initiatives and its relationship to such initiatives gives carbon disclosure a more hybrid character. Some three thousand organizations in sixty-six countries around the world now measure and disclose their emissions and climate strategies through CDP (PricewaterhouseCoopers 2010).

The GRI is a nonprofit organization that produces one of the most prevalent standards for sustainability or corporate social responsibility (CSR) reporting. The GRI seeks to standardize corporate sustainability reporting by making it routine and comparable to financial reporting. More than four thousand organizations from sixty countries now use GRI guidelines to produce and disclose sustainability reports.

Disclosure initiatives such as the GRI and CDP are emerging institutions that provide governance in the broad sense of the term, as a multilevel, multiactor system of rules, norms, and standards that structure and constrain a field of action (Mol 2008; Utting 2002). Disclosure has become an important institution of governance, raising awareness about climate change, clean energy, and energy efficiency, and promoting the principle of external accountability. Importantly, the rise of voluntary environmental disclosure has demonstrated to business the feasibility and potential benefits of environmental measurement and reporting, such as reputation management, relationships with stakeholders, and controlling energy costs.

In this chapter, addressing the hypotheses on transparency uptake and institutionalization stated in chapter 1, we argue, first, that organizations such as CDP and GRI have created pressures for democratization of governance through disclosure, yet corporate uptake of such disclosure is being driven by marketization. Second, in relation to the hypothesis on the institutionalization of transparency, we claim that political space has indeed opened up for new actors, but that state regulation is not entirely decentered. Indeed, we argue that these private initiatives have laid the technical and institutional groundwork for state-led regulatory initiatives that mandate disclosure and formalize carbon accounting standards. Finally, we consider the effectiveness of CDP and GRI, finding strong evidence that those disclosing non-financial information are not yet changing their core product and market strategies.

Carbon disclosure plays a role in three modes of governance: regulatory compliance, carbon trading and management, and civil regulation through transparency (see also Dingwerth and Eichinger, this book, chapter 10). First, carbon disclosure is critical for regulatory compliance. Companies subject to mandatory cap-and-trade programs need to measure their carbon emissions in order to ensure compliance. In 2009, the US Environmental Protection Agency issued a requirement that facilities emitting large quantities of GHGs collect emissions data and submit annual reports. Second, carbon information is integral to carbon markets and corporate carbon management. Carbon markets are emerging as a key form of governance, imposing emission caps and putting a price on carbon. Carbon accounting systems are also integral to corporate carbon management and assessment of carbon-related risks in equity and debt markets. Indeed, carbon as an intangible tradable commodity is constructed purely from specific informational protocols, necessitating the development of carbon accounting systems (Knox-Hayes 2010a). A third way in which carbon disclosure operates as governance is to exert pressure on organizations for accountability and performance. Standardized information can be used for benchmarking and ranking, providing a channel for transparency and accountability, and enabling NGOs and government agencies to demand certain performance levels, reward practices considered socially responsible, and exert pressure on poor performers (Fiorino 2006; Florini 2003; Mol 2008).

These different forms of disclosure and modes of governance imply different "institutional logics," the corporate logic of carbon risk management and carbon trading, and a logic of compliance and accountability oriented toward civil society and the state (Levy and Newell 2006). Although the corporate logic has accelerated the uptake of carbon disclosure, it raises questions about the trajectory along which disclosure initiatives are evolving and their ultimate impact. We argue that disclosure-based governance is drifting toward a corporate logic, partly due to the dominance in this field of auditors, accountants, and consultants, and the corporate interests that they represent (see also Auld and Gulbrandsen, this book, chapter 12).

Our analysis suggests that the success of disclosure as a new institution of governance requires a supportive economic context and that economic pressures therefore shape the evolution of disclosure scope and practices. The value of carbon disclosure to corporate actors, and their dominance in the coalition of actors developing disclosure mechanisms, steers disclosure toward corporate management's needs for internal carbon measurement, control, and trading. Although this corporate logic enhances the diffusion of disclosure, it also weakens its potential to generate substantial cuts in GHG emissions. As a result, the CDP, for one, is failing to deliver value to various stakeholders, with implications for the procedural and substantive effects of transparency in this instance.

Embracing Transparency

The Emergence of Disclosure as a Mode of Governance
From carbon trading to labor and environmental standards, we are witnessing the emergence of international institutions and sources of authority that touch many aspects of business operations. Governance by disclosure is implicated in these processes as well. These structures of global governance—rules, norms, codes of conduct, and standards—constrain, facilitate, and shape business behavior and the markets in which businesses operate (Haggard and Simmons 1987). Simultaneously, larger companies and industry associations are increasingly engaged in developing the structures and processes of global environmental governance, in collaboration as well as conflict with governmental agencies, multilateral institutions, and nongovernmental organizations (NGOs). Indeed, the increasing recognition that markets themselves are powerful mechanisms of global

environmental governance highlights the centrality of business within the complex fabric of environmental governance (Levy and Newell 2002).

Large firms, in their roles as investors, innovators, information providers, manufacturers, purchasers, lobbyists, and employers, are critical players in developing the architecture of global environmental governance. They coordinate extensive global value chains, shaping the geographic profile of production and environmental impacts (Gereffi et al. 2005). They are prominent in negotiating formal intergovernmental regimes, particularly within technical and economic advisory panels. Corporations participate in quasi-private policy bodies such as the Trans-Atlantic Business Dialogue, which are becoming increasingly influential in trade and investment policy (Coen 1999). They shape public debate through funding research centers, commissioning reports from consultants and NGOs, and through public relations campaigns. They participate in networks with private and public partners to establish standards, codes of conduct, and to promote particular technologies such as renewable energy. Large firms are also significant players in the institutional development of carbon emissions markets (Clark and Knox-Hayes 2011).

The production, research, and marketing practices of large firms thus play a key role in shaping environmental policies, standards, and impacts. The active corporate role in global environmental governance is increasingly welcomed by governments and international organizations, which are enticed by corporate resources and expertise and concerned about an international "governance deficit" (Falkner 2005; O'Brien et al. 2000). International economic integration, with its associated transnational environmental and social impacts, creates greater demand for coordinated responses that strain existing institutional capacity (Slaughter 2004).

The corporate role is legitimatized through the prevalence of neoliberal discourses of market-based solutions and competitiveness, complemented by (although sometimes in tension with) discourses of CSR and stakeholder dialogue. This has led to a notable shift in the relationship between business and NGOs around regulatory issues. From a position of clear antagonism, there is increasing emphasis on partnerships and institutionalized forms of collaboration (Newell 2001). Contemporary large firms are increasingly embedded in webs of relationships that provide varied forms of governance across wide areas of economic and social life. They are political actors, in the broad meaning of the term, blurring distinctions between market and nonmarket activities.

Carbon markets, for example, combine private and public initiatives to operationalize the reduction of emissions through the creation of standards and financial and legal instruments. Carbon is an intangible commodity and credits are constructed as the absence of emissions, to be sold as either emissions permits or reductions. A range of tangible resources, including forests and biodiversity, are now becoming connected to carbon markets as sources of emissions reduction. Transparency is a critical component of these emerging forms of environmental governance (see also Gupta et al., this book, chapter 8).

Carbon markets consist of two major components: (1) regulatory and political structures that establish the rules, property rights, and institutions of markets and (2) financial and services structures that transact and operate the market. Governments and other public agencies such as the European Commission and the Clean Development Mechanism (CDM) executive board create the regulatory structures. Large financial intermediaries create the financial components. In addition to compliance parties, other entities are becoming active and generating demand for emissions credits, seeking trading profits, reputational benefits, and knowledge about the markets. Key intermediary actors aggregate and exchange offsets and allowances for these parties, once the credits have been created and registered by the CDM executive board (as offsets) or the European Commission (as allowances).

Carbon aggregators originate the carbon projects in developing countries in partnership with leading firms and aggregate the credits from projects back into Europe. The aggregators will often transfer credits to investment banks and utilities, which provide most of the finance to develop the projects and then bring the credits to market through carbon brokerages and exchanges. Carbon brokerages link buyers and sellers of the credits. Exchanges provide a forum for buyers and sellers to meet but also hedge the delivery risk associated with trying to register credits through the CDM. Emissions markets are thus constructed by public and private agencies, and their governance is contested among these actors. Given the complexity of carbon markets, carbon measurement and disclosure serves to standardize and legitimate carbon accounting, thus playing a key role in structuring the governance of energy systems more broadly.

The Aims of Disclosure as a Mode of Governance

Environmental arenas such as the energy system are complex sociotechnical systems, and in this context, global environmental governance can be viewed as a multilevel and multiactor system of rules, standards, norms, and markets that stabilize these systems in particular ways. Governance does not necessarily guarantee an outcome that serves the public interest; indeed, the differential power and interests of key actors ensure that public interest is only one of many goals served by governance. A corollary is that governance is not an external superstructure that regulates a field from the *outside* (Smith and Sterling 2006); rather, it comprises the actors, relationships, and processes that shape the functioning and structures of a field. Governance systems are integrated economic, political, and discursive systems in which market and political power are intertwined. In this way, disclosure functions to reinforce the sovereignty and legitimacy of corporations as dominant players in complex governance systems (Mason, this book, chapter 4; Mol, this book, chapter 2).

The Gramscian concept of hegemony is useful to describe the contingent stability that global environmental governance brings as well as the potential for actors to contest (and collaborate) over system governance and the distribution of benefits. Hegemony refers to a state of relative order based on an alliance of dominant players and an alignment of political, economic, and discursive forces. The notion of hegemony, in this sense, is similar to the concept of field stabilization in organizational theory (Levy and Scully 2007), and conveys a degree of consent to a negotiated outcome. Global environmental governance arenas resemble contested organizational fields in which actors struggle over the construction of economic relationships, institutional rules and norms, and discursive frames (Maguire et al. 2004; Rao et al. 2000).

This concept of hegemony as contingent stability is well illustrated by the inertia evident in the carbon intensity of global energy and transportation systems. Unruh (2000, 818) uses the term *carbon lock-in* to refer to the "interlocking technological, institutional and social forces ... that perpetuate fossil fuel-based infrastructures in spite of their known environmental externalities." Lock-in is, in part, an economic and technological phenomenon. Incumbent firms have substantial capabilities and assets tied to existing technologies, and benefit from a variety of barriers to entry relating to infrastructure, branding, patents, and economies of scale that protect them from low-carbon competitive threats. Stable governance systems have an important economic dimension and are predicated on "business models" that secure the participation of various actors by generating profits for firms and investors, wages for labor, taxes and economic growth for governments, and demand from consumers.

The economic and technological advantages of the fossil fuel–based system are reinforced by its political structure, a powerful array of organizations that Unruh calls a "techno-institutional complex," including unions, standards organizations, business associations, and governmental agencies that frequently align their interests with the sectors they regulate and support. The political influence of fossil fuel–related industry associations is legendary, of course (Gelbspan 1997; Leggett 2000; Levy and Egan 2003). The political economy of the network thus shapes the structures of property rights, land use, labor law, environmental policies, trade and investment policy, and subsidies (Goodell 2006). Lock-in has also affected the development of climate governance systems such as the emissions trading systems, locking their geography and operations into existing market centers and financial networks (Clark and Knox-Hayes 2011; Knox-Hayes 2009).

The emergence of private actors such as firms and NGOs, as well as the scientific communities in global governance, has been generally, though not uniformly, welcomed. The diffusion of authority is widely perceived to represent a positive development that promises greater democracy, accountability, and capacity to solve problems requiring collective action at the international level (Lipschutz 2005; Slaughter 2004). Keck and Sikkink (1998) argue that the networks constructed by economic actors, firms, scientists, and activists multiply channels of political access and make international resources available to actors in domestic struggles, helping to level the playing field. The participation of civil society led Murphy and Bendell (1999) to coin the term *civil regulation* to refer to the pressure for business to comply with norms and standards advocated by civil society actors. As they put it, "We believe that civil society organizations are also playing significant roles in promoting environmental and social management. The evidence of anti-logging, anti-oil and anti-child labor protests illustrates that NGOs are increasingly setting the political agenda within which business must work" (Murphy and Bendell 1999, 57).

The prominence of business actors in global environmental governance has also provoked critics to highlight the corporate-economic logic of private governance. As Cutler et al. (1999, 3) observe, "a significant degree of global order is provided by individual firms that agree to cooperate, either formally or informally, in establishing an international framework for their economic activity." These frameworks increasingly comprise voluntary private informational systems, such as the 4C industry code for coffee (Kolk 2005), standards for social and environmental reporting such as the Global Reporting Initiative and Carbon Disclosure Project, or product-labeling standards such as the Forestry Stewardship Council (Dauvergne 2005). Cutler et al. use the term *private regime* to refer to "an integrated complex of formal and informal institutions that is a source of governance for an economic issue area as a whole" (1999, 9). They express concern with the blurring of boundaries between the state and private authority and the tendency toward privatization of governance within a corporate logic.

Corporations often prefer more private forms of governance because self-regulation can serve to accommodate external pressures, construct the firm corporation as a moral agent (DeWinter 2001; Marchand 1998), deflect the threat of regulation, and marginalize more radical activists (Shamir 2004). These tensions in global environmental governance between democratic accountability and a more private, corporate managerialism are not mere academic debates but also represent active contestation over governance. As the corporate logic of governance establishes its precedence, accounting firms and consultants play a considerable role in shaping and managing discourse (Auld and Gulbrandsen 2010). The increasing dominance of a corporate logic in information disclosure is thus unsurprising, given that it resides within a wider "transnational space" of financial, corporate, and state governance that is constituted and structured by transnational elites, institutions, and ideologies (Faist 2000). For Morgan (2001, 118), this transnational space comprises transnational corporations, regulatory agencies, and cognitive and normative frameworks, which "have to be conceptualized in terms of the interplay between top-down projects of transnationalism, pursued by powerful actors, and bottom-up processes of mutual identification and collective awareness."

Institutionalizing Transparency

Information as Governance in the GRI and CDP

The institutionalization of standardized nonfinancial reporting systems, such as the GRI and the CDP, is a key element of global environmental governance, and serves a number of governance functions. For nascent institutions such as carbon markets, the creation of standards is essential to regulate market inconsistencies, improve comparability across companies and sectors, establish clear price signals and ensure better compliance. Standards such as the Gold Standard for carbon offsets help to ensure that carbon offsets meet additionality criteria and are accounted for consistently. The offsets are based on the assumption of carbon baselines that "would have otherwise happened." As such, the reductions produced by offsetting cannot actually be demonstrated. They must be assumed and can easily be generated with incomplete or unreliable data. Standards such as the Gold Standard ensure that the offsets are generated with the best practices of monitoring, verifying, and reporting. In short, the standards enhance the commensurability of offsets by ensuring that the information they contain has greater integrity.

Information disclosure can be viewed as a pervasive mode of power that emanates from the constitutive and disciplinary effects of discourse (Hewson and Sinclair 1999). Nonfinancial reporting thus represents a set of discursive texts and practices that construct corporate and NGO subjectivity, promoting CSR as a domain of legitimate action. Practices of social auditing and reporting represent a form of discipline that functions to standardize, rank, and categorize performance. For Foucault, this moment of "examination" represents "a normalizing gaze, a surveillance that makes it possible to qualify, to classify and to punish" (1977, 184). The specific form taken by these standards and reporting mechanisms reflects their discursive lineage from corporate financial accounting systems and their embeddedness in wider structures of governance.

Nonfinancial reporting, as a mode of governance in which private, voluntary efforts are prominent, also presents the same tensions and contested logics that characterize the growing importance of private actors in global environmental governance more generally. Advocates view information disclosure as a logic of "civil regulation," a mechanism to improve democratic accountability and empower civil society groups to play a more active and assertive role in corporate issue-level governance. The success of the 1987 Toxic Release Inventory in reducing toxic emissions from industrial plants in the United States is often cited to support this approach (Graham 2002). Corporate managers, by contrast, tend to emphasize the logic of "sustainability management," highlighting the instrumental value of social reporting to corporate management, the investor community, as well as auditing and consulting firms. These tensions are evident in GRI and CDP (Knox-Hayes and Levy 2011; Levy et al. 2010).

Strategic Intervention in a Governance Field

The actors who founded and promoted GRI and CDP conceived these initiatives as deliberate interventions in the field of social and environmental reporting. Indeed, some GRI supporters saw the goal as not just changing corporate practice but, more fundamentally, shifting the balance of power in corporate governance and related arenas toward civil society. The explicit goal of GRI was to harmonize the practice of nonfinancial reporting, thereby empowering various societal actors. The 1997 draft paper stated, "The GRI vision is to improve corporate accountability by ensuring that all stakeholders—communities, environmentalists, labour, religious groups, shareholders, investment managers—have access to standardized, comparable, and consistent environmental information akin to corporate financial reporting. Only in this fashion will we be able to: (1) use the capital markets to promote and ensure sustainable business practices; (2) measure companies' adherence to standards set from Ceres principles; and (3) empower NGOs around the globe with the information they need to hold corporations accountable" (Ceres 1997).

Disclosure initiatives such as CDP and GRI were thus conceived as nonconfrontational strategies that could develop collaborative partnerships to serve mutual interests, and shifting norms, focusing managerial attention, and mobilizing pressure from investors, peers, and activists for companies to change their norms and practices. The NGOs promoting information disclosure appear to have understood the dangers of a direct confrontation with well-entrenched global environmental governance systems encompassing powerful actors and rooted belief systems. Instead, they pursued what Gramsci termed a *war of position,* a dynamic long-term strategy to gain legitimacy and win new allies.

The entrepreneurs behind these disclosure initiatives employed several strategies to negotiate the tensions between the logics of civil regulation and corporate environmental performance. First, they relied on the ascendant win-win logic of corporate environmentalism and CSR, in which interests are congruent rather than conflictual, to frame nonfinancial reporting as mutually beneficial. Notably, the groups behind these initiatives did not pitch the value of disclosure just in terms of their own agendas of increasing corporate accountability. Rather, they forged a wider coalition, including powerful business and financial actors, and attempted to appeal to the diverse interests and goals of these actors. In Gramscian terms, information disclosure constructs and promotes the common interest, facilitating the emergence of a governance system with a hegemonic alliance of actors.

To meet the goals of these diverse stakeholders, CDP emphasized somewhat different facets and functions of carbon disclosure. For financial actors, carbon disclosure was described as analogous to financial accounting and an extension of corporate social and environmental reporting, activities that already have widespread legitimacy, clear authority structures, and recognized benefits for multiple groups. Accounting and consulting firms also realized that social and environmental reporting potentially represented a vast new market for measuring, reporting, and

auditing nonfinancial information. For business audiences, CDP emphasized the potential financial benefits from energy savings and good public
relations and the standardized yet voluntary nature of disclosure, which
provides flexible implementation with lower compliance costs and little
legal exposure. Investors were enticed with the claim that carbon disclosure would assist in valuing financial assets by revealing the degree of
climate risk. To appeal to NGOs and multilateral organizations such as
UNEP, the emphasis was placed on improving corporate accountability
and creating more inclusive and transparent governance mechanisms.

Despite the rapid uptake of carbon disclosure, there remain troubling
questions about the trajectory along which the institution is evolving and
its ultimate impact. Tensions exist between the two "institutional logics"
of marketization and democratization—a corporate logic of carbon risk
management and carbon trading and an NGO-oriented logic based on
transparency and accountability. We argue that the field is drifting toward a more corporate logic, and that although this enhances the diffusion of disclosure, it also weakens it as a tool for driving the substantial
cuts in greenhouse gas emissions needed to address climate change. Our
analysis also highlights that building new institutions requires not just
discursive strategies to frame issues in a particular way but also political
and economic strategies to construct an organizational coalition and a
"business model" for the new institution (Knox-Hayes 2010b; Levy and
Scully 2007).

Effects of Transparency

A Corporate Logic in Information Disclosure

Though information disclosure is a contested field of governance, the
corporate logic of "sustainability management" increasingly pervades the
field. This is likely due to the power balance among the actors in the field
as well as the strategic compromises adopted by advocates of information
disclosure. The stakeholders who derive the most tangible economic benefits from nonfinancial reporting initiatives such as GRI and CDP are the
auditors, consultants, and certifiers of corporate social performance reports. Traditional accountancy firms, who lost substantial chunks of their
consulting business in the wake of the Enron and WorldCom scandals
and ensuing financial regulation, have been eager to develop the market
for nonfinancial information systems, auditing, and reporting. PricewaterhouseCoopers and KPMG have been the main competitors in this market segment, which emphasizes the verification of managerial processes

and reports but does not generally attempt to *assess* sustainability performance. Nonprofit consultancies, such as AccountAbility and Forum for the Future, provide a broader range of services to companies related to improving, measuring, and assessing their social and environmental performance.

The GRI founders understood from the beginning the strategic potential for enrolling auditors and consultants, and they have remained among its most active participants and supporters. Carbon disclosure has likewise attracted the attention of accounting and consulting firms, and has spawned a number of more specialized software firms who develop corporate carbon management systems. Recently, larger and more established business information firms have acquired some carbon software firms, suggesting their mainstream acceptance. Actors who benefit from financialization of carbon credits thus enjoy considerable power in structuring carbon information systems and enjoy a privileged position in carbon governance (Bumpus and Liverman 2008; Knox-Hayes and Levy 2011).

Activists and nongovernmental organizations, by contrast, appear to be losing interest in nonfinancial reporting as a strategic lever. Levy et al. (2010) report that at the 2008 GRI annual meeting only sixty participants represented NGOs and four represented labor out of a total of one thousand or more attendees. The information in GRI reports is generally not particularly useful for activist campaigns because much of it is qualitative and difficult to compare across sectors and firms. Similarly, carbon disclosure is moving toward a format supporting mandatory compliance and corporate management's needs for internal carbon measurement and control over energy costs. CDP is losing ground to corporate carbon and energy software systems, because CDP reports carbon emissions data as organizational aggregates, which are not useful for managers who need to control energy costs at the facility and process level.

Moreover, aggregate data are hard to interpret across different industrial sectors and are not particularly useful for either investors or NGOs. In addition to quantitative disclosure of emissions, CDP reports use a narrative format to portray the extent to which firms are conducting carbon inventories, preparing for trading, investing in mitigation technologies, and establishing managerial responsibilities. Nevertheless, companies are still wary that CDP represents an activist agenda. Despite the talk of information disclosure initiatives representing multistakeholder initiatives, the information systems are increasingly shaped by accounting and consulting firms to address the needs of client companies for reputation and risk management and improved operational efficiency.

Disclosure's Transformative Potential

Although nonfinancial reporting has not transformed global environmental governance or corporate practice, it has scored important strategic gains that should be acknowledged. It has generated legitimacy for the principle of disclosure and accountability to external stakeholders and increased the visibility and voice of environmental advocates inside and outside corporations and among multilateral institutions. The carbon disclosure movement, in particular, has generated considerable momentum toward the formalization of carbon accounting standards, which are crossing over into the regulatory apparatus of agencies such as the Securities and Exchange Commission and the Environmental Protection Agency. Perhaps most important, carbon disclosure has demonstrated the feasibility and potential benefits of carbon management to policy makers and business, shifting the field of play and opening political space for further action.

Despite the widespread enthusiasm for private modes of governance, there are clearly some major limitations. The effectiveness of voluntary disclosure systems is weakened by the focus on managerial processes rather than outcomes, the lack of comparability across firms and sectors, and the lack of sanctions for noncompliance (Gupta 2008; Mason 2008). Gupta (2008, 5) notes, for example, that information is not neutral: the political economy of nonfinancial reporting leads to "conflicts over the source and nature of disclosed information, differing perceptions of its accessibility, usability, affordability and comprehensibility." Mason (2008, 10) cautions that "the normative agenda here, often un-examined, is the scaling back of mandatory environmental regulation (nationally and internationally), the privatization of environmental resources, and the framing of information disclosure options in terms of individual lifestyle." The dominant position of business and finance in information disclosure exemplifies Barley's (2007, 214) concern about the "privatization of functions that have historically been the mandate of local, state, and federal governments."

Carbon disclosure, for example, attempts to institutionalize best practices on the assumption that companies will then manage and reduce their emissions. Even more than with financial accounting systems, carbon measurement and reporting has sufficient flexibility to shield companies from strong forms of accountability. Crucially, the institutionalization of carbon reporting relies on a successful project of "commensuration," defined by Levin and Espeland (2002, 121) as "the transformation of qualitative relations into quantities on a common metric." Just as financial reporting translates myriad activities into a common monetary metric, so carbon reporting renders complex operations involving multiple gases, sources, and impacts into a common carbon metric, tCO_2e (tonnes of carbon dioxide equivalent). The commodification of carbon requires an extensive organizational infrastructure to define carbon units, allocate property rights, and establish rules for trading (Knox-Hayes 2009).

These rules and procedures are not just technical but also political questions. For example, the CO_2 produced by driving cars could be attributed to oil producers, refiners, the car manufacturer, or the final consumer. The release of a draft GHG Protocol in December 2009 for scope 3 emissions (activities upstream and downstream of the value chain) generated considerable concern in the business community. Although it was simple to agree, in principle, that carbon disclosure was a good idea, the devil is in the details. Companies are apprehensive about the complexity and costs, and about the implicit principle that they are responsible for emissions beyond their direct control. For one thing, companies often report on their home country or main markets, but are unsure of how to report global operations or data for the full range of business units. Second, the world's largest polluters have the expertise to conduct scope 3 reporting in-house, whereas smaller companies likely do not have the necessary resources or expertise (Balch 2009).

Emissions-trading systems such as the European Union Emissions Trading Scheme (EU-ETS) have done much to increase awareness of the carbon economy, but in the absence of a significant carbon price, with consumers who are apathetic or confused and investors unsure about the relevance of carbon information, carbon disclosure systems do not necessarily translate into substantial reductions. Indeed, this is acknowledged in a 2009 CDP report. This report highlighted a "carbon chasm" between national targets of GHG reductions between 15 to 30 percent by 2020 and the carbon commitments of the S&P 100, the one hundred largest companies based in the United States, which average an increase of about 4 percent over the same time period (Carbon Disclosure Project 2009). The lack of standardization or regulatory oversight in carbon markets has also created significant allegations of abuse and fraud that have plagued the EU-ETS and the CDM.

Conclusion

In sum, as the preceding discussion suggests, the very strategies that have enabled the successful launch of nonfinancial reporting systems contain tensions, contradictions, and compromises in the relationship between democratization and marketization as drivers of disclosure, which thus emerge as significant constraints that circumscribe more systematic transformation. The strategy of promoting win-win discourses and positioning nonfinancial reporting as an extension of financial accounting has helped to win powerful corporate allies and gain mainstream acceptance, but it has also resulted in the dominance of corporate actors and a market-oriented managerialist logic to disclosure, at the expense of more democratically oriented institutions and practices. This does not mean that the strategy was misconceived. Nonfinancial reporting would have made little progress had it directly challenged the primacy of profit maximization, the legal rights of shareholders, or the conventional corporate governance structure that excludes representatives of the community, the environment, or labor. The strategy recognizes instead that it is easier to create change within nested subsystems than within entrenched and resilient broader institutions of capitalism, particularly financial markets and legal structures of corporate governance.

If so, NGOs wishing to effect fundamental changes in the structures of global environmental governance face a difficult dilemma. The success of nonfinancial reporting is counterbalanced by the risk of cooptation and assimilation within these structures rather than success in transforming them. This does appear to be the emerging outcome. Companies are frequently willing to embrace nonfinancial reporting as a demonstration of their social concern, but have proven unwilling to tolerate a system that imposes democratic accountability by providing clear measures and rankings of their social and environmental performances (on this, see also Dingwerth and Eichinger, this book, chapter 10). As we have argued in this chapter, voluntary disclosure systems are limited by their focus on managerial process, the lack of comparability across firms, and the lack of sanctions for noncompliance. As disclosure shifts from an NGO-oriented logic that emphasizes accountability toward a corporate logic emphasizing managerial control, questions pertaining to the underlying merits of carbon disclosure and its effectiveness as a governance system remain. Nonfinancial reporting does not yet seem to affect core product or market strategies. Even so, the terrain of disclosure-based governance is shifting, leading to new possibilities and challenges.

References

Auld, Graeme, and Lars Gulbrandsen. 2010. Transparency in Nonstate Certification: Consequences for Accountability and Legitimacy. *Global Environmental Politics* 10 (3):97–119.

Balch, Oliver. 2009. Carbon Accounting—Emissions Disclosure Stacking Up. *Ethical Corporation News Articles*, July 21. Available at http://www.wbcsd.org/Plugins/DocSearch/details.asp?ObjectId=MzUxMzA, last accessed October 15, 2010.

Barley, Stephen R. 2007. Corporations, Democracy, and the Public Good. *Journal of Management Inquiry* 16 (3):201–215.

Bumpus, Adam G., and Diana M. Liverman. 2008. Accumulation by Decarbonization and the Governance of Carbon Offsets. *Economic Geography* 84 (2):127–155.

Carbon Disclosure Project. 2009. *The Carbon Chasm*. London: Carbon Disclosure Project. Available at https://www.cdproject.net/CDPResults/65_329_219_CDP-The-Carbon-Chasm-Final.pdf.

Ceres. 1997. *Global Reporting Initiative Concept Paper*. Unpublished working paper. Boston: Ceres.

Clark, Jennifer, and Janelle Knox-Hayes. 2011. *An Emerging Geography of Intangible Assets: Financialization in Carbon Emissions Credit and Intellectual Property Markets*. School of Public Policy Working Paper Series, 66. Atlanta: Georgia Institute of Technology.

Coen, David. 1999. The Impact of U.S. Lobbying Practice on the European Business-Government Relationship. *California Management Review* 41 (4):27–44.

Cutler, Claire A., Virginia Haufler, and Tony Porter, eds. 1999. *Private Authority and International Affairs*. Albany, NY: SUNY Press.

Dauvergne, Peter. 2005. The Environmental Challenge to Loggers in the Asia-Pacific: Corporate Practices in Informal Regimes of Governance. In *The Business of Global Environmental Governance*, ed. David L. Levy and Peter J. Newell. Cambridge, MA: MIT Press.

DeWinter, Rebecca. 2001. The Anti-Sweatshop Movement: Constructing Corporate Moral Agency in the Global Apparel Industry. *Ethics & International Affairs* 15 (2):99–115.

Faist, Thomas. 2000. *The Volume and Dynamics of International Migration and Transnational Social Spaces*. Oxford: Oxford University Press.

Falkner, Robert. 2005. The Business of Ozone Layer Protection: Corporate Power in Regime Evolution. In *The Business of Global Environmental Governance*, ed. David L. Levy and Peter J. Newell. Cambridge, MA: MIT Press.

Fiorino, Daniel J. 2006. *The New Environmental Regulation*. Cambridge, MA: MIT Press.

Florini, Ann. 2003. *The Coming Democracy: New Rules for Running a New World*. Washington, DC: Island Press.

Foucault, Michel. 1977. *Discipline and Punish: The Birth of the Prison.* New York: Random House.

Gelbspan, Ross. 1997. *The Heat Is On.* Reading, MA: Addison Wesley.

Gereffi, Gary, John Humphery, and Timothy Sturgeon. 2005. The Governance of Global Value Chains. *Review of International Political Economy* 12 (1):78–104.

Goodell, Jeff. 2006. *Big Coal: The Dirty Secret behind America's Energy Future.* Boston: Houghton Mifflin.

Graham, Mary. 2002. *Democracy by Disclosure: The Rise of Technopopulism.* Washington, DC: Brookings Institution Press.

Gupta, Aarti. 2008. Transparency under Scrutiny: Information Disclosure in Global Environmental Governance. *Global Environmental Politics* 8 (2):1–7.

Haggard, Stephan, and Beth A. Simmons. 1987. Theories of International Regimes. *International Organization* 41 (3):491–517.

Hewson, Martin, and Timothy J. Sinclair, eds. 1999. *Approaches to Global Governance Theory.* Albany: SUNY Press.

Keck, Margaret E., and Kathryn Sikkink, eds. 1998. *Activists beyond Borders: Advocacy Networks in International Politics.* Ithaca, NY: Cornell University Press.

Knox-Hayes, Janelle. 2009. The Developing Carbon Financial Service Industry: Expertise, Adaptation and Complementarity in London and New York. *Journal of Economic Geography* 9 (6):749–778.

Knox-Hayes, Janelle. 2010a. Constructing Carbon Market Spacetime: Climate Change and the Onset of Neo-modernity. *Annals of the Association of American Geographers* 100 (4):953–962.

Knox-Hayes, Janelle. 2010b. Creating the Carbon Market Institution: Analysis of the Organizations and Relationships That Build the Market. *Competition and Change* 14 (3–4):174–201.

Knox-Hayes, Janelle, and David L. Levy. 2011. The Politics of Carbon Disclosure as Climate Governance. *Strategic Organization* 9 (1):1–9.

Kolk, Ans. 2005. Corporate Social Responsibility in the Coffee Sector: The Dynamics of MNC Responses and Code Development. *European Management Journal* 23 (2):228–236.

Leggett, Jeremy. 2000. *The Carbon War: Dispatches from the End of the Oil Century.* London: Penguin Books.

Levin, Peter, and Wendy N. Espeland. 2002. Pollution Futures: Commensuration Commodification and the Market for Air. In *Organizations, Policy and the Natural Environment: Institutional and Strategic Perspectives,* ed. A. J. Hoffman and M. J. Ventresca, 119–147. Stanford: Stanford University Press.

Levy, David, and Maureen Scully. 2007. The Institutional Entrepreneur as Modern Prince: The Strategic Face of Power in Contested Fields. *Organization Studies* 28 (7):971–991.

Levy, David L., Halina S. Brown, and Martin de Jong. 2010. The Contested Politics of Corporate Governance: The Case of the Global Reporting Initiative. *Business & Society* 49 (1):88–115.

Levy, David L., and Daniel Egan. 2003. A Neo-Gramscian Approach to Corporate Political Strategy: Conflict and Accommodation in the Climate Change Negotiations. *Journal of Management Studies* 40 (4):803–830.

Levy, David L., and Peter Newell. 2002. Business Strategy and International Environmental Governance: Toward a Neo-Gramscian Synthesis. *Global Environmental Politics* 2 (4):84–101.

Levy, David L., and Peter Newell. 2006. Multinationals in Global Governance. In *Transformations in Global Governance: Implications for Multinationals and Other Stakeholders*, ed. Sushil Vachani. London: Edward Elgar.

Lipschutz, Ronnie. 2005. *Regulation for the Rest of Us: Globalization, Governmentality and Global Politics*. London: Routledge.

Maguire, Steve, Cynthia Hardy, and Thomas B. Lawrence. 2004. Institutional Entrepreneurship in Emerging Fields: HIV/AIDS Treatment Advocacy in Canada. *Academy of Management Journal* 47 (5):657–679.

Marchand, Roland. 1998. *Creating the Corporate Soul: The Rise of Public Relations and Corporate Imagery in American Big Business*. Berkeley: University of California Press.

Mason, Michael. 2008. Transparency for Whom? Information Disclosure and Power in Global Environmental Governance. *Global Environmental Politics* 8 (2):8–13.

Mol, Arthur P. J. 2008. *Environmental Reform in the Information Age: The Contours of Informational Governance*. Cambridge, UK: Cambridge University Press.

Morgan, Glenn. 2001. Transnational Communities and Business Systems. *Global Networks* 1 (2):113–130.

Murphy, David F., and Jem Bendell. 1999. *Partners in Time? Business, NGOs, and Sustainable Development*. Geneva: United Nations Research Institute for Social Development.

Newell, Peter. 2001. Environmental NGOs, TNCs, and the Question of Governance. In *The International Political Economy of the Environment*, ed. Dimitris Stevis and Valerie J. Assetto. Boulder, CO: Lynne Rienner.

O'Brien, Robert, Anne Marie Goetz, Jan Aart Scholte, and Marc Williams. 2000. *Contesting Global Governance: Multilateral Economic Institutions and Global Social Movements*. Cambridge, UK: Cambridge University Press.

PricewaterhouseCoopers. 2010. *Carbon Disclosure Project 2010: Global 500 Report*. Available at https://www.cdproject.net/CDPResults/CDP-2010-G500.pdf.

Rao, Hayagreeva, Calvin Morill, and Mayer N. Zald. 2000. Power Plays: How Social Movements and Collective Action Create New Organizational Forms. *Research in Organizational Behavior* 22:239–282.

Shamir, Ronen. 2004. The De-Radicalization of Corporate Social Responsibility. *Critical Sociology* 30 (3):669–689.

Slaughter, Anne-Marie. 2004. *A New World Order*. Princeton, NJ: Princeton University Press.

Smith, Adrian, and Andy Sterling. 2006. *Moving Inside or Outside? Positioning the Governance of Sociotechnical Systems.* SPRU Electronic Working Paper Series.

Unruh, Gregory C. 2000. Understanding Carbon Lock-In. *Energy Policy* 28 (12):817–830.

Utting, Peter, ed. 2002. *Voluntary Approaches to Corporate Responsibility.* Geneva: United Nations Non-Governmental Liaison Service.

10

Tamed Transparency and the Global Reporting Initiative: The Role of Information Infrastructures

Klaus Dingwerth and Margot Eichinger

The politics of information disclosure are often associated with high hopes.[1] Disclosed information is expected to improve environmental performance, "thicken" democracy, and/or empower a broad range of stakeholders vis-à-vis corporations (for an overview, see Gupta and Mason, this book, chapter 1; Mol, this book, chapter 2). In this article, we investigate the "empowerment thesis" in relation to the Global Reporting Initiative (GRI), a private transnational institution that explicitly aims to improve the quality of corporate sustainability disclosure. In doing so, we build on our earlier research on GRI disclosure (Dingwerth and Eichinger 2010), wherein we introduced the notion of *tamed transparency* and argued that the transformative potential of transparency as practiced in the GRI remained unfulfilled—and hence tamed—in several ways. First, the GRI remained ambivalent in its transparency language. More precisely, it failed to specify what constitutes transparency and what purposes transparency is meant to serve. Second, the information that different corporations disclosed in their GRI reports was largely not comparable. It was therefore of limited value for report users. Third, the information infrastructure surrounding the GRI remained weak. In contrast to disclosure schemes such as the US-based Toxic Release Inventory, few civil society actors gathered around the GRI to translate the data contained (and often hidden) in sustainability reports into more valuable, accessible, comprehensible, and comparable—in short, into more actionable—information.

In this chapter, we extend our analysis of the GRI as a prime example of "tamed" rather than "targeted" transparency. We do so by developing further our argument regarding information structures and intermediaries surrounding GRI disclosure. More specifically, we go beyond an analysis of how *civil society* intermediaries use (or do not use) the information provided through GRI reports to consider the role of *commercial* intermediaries as well. In so doing, our interest here is in analyzing the broader *information infrastructure* within which the GRI, as one of the major sites of the transparency turn (Gupta and Mason, this book, chapter 1) in global environmental politics, is embedded.

We do so in three broad steps. First, we briefly introduce the GRI and its place in the wider transparency turn. Second, we summarize—and update when appropriate—the empirical findings of our earlier study in relation to the transparency rhetoric and policies of the GRI and the comparability of actual GRI reports. Third, we discuss the extent to which two different types of commercial intermediaries—namely, financial investment consultancies such as *IW Financial* and *MSCI* and consumer-oriented "for-benefit" corporations such as *GoodGuide*—contribute to making GRI-based information more valuable, accessible, comprehensible, and comparable. Our discussion shows that commercial intermediaries do make GRI reports more useful and add pressure on corporations to disclose more information about their social and environmental performance. At the same time, such "marketization" of transparency narrows the scope for noncommercial organizations. It makes it difficult for them to enter the field of information intermediaries with their own visions of how and to what end corporate transparency should be organized.

Embracing Transparency

The GRI was established as an independent nongovernmental organization in 2002 and is headquartered in Amsterdam, the Netherlands. It aims to develop and promote a coherent framework for nonfinancial reporting by corporations. To this end, the GRI regularly updates its *Sustainability Reporting Guidelines* in complex, multistakeholder processes that include the participation of business, organized civil society, labor, consultancies, academics, and representatives of governmental as well as intergovernmental organizations.[2]

The *Sustainability Reporting Guidelines* are at the core of the GRI reporting framework. We analyze the G3 (third generation) of these guidelines in this article. The G3 are composed of reporting principles and performance indicators. The *reporting principles* define the report content and quality and provide guidance on how to determine the boundary of a report. The *performance indicators* specify which aspects of an organization's activities and impacts are to be covered. The indicators embrace different substantive areas, including economic and environmental impacts, impacts on labor practices and human rights, and the broader issue of product responsibility. Examples include the economic indicator EC 4

"Significant financial assistance received from government"; the environmental indicator EN 15 "Number of IUCN Red List species and national conservation list species with habitats in areas affected by operations, by level of extinction risk"; and the labor relations indicator LA 14 "Ratio of basic salary and remuneration of women to men by employee category, by significant locations of operations" (Global Reporting Initiative 2011). Finally, the reporting principles and performance indicators are complemented by *indicator protocols* that specify how data on particular indicators are to be calculated and presented and by *sector supplements* that detail the reporting needs for a range of business sectors, including the automotive industry, the financial services sector, and airports (see table 10.1).

Reporting organizations are required to declare one of three *application levels*. Reports receive an A if they include information on all indicators of the G3 and the relevant sector supplement, as well as a statement on the company's management approach to each indicator category. The level B is awarded for organizations that report on a minimum of twenty indicators as well as on their management approaches for the different indicator categories. C signifies that a report covers at least ten indicators but not necessarily a statement on a corporation's management approaches. The status of plus (+) may be added to the application level, indicating that the report has been "externally assured." External assurance providers assess the quality of the report and the information contained within it.

In terms of *relevance,* the GRI is commonly regarded as the world's leading voluntary scheme for corporate nonfinancial reporting. In 2011, 95 percent of the 250 largest global companies reported on their activities (KPMG International 2011, 7). Eighty percent of them applied the GRI guidelines, thereby consolidating GRI's position as a global standard for CSR reporting (KPMG International 2011, 21). Moreover, a range of governments have either encouraged GRI reporting or established regulations based on the GRI framework, thus providing at least a thin "shadow of hierarchy" for the GRI and its regulatory framework (e.g., Commission of the European Communities 2002, 14; King Committee on Corporate Governance 2002, section 5; Global Reporting Initiative 2012a).

Institutionalizing Transparency

In the following, we briefly summarize the main findings of our earlier analysis of the GRI's *rhetoric* and *policies* on transparency and of the

Table 10.1
Elements of the GRI Reporting Framework

Element	Function	Example(s)
Reporting principles	To define the report content and quality	Content: materiality, stakeholder inclusiveness, sustainability context, completeness Quality: balance, comparability, accuracy, timeliness, reliability, clarity
Indicators	To define the areas in which organizations are asked to report and the measures to use	EN 15 "Number of IUCN Red List species and national conservation list species with habitats in areas affected by operations, by level of extinction risk"
Indicator protocols	To provide guidance for reporting on individual indicators	Indicator protocols set economic, indicator protocols set environmental, indicator protocols set human rights, indicator protocols set labor, indicator protocols set product responsibility, indicator protocols set society
Sector supplements	Provide guidance for individual industry sectors	Electric utilities sector supplement, automotive sector supplement, mining and metals sector supplement, NGO sector supplement
Application level	Defines how closely the reporting framework has been followed in the preparation of a report	Level B: an organization has reported on at least twenty indicators and on their management approaches for the different indicator categories

actual comparability of GRI reports (Dingwerth and Eichinger 2010). Our analysis provides support for the hypothesis on institutionalization, presented in chapter 1 of this book (Gupta and Mason), in that GRI decision-making on transparency is not state-led and has opened up political space for new actors. However, we also demonstrate that the transparency generated by the GRI is "tamed" at all three levels of rhetoric, policies, and comparability of reports.

Rhetoric

From its very beginning, the GRI has made transparency the anchor of its public communication. At the inauguration of the GRI in 2002, for instance, high-level speakers from international organizations, trade unions, business, and academia emphasized in their ceremonial statements the transformative power of information that would be generated by an organization such as the GRI (Global Reporting Initiative 2002). Beyond grand claims in support of transparency, the notion is also central to the everyday communication of the GRI, for example, when conferences or board declarations are titled "The Amsterdam Global Conference on Sustainability and Transparency" or the "Amsterdam Declaration on Transparency and Reporting." Yet, although virtually all GRI communications revolve around the term *transparency*, the organization commonly refrains from explicitly defining it. One exception is the *Sustainability Reporting Guidelines* in which transparency is said to refer to "the complete disclosure of information on the topics and Indicators required to reflect impacts and enable stakeholders to make decisions, and the processes, procedures, and assumptions used to prepare those disclosures" (Global Reporting Initiative 2011, 6).

Here, transparency is centered on the desire of stakeholders to make informed decisions and on the notion that the choices stakeholders make differ from those they would make if they had information that was more complete. Because transparency is linked to personal autonomy, it becomes a normatively loaded term. It requires those organizations that have relevant economic, environmental, social, or other impacts to "completely disclose" all information that stakeholders need to make a decision to buy or not to buy, to invest or not to invest, or to collectively organize against a company or refrain from doing so.

Yet this normatively demanding definition of transparency only vaguely informs other communications of the GRI. Our analysis reveals instead a heterogeneous communicative practice in which the GRI presents at least four different uses and justifications for transparency. Only one of these is based on the previously mentioned definition; moreover, this particular use of transparency as *inherently valuable* rarely appears in GRI communications that deal with the corporate sector (as opposed to communications dealing with public agencies or civil society organizations). The other three uses refer to transparency as *instrumental,* as *somehow related to sustainability,* or as an *element of contemporary world culture* and provide very different rationalities for subscribing to transparency. In the *instrumental justification,* transparency is simply advertised as useful for reporting organizations, either because information disclosure helps to identify potentials for efficiency gains or because particular audiences on whose support an organization depends demand it. Essentially, disclosure is a business practice that is reasonable because (and hence only as long as) there is a "business case" for it.

The communications that *relate transparency to sustainability* remain most elusive about what constitutes transparency and why it is useful. Here, transparency is portrayed as a logical precondition, a corollary, or as otherwise inherently related to sustainability. Because transparency is not justified on its own terms, it is portrayed as something that does not require justification and must, as a result, either be self-evidently valuable or be useful as a means to the otherwise self-evidently valuable objective of sustainability. Finally, GRI communications that refer to transparency *as a social norm* describe information disclosure as a socially appropriate practice for corporations, for instance, when they stress the "great relevance" of the GRI's reporting standard "in today's world where disclosure and transparency *is considered a key responsibility of financial institutions*" (Global Reporting Initiative 2008, emphasis added).

In sum, the GRI defines transparency in a coherent and normatively demanding way but does not stick to this definition and justification of transparency in its own communications. Instead, it offers a range of different uses of transparency that come with different justifications and, as a result, with different implications for the scope and quality of information disclosure deemed necessary. Although the GRI's explicit definition of transparency in the *Sustainability Reporting Guidelines* demands disclosure of all information that is potentially relevant in terms of stakeholders' personal autonomy, the instrumental conception calls for disclosing only those pieces of information that help to secure market leadership or support "global well-being." The third use of transparency requires disclosure "for sustainability purposes" and leaves it largely to the reporting entities to define what this means in practice. Finally, the fourth use determines the optimal scope of disclosure in relation to corresponding practices of peer groups and expectations of actors with which an organization interacts. A *transformative ambition* may thus be included in the official definition in the G3, but it plays a much weaker role in the communicative routines of the organization.

Policies

At a second level, transparency is also tamed in relation to the GRI's policies. If we accept the view that certain "enabling conditions"—most notably value, accessibility, comprehensibility, and comparability—define whether or not transparency policies can fulfill their transformative potential, two major limitations become visible.[3] Notably, although the GRI addresses the preconditions for "effective transparency" in its policies, its compliance management with the reporting principles remains weak. Moreover, the development of policies and tools to enhance comparability among reports proceeds only slowly.

Value of disclosed information is discussed under the reporting principle of *materiality* in which the G3 requires the information in a report to "cover topics and Indicators that reflect the organization's significant economic, environmental, and social impacts, or that would substantively influence the assessments and decisions of stakeholders" (Global Reporting Initiative 2011, 8). In practice, however, the reporting principles offer only a soft guideline for preparing a sustainability report. Moreover, only those organizations that seek the highest application level need to provide reasons for considering immaterial a performance indicator on which they do not disclose information.

The *accessibility and comprehensibility* of GRI reports are discussed under the reporting principle of *clarity.* Clarity of disclosed information requires that "information should be made available in a manner that is understandable and accessible to stakeholders using the report" (Global Reporting Initiative 2011, 16). Accessibility as defined by the GRI includes the physical accessibility of a report—for instance the free availability of sustainability reports on the Internet—but also the arrangement and presentation of information. In short, the GRI stipulates that "a stakeholder should be able to find desired information without unreasonable effort" (Global Reporting Initiative 2011, 16). The principle is fairly demanding in the sense that "those with particular accessibility needs (e.g., differing abilities, language, or technology)" should also be given access to information (Global Reporting Initiative 2011, 16). In practice, meeting this particular criterion might require translations of reports into various languages and the preparation of reports with different levels of complexity. Yet, in the absence of clear-cut criteria, compliance with the principle of clarity is difficult to verify. As a result, it does not play a role in the assignment of application levels that qualify a GRI report as more or less valuable, and compliance with the spirit of the principle remains largely voluntary for reporting organizations.

Finally, *comparability* is dealt with in a reporting principle with the same title. The principle acknowledges that "comparability is necessary for evaluating performance" and stipulates that "reported information should be presented in a manner that enables stakeholders to analyze changes in the organization's performance over time, and could support analysis relative to other organizations" (Global Reporting Initiative 2011, 14). The G3 guidelines further elaborate that reports "should include total numbers (i.e., absolute data such as tons of waste) as well as ratios (i.e., normalized data such as waste per unit of production) to enable analytical comparisons" (Global Reporting Initiative 2011, 14).

Comparability also plays an important role in other GRI communications. This relates to the fact that the absence of *comparable* sustainability reports rather than the absence of sustainability reports as such was the major problem that gave rise to the GRI in the first place. The GRI has sought to improve the comparability of GRI reports not only through the development of a unified reporting standard but also through development of technical solutions and software products that would enable report readers to more easily compare an organization's performance data with the same data of other corporations. In relation to this aspect, in 2004 the GRI Stakeholder Council already identified the following: "clear gaps between report preparers and GRI-based report users' and recommended the development of a software format that should facilitate the reporting process (make it easier), enhance the value of reporting (facilitate monitoring, management and governance of sustainability effects on business results and vice versa), and offer greater functionality to report readers and information users (e.g., search and benchmarking facilities)" (Global Reporting Initiative 2004, 11).

The development process of the G3 guidelines thus envisioned a technical interface through which information on each indicator could easily be identified and compared with other companies, but progress toward this goal has been slow from the outset.

In late 2011, the GRI launched a *Sustainability Disclosure Database* that enabled users to "compare levels of disclosure among GRI reporting organizations without having to study individual reports" (Global Reporting Initiative 2012c). The reporting practices on single indicators could be benchmarked according to country and sector, but the scope of the database is limited to the question of *whether or not* a corporate report provides information on a particular indicator. It thus provides information about who reports on indicator "EN 16—Total direct and indirect greenhouse gas emissions by weight," for example, but not about the quantity of greenhouse gas emissions reported by companies.

In addition, GRI is seeking to incorporate elements of the "eXtensible Business Reporting Language" (XBRL) into its reporting, a widely used standard to communicate and exchange business information in the context of financial reporting. Using the taxonomies of the XBRL format, computers can recognize elements of the report and select, analyze, store, and exchange information. The GRI initiated a taxonomy project in order to enable organizations to tag their sustainability data in their reports and apply the XBRL to GRI reports. In April 2012, GRI published the new XBRL taxonomy that enables investors, regulators, and analysts to find and analyze data more easily (Global Reporting Initiative 2012b). If taken up by reporting organizations, it promises to significantly enhance the comparability of data contained in corporate sustainability reports.

To summarize, the GRI is aware that corporate disclosure is most useful to users if the reported information is valuable, accessible, comprehensible, and comparable. It acknowledges this assumption in its reporting principles but the principles themselves remain soft. Thus far, the rhetorical emphasis on comparability is also at odds with the slow progress toward technical solutions that would enable report users and intermediaries to compare sustainability data more easily across time and business sectors. The development of an XBRL taxonomy has a potential to change the picture, but it remains to be seen how reporting organizations respond to this option.

Actual Comparability of GRI Reports

The limitations discussed in the previous sections have implications for how *actual GRI reports* fare in terms of criteria such as value, accessibility, comprehensibility, and comparability. To shed light on this question, we examined in our earlier work the sustainability reports of the ten largest automobile manufacturers (based on Fortune 500 data as of July 21, 2008) that compiled a GRI report (Dingwerth and Eichinger 2010). Because one of the largest and most widely accepted environmental challenges lies in reducing greenhouse gas (GHG) emissions, we used reduced GHG emissions as a proxy to assess corporate sustainability performance. More precisely, our analysis focused on the comparability of information in relation to three indicators included in the G3, namely total direct and indirect CO_2 emissions by weight (EN 16), other relevant indirect GHG emission by weight (EN 17), and initiatives to reduce GHG emissions and reductions achieved (EN 18). Our analysis suggests that even though all companies claim full coverage of the GHG indicators, the information they provide is of limited practical use.

The Sustainability Disclosure Database provides us with the information that 60 percent of the five automotive companies that have reports registered since January 1, 2011, fully reported on EN 16, 40 percent on EN 17, and 60 percent on EN 18. Looking into the reports reveals difficulties in comparing the data because not all reports follow the indicators' distinction between direct and indirect emissions. Furthermore, reporting periods differ and the comparison of absolute values is of limited value because production volumes vary. Glancing at percentage change appears better at first sight but rewards past inefficiencies and is equally influenced by changes in production volumes.

The best option to evaluate the CO_2 emissions might thus be to relate the value produced (e.g., manufactured vehicles) to the harm done (e.g., CO_2 emissions) (Isaksson and Steimle 2008). Although it is not prescribed for the specific indicator, this approach is suggested by the G3 reporting principles (Global Reporting Initiative 2006, 14–15). Of the ten producers analyzed, six provided value-per-harm data. Of these, only three were comparable because the others showed only imprecise graphs differentiated by car, truck, van, and bus (Daimler); only included direct GHG emissions (Peugeot); or provided CO_2 values in relation to financial profits but not to vehicles produced (Hyundai).

Finally, information about targets and strategies for the future suffered from the same problems, given that only some companies provided quantitative targets. Furthermore, the qualitative information provided in the report was more akin to corporate brand management and thus made it virtually impossible to extract the sincerity and the sustainability effects of any of the reported measures, let alone make reasonable comparisons across companies.

An investigation into other indicators tends to confirm our conclusion that even reports with application level A or A+ are no guarantee for comparability. Quantitative data are not always systematically gathered and completely reported, whereas qualitative information appears unbalanced and often fails to include a credible assessment of the sustainability impacts of various measures taken by a reporting organization. For instance, a GRI study on human rights reporting concludes that only 7 percent of all reports examined complied with the information requirements of quantitative human rights indicators (Global Reporting Initiative and Roberts Environment Center 2008). Part of the reason for the low comparability might be that neither the reporting entity nor the assurance providers have a strong interest in interpreting the reporting principles and assurance guidelines in very strict terms. As reporters gain leeway through a broader interpretation, assurance providers risk losing their contracts to competitors if they interpret their tasks more strictly than their clients.

Effects of Transparency

Our discussion thus far suggests that if we were to look exclusively at the GRI itself, then the transformative potential that the organization as well as many of its stakeholders associate with transparency is tamed in several ways. Yet information disclosure may also lead to empowerment if actors *outside the GRI system* fill the "actionable disclosure" gap. Such actors would need to figure as intermediaries between the GRI and the alleged beneficiaries of transparency through the extraction, collection, and reconfiguration of information contained in GRI reports so that it can be used more efficiently and acted on by various communities (see also SustainAbility 2011, 6).

In this section, we thus provide a first sketch of the landscape of intermediary organizations that use GRI data for their own communications. Our initial analysis identifies two major types of organizations within the ratings value chain, namely, providers of financial and investment services and "for-benefit" corporations that address consumers' information needs and thus come closer to the ideas and practices characteristic of the third sector (here, the GoodGuide). The selection of these categories is based on the observations that, first, corporate sustainability reporting combines business-to-business and business-to-consumer communications, and second, that civil society–based intermediaries are virtually absent in the case of the GRI. The selection of individual "cases" within the two categories is based on information collected by one of the authors at the ISEAL Public Day Annual Conference 2011, information provided by organizations initially contacted, and an Internet search for organizations that use GRI data in their own communications. Finally, our analysis is informed by our communications with the organizations, either through their responses to a short questionnaire or through telephone interviews, as well as on the information the organizations provide online. Our assessment of these initial case studies supports the directional thesis on transparency effects, stated in the introduction to this book, that the adoption of governance by disclosure in liberal environmental contexts will have minimal market-restricting effects. As we now show, in a context in which transparency is largely shaped by private sector disclosers and intermediaries, the GRI in fact promotes a "marketization of transparency."

Financial Service Providers: The Marketization of GRI Data

One important audience of sustainability reports consists of investors and analysts who, as a group, increasingly consider sustainability issues in their investment decisions. Socially responsible investment (SRI) incorporates environmental, social, and corporate governance (ESG) factors into traditional investment decision-making processes and has gained relevance during the last few years, making up about 10 percent of all investments in the United States (US SIF 2012). Investors usually rely on data feeds and analyses by specialized companies who act as intermediaries between the investment community and companies. Such firms have also developed in the SRI scene, where they collect and analyze corporate data for investor clients and produce ratings and rankings based on proprietary algorithms. In many cases, these companies also generate market and credit risks analytics in addition to ESG products. In what follows, we first describe their activities and then analyze how ESG research firms use and translate GRI data.

Description   Intermediaries in the field compile and analyze nonfinancial data and provide tools for analysts, asset managers, and investors to integrate sustainability data into their investment decisions. The degree to which these firms analyze and interpret data differs. Some companies, such as Bloomberg, primarily act as data compilers and providers, collecting and aggregating data from different sources such as annual reports, NGO websites, media coverage, and CSR reports. These findings are rendered into a comparable and consistent format for clients, who may select those indicators that are most relevant for them. Other firms go a step further and give an interpretation and investment recommendation or a rating. Important ESG research companies in this sector are MSCI ESG Research, Jantzi Sustainalytics, EIRIS, IW Financial, and others. Some companies such as Reuters Asset4 offer both kinds of services. Our analysis is especially informed by communications with MSCI ESG Research and IW Financial.

Typical approaches are negative and positive screenings and rankings. Negative screenings point to companies that engage in controversial activities, such as the arms trade, tobacco, gambling, or those violating the UN Global Compact (for instance MSCI ESG Business Involvement Screening Research and MSCI ESG Impact Monitor). The application of positive criteria by contrast compiles rankings and thereby identifies leading companies ("best in class"). In addition, ESG research firms provide rankings and ratings that focus on specific sectors or indicators tailored to clients' demands.

In general, the trend among ESG researchers is toward a consolidation of indicators: not the quantity of indicators but their relevance is important. Although some ESG firms used to collect as many as nine hundred indicators, today most focus on a few select indicators that are relevant to a specific sector and are proven to be material (Aachener Stiftung Kathy Beys 2012). MSCI for instance developed the so-called MSCI ESG Intangible Value Assessment, which identifies a handful of factors that are most relevant materially for ESG-related risks and opportunities within a sector, and compares them across companies.[4] In addition to collecting reliable data, the essential task for ESG research firms is thus to choose relevant indicators and develop an appropriate weighting scheme. Because this methodology is regarded as its core business, it is often kept confidential. The chasm between the push for corporate disclosure and the opaqueness of rating schemes is the critical issue in this regard, which we discuss further in the following section.

Analysis   For their products, ESG research firms rely on a broad range of data sources, including reports by civil society organizations, governmental information, media coverage, annual reports, and corporate sustainability reports. Reuters Asset4, for instance, states that it includes more than 750 data points in its assessment. CSR reports thus constitute one supplementing source among many others.[5]

Hence, information disclosed in corporate GRI reports is commonly integrated into the databases and assessment models of ESG firms, who consider the holistic reporting framework and indexing system as the main value of GRI reports. At the same time, even though the indexing system provides a short cut to the relevant data, the "... cost of labor to extract the data from the text of the reports and integrate it in to ... data systems" is still considered high.[6] Moreover, the trend with ESG research firms toward more sector-specific data makes all-encompassing GRI data sometimes too unspecific. One interviewee thus argued that "as GRI reports cover a broad range of factors, they are sometimes lacking those more specific factors that are relevant."[7] The sector supplements developed by GRI are seen as a tool to address this issue, but the pace of their development is considered insufficient.

If we assess the activities of ESG researchers against our criteria of value, accessibility, comprehensibility, and comparability of disclosed information, we can see that they contribute in several ways. ESG research companies add to the *value* as they merge data from different sources and check its consistency and plausibility. The more-focused analyses also choose certain key performance indicators (KPI) for their clients. The spotlight on indicators that materially influence financial and reputational risk are valuable for profit-oriented investors, even though they tend to underrate social and environmental factors that do not directly influence market performance.

In terms of *accessibility*, the assessment is double-edged. On the one hand the aggregation of data improves its accessibility, because it is easier for stakeholders to analyze one data set rather than hundreds of different company reports. On the other hand, this benefit has a price tag attached to it that restricts access to it. Data feeds from ESG research firms cost from US$2,000 to over US$100,000 per year, whereas individual reports range between US$200 and US$2,000 per company (CSRHUB 2010). Third, arguably the data are more *comprehensible,* because they are translated into a ranking system and numerical values that correspond with the value systems of investors and analysts. Finally, the largest impact is in the area of *comparability.* The aim of ESG research firms is to provide data and/or tools that help investors to come to a decision. Comparability of the data is thus key, and ESG firms reconfigure corporate sustainability data so that they are stated, for instance, in the same units or cover the same reference period and enable a transformation into benchmarking and ratings. Yet, this comparability through rankings must be treated with caution, because comparability between different sectors and even within one sector remains problematic.

In sum, ESG research companies are an important intermediary for GRI data. GRI data are integrated into their databases and hence enter into rankings, ratings, and investment decisions. With the work of ESG research companies, the data become more valuable, more comprehensible and, above all, more comparable. The accessibility is not necessarily enhanced because most firms sell their analyses to their customers to earn profit. Although enhanced transparency is enabled by incoming revenues from paying clients, downstream transparency is limited. As a result, most of the information flow is business-to-business.

Some organizations, such as CSRHUB, act however as "second-order intermediaries" that aggregate "some of the best, most objective corporate responsibility ratings" (CSRHUB 2012) by leading ESG research firms and other sources. Although basic membership is free, a subscription to CSRHUB enables access to an additional level of information at US$18 to US$89 per month. CSRHUB does not investigate the underlying ratings methodology of the ESG research firms but only serves as a hub for the information. This is also in the interest of ESG research firms, because their analytical model is "essential to the final product and therefore requires some degree of confidentiality" (NAEM 2011, 6). Therefore, the ESG research companies, although pushing for transparent business disclosure, also have a business interest in not making their own models and data too easily publicly available. However, the logic of keeping the methodology as a black box is increasingly being challenged and a second layer of transparency is evolving: in 2011, the Ceres and Tellus Institute, the founding organizations of the GRI, launched the Global Initiative for Sustainable Ratings. The initiative is modeled after the GRI and aims to develop a standard for rating the sustainability of companies (Tripoli 2011).

Empowering Consumers? The Use of GRI Data by GoodGuide

Whereas the preceding examples primarily deal with business-to-business communication, a second category of intermediaries is concerned with business-to-consumer communication. The major example of an organization that uses GRI data to inform and thereby empower consumers is GoodGuide. In the following, we first describe and then analyze the organization's efforts in translating the data contained in GRI reports into actionable information in terms of our analytical framework.

Description   Founded in 2007 by Dara O'Rourke, GoodGuide evaluates consumer products sold in the US market in terms of their health, environmental, and societal impacts. The current database includes over 120,000 evaluated products in categories such as personal care, food, household, child care, pet food, apparel, electronics, appliances, and cars. GoodGuide also offers an online toolbar and a mobile application to allow consumers to obtain information instantly about a product and its competitors. Users obtain a "scientific rating" of the product as a whole, which combines the health, environmental, and societal dimensions along with individual ratings for each dimension. The information contained in the ratings is heavily condensed and uses a simple scale from 0 to 10, with a score of 5 indicating an average performance and scores of 0 and 10 signaling that a product or company is the worst and best in its category, respectively.

If you point the camera of your mobile phone to the barcode of a can of Del Monte cinnamon-flavored pear halves, for example, your Good-Guide mobile application will inform you that the overall product rating is 4.2, with health at a 2.1 low, and environment and society at 5.5 and 5.2, respectively. The environment rating comes without a qualitative comment, but brief elaborations are added to the other two dimensions. On health, GoodGuide states that "this product has a high level of sugar, known to increase the risk of obesity, diabetes, and heart disease"; on the society rating, it adds, "this company's social policies, practices and performance are average." Finally, the instant information reveals that the product is ranked 123rd out of 252 canned fruits (GoodGuide 2012c).

For those who wish to learn more about a product or a company, GoodGuide offers several additional options. First, the three dimensions are broken down into individual indicators. For the product under consideration, the rating for health is composed, for instance, of two indicators, namely, the "ratio of recommended to restricted food components" and the indicator "sugar" that measures "whether this product exceeds the limit on sugar recommended by the World Health Organization." Environment, in turn, is measured at the company level rather than the product level and includes the subcategories transparency, resource use, environmental impacts, and environmental management, with the latter three all composed of several additional subcategories and indicators. Finally, the society dimension is also measured at the firm level and includes indicators in categories such as management, transparency, consumer, and worker (GoodGuide 2012a). Users can easily access the product or company score for each indicator.

Second, although the overall ratings reflect the relative weight that GoodGuide researchers have assigned to individual indicators, a personal filter allows users to decide which aspects of a product are more or less important to them. Once this filter is set, the product ratings that appear on the screen are adapted to the user's personal values. Third, the online database allows visitors to compare not only products but also companies and brands in terms of their environmental and social performance. A quick comparison of forty car companies thus informs that BMW and Rolls Royce perform best in terms of the environmental and social criteria selected by GoodGuide, scoring a weighted average of 7.3 on environmental indicators and 5.8 on social indicators. In contrast, Saab is the worst environmental and social performer, with a score of 3.2 and 3.0 in the two categories. The data on which ratings for each individual indicator are based are collected from various sources. Company-level information for public firms, for instance, "is primarily obtained from rating services that serve the socially responsible investment market" (GoodGuide 2012b), that is, from the previously discussed firms.

Organizationally, GoodGuide is incorporated as a "for-benefit" (rather than "for-profit") corporation that commits itself to social and environmental responsibility. Its revenues derive from two sources, namely, from selling advertising opportunities on its Internet pages and mobile application and from the sale of business intelligence reports that integrate data for individual companies or compare information for different companies. In terms of impact, a news report from *USA Today* (2011) suggests that GoodGuide's mobile application was downloaded six hundred thousand times between 2008 and 2011, whereas GoodGuide staff estimate that the organization's information on product ratings, company ratings, and purchase recommendations is transmitted to "over one million US consumers per month via our website, browser extensions and mobile applications."[8]

Analysis   GRI reports inform GoodGuide ratings primarily in two ways. First, the information contained in GRI reports enters the assessments of organizations such as IW Financial or Thomson Reuters Asset4, from which GoodGuide purchases data for its ratings. Second, GoodGuide analysts also use GRI reports for their own assessments of a company's social or environmental performance in relation to specific indicators, most notably a company's programs and policies. As a result, the organization considers GRI reports a "key source" for their evaluations of products, companies, and brands.[9]

To move closer toward an automatic import of evidence from GRI reports into the organization's own data management system for scoring, GoodGuide has also aligned its own issue framework with the GRI format. This is intended to reduce two significant direct costs associated with using GRI reports as a basis for company ratings. The first is the need to "manually extract data from reports that are published in different publication formats at different locations on different company websites." The second is the work required "to transform quantitative performance data included in GRI reports into normalized metrics (e.g., direct GHG emissions per dollar of annual revenue) that can be utilized to compare performance across companies."[10]

Overall, GoodGuide staff consider the standardized structure for sustainability reports provided by GRI to be a "key value added." The access to a "library of reports" on its website, combined with the indexing requirement of GRI reports, provides at least some service to data users. Nonetheless, the organization notes that its usefulness can be expanded in at least two ways. First, a "more granular tagging of the data elements used to describe a company's performance on any given GRI issue" is considered helpful to locate information related to a specific indicator more easily and to enable automatic import of information in report users' own databases. This relates, for instance, to tags that indicate whether a company is describing a policy, a program, or a quantitative performance target. Second, a "structured database containing report elements" is considered to be of significantly greater use than a mere collection of hyperlinks to corporate GRI reports.[11]

The translation efforts of GoodGuide contribute in several ways to our criteria of value, accessibility, comprehensibility, and comparability. In terms of *value*, one might argue that the integration of data from different sources and the weighting of individual indicators by the GoodGuide scoring framework promote materiality in the sense that the final score provides information about those aspects of a company's performance that "really matter." At the same time, the choices made in the scoring framework are open to the challenge that they underrate or overrate specific aspects and thus undermine the value or materiality of the information contained in the score for a product or company. Yet the availability of personalized filters offers at least a partial solution to this challenge. Second, the *accessibility* of information about the social and environmental performances of a company, as well as about performance on individual indicators, is enhanced as a result of the integration of different information sources in one place and user-friendly tools such as the online toolbar or the mobile application. At the same time, the information "behind the number" is not always accessible, depending on the sources from which a scoring is derived. Third, information is more *comprehensible* in the sense that a number or label such as "best," "below average," or "very poor" contains simplified and condensed information that is easily understood by laypeople. Finally, the central and most obvious advantage vis-à-vis the GRI's own work lies in the fact that the various tools developed by GoodGuide enable users to *compare* sustainability data of different companies on the basis of a common metric.

In terms of accessibility, an interesting additional dynamic is that, in a similar way as civil society–based online portals such as Rank a Brand,[12] GoodGuide puts a high premium on corporate information disclosure in its own ratings. Although a lack of publicly accessible data can hardly be read as an indicator of poor social or environmental performance, GoodGuide argues that "the pervasive lack of transparency about product attributes and company operations undermines the public's ability to evaluate performance." The organization thus includes transparency indicators that "measure the relative amount of information available from a company for assessing its environmental or social performance" and states that "companies exhibiting multiple data gaps are penalized in our scoring system for their lack of transparency." Because transparency indicators account for 25 percent of the weighted environmental score and for 20 percent of the weighted society score, the sanction for low corporate transparency can be considerable (GoodGuide 2012b). Furthermore, the GRI application level is used as one of the transparency indicators (with application levels A, B, and C leading to a score of 9, 8 and 7, respectively). Thus, companies that desire a good score for their products are encouraged not only to disclose information about their social and environmental performance but also to make use of the GRI reporting format (GoodGuide 2012d).

Conclusion

As discussed in our earlier work, the GRI itself promotes only a thin or "tamed" version of transparency through its rhetoric, policies, and institutional practices. Intermediary organizations from civil society are largely unable to fill the gap through a more "targeted" translation of the data contained in GRI reports (Dingwerth and Eichinger 2010). Adding commercial intermediaries to the analysis changes the overall picture somewhat. It does so in at least three ways. First, commercial intermediaries make the information contained in GRI reports more valuable, comprehensible, and comparable to information users. They therefore help to create conditions under which information becomes "actionable." Yet because making information valuable, comprehensible, and comparable is the very business model of commercial intermediaries, their services are usually limited to those who pay for them. In short, transparency thus understood empowers only some actors—namely, the intermediaries themselves and the users of their services. Both groups can put enhanced pressure on corporate actors based on the information they collect or acquire.

Second, commercial intermediaries pressure corporations to disclose more specific and thus more useful information. At the same time, they promote a particular kind of informational disclosure, namely, disclosure of information that is most sought by their audiences, whether investors or consumers. In business-to-business transparency, the materiality of the factors is assumed to be of central importance and therefore broader societal interests enter the scoring, rating, and ranking models by ESG consultancies only indirectly, when they are linked to an assumed reputational risk. Who defines transparency and on what terms thus becomes inherently linked to who can put the reputation of a corporation or a brand at risk and on what grounds. In the business-to-consumer model, societal concerns are more directly incorporated, but because GoodGuide is thus far limited to products sold on the US market, the models are primarily informed by values held by US consumers. As a result, even when US consumers might care about workers in producing countries, such concerns are only represented through the assumptions that US consumers (or GoodGuide staff) make about what workers in Bangladesh or China might care most about. In the end, even when transparency empowers consumers (or those who can put corporate reputation at risk) this does not mean it empowers those who are weak. In fact, at least those who can put corporate reputation at risk are often already quite powerful, even in the absence of full disclosure.

Third, in as much as information disclosed by GRI reporters becomes a tradable good, the strong role of commercial intermediaries we have described in this chapter lends strong support to the notion of a "marketization of transparency" (Gupta and Mason, this book, chapter 1). This marketization trend should not be condemned all too quickly, however. In contrast, we argue here that it generates a dynamic that leads to a fuller realization of at least some of the promises that are so frequently associated with disclosure policies. At the same time, as marketization becomes a defining feature of the field of information intermediaries, noncommercial organizations find it increasingly difficult to enter that field with their own alternative visions of how and to what end corporate transparency should be organized. Given the presence of powerful commercial intermediaries, civil society intermediaries may fail to persuade funding agencies of the need for their alternative services, signaling the narrowing effect of marketization. Broadly in line with the loss- of-innocence thesis laid out elsewhere in this book (Mol, this book, chapter 2), *what transparency is* and *what transparency is for* thus becomes increasingly defined in the "market for transparency."

Fourth, we can observe that the powerful market position that commercial intermediaries have acquired also gives rise to an additional layer of transparency. Whereas primary transparency focuses on disclosure by corporations, increasingly information brokers themselves become subject to scrutiny. As intermediaries are required to make their own practices and methodologies transparent, the disclosure system gains a level of complexity and reflexivity (Mol, this book, chapter 2) that might also affect its transformative potential.

Notes

1. This chapter builds on our earlier article "Tamed Transparency: How Information Disclosure under the Global Reporting Initiative Fails to Empower"

published in *Global Environmental Politics* 10 (2010): 74–96. For comments on earlier drafts, we are particularly grateful to Aarti Gupta, Michael Mason, and participants of the authors' workshop held at the London School of Economics and Political Science in September 2011. Klaus Dingwerth undertook some of the research reported here as a part of the project "Changing Norms of Global Governance" (grant no. DI1417/2-1). He gratefully acknowledges funding for this project from the Deutsche Forschungsgemeinschaft. The views expressed in this contribution are solely those of the authors; they do not represent the official opinion of GIZ.

2. On the GRI, see Brown, de Jong, and Levy 2009; Brown, de Jong, and Lessid-renska 2009; Dingwerth 2007; Pattberg 2007.

3. On the notions of value, accessibility, comprehensibility, and comparability see Fung et al. 2007, 55–65; Dingwerth and Eichinger 2010.

4. Telephone interview with Mike Langlais, ESG product development at MSCI, January 2012.

5. Thomson Reuters (2011) and telephone interview with Mike Langlais, ESG product development at MSCI, January 2012, and e-mail communication with Dan Porter, founder and vice president of marketing at IW Financial, Inc., December 2011.

6. E-mail communication with Dan Porter, founder and vice president of marketing at IW Financial, Inc., December 2011.

7. Telephone interview with Mike Langlais, ESG product development at MSCI, January 2012.

8. *USA Today* (2011) and e-mail communication with Bill Pease, chief scientist at GoodGuide, December 2011.

9. E-mail communication with Bill Pease, chief scientist at GoodGuide, December 2011.

10. Ibid.

11. Ibid.

12. Rank a Brand is an NGO incorporated in the Netherlands. It relies on "trained volunteers" to rank brands on the basis of a common set of questions for each industrial sector, with each question answered with "yes" (e.g., signaling the existence of a policy to curb greenhouse gases), "no" (e.g., signaling the absence of the latter), or "?" (signaling that no information on this item is available on the company's Internet pages). Because "no" and "?" are treated as a negative result in the scoring process, lack of information is strongly penalized; see http://www.rankabrand.org.

References

Aachener Stiftung Kathy Beys. 2012. *Konsolidierungswelle im Nachhaltigkeitsre-search.* Available at http://www.nachhaltigkeit.info/artikel/konsolidierungswelle_im_nachhaltigkeitsresearch_1671.htm.

Brown, Halina Szejnwald, Martin de Jong, and Teodorina Lessidrenska. 2009. The Rise of the Global Reporting Initiative as a Case of Institutional Entrepreneurship. *Environmental Politics* 18 (2): 182–200.

Brown, Halina Szejnwald, Martin de Jong, and David L. Levy. 2009. Building Institutions Based on Information Disclosure: Lessons from GRI's Sustainability Reporting. *Journal of Cleaner Production* 17 (6): 571–580.

Commission of the European Communities. 2002. *Communication from the Commission concerning Corporate Social Responsibility: A Business Contribution to Sustainable Development*. [COM (2002) 347, July 1] Brussels: Commission of the European Communities.

CSRHUB. 2010. *Crowds of Ratings: The Financial Folks*. Available at http://www.triplepundit.com/2010/12/crowds-ratings-financial-csr/.

CSRHUB. 2012. *About CSRHUB*. Available at http://www.csrhub.com/content/about-csrhub.

Dingwerth, Klaus. 2007. *The New Transnationalism: Transnational Governance and Democratic Legitimacy*. Basingstoke, UK: Palgrave Macmillan.

Dingwerth, Klaus, and Margot Eichinger. 2010. Tamed Transparency: How Information Disclosure under the Global Reporting Initiative Fails to Empower. *Global Environmental Politics* 10 (3): 74–96.

Fung, Archon, Mary Graham, and David Weil. 2007. *Full Disclosure: The Perils and Promise of Transparency*. Cambridge, UK: Cambridge University Press.

Global Reporting Initiative. 2002. *A Historic Collaborative Achievement: Inauguration of the Global Reporting Initiative*. Amsterdam: Global Reporting Initiative.

Global Reporting Initiative. 2004. *GRI Stakeholder Bulletin*11, July 5. Amsterdam: Global Reporting Initiative. (Document on file with author.)

Global Reporting Initiative. 2006. *G3: Sustainability Reporting Guidelines*. Amsterdam: Global Reporting Initiative.

Global Reporting Initiative. 2008. *News 2008: Finalized and Ready for Use; The GRI Financial Services Sector Supplement*. Available at http://www.globalreporting.org/NewsEventsPress/LatestNews/2008/NewsMonth08FSSS.htm.

Global Reporting Initiative. 2011. *G3.1: Sustainability Reporting Guidelines*. Amsterdam: Global Reporting Initiative.

Global Reporting Initiative. 2012a. *GRI Sustainability Reporting Statistics*. Publication year 2011. Available at https://www.globalreporting.org/resourcelibrary/GRI-Reporting-Trends-2011.pdf.

Global Reporting Initiative. 2012b. *New XBRL Reporting Format Helps Reveal Sustainability Data More Easily*. Available at https://www.globalreporting.org/information/news-and-press-center/Pages/New-XBRL-reporting-format-helps-reveal-sustainability-data-more-easily.aspx.

Global Reporting Initiative. 2012c. Sustainability Disclosure Database. *About This Site*. Available at http://database.globalreporting.org/pages/about.

Global Reporting Initiative and Roberts Environment Center. 2008. *Reporting on Human Rights: A Survey Conducted by the Global Reporting Initiative™ and the Roberts Environment Center (Claremont McKenna College).* Amsterdam: Global Reporting Initiative.

GoodGuide. 2012a. *GoodGuide Ratings.* Available at http://www.goodguide .com/about/ratings.

GoodGuide. 2012b. *Methodology Overview.* Available at http://www.goodguide .com/about/methodologies.

GoodGuide. 2012c. *Rating for Del Monte Cinnamon Flavored Pear Halves.* Available at http://www.goodguide.com/products/403793-del-monte-cinnamon -flavored.

GoodGuide. 2012d. *Scoring Rules.* Available at http://www.goodguide.com/ about/methodologies.

Isaksson, Raine, and Ulrich Steimle. 2008. *What Does GRI-Reporting Tell Us about Corporate Sustainability?* Unpublished Paper Presented at the 11th Quality Management and Organizational Development Conference, Helsingborg, Sweden.

King Committee on Corporate Governance. 2002. *King Report on Corporate Governance for South Africa.* Cape Town: King Committee.

KPMG International. 2011. *KPMG International Survey of Corporate Responsibility Reporting 2011.* Available at http://www.kpmg.com/Global/en/IssuesAnd Insights/ArticlesPublications/corporate-responsibility/Documents/2011-survey .pdf.

NAEM. 2011. *Driving ESG Reporting Progress through Dialogue.* Available at http://www.naem.org/page/ESG.

Pattberg, Philipp. 2007. *Private Institutions and Global Governance: The New Politics of Environmental Sustainability.* Cheltenham, UK: Edward Elgar.

SustainAbility. 2011. *Rate the Raters Phase Four: The Necessary Future of Ratings.* Available at http://www.sustainability.com/library/rate-the-raters-phase-four.

Thomson Reuters. 2011. *Asset4 ESG Data.* Available at http://cdn1. im.thomsonreuters.com/wp-content/uploads/2012/04/ASSET4-ESG-Data -Factsheet.pdf.

Tripoli, Stephen. 2011. *Ceres, Tellus Unveil Global Initiative for a Standardized, Comprehensive Corporate Sustainability Rating Standard.* Available at http:// www.ceres.org/press/press-releases/a-single-measure-unbiased-results-ceres-tellus -unveil-global-initiative-for-a-standardized-comprehensive-corporate-sustainabi lity-rating.

USA Today. 2011. GoodGuide App Helps Navigate Green Products. Available at http://www.usatoday.com/tech/products/2011-05-12-GoodGuide-app_n.htm.

US SIF. 2012. *Sustainable and Responsible Investing Facts.* Available at http://us sif.org/resources/sriguide/srifacts.cfm.

11

Transparency in Energy Governance: The Extractive Industries Transparency Initiative and Publish What You Pay Campaign

James Van Alstine

This chapter explores the challenges, opportunities, and outcomes of transparency-based energy governance through analyzing the multistakeholder Extractive Industries Transparency Initiative (EITI) and Publish What You Pay (PWYP) campaign. The chapter begins with a discussion of how transparency has evolved into a powerful international norm within the field of energy and nonenergy mineral governance. It then explores, using new petro-economy Ghana as a case study, how transparency is institutionalized and functions in practice.

Since the early 2000s, an increased demand for raw materials, partly driven by the growth of Asian economies, has fueled a global commodity boom (UNCTAD 2007). Energy and nonenergy mineral prices have rebounded quickly after the 2008–2010 recession (UNCTAD 2011). Higher commodity prices have spurred an increase in foreign direct investment into the world's poorest economies, driving speculation that a significant window of opportunity exists for these mineral-rich but poor economies to accelerate their development (UNCTAD 2007, iii). The proponents of resource-led development (for example, host-country governments, international financial institutions, and donor governments) highlight the importance of resource extraction as a source of foreign exchange, raw materials and energy, infrastructure development, revenues (for example, from taxation), and poverty alleviation (Humphreys et al. 2007; ICMM 2005; MMSD 2002; UNCTAD 2007; World Bank 2004). However, the concept of resource-led development, that is, how extractive industries contribute to poverty alleviation in the developing world, is poorly understood (Oxfam America 2001; Pegg 2006). African economies dependent on exploitation of natural resources are often characterized by poor economic growth, low living standards, corruption, and political authoritarianism (Gary and Karl 2003; Hilson and Maconachie 2009).

Given its positive development trajectory, commitment to democracy, and track record of transparency initiatives, Ghana is an exceptional case in the context of resource-rich sub-Saharan Africa. Having a substantial history in the extraction of nonenergy minerals (for example, gold), it is uniquely placed to reap the benefits from its offshore oil fields and resource-led development. As demand for energy and nonenergy minerals continues to rise, reserves will be exploited in more remote and technically, socially, and environmentally risky places. How energy governance evolves within a new petro-economy in sub-Saharan Africa is thus highly relevant to examine. This chapter adopts a moderate constructivist approach (Jones 2002) to identify how key logics, or collective action frames, related to transparency in Ghana have emerged and evolved over time. Energy governance, within the context of this chapter, can be defined as the formal and informal rules that shape the way that energy minerals contribute to sustainable development and poverty alleviation within host countries (e.g., Levy and Newell 2005).

I proceed as follows. The chapter first traces the evolution of the EITI and PWYP campaigns and notes how Ghana has become a hub of best practice learning and capacity building on transparency within the extractive industries. I next assess the normative, procedural, and substantive effects of transparency within the emerging oil sector in Ghana. I highlight four key findings: the limited transformative potential of transparency in energy governance, the hybrid voluntary-mandatory character of transparency mechanisms and a resultant rescaling of sovereignty and authority, the limitations of the World Bank's conceptualization of the extractive industry value chain, and the influence of resource materiality on opportunities and impacts of transparency interventions.

The analysis is based on primary and secondary data collected during fieldwork undertaken in oil-bearing communities in Ghana's western region in July 2010; attendance at the Fifth EITI Global Conference in Paris, March 2011; and telephone interviews with key stakeholders in Ghana in July–August 2011. Primary data include semistructured interviews and conference notes, and secondary data include EITI country reports, PWYP reports, media articles, NGO and think tank reports, corporate reports, and government documents.

Embracing Transparency

The transparency and good governance agenda in the arena of resource extraction has emerged because of intersecting ideas driven by transnational networks concerned with corruption, conflict, and corporate social responsibility (Haufler 2010, 54). The diffusion of these transparency norms has become institutionalized through agenda setting and coalition building by NGOs, often originating in the North, wielding significant discursive power (Haufler 2010, 57). It can also be argued that reputational concerns of Western governments, international financial institutions, and transnational extractive firms, driven by NGO advocacy, have facilitated the emergence of this international agenda (Gillies 2010). Indeed, the global normative environment favors governance by disclosure as a "light-touch" way of correcting market failures. In relation to the hypothesis on the uptake of transparency, as stated in chapter 1 of this book (Gupta and Mason), the drivers of disclosure within this context include marketization and to a lesser degree democratization.[1] As discussed in the following, though, recent host-country and extraterritorial legislation for transparency in energy governance has begun to counter pressures for market-based environmental governance.

In the wake of growing momentum for natural resource governance (Global Witness 1999; MMSD 2002; World Bank 2003) and in the spirit of public-private partnerships, the EITI was launched by then–UK prime minister Tony Blair at the World Summit on Sustainable Development in 2002. The initiative has evolved into a voluntary international standard with a secretariat based in Oslo, which seeks to strengthen governance in the extractives sector by improving transparency and accountability through the disclosure of company payments and government revenues (EITI 2011b). A distinguishing feature of the EITI is that it is a government-driven process. In order to become an EITI candidate country, governments must meet five sign-up requirements, which include a public statement of intention, a commitment to work with civil society and companies, and the establishment of a multistakeholder group to oversee implementation. To achieve EITI-compliant status or to extend candidate status beyond two and a half years, governments must complete an EITI validation. An independent validator conducts this validation process, using the methodology defined in the EITI rules. A country is recognized as EITI compliant if, according to the EITI international board, it meets all requirements. If a country has made good progress, it may be able to retain its candidate status; if not, a country's candidate status will be revoked by the board (EITI 2011b). As of August 2011, the EITI was supported by thirty-nine countries (eleven compliant, twenty-four candidate, and four interested countries), more than forty-nine companies, and a wide variety of other stakeholders, including NGOs, international finance institutions, and academic partners (EITI 2011b).

In 2002, Global Witness, along with five other founding members (CAFOD, Open Society Institute, Oxfam GB, Save the Children UK, and Transparency International UK) also publicly launched the PWYP campaign, which calls for transparency of company payments and government revenues, government expenditures, and contracts and licensing procedures (PWYP 2011b). The aim of PWYP is not transparency as such. The aim is to "improve the lives of ordinary citizens in resource-rich countries," and it seeks to achieve this end through advocacy, training, and capacity building (PWYP 2011b). The PYWP initiative has evolved into a global network made up of more than six hundred civil society organizations in sixty-one countries.

The EITI and PWYP have acted as key catalysts in mainstreaming a growing consensus in favor of transparency in the extractive sector. The two initiatives are complementary yet distinct. The EITI, in its current form, focuses quite narrowly on seeking publication and verification of company payments and government revenues from the extractives sector, whereas PWYP broadens the remit to engage more directly with transparency in other areas of the extractive industries value chain and calls for mandatory transparency interventions.

The World Bank launched an initiative known as EITI++ in 2008, which sought to go beyond the EITI to offer World Bank assistance in contract design, tax collection, regulation and monitoring of operations, and revenue management and allocation (World Bank 2008). Although, according to discussions with World Bank officials, the formal EITI++ initiative has been discontinued, the bank still actively assists resource-rich countries in implementing transparency initiatives throughout the extractive industries value chain (Alba 2009). According to a 2009 World Bank working paper (Alba 2009), good governance needs to be institutionalized throughout the extractive industries value chain, which includes five core components:

1. Award of contracts and licenses
2. Regulation and monitoring of operations
3. Collection of taxes and royalties
4. Revenue management and allocation
5. Implementation of sustainable development policies and projects

Thus, EITI exists as an international standard with codified rules, processes, and a secretariat, whereas PWYP is an advocacy organization that uses a variety of different campaigning strategies to further its objectives.

A key distinction is that PWYP seeks to influence hard law, and EITI promotes voluntary and incremental reform. As Auld and Gulbrandsen argue in comparing transparency in the voluntary certification programs of the MSC and FSC (Auld and Gulbrandsen, this book, chapter 12), the EITI and PWYP too use different approaches to legitimize their organizations: transparency is seen as an end in itself by the EITI, whereas the PWYP uses transparency more instrumentally to further other ends.

These transparency and anticorruption initiatives have made significant progress since the new millennium. A move from soft to hard law is now apparent in the governance of resource extraction. For example, in 2007, good governance and revenue transparency made it to the top of the global natural resource governance agenda, when the G8 endorsed good governance and anticorruption initiatives such as the EITI (Benner and Soares de Oliveira 2010, 288). In 2011, the G8 went further and endorsed mandatory disclosure of oil, gas, and mining payments to governments (PWYP 2011a). This G8 endorsement followed the passing of the US Dodd-Frank Financial Reform and Consumer Protection Act in July 2010, which requires oil and mining companies listed on US stock exchanges to report their payments to US and foreign governments (PWYP 2011a). The European Commission is also planning to put forth similar extraterritorial legislation requiring extractive firms to publish information about their activities (PWYP 2011a).

Although the EITI and PWYP coalitions have made significant progress in a variety of countries, a number of limitations remain. First, the assumption that more information is better does not always hold, and the implementation of transparency does not always achieve its desired result (Fung and others 2007; Haufler 2010). Similar to analyses in this book of the Global Reporting Initiative (see Dingwerth and Eichinger, chapter 10) and corporate disclosure systems (see Knox-Hayes and Levy, chapter 9), early studies found that EITI member states do not perform better in corruption rankings than nonmember states (Aaronson 2011; Haufler 2010). The EITI and transparency in and of itself may not be capable of facilitating good governance (Hilson and Maconachie 2009). As discussed, the EITI addresses only one component of the extractive industries value chain. Various authors recommend that transparency reform should focus on expenditures rather than revenues (Frynas 2009; Kolstad and Wiig 2009).

Second, the quality of EITI data has been problematic. Despite auditing requirements, member states and companies do not produce complete and reliable data (Dykstra 2011; Gillies 2011; Ravat and Ufer 2010). For example, a Revenue Watch Institute report in March 2011 highlighted various aspects of EITI implementation requirements that were not being met by a high percentage of EITI candidate countries (Dykstra 2011, 6). Third, lack of a strong domestic civil society that can fully participate in the EITI process may hinder the effectiveness of revenue transparency. Foreign aid programs have tried to target building capacity within civil society, but these may not have lasting impacts (Haufler 2010; Ottaway and Carothers 2000). Civil society in some participating countries is not allowed to participate fully in the EITI process, and intimidation and harassment of civil society in some candidate countries remains a significant concern (Aaronson 2011; Dykstra 2011; Smith et al. 2012).

Fourth, the shared vision and communication of EITI within participating countries may negatively affect its effectiveness. For example, there may be differing perspectives from government, industry, and civil society on its aims and objectives (Smith et al. 2012), and in many EITI countries, the public and legislators may not even be aware of its existence (Aaronson 2011). Fifth, governance by disclosure within the extractive industries may be the "default option" because more contested options, such as mandatory restrictions or regulation, are politically precluded (Haufler 2010). Therefore, transparency in resource governance is not likely to challenge the political and economic structural constraints characteristic of extractive contexts (Benner and Soares de Oliveira 2010), nor will it function successfully without certain preconditions, such as an independent media and an active and free civil society (Frynas 2009).

In chapter 1 of this book, Gupta and Mason put forward the hypothesis that the institutionalization of transparency decenters state-led regulation and opens up political space for new actors. Given that EITI is a state-driven process, assessing this hypothesis requires examining the nature and scope of oil and gas governance in Ghana and the role of disclosure therein.

Institutionalizing Transparency

As discussed, diffusion of transparency norms has occurred at the international scale in the extractive sector. I have identified how the *institutional logics* related to transparency have emerged and evolved over time in this realm. As McAdam and Scott (2005, 15) highlight, "It is possible and useful to identify dominant logics that reflect the consensus of powerful actors as well as secondary and/or repressed logics representing other, subordinated or emergent interests." The construction of institutional logics is very similar to the process of strategic framing, which "denotes an active, processual phenomenon that implies agency and contention at the level of reality construction" (Benford and Snow 2000, 614). A process of strategic framing may actively seek to construct shared understanding around issues and viable courses of action (Campbell 2005, 49). As Scott (2008, 188) highlights, the concept of a strategic frame is very similar to an institutional logic: "Issues of how things are interpreted and represented connect fairly seamlessly to considerations how things are to be done." I track the emergence here of the logics of transparency in relation to the nascent petroleum industry in Ghana in order to assess their normative, procedural, and substantive effects. The advent of EITI and PWYP is central to this discussion.

Commercially viable offshore oil was discovered in Ghana in 2007, with predicted reserves of three billion barrels. As of December 2010, commercial oil production began in the Jubilee field and was scheduled to reach a plateau of 120,000 barrels per day by August 2011 (Oxfam America 2011). Further exploration is going on and it is likely that Ghana will be producing 250,000 barrels per day by 2014, making it the six largest producer of oil in sub-Saharan Africa (Oxfam America 2011). Expectations are on the rise since commercial production in Ghana began. The Jubilee field is located approximately sixty kilometers offshore of Ghana's western region, and has expected recoverable reserves of eight hundred million barrels of light crude oil (GNPC n.d.). Tullow Ghana Limited, an Anglo-Irish company, is leading the consortium of Jubilee partners, coordinating the development of the Jubilee field as well as the implementation of the Jubilee partners' corporate social responsibility strategy.

Ghana is the darling of donors with an enviable record of a peaceful and stable democracy. With economic growth rates consistently exceeding 6 percent over recent years, it is making good progress toward becoming a middle-income country by 2015 (CIDA 2011). Ghana ranks sixty-second on Transparency International's 2010 Corruption Perceptions Index, and seventh out of forty-seven sub-Saharan African countries. However, it remains at 136th out of 187 countries on the UNDP 2011 Human Development Index (UNDP 2011). Its primary export commodities include cocoa, gold, and timber, with gold representing 34 percent of the country's exports (12 percent of GDP) from 2000 to 2003 (EITI 2011a). As Ian Gary, senior policy manager for extractive industries at Oxfam America, highlights, Ghana's trajectory as an oil-producing country may advance differently than that of other sub-Saharan countries: "So I think the challenges are great. I think often the challenges are underestimated in Ghana by government actors. But there is a completely different environment in terms of how the law is developed, the interaction with civil society and government, free media and vibrant media, that at least gives some foundation that things can go forward differently" (Oxfam America 2011, n.p.).

One of the unique aspects about Ghana is that it had already established an active PWYP coalition and was an EITI candidate country for its mining sector when offshore oil was discovered in 2007. The logics of transparency in Ghana's extractives sector began to be institutionalized in the early 2000s. Ghana announced it would pilot EITI in its mining sector in June 2003 (EITI 2011a). It was the first candidate country to engage only with its mining sector, because most other pilot countries were oil and gas producers (Nguyen-Thanh and Schnell 2009). It was one of the test cases for adapting the EITI rules to conventional mining. The Ghana EITI (GHEITI) process has produced seven reports covering payments, receipts, disbursements, and validation on the mining sector since 2007. In October 2010, Ghana's mining sector was successfully validated and designated as EITI compliant (EITI 2011a).

Driving the institutionalization of revenue transparency within Ghana's mining sector were a variety of different factors, including Ghana's history of good governance and anticorruption drives, international revenue transparency networks working with domestic NGOs, and donor and NGO-funded capacity-building activities targeting government and civil society (ISODEC 2009; PWYP—Ghana n.d.).

PWYP—Ghana sought to operate as a decentralized network and include representatives from mineral producing regions. Of interest here is the role of PYWP—Ghana in galvanizing the citizenry in engaging with the GHEITI process, as well as focusing the initiative on the impacts and revenue-royalty transparency at the subnational level. Early in the implementation process, Ghana demonstrated candidate country best practice by extending its EITI report requirements to subnational revenue flows (Nguyen-Thanh and Schnell 2009). Driven by international revenue transparency logics, development partners and international NGOs provided financial and technical support not just to civil society but also to government representatives and members of Parliament. The institutionalization of GHEITI and voluntary revenue transparency mechanisms were well established for the mining sector when commercially viable oil was discovered in 2007.

Developments in Ghana thus qualify the second hypothesis posited in the introduction to this book (Gupta and Mason, chapter 1) insofar as institutionalization of transparency opens up political space for new actors, but does not necessarily decenter state-led regulation. As discussed in the next section, transparency has actually rescaled sovereignty and bolstered state-led regulation and authority through active civil society engagement and advocacy away from soft law, such as voluntary good governance practices, toward hard law or binding regulation.

Effects of Transparency

Referring back to the framework of analysis set out in chapter 1, I turn next to assessing the normative, procedural, and substantive effects this revenue transparency agenda has had on Ghana's oil and gas sector.

Normative and Procedural Effects

With regard to normative and procedural effects of disclosure, or the extent to which transparency informs and empowers various stakeholders, there has been significant progress. With newly discovered oil in 2007, civil society leaders embarked on a "sensitization" campaign to inform the public about the pitfalls and opportunities for the transparency and good governance agenda to apply throughout the extractive industries value chain. The publication of *Ghana's Big Test—Oil's Challenge to Democratic Development* by the Integrated Social Development Centre and Oxfam America in January 2009 gained international media attention (Oxfam America 2009). Also in 2009, GHEITI's National Steering Committee began meeting with officials from the Ministry of Energy to share experiences from GHEITI in mining and discuss extending it to oil and gas. Numerous capacity-building and information-sharing workshops were held during this time, often spearheaded by civil society leaders. In March 2010, the Civil Society Platform on Oil and Gas (CSPOG) was created, which is a broad coalition with about 120 members, including civil society organizations, academic and research institutions, and individuals.

After a citizen's summit in June 2010 to consolidate views and positions, CSPOG issued a communiqué to government on the petroleum regulatory framework, the Petroleum Revenue Management Bill, and local content–local participation policy. Here the logic of transparency was applied in the context of mandatory policy and legislation. Although PWYP advocates for mandatory transparency interventions throughout the value chain of the extractive industries, it was a significant move beyond the voluntary remit of GHEITI. Also during this time, a multistakeholder workshop was held to discuss extending GHEITI to oil and gas. This expansion was completed in August 2010, when the GHEITI National Steering Committee was restructured to include oil, gas, and mining stakeholders (EITI 2011a).

In the run up to first oil exploration in December 2010, CSPOG took an active role organizing events, such as a regulatory roundtable in November 2010 to deliberate clauses of the Petroleum Revenue Management Bill and Petroleum Exploration and Production Bill. It also published materials such as newsletters and a working paper to educate the public on challenges and opportunities associated with the production of oil and gas (CSPOG 2010). International headlines were garnered in April 2011 when CSPOG published the *Readiness Report Card*, in conjunction with Oxfam America, which measured the performance not only of Ghana's government but also of development partners such as the World Bank, IMF, Ghana's Parliament, industry, and civil society itself (CSPOG 2011). The report was launched in Accra, London, and Washington DC (Oxfam America 2011).

Transparency within Ghana's emerging oil and gas industry has had significant procedural and normative effects (see table 11.1). For example, Ghana has emerged as a central node in a regional extractive industries capacity-building process. The Africa Regional Extractive Industries Knowledge Hub is hosted by the Ghana Institute of Management and Public Administration, which organized a roundtable meeting on contract transparency in April 2011 (Public Agenda 2011). The Ghana Institute of Management and Public Administration has also been hosting a "summer school" since 2009 on the governance of oil, gas, and mining revenues, which has been cosponsored by the Revenue Watch Institute and the German Organization for Technical Cooperation (GTZ). Other information and capacity-building activities are ongoing. In July 2011, for example, a workshop was organized by CSPOG and Public Agenda for journalists on reporting oil and gas issues and a revenue-monitoring tool was developed in 2011 by CSPOG.

Civil society has actively engaged with governance of the emerging oil and gas sector in Ghana to inform and empower multiple stakeholders at various levels. Nonetheless, Mohammed Amin Adam, oil coordinator for PWYP—Ghana and CSPOG steering committee member, warned that weaknesses remain: "Then on the part of civil society, we are weak. We are very weak in technical capacity to understand contracts, to monitor the contracts. We are also weak in our ability to track revenues because beyond oil production, what is important for civil society to do is how the

Table 11.1
Effectiveness of Transparency Initiatives in Ghana's Oil and Gas Sector

Types of Effects	Means	Ends
Normative: the extent to which transparency informs	• Press releases, newsletters, and regular civil society contributions to newspaper, radio, and television discussions • Community workshops and capacity-building activities • Domestic and international publications	• General public made aware of issues relating to oil and gas industry, such as legislation and operations, for example: • Memorandums on Petroleum Commission, Petroleum Revenue Management Bill, and Petroleum Exploration and Production Bill • Informed public of faulty flow meters and disputes over oil spill cleanup • GHEITI extended to include oil and gas sector
Procedural: the extent to which transparency empowers	• E-petitions, community meetings, and radio and television discussions • CSPOG members participate in the drafting of memorandums, attend regular membership meetings and multistakeholder events • PWYP consults with community environmental monitoring and advocacy groups on issues in the western region • PWYP coalition members visit other implementing countries	• Multistakeholder meetings provide opportunity for attendees to hold governing actors accountable. • E-petitions and memorandums enable participants to lobby governing actors and potentially hold them accountable. • Revenue-monitoring tools and networking builds capacity of civil society to hold government and companies accountable. • Oil and gas civil society representatives are included on the GHEITI Steering Committee. • Traditional authorities and community leaders in the western region demand greater benefits from the presence of the oil industry.
Substantive: the extent to which transparency improves governance outcomes	• Memorandums on Petroleum Commission, Petroleum Revenue Management Bill, and Petroleum Exploration and Production Bill • Lobbying and capacity building for government and parliamentary members by civil society leaders and donors	• Following the release of a Petroleum Revenue Management Bill memorandum, changes were made, including the inclusion of a Public Oversight Committee (passed in March 2011). • After civil society influence, the Petroleum Commission Bill established an independent regulator (passed in June 2011). • As part of GHEITI, disclosure of oil revenues and payments started in 2011 (with the first national report published in 2013)

revenues flow into the budget and how the revenues impact on living conditions. Civil society doesn't have the capacity yet to track the revenues" (Oxfam America 2011, n.p.).

Here Adam highlights the imperative to extend the logic of transparency beyond payments and rents to other aspects of the petroleum value chain. It is interesting that civil society has moved beyond the voluntary logics of GHEITI to engage with mandatory policy and legislative initiatives. Substantive effects of transparency are found in the space of these mandatory initiatives. As Dr. David Nguyen-Thanh of GTZ has cautioned, "the measure of success is not the number of workshops and seminars organized but the creation of benchmarks to measure costs and benefits of training over time, and the influence of various actors in improving the lives of individuals and communities" (Revenue Watch Institute 2010, n.p.). The question remains to what extent the logics of transparency in relation to the emerging oil and gas sector in Ghana are having substantive effects at national and local levels.

Substantive Effects

Particularly at the national level, significant interaction has occurred between the voluntary revenue transparency agenda (that is the EITI) and mandatory regulatory initiatives throughout the oil and gas industry value chain. A drive was underway to get a regulatory framework in place before the beginning of oil production. Although substantial progress was made, major petroleum legislation was still being debated in Parliament when Ghana's first oil began to flow in December 2010. However, in March 2011, the Petroleum Revenue Management Bill was passed and CSPOG successfully lobbied for broader participation in the Public Interest and Accountability Committee to monitor oil revenues. Civil society leaders hailed Ghana's Petroleum Revenue Management Law as one of the best in the world because of its transparency provisions and citizen oversight. As Adam highlighted: "I'm happy to mention that about 15 recommendations that we made to government to improve and develop a transparent process of managing oil revenues were all taken on board by the government, and they all are in the revenue management law as we speak today" (Oxfam America 2011, n.p.).

Ghana's revenue management law goes beyond the EITI voluntary agenda; it covers spending transparency and accountability in addition to revenue transparency. Another success for civil society leaders came in June 2011 when the Petroleum Commission Bill was passed, which established an independent regulator of the petroleum sector.

Transparency advocates have begun to argue that it is not just important to know how much firms pay but also the fiscal terms of the contract that companies sign with host countries (Cotula 2010). They argue that contract disclosure will enable EITI-implementing countries to establish what companies do not pay (Public Agenda 2011). Contract transparency has become a top advocacy priority for PWYP. In Ghana, the EITI multistakeholder group required the auditor to reconcile payments with the fiscal terms contained in the mining contracts of EITI-participating companies. However, it was not until 2011 that Jubilee field contracts were disclosed. In May 2011 Kosmos disclosed its contract together with joint production agreements with other Jubilee partners because of its initial public offering at the US Securities and Exchange Commission (Revenue Watch Institute 2011). This action forced the Ghanaian government and Tullow Oil also to disclose these contracts (Public Agenda 2011). Ghana is demonstrating its commitment to contract transparency and its willingness to do business differently from other African oil-rich countries, because it intends to provide legal backing to contract disclosure in its draft Petroleum Exploration and Production Bill (Public Agenda 2011).

What is interesting here is how governance mechanisms, at and between different levels, have interacted to raise revenue transparency on the agenda and enact institutional change. Vibrant advocacy networks, information-sharing, training, and capacity-building events have driven transparency forward and permitted engagement with new issues areas within the extractive industries value chain.

Civil society leaders have also increased pressure on members of Parliament, after the success of the Petroleum Revenue Management Bill, to close transparency gaps in how the revenue is generated. The Petroleum Exploration and Production Bill was actually submitted to Parliament but then withdrawn for repackaging. Civil society leaders felt it was quite nontransparent and hoped the delay would bring positive changes, and they lobbied for a contract disclosure requirement to be included in the bill, in addition to a competitive bidding process for allocating oil concessions (Oxfam America 2011).

As highlighted, an interesting trend in governance by disclosure in Ghana is the interaction between soft and hard law in extractive industry disclosure. Within the context of transparency, soft law is defined as voluntary norms, standards, and good governance initiatives such as the EITI, whereas hard law is the move toward incorporating transparency accountability mechanisms into binding laws and regulations. At least at the national level in Ghana, the transparency agenda has moved well beyond voluntary disclosure of payments and revenues by firms and government and has made its way into the legislative framework that governs petroleum revenue management and possibly exploration and production. However, with regard to substantive effects of transparency in Ghana's emerging oil and gas sector, it remains to be seen how transparency influences on-the-ground changes such as the lives of ordinary citizens in Ghana and other resource-rich countries (PWYP 2011b). Future research should address this knowledge gap (e.g., Scanteam 2011).

Transparency's Transformative Potential?

As is evident from the foregoing discussion, the transparency agenda has had significant normative and procedural impacts on the governance of the emerging oil and gas industry, and some limited substantive impacts, such as through the interaction between soft and hard law. In concluding, I consider some of the gaps and opportunities emerging within the transparency in energy governance agenda in Ghana. Figure 11.1 outlines various dimensions of transparency in energy governance within the context of Ghana's emerging oil and gas sector, which help to illustrate the chapter's key findings.

To begin with, returning to one of the main themes of the book, *the degree to which transparency in energy governance has been transformational is limited in the case of Ghana.* However, distinct from the findings on the Global Reporting Initiative (see Dingwerth and Eichinger, this book, chapter 10), a vibrant internationally networked NGO community has evolved in the context of the EITI and PWYP campaigns. Although initial success occurred through civil society engagement with the emerging regulatory framework in Ghana, limitations to the transparency and good governance agenda at the national level remain. These include lack of a long-term national development plan, a weak oil spill response plan, no strategic environmental assessment for the oil and gas sector, lack of technical capacity in Parliament to scrutinize contracts and monitor the oil and gas industry, no guidelines on how oil and gas revenues fit into the overall budget, and the potential of national security exemptions in the Freedom of Information Bill, which is pending in Parliament (Oxfam America 2011). In addition to these challenges at the national level, there are significant concerns at the subnational level within Ghana's western region.

There is little evidence that civil society organizations and/or donors have engaged in rigorous and critical research with the aim to understand baseline conditions and implement transparency, capacity building, and

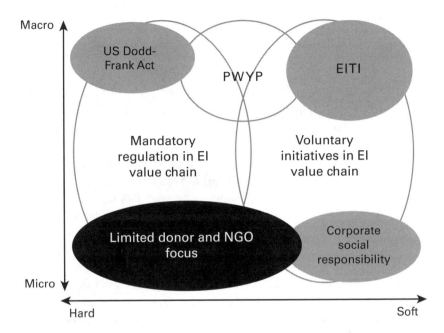

Figure 11.1
Dimensions of Transparency in Energy Governance

accountability mechanisms at the district level within the western region. Tullow and government agencies have held public consultations in the western region, and Tullow and the Jubilee partners have made corporate social responsibility investments (Oxfam America 2011). Community environmental monitoring and advocacy groups have been established in each district, but it remains to be seen to what extent transparency and accountability mechanisms have been institutionalized at the local level. In the context of Ghana's emerging oil sector, there is a significant opportunity for civil society organizations and development partners to fill this gap, as Nana Ama Yirrah has stressed: "So we on the Civil Society Platform are saying that, yes, the laws are important. The legislation to guide oil exploration and production, oil revenue, and revenue management are important. But what is even of more importance to us is to see how this generation of revenue … this protection of the revenue sources translates into development—real development for the people (Oxfam America 2011, n.p.).

In response to growing concern, the government announced it would set up a Western Corridor Development Authority to address development issues in the region, but local civil society leaders remained skeptical that the intervention would confront the specific issues of concern to the front-line communities in the oil region (Oxfam America 2011). Thus, there appears to be a disconnect between efforts at the national and local levels.

A second significant finding is *the hybrid character of voluntary and mandatory transparency logics.* As indicated in figure 11.1, a dynamic institutionalization process has rescaled state sovereignty and authority through active civil society engagement and advocacy away from soft law, such as voluntary good governance practices, toward hard law, or binding policy and regulation. This move from voluntary to mandatory rules brings with it risks and opportunities: who exercises authority and to what extent are they transparent and accountable to Ghanaian citizens? Governance gaps exist at the local level and, at the national level, there are concerns about the extent to which the Freedom of Information Bill will be subject to national security exemptions for the petroleum industry and whether the Petroleum Exploration and Production Bill will embrace contract transparency and a competitive bidding process, among others. At the international level, an interesting new development is that the US Dodd-Frank Act may require US-listed oil companies (for example, Kosmos in Ghana) to disclose their payments to the Ghanaian government. Although Ghana is a signatory to the EITI, this is an important example of how extraterritorial legislation may rescale state sovereignty. This hard law should benefit Ghanaian citizens as well as US citizens, but Ghanaians are not the intended beneficiaries.

Processes of scaling and rescaling are indicative of the structural context within which the diffusion of transparency logics takes place. The social construction of scale, how scalar configurations are in fact "the outcomes of socio-spatial processes that regulate and organize social power relations" (Swyngedouw 2004, 26), is particularly relevant. As Haufler points out, the good governance and transparency agendas sit quite comfortably alongside the "neoliberal norms of market efficiency and bureaucratic rationality" (2010, 56). The NGOs that have engaged in this neoliberal form of market governance have attempted to fill a governance gap in the value chain of the extractive industries. It can be argued that the revenue transparency agenda is a reformist initiative seeking only incremental change (Benner and Soares de Oliveira 2010), yet it can also be viewed as an important first step in the governance of resource extraction.

Third, *the World Bank's conceptualization of the extractive industry value chain as a template for transparency interventions has limitations.*

For example, in the World Bank's working paper, *The Extractive Industries Value Chain,* the value chain is depicted as a linear process that proceeds from awarding contracts and licenses, to regulating and monitoring operations, to collecting taxes and royalties, to revenue management and allocation, to implementing sustainable development policies and projects (Alba 2009). This linear typology misses the scalar and temporal dynamics of the industry, particularly in a "new oil" country context such as Ghana. For example, sustainable development and long-term poverty reduction policies should be established before the petroleum regulatory framework is put into place. In addition, the World Bank's value chain typology does little to elaborate on jurisdictional levels, such as to what extent these links in the chain need to be implemented at national versus local levels. Regulation and monitoring of operations, collecting taxes and royalties, and revenue allocation, in addition to implementation of sustainable development polices and projects, should occur at and between national and local levels. The risk here is that NGOs and development partners focus on certain links of the chain without recognizing the need for interventions at multiple levels, from exploration to production and closure throughout the operational time frame of the industry. The NGO and international community focus on getting the regulatory framework in place before first oil was important. Yet what appears to have occurred as a knock-on effect is lack of understanding about impacts of the emerging petroleum sector in the western region and a relatively naive corporate social responsibility strategy in the frontline communities by Jubilee partners (Sam et al. forthcoming).

Finally, one of the key themes emerging from this analysis is *the impact a resource's materiality has on transparency processes and outcomes.* For example, oil has unique material qualities that pose significant governance challenges (see Bridge 2008; Le Billon 2001; Ross 2004; Watts 2007). For one, Ghana's oil is located sixty kilometers offshore, and is sweet and light crude, which is easy to transport and is sought after by Western and emerging economies for its low sulfur content and refining ease. The Ghanaian government centrally controls the rents, without any earmarking for the western region (a different model than that of Ghana's gold-mining sector). The oil sector provides few domestic jobs compared to conventional mining, and the types of international oil companies operating in Ghana tend to be junior players, with relatively little experience of moving from exploration into production and managing the subsequent social, economic, and environmental impacts on so-called host communities. Indeed, the material properties of this energy mineral are very different from those of nonenergy minerals, such as gold, which leads to differing governance and development outcomes. For example, Hilson and Maconachie (2009) organize African resource-rich countries into three different categories: petro-economies (oil and gas), "lootable" economies (diamonds and gemstones), and "conventional" mineral producers (copper, gold, and other nonlootable minerals). This is a relevant typology and points to the need for further comparative research on what governance mechanisms and policy frameworks may be best suited for each type of resource. The extent to which transparency mechanisms depend on the resource being governed thus requires much more sustained scrutiny.

Conclusion

In the introduction to this book, Gupta and Mason query whether transparency in global environmental governance can be transformational, including whether it is a red herring, distracting from opportunities to make more substantive change, or serves rather as an approach with necessarily limited transformative powers because of a variety of challenges, but nonetheless as the "best game in town." Given the interaction between voluntary and mandatory transparency logics in Ghanaian revenue transparency, it does not appear that this good governance agenda has "distracted" attention from opportunities to make substantive change, nor, however, has it been "transformational" within Ghana's extractive sector. Voluntary governance by disclosure has not been the "default option" here (Haufler 2010). Rather it has been one of a variety of pathways chosen for institutionalizing good governance within its extractive sector. Nonetheless, significant challenges remain. The logics of transparency, accountability, and community benefits in the western region are underrepresented, and the Petroleum Exploration and Development Bill and the Freedom of Information Bill are held up in Parliament, with civil society concerned that transparency mechanisms within these may be compromised.

Concern has also been raised in the literature that lack of a strong domestic civil society may hinder the effectiveness of revenue transparency, and that difficulties in agreeing on a shared vision and communication of EITI within participating countries may negatively affect its success (Aaronson 2011; Smith et al. 2012). The evidence from Ghana suggests that civil society has demonstrated a common voice at the national level with regard to the emerging petroleum sector and has actively and strategically engaged with the issue of revenue transparency within the framework of GHEITI and disclosure throughout the value chain. Thus, the-best-game-in-town thesis for disclosure-based governance best fits the Ghanaian case: transparency in energy governance is having some success, but it is still very early days for the industry within the country. The tremendous knowledge sharing that is occurring in this domain, with Ghana as the key node within a growing transnational network of civil society activists, development partners, and other stakeholders, is promising. However, evidence is lacking on how transparency in energy governance influences on-the-ground pro-poor change in Ghana and other resource-rich countries within and beyond sub-Saharan Africa, pointing to an important research agenda in transparency studies.

Note

1. EITI-compliant countries are characterized by a range of regimes. Using The Economist Intelligence Unit's 2012 Democracy Index, four out of the seventeen compliant EITI countries as of April 2013 are authoritarian regimes, seven are hybrid regimes, five are flawed democracies, and only one is a full democracy. More research is needed to determine whether the adoption of the EITI influences democratization.

References

Aaronson, Susan Ariel. 2011. Limited Partnership: Business, Government, Civil Society, and the Public in the Extractive Industries Transparency Initiative (EITI). *Public Administration and Development* 31 (1): 50–63.

Alba, Eleodoro Mayorga. 2009. *Extractive Industries Value Chain.* Extractive Industries for Development Series #3. Africa Region Working Paper Series #125. Washington, DC: The World Bank.

Benford, Robert D., and David A. Snow. 2000. Framing Processes and Social Movements: An Overview and Assessment. *Annual Review of Sociology* 26: 611–639.

Benner, Thorsten, and Richardo Soares de Oliveira. 2010. The Good/Bad Nexus in Global Energy Governance. In *Global Energy Governance: The New Rules of the Game,* ed. Andreas Goldthau and Jan Martin Witte. Berlin: Global Public Policy Institute and Brookings Institution Press.

Bridge, Gavin. 2008. Global Production Networks and the Extractive Sector: Governing Resource-Based Development. *Journal of Economic Geography* 8 (3): 389–419.

Campbell, John L. 2005. Where Do We Stand? Common Mechanisms in Organizations and Social Movements Research. In *Social Movements and Organization*

Theory, ed. Gerald F. Davis, Doug McAdam, W. Richard Scott, and Mayner N. Zald, 41–68. New York: Cambridge University Press.

CIDA. 2011. *Ghana Overview*. Ottawa: Canadian International Development Agency.

Cotula, Lorenzo. 2010. *Investment Contracts and Sustainable Development: How to Make Contracts for Fairer and More Sustainable Natural Resource Investments*. Natural Resource Issues, No. 20. London: International Institute for Environment and Development.

CSPOG. 2010. *A Brief Guide to Oil and Gas in Ghana*. Ghana Oil and Gas Watch. Accra: Civil Society Platform on Oil and Gas.

CSPOG. 2011. *Ghana's Oil Boom—a Readiness Report Card*. Accra: Civil Society Platform on Oil and Gas.

Dykstra, Page. 2011. *Learning from Success and Challenges*. EITI 2011 Briefing. New York: Revenue Watch Institute.

EITI. 2011a. *EITI Countries—Ghana*. vol. 2011. Extractive Industies Transparency Initiative. Oslo: EITI Secretariat.

EITI. 2011b. *Extractive Industries Transparency Initiative Website*. vol. 2011. Oslo: EITI Secretariat.

Frynas, Jedrzej George. 2009. *Beyond Corporate Social Responsibility*. Cambridge, UK: Cambridge University Press.

Fung, Archon, Mary Graham, and David Weil. 2007. *Full Disclosure: The Perils and Promise of Transparency*. Cambridge, UK: Cambridge University Press.

Gary, Ian, and Terry Lynn Karl. 2003. *Bottom of the Barrel: Africa's Oil Boom and the Poor*. Washington, DC: Catholic Relief Services.

Gillies, Alexandra. 2010. Reputational Concerns and the Emergence of Oil Sector Transparency as an International Norm. *International Studies Quarterly* 54 (1): 103–126.

Gillies, Alexandra. 2011. *What Do the Numbers Say? Analyzing Report Data*. EITI 2011 Briefing. New York: Revenue Watch Institute.

GNPC. n.d. *Exploration and Production Current Operations*. GNPC Website. Ghana National Petroleum Corporation.

Global Witness. 1999. *A Crude Awakening*. London: Global Witness.

Haufler, Virginia. 2010. Disclosure as Governance: The Extractive Industries Transparency Initiative and Resource Management in the Developing World. *Global Environmental Politics* 10 (3): 53–73.

Hilson, Gavin, and Roy Maconachie. 2009. "Good Governance" and the Extractive Industries in Sub-Saharan Africa. *Mineral Processing and Extractive Metallurgy Review* 30 (1): 52–100.

Humphreys, M., Jeffrey D. Sachs, and Joseph E. Stiglitz, eds. 2007. *Escaping the Resource Curse*. New York: Columbia University Press.

ICMM. 2005. *Community Development Toolkit*. London: ICMM, World Bank, ESMAP.

ISODEC. 2009. *Civil Society and EITI Implementation in Ghana.* Dodowa Workshop. Dodowa: Integrated Social Development Centre.

Jones, Samantha. 2002. Social Constructionism and the Environment: Through the Quagmire. *Global Environmental Change* 12 (4): 247–251.

Kolstad, Ivar, and Arne Wiig. 2009. Is Transparency the Key to Reducing Corruption in Resource-Rich Countries? *World Development* 37 (3): 521–532.

Le Billon, Philippe. 2001. The Political Ecology of War: Natural Resources and Armed Conflicts. *Political Geography* 20 (5): 561–584.

Levy, David L., and Peter Newell. 2005. *The Business of Global Environmental Governance.* Cambridge, MA: MIT Press.

McAdam, Doug, and Richard W. Scott. 2005. Organizations and Movements. In *Social Movements and Organization Theory,* ed. Gerald F. Davis, Doug McAdam, Richard W. Scott, and Mayner N. Zald, 4–40. Cambridge, UK: Cambridge University Press.

MMSD. 2002. *Breaking New Ground: Mining, Minerals and Sustainable Development; The Report of the MMSD Project.* London: Earthscan.

Nguyen-Thanh, David, and Maya Schnell. 2009. Reviewing Half a Decade of EITI Implementation in Ghana's Mining Sector. In *Advancing the EITI in the Mining Sector: A Consultation with Stakeholders,* ed. Christopher Eads, Paul Mitchell, and Francisco Paris. Oslo: EITI.

Ottaway, Marina, and Thomas Carothers. 2000. *Funding Virtue: Civil Society Aid and Democracy Promotion.* Washington, DC: Carnegie Endowment for International Peace.

Oxfam America. 2001. *Extractive Sectors and the Poor,* ed. Michael Ross. Washington, DC: Oxfam America.

Oxfam America. 2009. *Ghana's Big Test: Oil's Challenge to Democratic Development.* Washington, DC: Oxfam America.

Oxfam America. 2011. *Oxfam America Holds a Discussion on the Findings of a New Report Analysing Ghana's Preparedness to Manage Its New Wealth and "Address the Problems That Face So Many Oil Booming African Countries"—Final.* Washington, DC: Oxfam America.

Pegg, S. 2006. Mining and Poverty Reduction: Transforming Rhetoric into Reality. *Journal of Cleaner Production* 14 (3–4): 376–387.

Public Agenda. 2011. Ghana: Expanding the Frontiers of Good Governance. *Africa News.* Accra: AllAfrica, Inc.

PWYP. 2011a. *G8 Endorses Mandatory Oil, Gas and Mining Payment Transparency.* London: Publish What You Pay International.

PWYP. 2011b. *Publish What You Pay Website.* vol. 2011. London: Publish What You Pay.

PWYP—Ghana. n.d. *The Formal Launch of the Campaign.* Accra: Publish What You Pay—Ghana.

Ravat, Anwar, and Andre Ufer. 2010. *Toward Strengthened EITI Reporting: Summary Report and Recommendations, Extractive Industries for Development Series*. vol. 14. Washington DC: World Bank Group's Oil, Gas, and Mining Policy Division.

Revenue Watch Institute. 2010. *Africa Regional Knowledge Hub for Extractive Industries Re-Launches with 2010 Summer Session*. Accra: Revenue Watch Institute.

Revenue Watch Institute. 2011. *Ghana Jubilee Field Contracts, Revenue Watch Institute Resource Center*. New York: Revenue Watch Institute.

Ross, Michael. 2004. What Do We Know about Natural Resources and Civil War. *Journal of Peace Research* 41 (3): 337–356.

Sam, Gilbert, Kyei K. Yamoah, Bright Yeboah, and James Van Alstine. Forthcoming. Seeking Benefits and Avoiding Conflicts: A Community-Company Assessment of Ghana's Hydrocarbon Industry. In *Rights, Risk and Responsibilities: Building Capacity for Community-Company Engagement*, ed. James Van Alstine and A. Rani Parker. Leeds, UK: University of Leeds.

Scanteam. 2011. *Achievements and Strategic Options: Evaluation of the Extractive Industries Transparency Initiative*. Oslo: Scanteam.

Scott, Richard W. 2008. *Institutions and Organizations*. 3rd ed. Thousand Oaks, CA: Sage.

Smith, Shirley M., Derek D. Shepherd, and Peter T. Dorward. 2012. Perspectives on Community Representation within the Extractive Industries Transparency Initiative: Experiences from South-East Madagascar. *Resources Policy* 37 (2): 241–250.

Swyngedouw, Erik. 2004. Globalisation or "Glocalisation"? Networks, Territories and Rescaling. *Cambridge Review of International Affairs* 17 (1): 25–48.

UNCTAD. 2007. *Transnational Corporations, Extractive Industries and Development*. World Investment Report. Geneva: United Nations Conference on Trade and Development.

UNCTAD. 2011. *Commodities at a Glance*. Geneva: United Nations Conference on Trade and Development.

UNDP. 2011. *Sustainability and Equity: A Better Future for All, Human Development Report*. New York: United Nations Development Programme.

Watts, Michael. 2007. *The Rule of Oil: Petro-Politics and the Anatomy of an Insurgency, Oil and Politics Conference*, 1–34. London: Goldsmiths College, University of London.

World Bank. 2003. *Striking a Better Balance: The Extractive Industries Review*. Washington, DC: The World Bank Group.

World Bank. 2004. *Striking a Better Balance—the World Bank Group and Extractive Industries: The Final Report of the Extractive Industries Review*. Washington, DC: World Bank.

World Bank. 2008. *World Bank Group and Partners Launch EITI++*. Press Release No. 2008/269/AFR. Washington, DC: World Bank.

12

Learning through Disclosure: The Evolving Importance of Transparency in the Practice of Nonstate Certification

Graeme Auld and Lars H. Gulbrandsen

Certification programs—organized and coordinated by nonstate actors to address social and environmental challenges in numerous economic sectors—exemplify efforts to govern by disclosure.[1] Some hope certification will be a tool for NGOs, investors, governments, and consumers to, via labeled products, identify and support high performers and, hence, place upward pressure on sectorwide practices. Beyond this simple appraisal, however, unanswered questions remain concerning the practice and consequences of transparency by nonstate certification.

This chapter presents a critical comparative analysis of transparency in nonstate certification in two ways. First, we compare certification initiatives in the forest and fisheries sectors, primarily focusing on the Forest Stewardship Council (FSC) and the Marine Stewardship Council (MSC) to assess *transparency of* and *for* private governance and its consequences for legitimacy and accountability (Mitchell 2011). To do so, we assess not only what information is disclosed but also, via rules for participation, which actors define, control, and have access to it. Through this lens, important differences across programs emerge. As a membership organization, the FSC allows direct participation in rule-making processes through, for instance, national initiatives charged with localizing the program's global standard. The MSC, by contrast, formed as a partnership initiative of the World Wide Fund for Nature (WWF) and Unilever, which sought to create an FSC-type organization for seafood (Fowler and Heap 2000). Other stakeholders were quickly included via workshops and outreach seeking feedback on standards development. Yet, the partners purposefully avoided copying the FSC's approach to membership and its national affiliates for localizing global standards (Auld 2009). The contrasting paths of the FSC and MSC shed light on the relationships between transparency and participation and resultant links to legitimacy and accountability. The MSC's pursuit of legitimacy involves a more instrumental use of transparency and participation: they are used here to inform stakeholders of the program's activities and to solicit advice to make fisheries assessments credible. The FSC, by contrast, treats transparency and participation more as ends unto themselves.

These differences uncover a nuanced view of the role that democratization plays in driving transparency in global environmental governance (Gupta and Mason, this book, chapter 1). Although the FSC's embracing of inclusive stakeholder governance is consistent with a democratization driver of disclosure, the MSC roots its transparency practices more in norms of scientific expertise and instrumental knowledge. With accountability, the two programs are more similar, both treating transparency as an important tool for accountability. Each has continually increased the checks on and openness of auditing practices by introducing new requirements for certifiers and methodologies for ensuring consistency across assessments. Here, both programs thus support the postulate, advanced in the introduction to this book, that institutionalization of transparency can decenter state-led regulatory processes and open up political space for other actors.

Our second comparative focus examines how the transparency provisions of individual nonstate certification programs interact to affect the learning potential of the private regulatory field. We find uneven diffusion of the disclosure practices undertaken by the MSC and FSC, particularly the disclosure of auditing reports. Carbon-offset verifiers, such as the American Carbon Registry, Verified Carbon Standard, and Climate Action Reserve, have adopted this practice. However, other programs within the forestry and fishery sector have not done so nor has the joint initiative of the Rainforest Alliance and the Sustainable Agriculture Network, a program active in certifying many agricultural commodities.

This inconsistency has implications for the learning capacity of nonstate certification programs. We find that later programs benefit from the transparency of earlier programs, but do not disclose their own lessons to inform future developments of the certification field as a whole. As such, we stress here that the *marketization of information*—that is, how knowledge about the operation of nonstate certification is becoming privately controlled and exchanged—requires careful attention if the transformative potential of both transparency and certification is to be realized (on this point, see also Mol, this book, chapter 2).

Our analysis proceeds in four parts. First, we review the links between transparency and (1) programmatic legitimacy and accountability, and (2) learning within and across nonstate certification initiatives by drawing an analytic distinction between procedural and outcome transparency. Second, we examine the transparency requirements of the MSC and FSC. Third, we explore the effects of procedural and outcome transparency for goals of legitimacy and accountability and then assess links between outcome transparency and the field-level learning capacity of nonstate certification programs.

Embracing Transparency

The information provided by an eco-label is only one reason and—in our assessment—not the most important reason why certification is an example of governance by disclosure (Gupta 2008). First, eco-labels provide limited information; consumers who buy labeled products essentially have to *trust* the label. Absent public outreach and marketing, most consumers cannot be expected to critically assess labeling requirements and then make informed choices about whether or not to buy a labeled product. Although some labels provide extensive on-product information—nutritional labels for instance—this approach is rare among nonstate certification programs. Second, research shows that NGO targeting of major buyers that then demand certified products from their supply chains has contributed more to the growth and spread of nonstate certification programs than has consumer demand (Cashore et al. 2004; Gulbrandsen 2006; Sasser 2003). Third, eco-labels are only a small part of the information that nonstate certification programs disclose; information about the procedures and outcomes of rule making and auditing—that is the *transparency of* and *for* governance (Mitchell 2011)—reveals a lot more about the consequences of transparency in certification programs than does the label itself.

This chapter, then, focuses on procedural and outcome transparency and their implications for the accountability and legitimacy of certification programs, and for the learning capacity of private regulatory fields (Auld and Gulbrandsen 2010). By procedural transparency, we mean the openness of governance processes, such as decision making or adjudication (Vermeule 2007, 187). Transparency of this type is often used to improve the legitimacy of global governance arrangements; open procedures are postulated to legitimize governors not supported by norms of popular sovereignty (Esty 2006, 1514; Gupta 2008; Mitchell 2011). Outcome transparency involves information about regulated or unregulated behaviors; for instance, a law might require disclosure of the environmental or health risks of a product or manufacturing process (Mitchell 2011). It deals directly with a policy's substantive ends and has consequences for identifying and managing environmental and social problems by providing information to concerned actors with the aim of affecting behavior and/or increasing accountability (Vermeule 2007, 187; see also Mitchell 1998). Although outcome and procedural transparency can occur simultaneously, they may not. A process with no procedural transparency could establish a rule requiring extensive outcome transparency for some regulated party; hence, they are useful to disentangle.

With certification, the focal actors for procedural transparency are decision makers. Information about decision-making processes made public can be a means to meet all the previously mentioned policy goals. First, accountability may improve, because information about decision-making processes enables program members and the public to ask relevant questions and demand answers. Second, by appealing to shared norms of openness and fairness, support for certification by producers, NGOs, local communities, and other relevant audiences can increase, thus enhancing legitimacy (Bernstein 2004; Bernstein and Cashore 2007). Finally, information about decision-making processes can facilitate buy-in from a broad base of participants to ensure effective implementation of policy choices. Because participation is voluntary, procedural transparency can help convince participants that decision making is conducted in an open, balanced, and fair manner.

With outcome transparency, the focal actors are those being regulated. Information about their activities disclosed to the public and stakeholders can enhance accountability and legitimacy. First, better accountability can result because NGOs use audit reports to hold certified companies to account for their practices and performance (Meidinger 2006, 82). Second, improved legitimacy can result if information about auditing and monitoring convinces relevant audiences that assessments are credible and that the system for monitoring practices, verifying compliance, and responding to noncompliance can be trusted (O'Rourke 2006; Raynolds et al. 2007). Finally, by generating information about the practices and performance of certified companies, outcome transparency can influence behavior and ultimately may facilitate better environmental and working conditions or other relevant improvements (O'Rourke 2003).

Procedural and outcome transparency do not act in isolation; other policies and the environment within which information is disclosed condition their consequences. First, procedural transparency may not empower all stakeholders equally (Langley 2001; see also Vermeule 2007, 192). Who is selected as a participant, what form of information is exchanged and through what means, and who holds decision-making power are important questions. How they are answered matters for how transparency affects accountability and legitimacy (Fung 2006).

Second, the outcome and procedural transparency practices of individual certification programs interact to affect the learning capacity of the broader field of private regulators. There are two competing incentives at play. On the one hand, individual programs have incentives to control their information disclosures; they confront market norms about information such as commercial confidentiality and intellectual property rights, which favor private, restricted, or paid-for access to information. On the other, the collective-learning and innovation capacity relies on open access. Without information on what does and does not work, learning across programs will be limited.

Various scholars interested in the aggregate effects of self-organized governance or policy experiments underscore this point (Keohane and Victor 2011; Victor et al. 2005). As stated by Overdevest et al. (2010, 286), "Experimentalism seeks to encourage local jurisdictions or communities to experiment with ways of achieving standards for environmental quality (air quality, water quality, adequate participation), while it calls for the broader pooling and sharing of information across experiments to help improve public understanding and accountability." The key point for us is the "pooling and sharing of information," which relies on the transparency.

These insights highlight a key challenge. Nonstate certification programs are innovating new governance arrangements, mechanisms, and norms with broad value for collective efforts to manage earth systems. Tracking systems developed in forestry, for instance, have become critical for advancing efforts to fight illegal timber trade (Auld et al. 2010). However, incomplete or uneven transparency across the field of nonstate certification programs presents problems for this collective model of innovation. It may mean certain programs gain from the experiences of others, without reciprocating with information about their own successes and failures. Hence, we suggest that open source governance models—from computer software in particular—provide important lessons for the future evolution of nonstate certification programs (Boyle 2008; Braithwaite 2008).

This second part of our analysis is, then, a plausibility probe for the argument that without disclosure about the effects of nonstate certification, collective learning to advance effectiveness will be difficult. Absent disclosure requirements, later programs can copy aspects of early programs without having to disclose their own lessons learned, thus hampering learning and innovation. Though many design characteristics may be copied (Dingwerth and Pattberg 2009; Gulbrandsen 2010), we focus on outcome transparency because it is arguably critical for learning about programmatic effects.

Institutionalizing Transparency

This section reviews procedural and outcome transparency provisions in the FSC's and MSC's rule-making and auditing processes (table 12.1).[2] In so doing, we also consider how the institutionalization of transparency in these schemes might be opening up political space for new actors.

Rule Making

Ultimate decision-making authority resides with different bodies in the two programs. With the FSC, authority is held by the organization's membership, over 853 in February 2013 (Forest Stewardship Council 2013). Member organizations and individuals are separated into three interest-based chambers (environment, social, and economic), each of which now control one-third of the total voting rights. Parity between northern and southern interests is also required within each chamber. The secretariat is the FSC's central organizational body. Led by the executive director, it manages operational issues, carrying out the membership's motions and the board of director's strategic plans (Forest Stewardship Council 1995).

By contrast, with the MSC, ultimate decision-making authority is held by a board of trustees, which also acts as the organization's public face. Initially, the MSC was run by a secretariat that coordinated the activities of a standards council, advisory board, and national working groups (Fowler and Heap 2000, 141). The advisory board was partitioned into three chambers: one for economic interests, a second for environmental groups and government bodies (domestic and international), and a third for educational, social, and consumer interests (Marine Stewardship Council 2000; see also Fowler and Heap 2000, 141). It was the closest analog to FSC's membership, being "open to any individual with an interest in fisheries and their certification irrespective of their own background" (Marine Stewardship Council 1999). Following a review in 2001, the MSC expanded its board of trustees and replaced the standards council with a technical advisory board designed to give advice on standards, chain of custody, and logo licensing. Finally, the advisory board was replaced by a stakeholder council comprising thirty to fifty members

Table 12.1
Transparency Used by the FSC and MSC

Types of Transparency	Focal Actors	Use and Consequences for FSC — Means	Use and Consequences for FSC — Ends	Use and Consequences for MSC — Means	Use and Consequences for MSC — Ends
Procedural	National initiatives	• Broad participation in standards development • Stakeholder and public meetings • Comment periods on draft standards	• Standards accountable to members and public • Legitimate standard, congruent with local conditions • Buy-in from participants to ensure legitimacy and implementation		
	Certifier, assessment team	• Seven years of records available to FSC • Assessment records available to stakeholders • Documenting and responding to stakeholder comments, keeping identities anonymous	• Certifiers accountable to stakeholders and FSC • Credible assessments and legitimacy of program	• Public notice for operations entering full assessment • Thirty-day comment period on assessment standard • Documenting and responding to stakeholder comments	• Standards accountable to public • Legitimate standard, congruent with local conditions, based on expert knowledge and stakeholder consultation
Outcome	Fishery or forestry operation	• Disclose information to certifier for evaluation against P&C • Assessment summarized and publicized on certifier's website; full report provided to FSC	• Certifiers and operation accountable to stakeholders and FSC • Credible assessment and legitimacy of program • Compliance with standard	• Disclose information to certifier for evaluation against P&C • Assessment summarized and publicized on MSC website	• Certifier and company accountable to stakeholders and MSC • Credible assessment and legitimacy of program • Compliance with standard

who met annually to provide the board guidance. Two members from the council and one member of the technical advisory board hold seats on the board of trustees, which continues to hold rule-making authority (Marine Stewardship Council 2001b).

The core rules the FSC and MSC establish are those governing the practices of audited operations in the respective sectors. Both programs took similar approaches to establishing global standards, but differed in how they made these standards appropriate for different local fisheries and forestry contexts. The FSC decentralized the process. After spending four years drafting the international Principles and Criteria (P&C), which involved worldwide consultation, groups of interested stakeholders in a specific country—or region within a country—were given official status and charged with developing locally appropriate indicators and verifiers for the P&C.[3] The FSC set stringent requirements for transparency of these initiatives. As stated in Evison (1998, 29), the belief was that "in order for the FSC as a whole to maintain its credibility and transparency, the organization and its National Initiatives must act in an open and participatory fashion." Likewise, with the national initiatives' standards development work, the FSC required procedural transparency for standards it will endorse. This meant that "the consultative process [has to] be transparent and accountable, both to working group members, and to the wider public. Minutes of all meetings and draft standards [are to] be made available to any interested party" (Evison 1998, 29).

Meeting these procedural requirements has been time and resource intensive, and as a result, endorsed standards lag behind the spread of forest management certificates.[4] By 2010, FSC-certified forests existed in eighty-two countries, nearly four times the number of endorsed standards (given some countries, particularly the United States, have several subnational standards endorsed) (Forest Stewardship Council 2007a). Because certifiers were operating before the FSC launched, and in order not to restrict participation in areas where standards remain incomplete, FSC-accredited certifiers may assess operations against locally adapted "generic" standards (Forest Stewardship Council 2004d). Here, too, FSC requires stakeholder consultation. This includes soliciting input from any FSC national initiative operational in the country or region, relevant government bodies, interested domestic and international NGOs, representatives of relevant indigenous peoples and forest dwelling or using communities affected by the operations, labor unions, contractors, and representatives of forest industry and forest owners (Forest Stewardship Council 2004e; Forest Stewardship Council 2004d, clause 3.1.3). In a language readily understood in the region, the certifier must contact stakeholders about the assessment and indicate that their input will inform the localization of the generic standard for the assessment. The standard must also be made available on the certifier's website (Forest Stewardship Council 2004d).

The MSC, although emulating the FSC's approach to setting global principles and criteria, has given the role of localization to certifiers (Murphy and Bendell 1997). Similar to the FSC, applicants can undergo a confidential preassessment that identifies steps the operation will need to take prior to a full assessment (Chaffee et al. 2003, 64). Public notice is required prior to the full assessment, which is when work similar to that done by FSC national initiatives begins. Initially, expert assessment teams were given discretion to develop performance indicators and scoring guideposts for evaluating the candidate fishery. Although guided by previous assessments, the aim was to have operation-specific measures. Since 2001, however, the MSC has been working on the consistency and reliability of assessments. In July 2008, it introduced a new fisheries assessment methodology that provides a default assessment tree from which certifiers must now build performance indicators and scoring guideposts (Marine Stewardship Council 2008a, 2008b; see also Gulbrandsen 2010, 126).

During the assessment, the applicant fishery is required to provide information that will enable the assessment team to score the fishery; the assessment team interviews relevant stakeholders and takes account of concerns relating to management and sustainability of the fishery. Procedural transparency is facilitated by a comment period in which interested stakeholders get thirty days to make suggestions about performance indicators and scoring guideposts. The final versions must incorporate this feedback and be made public before the assessment begins (Chaffee et al. 2003, 70).

Auditing

Independent certification bodies (certifiers) conduct the certification assessments—or audits—for both programs. Both programs also use the same external organization—Accreditation Services International (ASI)—to conduct the assessments. ASI was originally set up by the FSC in March 2006.

For the FSC, the basic rules for what auditors must disclose have been the same since late 2004; however, ASI now posts public summaries of the accreditation reports on its website. The requirements for procedural transparency are extensive. Each accredited certifier must maintain seven years of records on a wide range of issues, and all this information must be made available to the FSC on request. The records must cover, among other considerations, information on the certifier's staff including their qualifications, potential conflicts of interest and training records; information on its decision-making processes and operations including committee work, evaluation and certification contracts, reporting, and approvals for use of the FSC trademark; details on all certificate holders and their products; and meeting minutes or notes from all committees overseeing certification and dispute-resolution decisions (Forest Stewardship Council 2004c, clause 9). Additionally, the rules require that certifiers provide interested stakeholders information on the names and qualifications of those responsible for, among other things, the certifier's overall performance, decision making, and dispute resolution (Forest Stewardship Council 2004c, clause 3.3).

A first step for applicants is typically a confidential preassessment. During the full assessment, stakeholders are to be consulted to aid in determining whether the operation is in "compliance with the environmental, legal, social, and economic requirements of the Forest Stewardship Standard" (Forest Stewardship Council 2004e, clause 1.1). With the exception of small forest owners (operations eligible for FSC's small and low-intensity managed forests program), FSC defines stakeholders as previously noted. The FSC also requires that certifiers document all input, with explanations for how these comments affected the certification outcome. Should the certificate be awarded, the certifier must contact stakeholders to inform them of the outcome and explain how the stakeholders' specific concerns were addressed. These details are sometimes present in the public summary report, but none of the opinions of stakeholders are made public without prior written consent (Forest Stewardship Council 2004e).

When assessments use either a generic or an endorsed standard, the results are summarized and posted on the certifier's website. At minimum, the report must disclose a description of the forest and its land-use history, details on the forest management systems in use, a summary of the operation's management plan in terms of FSC's requirements (criterion 7.1), details of the operation's monitoring and assessment procedures consistent with FSC requirements (criterion 8.2), and a description of the audit's scope and justification for any areas not assessed. The report must also note the assessment standard, details of the evaluation process, general observations made to make the certification decision, and a clear statement of the certification outcome, including any conditions or preconditions (Forest Stewardship Council 2004a). This is in addition to a longer report detailing the operation's full assessment, which is provided to the FSC (Forest Stewardship Council 2004b). Discussion of the evaluation process typically explains how and with whom the team consulted.

For the MSC, as previously noted, a preassessment is a necessary first step. The preassessment is fully confidential, but sometimes clients publicize the outcome on the web to show stakeholders identified areas for improvements (Gulbrandsen 2010, 125). If an applicant fishery wants to undergo a full assessment, this must be publicized—in a local newspaper, for example—and all relevant stakeholders need to be notified. By 2004, less than half of the fisheries that had undergone preassessments proceeded to a full assessment (Bridgespan Group 2004, 4). Still, as of December 2011, there were 135 fisheries in some stage of full assessment and 109 already certified. An average full assessment takes one and a half years from announcement to the final decision (Auld and Gulbrandsen 2010).

The certifier appoints the full-assessment team that comprises experts in fishery stock assessments, ecosystem management, and fishery management. The assessment involves significant stakeholder engagement. Some assessments have even provided opportunities to comment on potential expert assessors (Scientific Certification Systems 2000). Any stakeholder can comment on the process, and the team must demonstrate that these comments have been considered in their final report. The assessment team also arranges meetings with stakeholders throughout the process, and groups they have met with are listed in the public summary report. The reports also list comments considered by the team. With the western Australian rock lobster fishery, conservation groups expressed concern about by-catch; consequently, the fishery was required to create, within twelve months, a better system for tracking by-catch and documenting the fishery's interactions with marine life (Scientific Certification Systems 2000, 26).

In the end, the assessment team makes the certification decision. The team members score the fishery according to the assessment tree and issue a preliminary report for peer review and public comment. Stakeholders may also object to the final certification decision, which activates an objections procedure. All relevant assessment documents are posted on the MSC webpage. These documents include a number of stakeholder notifications, a public comment draft report, final report and determination, a public certification report, and annual surveillance reports. When relevant, a summary report of the objections panel and other relevant documents from the objections procedure are also posted on the website (Marine Stewardship Council 2009).

Our discussion thus far reveals how the "intermediaries or infrastructures [of transparency]" (Gupta and Mason, chapter 1, this book) are functioning comparatively in these two certification schemes, one effect of which has been to expand this governance realm to include an array of new actors, such as auditing institutions. We turn next to assessing how such forms of institutionalized transparency shape the normative, procedural and substantive effects of governance by disclosure in these cases.

Effects of Transparency

Procedural and outcome transparency do not act in isolation. Which actors are considered legitimate stakeholders and which actors have decision-making authority affect how transparency influences a program's accountability and legitimacy. An assessment of transparency alone may miss these important interactive effects. With this point in mind, this section focuses on the connections between transparency and participation, on the one hand, and accountability and legitimacy on the other. We assess how outcome transparency affects the learning capacity of the field of nonstate certification programs.

Legitimacy

The MSC and FSC have pursued divergent paths in connecting transparency and participation to programmatic legitimacy. The comparison makes clear that the MSC's decision to avoid membership affected how transparency policies functioned in legitimating the program. Early concerns about the MSC centered on its governance. These came even though it was also being championed for its transparent consultation process (e.g., O'Riordan 1997, 10). Still, a series of articles in *Samudra* (a periodical of the International Collective in Support of Fishworkers) between 1996 and 1998 raised numerous criticisms of the MSC, including the concern that it would marginalize small-scale fishers, particularly in the South. In this respect, it was not a matter of whether consultations were transparent, but rather whether stakeholders were adequately involved in discussions about MSC's goals.

The MSC was responsive to these concerns. Indeed, an MSC founder contributing to the *Samudra* debates noted that membership had been discussed during the standards-development workshops and was still under consideration (Sutton 1998). It was then addressed in the 2001 governance review, which considered membership a possible way to increase the active engagement and investment of NGOs and retailers in the MSC (Marine Stewardship Council 2001a). Yet, instead of promoting membership, the review reaffirmed the value of a streamlined governance organization. At the time, the MSC explained, "many funders and NGOs in particular raised the question of a "democratic deficit" in the organization's structure. Comparisons were made with the seemingly more open Forest Stewardship Council (FSC). Some felt that in order for the MSC to be truly accountable to all its stakeholders, the organization should be membership based. This was, rightly in the view of many, rejected and some argue that the FSC's experience has vindicated that decision" (Marine Stewardship Council 2001a). Consistent with our argument, this exemplifies the different approach the MSC has taken to garnering support as a governance organization.

Turning to the FSC, the choice to devolve some authority to National Initiatives and to base the program's legitimacy more completely on the support of members is an alternative approach. One implication has been that stakeholders supporting the FSC have had an easier time using the language of transparency and participation as a point of contrast with competing, producer-backed certification initiatives. The themes identified by Overdevest in her analysis of reports comparing the FSC and competitors are informative (Overdevest 2005). A report by the Certified Forest Products Council (a group of North American companies committed to buying third-party certified forest products) emphasized, for example, the openness and transparency of standards development as a key measure of comparison. A more recent Greenpeace report explains: "Key strengths of the FSC network and organization have been its transparency and its ability to pioneer approaches and adaptations of certification. [...] It is in effect an elaborate conflict resolution mechanism for reconciling many differing views and values in relation to forests and some plantations" (Rosoman et al. 2008, 3). Guidelines established to separate credible from noncredible certification initiatives, such as those of the World Bank/WWF Global Forest Alliance, also consider procedural transparency in rule making and auditing as critical (WWF/World Bank Global Forest Alliance 2006, 16). The point for our assessment concerns how transparency relates to other governance issues, such as who eligible stakeholders are and who gets decision-making power. Perceptions that the FSC was transparent stemmed, arguably, from its openness to stakeholder involvement, the power of membership provisions, and the devolution of authority to national initiatives; not, by contrast, from any specific efforts to disclose information on how decisions were being made.

This divergence is clearest in the practice of localizing standards, when global standards are made appropriate to local social and environmental conditions.[5] The purpose this process serves for each program differs in a subtle but important way. With the MSC, localization has been more a means to an end: experts with knowledge about a fishery's ecology and biology are used to help the assessment team build a credible standard. Drawing on expert knowledge is a central aim of the MSC. As a recent document entitled "A Stakeholder's Guide to the Marine Stewardship Council" explains, stakeholders are a critical "source of information needed to conduct a meaningful assessment." It is particularly important that they ensure that stakeholder issues are considered in the assessment, the assessment "is well-informed and comprehensive," and that the assessment's outcome "is consistent with the rigorous MSC standard" (Marine Stewardship Council 2009, 4). This aim is also apparent in audit reports. For instance, the public report for the Alaska salmon fishery noted concerns voiced by Canadian academics, NGOs, and commercial interests about stocks affected by Alaska's interception fishery. The report notes that "one of the key components of the stakeholder consultation process is to help extend the evaluation team's discovery capabilities. This helps ensure that the evaluation team gets access to all available data/information about a fishery. [...] Unfortunately, while the Canadians we were able to speak to were quick to voice concern, none of the Canadian stakeholders presented evidence that the often identified suspicions about problems in Alaska's interception fisheries were correct or founded" (Scientific Certification Systems 2000, 56).

This is a legitimate criterion for evaluating input, and as the previous section noted, auditors are required to state how they account for stakeholder input. Still, it exemplifies an instrumental view of the consultation process and illustrates how MSC processes envision consultation more as a means to legitimize assessment outcomes.

This is also true for the FSC, but, in addition, the process of developing local standards via national initiatives is an end unto itself. Empowering stakeholders to take ownership of local standard development appropriate to their forests has been central to the FSC and its claims to legitimacy (Cashore et al. 2004; Tollefson et al. 2008). However, the time taken for national initiatives to submit standards to the FSC for approval constitutes a problem. Recall that the FSC grants considerable authority to certifiers to apply generic standards in situations when endorsed national standards are not yet in place. This discretionary power has been criticized because it purportedly undermines the credibility of the FSC, given lack of effective control mechanisms (Counsell and Loraas 2002). Additionally, it relates to a broader concern that too much power for auditors undermines the authority given to national initiatives. The two different approaches to standard setting offered by the FSC have meant that, in certain cases, stakeholder involvement has been extensive and rich, whereas in other cases standard setting has been much less visible and participatory. This is tricky for the FSC. The national initiatives and their extensive engagement with national stakeholders are partly the basis for its legitimacy. Yet, the national initiatives have often been hard to coordinate, they are resource-intensive to maintain and slow at getting standards drafted.[6] In response, the FSC has been reaffirming its commitment to its global network and focusing on ensuring "integrity, credibility and transparency of the FSC system" (Forest Stewardship Council 2007b, 10). This has included introducing some flexibility by permitting standards work to occur in countries without national initiatives (Forest Stewardship Council 2009a). The new standard for FSC accreditation that became operational in January 2010 also increases provisions for stakeholder engagement in the adaptation of a certifier's generic standard for a given assessment (Forest Stewardship Council 2009b).

In sum, the MSC and FSC pursued different means of legitimation: one that uses procedural transparency and stakeholder consultation instrumentally and the other in which these provisions are ends unto themselves.

Accountability

The MSC and FSC treat auditing as a means for accountability. However, after early scrutiny from concerned stakeholders, both programs prescribed transparency and participation as necessary to ensure their legitimacy.

For the MSC, the western Australian rock lobster fishery (certified in March 2000) and the New Zealand hoki fishery (certified in March 2001) provoked concern. Participants of the just-formed stakeholder council aired these concerns, noting the arm's-length, opaque relationship between the MSC and the certifiers. One issue was the confidentiality of preassessments. A June 2002 meeting of the stakeholder council pushed the MSC to exert greater control over the preassessments, viewing these as a credibility issue for the organization. The meeting gave four recommendations to the board. These included, for example, that certifiers be required to "notify the MSC of all formal applications for pre-assessment" and ensure that clients know if they are considered controversial. It also noted that MSC ought to work with certifiers on preassessments, including helping identify relevant stakeholders, and have confidential access to preassessment reports for those fisheries undergoing a full assessment (Marine Stewardship Council 2002, 9). The council's August 2003 meeting then discussed possible forms of oversight and transparency for accredited certifiers, including the possible publication of the accreditation reports or, at least, information on nonconformities with MSC requirements. The meeting notes outlined an action point to "discuss options" on how to improve transparency (Marine Stewardship Council 2003). Likewise, a report commissioned by the Homeland Foundation, Oak Foundation, and Pew Charitable Trusts released in 2004 urged the MSC to address several issues, with some focused specifically on the accreditation and certification processes, including, "Ensure transparency in all documents and decision-making as much as possible" (Highleyman et al. 2004, 31).

The FSC faced similar early criticism. One of the first was Smart-Wood's certification of Flor y Fauna in 1995 (Donovan 1996). The issues surrounded preexisting scrutiny of the company in the Netherlands; links between the WWF Netherlands, a Dutch insurance and banking group, and the FSC, all of whom were endorsing Flor y Fauna; and questions about the company's growth-and-yield and pricing expectations (Centeno 1996). Although the assessment began in 1993—before the FSC accredited SmartWood—it still raised concerns about the credibility of the assessment processes. This was followed in 1996 and 1997 by disquiet over an SGS assessment of Leroy Gabon. This was related to the company's operations near a forest reserve, but also to the limited stakeholder consultations and insufficient management plan (IPS-Inter Press Service 1997). In this case, the FSC eventually suspended SGS's forest-management accreditation pending certain changes to its procedures, and it requested that all accredited certifiers respect a six-month moratorium on certifying primary forests (Tickell 1997).

Responding to these concerns, the MSC and FSC have modified their accreditation processes, increasing procedural and outcome transparency such as requiring the disclosure of the public summary reports for certification assessments. This advances accountability as skeptical groups and individuals are able to trace the corrective action requirements imposed on companies and see how they are eventually resolved. Moreover, the summary reports facilitate the work of outside critics because they can access information previously unavailable and raise their concerns more forcibly. For example, data for a report critical of FSC's accreditation and auditing practices, issued by the Rainforest Foundation, would have been difficult to compile had the public summary reports not been available (Counsell and Loraas 2002).

The MSC and FSC have not perfectly converged in their approach to using transparency for accountability. Unlike the FSC, the MSC does not make accreditation reports available on its website. Still, both programs have been consistently increasing checks on and openness of their auditing processes through new stakeholder engagement requirements during the assessment process (Auld and Gulbrandsen 2010). This underscores the general connection within nonstate certification between transparency and participation, on the one hand, and accountability on the other.

Learning Capacity

Turning the lens to the field-level effects of transparency, here we examine other programs in the forest and fishery sectors. Considerable work has documented how later-emerging programs have learned from first movers, both within issue areas and across them. Dingwerth and Pattberg show, for instance, that membership in the International Social and Environmental Accreditation and Labeling (ISEAL) Alliance affects the transparency of certification programs, particularly with regard to rule-making procedures (Dingwerth and Pattberg 2009). ISEAL has worked to improve the operations of lead nonstate certification programs and now includes thirteen members.[7] Each instance of emulation has significance. Here, however, we focus only on the diffusion of outcome transparency given its connection to learning and innovation.

Table 12.2 details the disclosure practices of forest and fishery certification programs. Three key points emerge. First, across all the programs, procedural transparency for auditing has become a norm. Although the practice varies, all the programs disclose on their websites the specific steps an audit will involve and information on when consultation and stakeholder engagement are to occur. The Program for the Endorsement of Forest Certification (PEFC), for instance, requires that "the audit evidence to determine the conformity with the forest management standards shall include relevant information from external parties (e.g., government agencies, community groups, conservation organizations, etc.) as appropriate" (PEFC 2007, 4). It leaves open, however, who these groups should be and what information must be provided to them by the certifier. There is also variability between different PEFC-endorsed schemes.[8] Second, there are differences in the extent to which outcome transparency is diffusing within the fishery and forestry sectors. Aquaculture programs are

Table 12.2
Transparency Provisions Forest and Fishery Certification Audits

Programs	Sector	Date established	Transparency Provisions	
			Auditing Procedures Public	Audit Outcomes Public
Forest Stewardship Council*	Forestry	1993	Yes	Yes
Marine Stewardship Council*	Fisheries	1997	Yes	Yes
Program for the Endorsement of Forest Certification	Forestry	1999	Yes	Yes
Global Aquaculture Alliance	Fisheries	1997	Yes	No
Rainforest Alliance/ Sustainable Agriculture Network*	Forestry	1989/1993	Yes	Yes (forestry and carbon)/ No (agriculture)
Friend of the Sea	Fisheries	2006	Yes	Yes (capture fishery)/ No (aquaculture)
Naturland	Fisheries	1982	Yes	Yes (capture fishery)/ No (aquaculture)
Aquaculture Stewardship Council**	Fisheries	2009	Yes	To be determined
ISO 12877	Fisheries	2007	Partially; available, but at a cost	To be determined

Notes: Data for table is obtained from the organizations' websites. *Indicates that the program is a member of the ISEAL Alliance. **Associate member in ISEAL Alliance.

not disclosing audit reports, whereas ocean-capture programs are. Certain agriculture programs are not disclosing audit reports, whereas forestry programs are. Third, for those schemes requiring outcome disclosure, the quality of information varies. With the PEFC, for instance, a public summary report is required, but the specifics of the report are determined by individual schemes (PEFC 2007).

What do these differences mean? First, as previously noted, outcome transparency provides information to stakeholders for assessing the performance of the certification process, holding to account the program or the operator when practice falls short of the rules. Numerous studies assess the FSC's public summary reports to elucidate where improvements have and have not been made (Auld et al. 2008). By contrast, studies of rule compliance for aquaculture programs are notably absent, and evaluations of programs with lower-quality public reports are equally thin. Without this information, it is very difficult to assess whether the choices certification programs are making are advancing rule compliance in the management practices. This issue is even more important when one considers that even when disclosed information is somewhat detailed, as with the FSC, the challenge of connecting rule compliance with actual improvements in performance persists.

An evolving understanding of this challenge appears to be emerging. ISEAL has recently developed an impact code for its members, which aims to improve, among other things, the ability of certification programs to track performance. As the code notes, programs should assess their impacts to "enhance societal learning by feeding results into the standards landscape to understand the cumulative impacts of voluntary standards systems" (ISEAL Alliance 2010, 3). If we take the insights of open source governance models and those from experimental governance seriously, ISEAL would do well to require members disclose like information.

Conclusion

Procedural and outcome transparency are crucial program elements for nonstate certification, even if they serve different ends for individual programs. We have argued that MSC's choice to avoid membership affected how transparency policies functioned in legitimating the program. Facing criticism for giving stakeholders less decision-making power than the FSC, the MSC continues to base its legitimacy on efficient and transparent procedures, balance, and expertise. It has bolstered stakeholder outreach, but remains committed to its leaner governance model. Rather than bringing all relevant stakeholders under its umbrella, it has chosen to inform stakeholders of its activities and draw on their expertise and concerns when needed to make individual assessments credible. This instrumental view of participation and the reliance on expertise are different from the democratization hypothesis outlined in this book. Here, the MSC appeals more to the norm that expert decisions can be more appropriate than those guided by participatory democratic outcomes (for a similar emphasis on a techno-statist imperative for transparency in a multilateral governance context, see Jansen and Dubois, this book, chapter 5).

The FSC, by contrast, and more aligned with the democratization-as-driver hypothesis, bases its legitimacy on a broader sense of stakeholder engagement and inclusiveness, as illustrated by two program features. First, the choice to develop transparent procedures that devolved considerable rule-making authority to national stakeholders influenced how stakeholders viewed the organization. As well, it meant that political controversy over acceptable practices centered on a different aspect of the certification procedure than occurred in fisheries. Developing national (sometimes subnational) FSC standards has been one of the most prolonged and arduous aspects of its work. Second, the choice to grant ultimate decision-making authority to FSC members influenced perceptions of the program's transparency. The view of FSC as transparent emerged as much from its openness to stakeholders, the power of membership provisions, and the devolution of decision-making power to national initiatives as from its specific requirements for procedural and outcome transparency.

Both programs have sought to improve accountability by using procedural and outcome transparency, such as publicizing summarized assessment reports and increasing online disclosure of audit outcomes. Whereas this increased disclosure may boost credibility of forest and fisheries certification to some while reinforcing the skepticism of others, with few exceptions it has been a critical tool for furthering MSC and FSC accountability. Our claim is that although increased disclosure might not have convinced skeptical stakeholders of the merits of certification, most stakeholders would agree that it has enhanced their ability to scrutinize accreditation and certification practices. Procedural and outcome transparency have improved the conditions for holding certifiers and companies to account for their practices. In this respect, we find support for the book's hypothesis that the institutionalization of transparency can decenter state-led regulatory processes and open up political space for new actors. Procedural and outcome transparency have fostered a broader political space in which debate and contest occur over the appropriate practices of forest and fisheries operators.

This final point is crucial when we turn to assessing the diffusion of disclosure among a broader set of nonstate certification programs. In this comparator group, the MSC and FSC emerge as leaders, because few other initiatives disclose audit reports with similar detail. This incomplete disclosure presents challenges for fostering learning within this private governance field, because only certain lessons are taken up to inform future reforms. In the open source software model, the licensing agreements stipulate that parties may openly use and modify software, but that subsequent innovations need to be fed back into the commons to facilitate future innovation and growth. Devising ways to emulate this practice appears to be an important challenge nonstate certification programs face in ensuring market norms of private and paid-for access to information do not take away from the transformative learning that private regulatory fields may be able to inspire.

Notes

1. This chapter represents a significantly revamped and extended version of Auld and Gulbrandsen (2010).

2. We draw in this section from Auld and Gulbrandsen (2010).

3. There are now fifty-seven national initiatives: fifteen in Africa, two in North America, nine in Latin and Central America, twenty-three in Europe (including Russia), and eight in Asia and Oceania.

4. For a fuller discussion of how long standards have taken to receive endorsement, see Auld and Gulbrandsen (2010).

5. Localization also raises concerns about consistency across the rules and requirements of nonstate certification. On this concern, the MSC and FSC have charted a similar course. For more discussion, see Auld and Gulbrandsen (2010).

6. Interview, FSC staff, December 2007.

7. See http://www.isealalliance.org/our-members for a current list of members.

8. For instance, on the inclusion of information from external parties, the Austrian scheme notes that the evaluation will comprise "consideration of relevant information from external interest groups (government bodies, associations, environmental groups, etc.), in as far as *sensible* and appropriate" (emphasis added) PEFC Austria (2006, 23).

References

Auld, Graeme. 2009. *Reversal of Fortune: How Early Choices Can Alter the Logic of Market-Based Authority.* PhD dissertation. New Haven, CT: Yale University.

Auld, Graeme, Benjamin Cashore, Cristina Balboa, Laura Bozzi, and Stefan Renckens. 2010. Can Technological Innovations Improve Private Regulations in the Global Economy? *Business and Politics* 12 (3): article 9.

Auld, Graeme, and Lars H. Gulbrandsen. 2010. Transparency in Nonstate Certification: Consequences for Accountability and Legitimacy. *Global Environmental Politics* 10 (3): 97–119.

Auld, Graeme, Lars H. Gulbrandsen, and Constance McDermott. 2008. Certification Schemes and the Impacts on Forests and Forestry. *Annual Review of Environment and Resources* 33 (1): 187–211.

Bernstein, Steven. 2004. Legitimacy in Global Environmental Governance. *Journal of International Law and International Relations* 1 (1–2): 139–166.

Bernstein, Steven, and Benjamin Cashore. 2007. Can Non-state Global Governance Be Legitimate? An Analytical Framework. *Regulation and Governance* 1 (4): 347–371.

Boyle, James. 2008. *The Public Domain: Enclosing the Commons of the Mind.* New Haven, CN: Yale University Press.

Braithwaite, John. 2008. *Regulatory Capitalism: How It Works, Ideas for Making It Work Better.* Cheltenham, UK: Edward Elgar.

Bridgespan Group. 2004. *Fishery Certification: Summary of Analysis and Recommendations.* Boston: The Bridgespan Group.

Cashore, Benjamin, Graeme Auld, and Deanna Newsom. 2004. *Governing through Markets: Forest Certification and the Emergence of Non-state Authority.* New Haven, CT: Yale University Press.

Centeno, Julio Cesar. 1996. *Forest Certification as a Tool for Greenwashing.* Treemail, November 4. Available at http://www.treemail.nl/teakscan.dal/files/greenwas.htm.

Chaffee, Chet, Bruce Phillips, and Trevor Ward. 2003. Implementing the MSC Programme Process. In *Eco-Labelling in Fisheries: What Is It All About?* ed. Bruce Phillips, Trevor Ward, and Chet Chaffee, 63–79. Oxford: Blackwell Publishing.

Counsell, Simon, and Kim Terje Loraas. 2002. *Trading in Credibility: The Myth and Reality of the Forest Stewardship Council.* London: Rainforest Foundation.

Dingwerth, Klaus, and Philipp Pattberg. 2009. World Politics and Organizational Fields: The Case of Transnational Sustainability Governance. *European Journal of International Relations* 15 (4): 707–743.

Donovan, Richard. 1996. *Smart Wood Statement on Flor y Fauna.* Posted comment. Forest List Archive, March 12. Available at http://www.metla.fi/archive/forest/1996/03/msg00060.html.

Esty, Daniel C. 2006. Good Governance at the Supranational Scale: Globalizing Administrative Law. *Yale Law Journal* 115 (7): 1490–1563.

Evison, Irene J. 1998. *FSC National Initiatives Manual*. Oaxaca, Mexico: Forest Stewardship Council.

Forest Stewardship Council (FSC). 1995. *FSC Statutes*. Document 1.3. Forest Stewardship Council. Archival web page. Available at http://web.archive.org/web/19991009014300/fscoax.org/html/noframes/1-3.htm.

Forest Stewardship Council (FSC). 2004a. *Forest Certification Public Summary Reports—FSC-Std-20–009 (V2–1) En*. Bonn: Forest Stewardship Council.

Forest Stewardship Council (FSC). 2004b. *Forest Certification Reports—FSC-Std-20–008 (V2–1) En*. Bonn: Forest Stewardship Council.

Forest Stewardship Council (FSC). 2004c. *General Requirements for FSC Accredited Certification Bodies: Application of ISO/IEC Guide 65: 1996 (E)—FSC-Std-20–001 (V2–1) En*. Bonn: Forest Stewardship Council.

Forest Stewardship Council (FSC). 2004d. *Local Adaptation of Certification Body Generic Forest Stewardship Standards—FSC-Std-20–003 (V2–1) En*. Bonn: Forest Stewardship Council.

Forest Stewardship Council (FSC). 2004e. *Stakeholder Consultation for Forest Evaluation—FSC-Std-20–006 (V2–1) En*. Bonn: Forest Stewardship Council.

Forest Stewardship Council (FSC). 2007a. *FSC Accredited Forest Stewardship Standards*. March 30. Available at http://www.fsc.org/fileadmin/webdata/public/document_center/accreditation_documents/national_standards/2007_03_30_FSC_Accredited_Standards.pdf.

Forest Stewardship Council (FSC). 2007b. *Strengthening Forest Conservation, Communities and Markets: The Global Strategy of the Forest Stewardship Council*. Bonn: Forest Stewardship Council.

Forest Stewardship Council (FSC). 2009a. *Process Requirements for the Development and Maintenance of National Forest Stewardship Standards*. Bonn: Forest Stewardship Council.

Forest Stewardship Council (FSC). 2009b. *New Accreditation Standards to Strengthen FSC Certification System*. September 29. Available at http://www.fsc.org.vm-fsc-entw.tops.net/news.html?&no_cache=1&tx_ttnews%5Btt_news%5D=415&cHash=76cdc33f7aa67131cda81933773f0ca6.

Forest Stewardship Council (FSC). 2013. *Consolidating Gains, Strengthening Leadership: Forest Stewardship Council Annual Report 2012*. Bonn: Forest Stewardship Council.

Fowler, Penny, and Simon Heap. 2000. Bridging Troubled Waters: The Marine Stewardship Council. In *Terms of Endearment: Business, NGOs, and Sustainable Development*, ed. Jem Bendell, 135–148. Sheffield, UK: Greenleaf Publishing.

Fung, Archon. 2006. Varieties of Participation in Complex Governance. *Public Administration Review* 66 (1): 66–75.

Gulbrandsen, Lars H. 2006. Creating Markets for Eco-Labelling: Are Consumers Insignificant? *International Journal of Consumer Studies* 30 (5): 477–489.

Gulbrandsen, Lars H. 2010. *Transnational Environmental Governance: The Emergence and Effects of the Certification of Forests and Fisheries*. Cheltenham, UK: Edward Elgar.

Gupta, Aarti. 2008. Transparency under Scrutiny: Information Disclosure in Global Environmental Governance. *Global Environmental Politics* 8 (2): 1–7.

Highleyman, Scott, Amy Mathews Amos, and Hank Cauley. 2004. An Independent Assessment of the Marine Stewardship Council. Sandy River Pit., ME: Wildhavens.

IPS-Inter Press Service. 1997. *Gabon-Environment: NGOs Want Eco-Label Stripped from German Firm*. January 26.

ISEAL Alliance. 2010. *Assessing the Impacts of Social and Environmental Standards Systems V1.0: ISEAL Code of Good Practices*. London: International Social and Environmental Accreditation and Labeling (ISEAL) Alliance.

Keohane, Robert O., and David G. Victor. 2011. The Regime Complex for Climate Change. *Perspectives on Politics* 9 (1): 7–23.

Langley, Paul. 2001. Transparency in the Making of Global Environmental Governance. *Global Society* 15 (1): 73–92.

Marine Stewardship Council (MSC). 1999. *MSC Structures: The Marine Stewardship Council Structure and Governance*. Archived web page. Available at http://web.archive.org/web/19990125101405/http://www.msc.org.

Marine Stewardship Council (MSC). 2000. *World's First Sustainable Seafood Products Launched*. Press Release. March 3. Available at http://www.msc.org/newsroom/news/world2019s-first-sustainable-seafood-products.

Marine Stewardship Council (MSC). 2001a. *Governance Review Commission*. January 18. Archived web page. Available at http://web.archive.org/web/20010118151300/http://www.msc.org/.

Marine Stewardship Council (MSC). 2001b. *MSC Announces New Governance Structure*. Press release. July 27. Available at http://www.msc.org/newsroom/news/msc-announces-new-governance-structure.

Marine Stewardship Council (MSC). 2002. MSC Stakeholder Council Meeting. London: Marine Stewardship Council.

Marine Stewardship Council (MSC). 2003. *Minutes from 3rd Stakeholder Council Meeting*. London: Marine Stewardship Council.

Marine Stewardship Council (MSC). 2008a. *Marine Stewardship Council Fisheries Assessment Methodology and Guidance to Certification Bodies*. London: Marine Stewardship Council.

Marine Stewardship Council (MSC). 2008b. *Simpler Faster and More Consistent*. Press release. July 21. Available at http://www.msc.org/newsroom/news/2018simpler-faster-and-more-consistent2019?fromsearch=1&newsquery=assessment+methodology&year=2008&month=July&isnewssearch=1.

Marine Stewardship Council (MSC). 2009. *A Stakeholder's Guide to the Marine Stewardship Council*. London: Marine Stewardship Council.

Meidinger, Errol. 2006. The Administrative Law of Global Private-Public Regulation: The Case of Forestry. *European Journal of International Law* 17 (1): 47–87.

Mitchell, Ronald B. 1998. Sources of Transparency: Information Systems in International Regimes. *International Studies Quarterly* 42 (1): 109–130.

Mitchell, Ronald B. 2011. Transparency for Governance: The Mechanisms and Effectiveness of Disclosure-Based and Education-Based Transparency Policies. *Ecological Economics* 70 (11): 1882–1890.

Murphy, David F., and Jem Bendell. 1997. *In the Company of Partners: Business, Environmental Groups and Sustainable Development Post-Rio.* Bristol, UK: Policy Press.

O'Riordan, Brian. 1997. Marine Stewardship Council: Who's Being Seduced? *Samudra* (18).

O'Rourke, Dara. 2003. Outsourcing Regulation: Analyzing Nongovernmental Systems of Labor Standards and Monitoring. *Policy Studies Journal: The Journal of the Policy Studies Organization* 31 (1): 1–29.

O'Rourke, Dara. 2006. Multi-stakeholder Regulation: Privatizing or Socializing Global Labor Standards? *World Development* 34 (5):899–918.

Overdevest, Christine. 2005. Treadmill Politics, Information Politics and Public Policy—toward a Political Economy of Information. *Organization & Environment* 18 (1): 72–90.

Overdevest, Christine, Alena Bleicher, and Matthias Gross. 2010. The Experimental Turn in Environmental Sociology: Pragmatism and New Forms of Governance. In *Environmental Sociology: European Perspectives and Interdisciplinary Challenges*, ed. Matthias Gross and Harald Heinrichs. New York: Springer.

PEFC. 2007. *Certification and Accreditation Procedures—annex 6.* Geneva: Program for the Endorsement of Forest Certification.

PEFC Austria. 2006. *Austrian Forest Certification Scheme—system Description.* Vienna: PEFC Austria.

Raynolds, Laura T., Douglas Murray, and Andrew Heller. 2007. Regulating Sustainability in the Coffee Sector: A Comparative Analysis of Third-party Environmental and Social Certification Initiatives. *Agriculture and Human Values* 24 (2):147–163.

Rosoman, Grant, Judy Rodrigues, and Anna Jenkins. 2008. *Holding the Line with the FSC.* Amsterdam: Greenpeace International.

Sasser, Erika N. 2003. Gaining Leverage: NGO Influence on Certification Institutions in the Forest Products Sector. In *Forest Policy for Private Forestry*, ed. Larry Teeter, Benjamin Cashore, and Daowei Zhang, 229–244. Oxon, UK: CAB International.

Scientific Certification Systems. 2000. *Public Summary for the MSC Certification of: The Western Rock Lobster Fishery, Western Australia.* Public Summary. Scientific Certification Systems Marine Fisheries Certification Program. April. Available at http://www.msc.org.

Sutton, Michael. 1998. Marine Stewardship Council: An Appeal for Co-Operation. *Samudra* (19).

Tickell, Oliver. 1997. FSC Cracks Down on Certifier Despite Approval. *Timber Trades Journal* (October 25).

Tollefson, Chris, Fred P. Gale, and David Haley. 2008. *Setting the Standard: Certification, Governance, and the Forest Stewardship Council.* Vancouver: UBC Press.

Vermeule, Adrian. 2007. *Mechanisms of Democracy: Institutional Design Writ Large.* New York: Oxford University Press.

Victor, D. G., J. C. House, and S. Joy. 2005. A Madisonian Approach to Climate Policy. *Science* 309 (5742): 1820–1821.

WWF/World Bank Global Forest Alliance. 2006. *Forest Certification Assessment Guide (FCAG): A Framework for Assessing Credible Forest Certification Systems/Schemes.* Washington, DC: World Bank and World Wide Fund for Nature.

13

Transparency and Environmental Equity: The International Finance Corporation's Disclosure Practices

Timothy Ehresman and Dimitris Stevis

Although a number of scholars postulate a connection between transparency and environmental justice, including several in this book, that relationship requires much more attention and empirical research. In this chapter, we explore whether transparency can be an effective strategy toward more equitable environmental governance and, specifically, a more equitable and transformative liberal environmental governance. In order to differentiate our approach from that of market liberalism, we start by clarifying social liberal international environmental justice and the kinds of disclosure practices consistent with three key approaches to it. We then ask why the International Finance Corporation (IFC)—part of the World Bank Group—has embraced transparency, how it has proceeded to institutionalize its transparency policies, and what the effects of its disclosure practices have been, in terms of advancing social liberal environmental justice. We conclude by revisiting the relationship between transparency and environmental justice.

In the introductory chapters in this book, the authors note the potential for transparency to enhance prospects for democracy, participation, and environmental improvements. Notably, for our purposes, Arthur Mol explicitly evokes the link between transparency and the "empowerment of the oppressed" (Mol, this book, chapter 2). He makes the key observation, however, that this promise of transparency is not a foregone conclusion and that more will be required for transparency to go beyond merely serving and legitimizing the scope of power and welfare inequalities so visible in our global society. It is in this sense that this chapter makes its contribution to the critical focus of this book. That is, recognizing the limitations of the market liberal model, we explore the potential of transparency to empower within a social liberal approach to international environmental justice. However this potential cannot be left to itself; indeed, as Mol contends, there are reasons to question whether more transparency is necessarily and always better, and whether or not there are structural challenges to be overcome for transparency to fully serve the interests and needs of environmental equity.

This tension is evident in existing scholarship. In the context of private corporate activity, for example, transparency has come to be hailed as an important regulatory tool in seeking to forestall and prevent significant environmental harm. The contribution of private corporate transparency to environmental equity has been considered at length in the legal literature following the tragic 1984 Bhopal incident in India with Union Carbide. For example, in 1986 the US Congress relatedly enacted the Emergency Planning and Community Right-to-Know Act,[1] which in part mandated the disclosure by manufacturing companies of the content and volume of toxic chemicals released at manufacturing sites. Companies falling under the purview of this statute are required to submit information to the US Environmental Protection Agency's annual Toxic Release Inventory (TRI)—identifying the release and/or transfer of "654 specified toxic chemicals, subject to reporting thresholds" (Rechtschaffen et al. 2009, 383; see also Johnson 2004, 197ff). This information is then released to the public in the form of an Internet-accessed database (Johnson 2004, 199).

Mandated disclosures of this type by private actors are also increasingly being instituted outside the United States. For example, TRI-like pollution release and transfer registers (PRTRs) are now diffusing across OECD countries.[2] Touted benefits include enhancing community awareness and environmental information acquisition. Parties to the PRTR Protocol to the Aarhus Convention are also required to adopt PRTRs that meet specified guidelines. There are currently more than thirty parties to the PRTR Protocol. The EU has passed similar requirements under EU Regulation No. 166/2006 of the European Parliament and Council, making the Aarhus PRTR Protocol part of EU law. Emitting corporations produce these facility-specific reports for public use to ensure that public and private actors are aware of the inherent threats of industrial activity to health.

The legal literature identifies additional benefits of information disclosure that speak directly to environmental equity concerns, and suggests thereby that Mol's guarded optimism is not entirely misplaced. Scholars note that mandated disclosures provide an empirical basis on which to determine whether poor and vulnerable communities are indeed burdened with greater levels of toxic effluence—a question confirmed by several empirical studies of precisely this sort (Johnson 2004, 225). Scholars also point to the benefits of increased corporate disclosure for the political mobilization and representation of poor and vulnerable communities as they negotiate with corporations over the nature and location of proposed "dirty" activities (Karkkainen 2001, 316ff). Here an increased democratization is seen to result from better quality information *and* the improved ability to identify actors implicated by such information. In addition, mandated disclosure invests affected communities with a legal *right to know* the content of disclosed information (Johnson 2004, 209ff; Rechtschaffen et al. 2009, 383), contributing, in the terminology of this book, to the normative effectiveness of transparency as a mechanism of governance.

A number of the contributors to this book have also made explicit references to the possibility that increased transparency will contribute to a stronger environmental justice. Michael Mason has evaluated the express purpose of the Aarhus Convention to recognize access to justice in environmental matters (Mason, this book, chapter 4). Similarly, Auld and Gulbrandsen have observed that nonstate certification programs, aimed at improving environmental outcomes, attend not only to environmental degradation but also to fairness (Auld and Gulbrandsen, this book, chapter 12). These chapters, like ours, reflect the broad framing of effectiveness informing this book, which equates the procedural effects of transparency with the prospects for empowerment (Gupta and Mason, this book, chapter 1). Our focus here is on justice as pertaining to the equitable quality of empowerment.

Other references in this book to the justice-related (procedural) effects of transparency are more implicit. In addition to Mol's reference to the possible but uncertain empowerment of the oppressed, Aarti Gupta observes that one key question in the domain of global environmental politics is whether transparency can reconfigure existing power asymmetries (Gupta, this book, chapter 6). Elsewhere she analyzes expressly whether the disclosure of information may itself be transformative, noting "transparency is premised on the notion that information ... can empower" (2008, 4). Florini and Jairaj find some evidence in their comparative study that national-level transparency by a state actor has helped to empower citizens, though transparency will always implicate power struggles (Florini and Jairaj, this book, chapter 3). As we noted at the outset, the suggestion that transparency can empower the relatively less powerful is fully reflective of concerns with equity and fairness.

This reveals that a variety of authors have postulated a link between transparency and environmental equity concerns. Our goal in this contribution is to advance the investigation of this link by focusing on whether and how transparency can advance social liberal international environmental justice. Given the hegemonic role of laissez faire or hyper-liberal thought and practice, this is an important question for those who adopt a social liberal rather than market liberal perspective. Is it possible to address questions of structural inequity within the parameters of social liberal politics, or do liberal politics aim merely to mitigate the harshest impacts, or, even worse, to legitimize them?

We employ the case of the IFC for several reasons. First, environmental justice concerns are particularly poignant in poorer regions of the world, and the IFC is concerned with this cross-section of countries. Second, the IFC is chartered to assist foreign direct investment in the developing world. Foreign direct investment is a central liberal prescription for growth and human well-being in developing countries. Finally, the IFC is a global leader among international financial institutions and private financial organizations in applying social and environmental requirements to the projects it sponsors. Thus if the IFC's disclosure practices cannot contribute to promoting a modicum of social liberal international environmental justice in its investment projects, other agencies and unsponsored corporations are unlikely to do much better.

We note at the outset that neither the IFC's disclosure policies nor its broader Sustainability Framework explicitly identify environmental equity as a dimension to its activities. However, the content of these policies and their institutionalization clearly address questions of environmental (and social) equity, as we develop more fully in the following. To pursue these questions we must first consider the contours of a social liberal, but not necessarily market liberal, environmental justice (for the latter, see Beckerman and Pasek 2001). Social liberalism does retain the emphasis on individual autonomy and liberty present in market liberalism, but also calls for social institutions and processes that constrain market liberalism in the interests of furthering individual flourishing and thus the liberal vision itself (Barry 2001; de-Shalit 1995; Richardson 2001; Wissenburg 2006). In the course of clarifying the various social liberal approaches to environmental justice, we are also reclaiming then the terrain from market liberal thought that obscures the variability within present and historical liberalism.

Embracing Transparency

Disclosure and International Environmental Justice
Social liberal international environmental justice may be understood according to three separate strands: distributive justice, capabilities justice,

and human rights justice (figure 13.1). Each of these embodies a liberal ethos, we contend, for two reasons. First, each strand is well represented in a literature that is fundamentally accepting of the existing liberal global political and economic order. Second, these strands are concerned, explicitly or implicitly, with the welfare of the individual. In this section, we discuss these three strands according to their relative practical strength for empowering the weak and making counterhegemonic claims in the transparency context. We also identify the kinds of disclosure practices congruent with each strand in order to enable a nuanced justice-oriented analysis of the IFC's goals and practices.

Distributive international environmental justice refers to a fair distribution of environmental burdens and decisional access. Okereke and Dooley (2010, 84) identify six distributive approaches to climate justice, for example. Employing their systematization, the form of distributive justice we refer to here is the liberal egalitarian approach. In this approach, a fair distribution of burdens and benefits among stakeholders refers to all parties receiving what is "fair" given their recognized claims in the specific case and assumes some significant degree of equality among the parties involved or affected in their capacity to employ disclosed information. Classically founded in the seminal work of John Rawls (1999), liberal egalitarian thought is receiving significant attention in scholarly work on international justice (e.g., Garcia 2003; Meyer and Roser 2006).

In application, distributive international environmental justice so understood would call for full disclosure by corporate investors regarding the environmental impacts and effects of their project. Distributive justice also entails consultation with affected stakeholders and participation by such stakeholders in discussions of project structure and impacts. The expectation is that those affected will be able to use that information to better advance their interests. There is no expectation, however, that this engagement between investors and affected parties will enable and entail actual joint decision making.

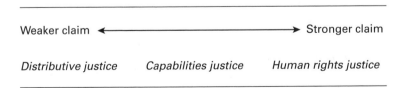

Weaker claim ◀——————————————▶ Stronger claim

Distributive justice   *Capabilities justice*   *Human rights justice*

Figure 13.1
Liberal Views of Justice Organized by Strength of Claim

The capabilities approach refers to building the necessary capabilities for individuals and their constituent communities to choose the lives they have reason to value, including what constitutes permissible and desirable uses of resources and the acceptable externalities of such uses (Schlosberg 2007). The capabilities approach is social for a variety of reasons. First, the life one has reason to value includes participating meaningfully in community life. Second, wealth is not an end but a means to other more important things (Sen 1999, 14). Third, Sen explicitly affirms the need for the formation of institutions to guide and inform individual freedoms (1999, 142). Even Adam Smith "did not hesitate to investigate economic circumstances in which particular restrictions may be sensibly proposed, or economic fields in which *nonmarket institutions* would be badly needed to supplement what the markets can do" (Sen 1999, 124: emphasis added). Fourth, Sen argues against relegating what are fairly considered "public goods" to the private market mechanism (1999, 128).

In this strand, the release of information needs to be accompanied by the meaningful sharing of decisional authority and not merely consultation over the activity, which is the subject of disclosure in order to facilitate real agency. This capability approach, therefore, affords greater justice because it specifies particular aspects of individual and community life and functioning, which must be accommodated and facilitated if individuals are to be enabled to live out justice in their own lives.

Finally, the human rights approach is the strongest strand, principally because of a global discourse on the importance of human rights. These rights are also enshrined in instruments of international and domestic law that facilitate their enforcement. Transparency in the human rights strand would be similar to that of the capabilities strand, with the addition of legal force associated with the release of information. Affected stakeholders would be entitled to have their concerns and interests substantively accommodated, even if that were to mean the investment project would not proceed, at least as proposed. Thus, the human rights approach would, by virtue of the scope of such entitlements, accord to affected stakeholders a right to grant or withhold consent to, and not only consult and negotiate regarding, the proposed project.

Embracing Transparency in the IFC

Pressures by NGOs regarding the World Bank's environmental record in the 1970s and 1980s, in particular with respect to two highly contested and publicized development projects in Brazil and India, resulted in the US government passing the so-called Pelosi Amendment in 1989.[3] The

Pelosi Amendment required that the US executive director to the bank cast a negative vote on any bank project for which an environmental assessment had not been completed and made available to the board at least 120 days prior to the board vote on the project. What ultimately resulted was the inception of the "Tuesday Group"—consisting of various governmental agencies and NGOs. The group constitutes something of an "early warning system" to alert the US executive director to potentially problematic projects (Park 2005b, 128).

The IFC underwent a similarly painful process of public scrutiny and protest in 1992 with respect to the Pangue Dam project in Chile. Having approved some $170 million in loans to the Pangue project, the IFC came under intense pressure from a variety of NGOs and Chilean citizens groups, articulating concern regarding the potential impacts of the dam network on surrounding peoples and environs. The Tuesday Group brought these concerns to the attention of the US executive director, who had also met personally with a number of the NGOs involved. In 1992, the director abstained from voting on the project (Park 2005a, 104–105).

In 1995, the IFC created the Operations Evaluation Group, tasked with conducting a postproject review of IFC compliance with bank safeguards. In 1999 the IFC also created the office of the independent Compliance Advisor/Ombudsman (CAO), specifically tasked to facilitate, consider, and report on claims by private persons and groups—including environmental injury claims—occurring as a result of IFC projects (Seymour and Dubash 2004). In 2001, IFC senior management asked the CAO to undertake a review of its 1998 safeguard policies.

As a result of the CAO report, in 2004 the IFC began its own review of its safeguard policies, ultimately resulting in the adoption on February 21, 2006, of the IFC's landmark Policy on Social and Environmental Sustainability, Performance Standards, and Disclosure Policy (collectively, the Sustainability Framework) (IFC 2009a, 1; see also Wright 2007). In addition, in 2007 the IFC published a road test document on human rights impact assessment (IFC 2007b), further expanding its scope of concern for social and environmental project impacts. In its 2007 annual report, the IFC began reporting on financial performance, environmental and social performance, and development impact—its triple bottom line—for the first time (IFC 2009a, 4).

In 2003, the IFC also joined ten private international banks to adopt the IFC sustainability approach[4] as standards to be applied to foreign direct investment project finance—the "Equator Principles" (Lawrence 2005, 6–7). As of October 2013, more than seventy-five "equator banks" representing more than 70 percent of global project finance in the developing world have acceded to these principles.[5]

The foregoing discussion reveals that the IFC has attained its present position as the result of external influence and pressure, and internal initiative and leadership. The impact of democratization on uptake of transparency is indeed evident in this, given the ascendant role of NGO scrutiny and pressure. However, the IFC has come to occupy, in its own right, a central position in global environmental and social practices with respect to foreign direct investment in the South.

Institutionalizing Transparency

We now turn to the application of these organizational changes and developments in specific IFC policies and programs, where it is evident that the institutionalization of transparency at the IFC has opened up space for local communities, including indigenous peoples, to enter the project approval and implementation process. The IFC follows the project environmental and social categorization scheme established initially by the bank: category A projects are those likely to have significant environmental and social impacts, which are "diverse, irreversible, or unprecedented." Category B projects are those with "limited" negative social and environmental impacts, which are considered to be remediable with existing technologies and management practices. Category C projects are those unlikely to have significant adverse social or environmental impacts; and financial intermediary projects are those that consist primarily of the funding of loan vehicles and finance institutions, although the IFC recognized in 2006 that some projects funded by involved institutions and funds may have potential impacts (IFC 2006g, 4). Of the 576 investment projects active as of IFC fiscal year 2012, only 17 are category A, 167 are category B, and 269 are category C. One hundred fifty-nine are financial intermediary projects (IFC 2013, 28).

We now trace the progression of the application of the Sustainability Framework and critical responses to it. The disclosure requirements set forth in table 13.1 have applied since 2006 to category A and category B projects.

The 2006 Sustainability Framework required disclosure of information by the IFC and by IFC clients for category A and category B projects. In the 2006 Policy on Disclosure of Information, the IFC refers specifically to its encouragement of its clients "to be more transparent about their businesses to help broaden understanding of their specific projects

Table 13.1
IFC Disclosure Framework 2006

Disclosing Group	What Information Is Disclosed	Disclosed to Whom?	Disclosed When?
IFC	1. Summary of proposed investment (IFC 2006f, para. 13) 2. Environmental and Social Review Summary (IFC 2006f, para. 14)	1. Disclosed on IFC website 2. Disclosed on IFC website	1. Prior to board approval 2. Category A projects at least sixty days prior to board approval (thirty days for category B projects)
IFC Compliance Advisor/ Ombudsman	1. Reports of complaints filed and the status thereof (IFC 2006f, para. 27)	1. Disclosed on the CAO website	1. When complaints are received
Clients	1. Relevant project information (IFC 2006g, paras. 10, 19) 2. Project contract payments (IFC 2006g, para. 22) 3. The existence and content of any client ESIA (IFC 2006a, para. 20) 4. For projects with potential risks and adverse impacts, full project disclosure to enable meaningful community consultation regarding the project (IFC 2006a, para. 21) 5. For projects with significant risks and adverse impacts, full project disclosure to enable "free, prior informed consultation" (IFC 2006a, para. 22) 6. Grievance mechanism (IFC 2006a, para. 23) 7. Must make periodic reports regarding client progress toward compliance with its environmental action plan (IFC 2006a, para. 26) 8. Grievance mechanism for labor complaints (IFC 2006b, para. 13) 9. Ongoing community engagement regarding community health and safety issues (IFC 2006c, para. 5) 10. Additional disclosures related to the physical or economic displacement of persons (IFC 2006d) 11. Distinct disclosure and engagement requirements regarding indigenous peoples (IFC 2006e, para. 9)	1. Affected communities 2. To the IFC and affected communities 3. To affected communities 4. To affected communities 5. To affected communities 6. To affected communities 7. To affected communities 8. To affected communities 9. To affected communities 10. To affected communities 11. To affected communities	1–5. For greenfield projects, prior to project implementation, otherwise, at inception of IFC involvement (except as noted) 6. And ongoing 7. Ongoing, at least annually 8-11. And ongoing

and of private sector development in general" (IFC 2006f, para. 6). In the view of the IFC, client commitment to accountability and transparency would increase overall project viability and profitability.

The 2006 Policy on Disclosure of Information identifies the types of information disclosed by the IFC, in particular information about the IFC and information about its activities. The stated purposes of these disclosures were to "enable its clients, partners and stakeholders (*including affected communities*) to understand better, and to engage in informed discussion about ... its contribution to development" (IFC 2006f, para. 8, emphasis added). The IFC adopted a presumption in favor of disclosure, with the limitations generally afforded financial institutions for client confidential and proprietary information (2006f, para. 9). Specific project documents provided by the IFC on its website for public scrutiny include the Summary of Proposed Investment, and Environmental and Social Review Summary, both to be made public prior to IFC board approval of the project (2006f, paras. 13, 14). These documents contain the IFC's categorization of the project, support for such categorization, and a description of the social and environmental impacts of the project to include development impacts and the particulars of community engagement.

As to client disclosure, the 2006 framework required sponsored corporations to disclose to and engage affected communities in a number of ways. In particular, the umbrella Policy on Social and Environmental Sustainability contemplated that the broad social and environmental aims of the IFC and its sponsored projects would best be met by the client's "regular engagement with local communities about matters that directly affect them" (IFC 2006g, para. 8). When projects had potentially "significant" negative impacts, whether a category A or B project, the IFC undertook to ensure "broad community support" (though not consent) among affected communities—a level of community solidarity assessed through the client's environmental impact assessment process (2006g, paras. 15, 20).

These aspirations and requirements, as embodied in the more general language of the 2006 Social and Environmental Sustainability Policy, were specifically implemented through the 2006 Performance Standards and the 2006 Policy on Disclosure of Information. In particular, Performance Standard 1 regarding social and environmental assessment and management required the client to engage affected communities and disclose to them any social and environmental impact assessment prepared by the client (IFC 2006a, paras. 19, 20). These disclosures were required to be made early in the project review process, before the commencement of project construction in any event, and throughout the project life. When projects retained potential risks and adverse (but not "significant") impacts to affected communities, clients were required to engage in a "consultation" process, based on prior disclosure of project data (2006a, para. 21).

Projects with "significant" adverse impacts required "free, prior and informed consultation" by which broad community support for the project was to be obtained (IFC 2006a, para. 22). As part of the ongoing transparency process, clients were also required to establish a grievance mechanism by which to obtain and respond to community complaints regarding the social and environmental impacts of projects (2006a, para. 23). This process was to be managed entirely by the client and is separate from the CAO program managed by the IFC, noted previously. Performance Standard 2 (labor and working conditions) required a specific grievance process to handle labor complaints (IFC 2006b, para. 13). Clients were required to submit periodic reports to affected communities reporting on progress in meeting their environmental action plan (IFC 2006a, para. 26). Performance Standard 4 (community health and safety) required clients to engage communities on an ongoing basis with reference to particular community health, safety, and security concerns (IFC 2006c, para. 5). Performance Standard 5 (resettlement) applied particular disclosure requirements to projects that required the economic or physical displacement of situated persons and communities (IFC 2006d). Performance Standard 7 (indigenous peoples) established specific disclosure and engagement procedures for projects that would affect indigenous peoples (IFC 2006e, para. 9).

The existence and operation of the CAO is also important in several respects. Reaching beyond mere distributive justice, the CAO enables local populations to wield a measure of power over clients and the IFC, holding them to account. This reflects capabilities and human rights justice by mediating the "enablement" called for by human rights scholars, and by advancing capabilities such as meaningful participation in the life of the community. Nonetheless, although e-mail complaints in any language are acceptable, anonymous complaints are not accepted, and going public by filing a CAO complaint still retains political and cultural barriers for many, mitigating somewhat the transparency benefits of the CAO program.

The IFC's own initiative in visiting project sites and meeting with community representatives, and requiring the same of clients, has resulted in some measurable empowerment of affected stakeholders. To that extent, capabilities and human rights international environmental justice is enhanced. Our study of some twenty category B projects, for example, revealed that in nearly every case, the IFC social and environmental staff made in-person visits to existing or projected project sites to meet with client personnel and affected communities. Indeed, the recent strengthening of the stakeholder engagement process, discussed in the following, deepens the reach of corporate transparency under the IFC by requiring clients to develop a specific stakeholder engagement plan and by the IFC's commitment to disclose its basis for finding "broad community support." These changes do not, however, fundamentally alter the emphasis of the IFC on client responsibility and initiative—an issue to which we return in the conclusion.

Effects of Transparency

The impacts of these disclosure policies at the IFC are perhaps clearest in the context of stakeholder feedback expressed in the Sustainability Framework review and revision process. When the IFC board approved the 2006 Sustainability Framework, it required the department responsible for the Sustainability Framework to undertake, within three years following implementation, a review of the policies and practices employed. In the course of conducting this review, the IFC engaged in significant levels of transparency. First, the IFC published its own *Report on the First Three Years of Application* (IFC 2009a), in which it engaged in a systematic analysis of the strengths and weaknesses of the framework. It also proposed a global and comprehensive process of consultations to obtain the views of government (including the members of the Tuesday Group) and civil society on needed areas of improvement (IFC 2009b). This included the solicitation of written comments on the shortcomings of the Sustainability Framework, web-based dialogues hosted by IFC social and environmental staff, and in-person consultations with interested persons, hosted by the IFC in many of the major cities around the world. The IFC also identified more than thirty specific communities affected by post-2006 projects to consult with regarding the effectiveness of the Sustainability Framework, the performance standards in particular (IFC 2009c).

Although the IFC did not make most submissions to it public, it did periodically summarize the overall content of comments and complaints received and made these summaries available on its website. In addition, some NGOs and government agencies posted their submissions on their own websites. One submission, endorsed by more than one hundred international NGOs, was delivered to the IFC in March 2010, relatively early in the consultation process (Civil Society Organizations 2010). In this submission, a number of issues with the Sustainability Framework were identified which implicated transparency issues explicitly. In particular, the NGO submission alleged specific implementation issues, particularly the need for the IFC to better ensure that clients have engaged affected communities as required, have disclosed environmental and social impact assessment results, and have established meaningful grievance programs. The NGO submission also noted that host communities are frequently "not made aware that the IFC has invested in a given project, that environmental and social requirements apply, and that they have rights to information and accountability" (Civil Society Organizations 2010, 4).

In its submission, the World Resources Institute (WRI) pointed out that the application of the community engagement requirement was uneven and episodic, and recent CAO complaints made it evident that this was an underlying source of discontent and tension between clients and affected peoples (WRI 2010, 3). The WRI also joined a number of other entities in calling for free prior informed consent (and not merely consultation) by indigenous peoples for projects that would affect them (2010, 4). Echoing the NGO submission, the WRI noted that the IFC should require clients to inform communities of the IFC's involvement and of the availability of the CAO process and service (2010, 6).

The US Department of Treasury also submitted recommendations to the IFC. In these comments, made public at that time on its own website, the Treasury noted the need for the IFC to require clients to disclose to affected communities in a timely fashion the IFC's own "free prior informed consultation" and "broad community support" requirements (US Department of Treasury 2010, 6). The submission also called for the IFC to be more transparent about its process and basis for findings of broad community support, and stated that the IFC needed to be clearer about just what constituted adequate disclosure to affected communities under Performance Standard 1. In particular, the Treasury was concerned that high-risk category B projects may as a practical matter undergo insufficient public consultation and disclosure, leaving the affected community with little recourse (US Department of Treasury 2010, 8).

In the IFC's own summaries of inputs received at the various stages of the consultation process, it identified a number of additional transparency and disclosure concerns by interested stakeholders. Some, for instance, were concerned that the notion of "broad community support" be balanced with host state sovereignty to approve or disapprove the project (IFC 2010c, annex I).

The IFC reported that some stakeholders argued disclosure should include applicable human rights and others suggested that the institution needed to improve its disclosure of postapproval project supervision and monitoring reports. The IFC's June 2010 consultation in Washington, DC, attended by more than sixty academics, NGO representatives, and members of the US government, reiterated many of these concerns (IFC 2010d).

Notably, at the June 15, 2010, and March 3, 2011, consultations in Washington, DC, a number of participants expressed concern that financial intermediary projects were not subject to meaningful social and environmental disclosure of the impacts of the projects they would ultimately fund with the finances obtained from the IFC (IFC 2010d).

The World Bank's Independent Evaluation Group—an internal watchdog agency—also prepared a study for the IFC's review process, in which it recommended improved disclosure to affected communities, such as making additional social and environmental disclosures even after board approval of the project. The Independent Evaluation Group also recommended a more "robust" approach to applying the performance standards to financial intermediary projects (Independent Evaluation Group 2010). Finally, the CAO reviewed five IFC projects with which to construct its own report containing a number of transparency-related recommendations for the IFC (Compliance Advisor/Ombudsman 2010).

In response to these concerns, the IFC ultimately adopted a number of changes, outlined in table 13.2. First, the 2006 Disclosure Policy was renamed the Access to Information Policy (IFC 2012a), highlighting the benefits to recipients of increased disclosure. Rather than one-time disclosure under the 2006 guidelines, the IFC has now committed to make substantive project disclosures over the life of the project. This means that the IFC will be making environmental, social, and development outcome disclosures repeatedly during the tenure of the IFC's financial association with an investment project, based on data generated by the client and the IFC itself. These requirements also apply to financial intermediary projects, with the result that stakeholders will be able to obtain information regarding the application of IFC bank finance funds following initial disbursement to borrower banks. Furthermore, the IFC expanded its project category scheme to require borrower banks to disclose the most environmentally sensitive projects (IFC 2012d, para. 40).

The IFC has also undertaken to accelerate the timing of disclosure of the environmental and social profiles of high-risk projects, even in advance of the completion of the IFC's own reports (IFC 2012a, para. 36). Under the Access Policy, the IFC also commits to disclosing more details regarding its process of confirming broad community support (IFC 2012d, para. 32) and, in a new requirement applicable to indigenous peoples under certain circumstances, free prior informed *consent* to proposed projects (IFC 2012d, para. 31; see also new Performance Standard 7, IFC 2012c). The IFC has also committed to disclose the greenhouse gas emissions aggregate of its loan and investment portfolio (IFC 2012a, para. 11). Finally, the IFC now requires contract disclosure for all extractive industry projects, regardless of size and income (IFC 2012a, paras. 49–51). Significantly, the IFC is clear on retaining its rights and indeed obligations to hold business-related and proprietary information confidential, in a fashion customary for lending institutions whose clients must make their way in a competitive marketplace (IFC 2012a). We consider further in the following the ways in which this partial transparency might be enhanced.

Table 13.2
2011 Revisions to IFC Disclosure Framework

Disclosing Group	What Information Is Disclosed	Disclosed to Whom?	Disclosed When?
IFC	1. Ongoing project disclosure regarding social and environmental impact (IFC 2012a, paras. 40ff.) 2. New disclosure requirements for FI projects (IFC 2012d, para. 40) 3. More detail regarding the IFC's process of identifying "broad community support" (IFC 2012a, para. 32) 4. GHG emissions profile of its investment portfolio (IFC 2012a, para. 11.)	1. Disclosed on IFC website 2. Disclosed on IFC website 3. Disclosed on IFC website 4. The public	1. Following IFC board approval 2. Prior to IFC board approval 3. Prior to IFC board approval 4. IFC annual report
Clients	1. Must obtain "free, prior informed consent" from indigenous peoples under certain circumstances (IFC 2012a, para. 31; 2012c) 2. Contract disclosure by all extractive projects (IFC 2012a, paras. 49–51) 3. Must involve affected communities in monitoring when appropriate (IFC 2012d, para. 22)	1. Affected communities 2. To the IFC and affected communities 3. Affected communities	1. Prior to IFC board approval 2. Prior to IFC board approval 3. Ongoing

In response to comments by the Independent Evaluation Group, CAO, and NGOs, the IFC has strengthened its community and stakeholder engagement and consultation requirements. Clients will be required to develop a stakeholder engagement plan to provide greater specificity to the consultation process (IFC 2011, para. 27). The IFC has also expanded its guidance on consultation, in particular when projects retain potentially significant adverse impacts (2011, paras. 30ff). Further, the IFC now requires clients to involve affected communities in the project-monitoring process "where appropriate" (IFC 2012d, para. 22).

Although not addressing an environmental human right per se, the recent movement of the IFC to recognize the obligation of private enterprise to partner in promoting and protecting human rights is noteworthy. One result is an extensive guidance document, the *Guide to Human Rights Impact Assessment and Management* published online in June 2010 for conducting human rights impact assessment (IFC 2010a). The IFC publishes the guide in concert with the International Business Leaders' Forum and the Global Compact, and with the participation and endorsement of John Ruggie in the context of his previous work as Special Rapporteur on Human Rights and Business to the UN Secretary General.

Normatively speaking, the IFC has broadened its role as a global trendsetter for project finance disclosure standards, altering what is fairly expected of corporate actors seeking investment opportunities in the developing world. The substance of IFC and client transparency requirements has been enhanced by the Sustainability Framework review and update sequence. In addition, with regard to process, the rights and opportunities of affected communities to participate and meaningfully affect the project process have been materially strengthened. In concluding, we assess the import of these policies and changes.

Conclusion

Do the disclosure policies of the IFC promote a social liberal international environmental justice? If so, to what extent and how is transparency limited? How are the IFC's transparency practices shaped by the investment context, and how do they relate to public-private authority? Finally, what is the transformative potential of transparency in North to South foreign direct investment? In this section, we offer some answers in the context of the justice positioning of the IFC.

Based on our evaluation in this chapter of the IFC's programs and policies, we find that transparency at the IFC does materially advance a social liberal form of international environmental justice. In particular, the IFC's Sustainability Framework, as revised, does appear to take significant account of distributive international environmental justice. The IFC's disclosure requirements result in the shifting of considerable knowledge creation and dissemination burdens onto the client and away from local communities. Environmental information is more equitably distributed in this process, and with strengthened IFC monitoring and project supervision, ongoing engagement should entrench these equity gains. From a social liberal perspective, a possible next step would be to permit the monitoring process to be periodically audited by an outside third party.

As to the nature of information disclosed, although we acknowledge the necessity of holding some amount of proprietary information confidential, we suggest that a social liberal justice could be enhanced. Presently appeals of IFC denials of requests for information are submitted first to the IFC's own staff (IFC 2012a, para. 59), with a secondary appeal right to a panel of outside experts nominated by IFC management and approved by the IFC board of directors (2012a, para. 65). A more transparent and equitable outcome would be realized if a relatively independent third party, along the lines of the CAO, was accorded the responsibility and authority to evaluate the IFC's own confidentiality decisions much in the same manner as this advisor/ombudsman is now empowered to consider stakeholder complaints on other grounds. Given the quasi-public mandate of the IFC as the originator of the Equator Principles and its multilateral state-level membership, an appropriate analog would be the formal appeals process available to requesters of information under the United States' Freedom of Information Act.[6] A social liberal position would justify giving outside stakeholders greater access to the very decision process of determining what information should be considered confidential.

We note that advances in capabilities and human rights justice are presently somewhat limited, because of the broader investment context. First, to the extent that affected communities have a right to grant or withhold broad community support for the project, a significant measure of capabilities justice is served because local persons and groups enjoy an enhanced ability to direct their own destinies, as compared with a non-IFC investment scenario. This adds to distributive international environmental justice by virtue of shaping the uses of disclosed information, and by enabling recipient communities to understand and meaningfully act on the information received. We thus find some measure of empowerment for affected communities. This is strengthened by the IFC's own new commitment to disclose the basis for its finding that the client indeed obtained broad community support, and also to disclose over the life of the project all information that would be necessary to update and modify its initial disclosures regarding the project.

However, one area in which a social liberal justice could be enhanced is for the IFC to disclose not only how it ascertained that broad community support exists but also how it identified "affected communities" for the purposes of making that determination. Performance Standard 1 defines affected communities as "local communities directly affected by the project" (IFC 2012b, para. 1). This definition is not, we suggest, specific enough to render the process of identifying affected stakeholders itself sufficiently transparent.

Second, for the full realization of capabilities and human rights, local populations must also have an even greater measure of authority over the specifics of the project, a level of agency that has not been attained except with respect to indigenous populations in specified circumstances. According indigenous peoples a consent right was compelling to the IFC in the 2010–2011 revision process, due in part to broad agreement among NGO advocates and presumably because indigenous interests and constituencies are easier to identify. A more general consent right would, we contend, materially enhance a social liberal justice. As argued by the World Resources Institute, ensuring pre-project consent, particularly with respect to the more socially and environmentally invasive projects, can serve the interests of both investor and host community (Herz et al. 2007).

Jansen and Dubois observe in this book (chapter 5) that an information-based prior informed consent right may itself be problematic because of knowledge disparities and variance in regulatory capacities between disclosing and recipient entities. Similarly, Gupta notes that the procedural elements of a prior consent right may not ensure substantively improved outcomes (Gupta, this book, chapter 6). For our purposes, these obstacles highlight the *level at which* a consent right could and should be established. That is, if a consent right fails to deliver anticipated benefits to affected stakeholders, which entity is best placed to construct and impose such a right?

A general consent requirement could be built into the policies of the IFC, particularly because the Sustainability Framework applies even when national-level requirements impose lower standards and because the framework already contains a consent right for indigenous peoples. However, given the relatively greater variance in community identity and decision making outside the indigenous context, and that such diverse local community decisional rights are part and parcel of political and cultural structures instituted and maintained by the state, a general consent provision would more appropriately reside (and endure) in national-level regulation, implemented locally. The human rights arena is instructive here. The IFC requires that clients respect and thus comply with human rights, but also accepts that states are ultimately the actors that must ensure and enforce human rights (IFC 2010b, 2011, 2012d). A general consent right is not presently established in international human rights law. Thus as a matter of implementation the revised Sustainability Framework's requirement for transparent broad community support could then well serve the needed balancing of the right and calling of the state to confirm and protect the human rights of its people with the IFC's own undertakings and responsibilities.

This is quintessentially the issue of the public-private distinction with respect to authority and accountability, namely, the appropriate relationship among the client, the IFC, the host community, and the host state government. Social liberalism expressly contemplates that private business activity is subject to public deliberation and policy and, thus, transcends mere corporate volition such as corporate social responsibility. That is, under a social liberal ethos there will be occasions in which formal regulation is called for in the interests of public welfare and equity. Thus to call for states to establish a consent process is entirely within the ambit of a social liberal understanding. As to substance, promoting such a policy at the national or global levels should be sensitive to differing capacities, state values, and cultural systems without leading to fragmentation and downward harmonization. As to process, various states may choose to go about establishing a general consent right in varying ways, whether by local referendum, formal legislation, or some hybrid thereof. We would note here that state-imposed consent rights—whether implemented at the national or local level—should nonetheless be consistent enough to ensure that one state or region's policies do not cancel out the effect and benefits of those of another state and/or region.

Finally, with regard to transformative potential, the social liberal approach enables us to identify improvements in a liberal justice, while acknowledging the parameters within which these improvements take place. As we have observed, it is inherent in the IFC-client relationship that the largest share of meaningful disclosure is to be undertaken by clients, initially and throughout the project's lifetime. Because the long-term implementation of IFC policies is dependent on the initiative and discretion of project personnel, there remain limitations on the promotion of capabilities or human rights justice. Although the IFC has committed to strengthening its monitoring programs, there is no substitute for daily contact between the clients and affected persons and groups. That is, although IFC monitoring in its strengthened form will work toward improved project transparency, the IFC and other project finance institutions are associated only with a project for the duration of applicable financing and are necessarily less involved than the client during this term. If the project standards imposed by the equator banks are to take hold and improve life chances and quality of individual and collective existence, the client-community interface must thrive and persist. We find that this limits the transformative potential of the IFC's transparency policies. If the impacts of the IFC's own guidelines are to be realized outside the portfolio of IFC projects, and indeed within the IFC portfolio, some significant measure of corporate commitment to ongoing and meaningful transparency, and the credible use of such disclosures by affected stakeholders, is required. We suggest that the full realization of this level of personal commitment by corporate leadership, although encouraged by the IFC's policies and programs, is in the end beyond the ability of the IFC to fully ensure. The social liberal model would contend that this allowance for corporate latitude, infused with social equity concerns, is fundamental to the individual freedoms that it envisions. More radical approaches, whether social-democratic or communitarian, would argue that this limitation of the IFC resides not in the realm of individual volition, but in the ontological primacy and autonomy of the individual and thus the very nature of social liberalism itself.

We conclude that there is at the IFC measurable progress toward a transparency-based social liberal justice in the context of North-South foreign direct investment, but not without limitations and room for improvement. We recognize that our analysis leaves fundamental questions unanswered—for example, questions regarding the legitimacy of transparency-driven structural changes within the social liberal model, the sufficiency of social liberal empowerment, and the extent to which we should accept that international financial entities such as the IFC are for the foreseeable future content to remain thoroughly liberal institutions. We suggest that answers to such questions turn more on prior normative commitments than on the example of the IFC itself.

Notes

1. EPCRA; 42 USC §§11001–11050.
2. See OECD PRTR website http://www.prtr.net.

3. 22 USC §§ 262m-7.

4. Now also the Performance Standards and IFC Environment, Health and Safety Guidelines; see IFC (2007a).

5. See http://www.equator-principles.com.

6. See 5 USC §§ 552(a)(4) and (6).

References

Barry, John. 2001. Greening Liberal Democracy: Practice, Theory and Political Economy. In *Sustaining Liberal Democracy: Ecological Challenges and Opportunities*, ed. John Barry and Marcel Wissenburg. London: Palgrave.

Beckerman, Wilfred, and Joanna Pasek. 2001. *Justice, Posterity, and the Environment*. Oxford: Oxford University Press.

Civil Society Organizations. 2010. Submission by Civil Society Organizations to the International Finance Corporation Commenting on the Social and Environmental Sustainability Policy, Performance Standards and Disclosure Policy (on file with authors).

Compliance Advisor/Ombudsman. 2010. *Advisory Note on Review of IFC's Policy and Performance Standards on Social and Environmental Sustainability and Policy on Disclosure of Information*. Washington, DC: Compliance Advisor/ Ombudsman.

de-Shalit, Avner. 1995. Is Liberalism Environment-Friendly? *Social Theory and Practice* 21 (2): 287–314.

Garcia, Frank J. 2003. *Trade, Inequality, and Justice: Toward a Liberal Theory of Just Trade*. New York: Transnational Publishers.

Gupta, Aarti. 2008. Transparency under Scrutiny: Information Disclosure in Global Environmental Governance. *Global Environmental Politics* 8 (2): 1–7.

Herz, Stephen, Antonio La Vina, and Jonathan Sohn. 2007. *Development without Conflict: The Business Case for Community Consent*. Washington, DC: World Resources Institute.

Independent Evaluation Group. 2010. *Safeguards and Sustainability Policies in a Changing World: An Independent Evaluation of World Bank Group Experience (CODE2010–0048)*. Washington, DC: Independent Evaluation Group.

International Finance Corporation (IFC). 2006a. *Performance Standard 1: Social and Environmental Assessment and Management Systems*. Washington, DC: International Finance Corporation.

International Finance Corporation (IFC). 2006b. *Performance Standard 2: Labor and Working Conditions*. Washington, DC: International Finance Institution.

International Finance Corporation (IFC). 2006c. *Performance Standard 4: Community Health, Safety and Security*. Washington, DC: International Finance Corporation.

International Finance Corporation (IFC). 2006d. *Performance Standard 5: Land Acquisition and Involuntary Resettlement.* Washington, DC: International Finance Corporation.

International Finance Corporation (IFC). 2006e. *Performance Standard 7: Indigenous Peoples.* Washington, DC: International Finance Corporation.

International Finance Corporation (IFC). 2006f. *Policy on Disclosure of Information.* Washington, DC: International Finance Corporation.

International Finance Corporation (IFC). 2006g. *Policy on Social and Environmental Sustainability.* Washington, DC: International Finance Corporation.

International Finance Corporation (IFC). 2007a. *Environmental, Health and Safety Guidelines.* Washington, DC: International Finance Corporation.

International Finance Corporation (IFC). 2007b. *Guide to Human Rights Impact Assessment and Management: Road-Testing Draft.* June. Washington, DC: International Finance Corporation.

International Finance Corporation (IFC). 2009a. *IFC's Policy and Performance Standards on Social and Environmental Sustainability and Policy on Disclosure of Information: Report on First Three Years of Application.* Washington, DC: International Finance Corporation.

International Finance Corporation (IFC). 2009b. *Overview of Consultation and Engagement Process.* Washington, DC: International Finance Corporation.

International Finance Corporation (IFC). 2009c. *Performance Standard Review and Update Process: Consultation with Directly Affected Communities.* October 26, 2009, Draft for Comment. Washington, DC: International Finance Corporation.

International Finance Corporation (IFC). 2010a. *Guide to Human Rights Impact Assessment and Management.* Washington, DC: International Finance Corporation.

International Finance Corporation (IFC). 2010b. *IFC Policy and Performance Standards on Social and Environmental Sustainability and Policy on Disclosure of Information: Review and Update of "The International Bill of Human Rights and IFC Policies and Performance Standards.* Washington, DC: International Finance Corporation.

International Finance Corporation (IFC). 2010c. *IFC Policy and Performance Standards on Social and Environmental Sustainability and Policy on Disclosure of Information: Review and Update of "Progress Report on Phase I of Consultation,"* January 11. Washington, DC: International Finance Corporation.

International Finance Corporation (IFC). 2010d. *Review and Update of the Policy and Performance Standards on Social and Environmental Sustainability and Policy on Disclosure of Information.* Washington, DC, Consultation, June 15. Washington, DC: International Finance Corporation.

International Finance Corporation (IFC). 2011. *Guidance Note 1—V 2: Assessment and Management of Social and Environmental Risks and Impacts.* Washington, DC: International Finance Corporation.

International Finance Corporation (IFC). 2012a. *Access to Information Policy.* Washington, DC: International Finance Corporation.

International Finance Corporation (IFC). 2012b. *Performance Standard 1: Assessment and Management of Environmental and Social Risks and Impacts.* Washington, DC: International Finance Corporation.

International Finance Corporation (IFC). 2012c. *Performance Standard 7: Indigenous Peoples.* Washington, DC: International Finance Corporation.

International Finance Corporation (IFC). 2012d. *Policy on Social and Environmental Sustainability.* Washington, DC: International Finance Corporation.

International Finance Corporation (IFC). 2013. *2013 Annual Report.* Washington, DC: International Finance Corporation.

Johnson, Stephen M. 2004. *Economics, Equity and the Environment.* Washington, DC: Environmental Law Institute.

Karkkainen, Bradley C. 2001. Information as Environmental Regulation: TRI and Performance Benchmarking, Precursor to a New Paradigm? *Georgetown Law Journal* 89: 257–370.

Lawrence, Shannon. 2005. *Retreat from the Safeguard Policies: Recent Trends Undermining Social and Environmental Accountability at the World Bank.* Washington, DC: Environmental Defense Fund Publication.

Meyer, Lukas H., and Dominic Roser. 2006. Distributive Justice and Climate Change: The Allocation of Emission Rights. *Analyse & Kritik* 28: 223–249.

Okereke, Chukwumerije, and Kate Dooley. 2010. Principles of Justice in Proposals and Policy Approaches to Avoided Deforestation: Towards a Post-Kyoto Climate Agreement. *Global Environmental Change* 20 (1): 82–95.

Park, Susan. 2005a. How Transnational Environmental Advocacy Networks Socialize International Financial Institutions: A Case Study of the International Finance Corporation. *Global Environmental Politics* 5 (4): 96–119.

Park, Susan. 2005b. Norm Diffusion within International Organizations: A Case Study of the World Bank. *Journal of International Relations and Development* 8 (2): 111–141.

Rawls, John. 1999. *A Theory of Justice.* Cambridge, MA: Belknap Press of Harvard University Press.

Rechtschaffen, Clifford, Eileen Gauna, and Catherine O'Neill. 2009. *Environmental Justice: Law, Policy and Regulations.* 2nd ed. Durham, NC: Carolina Academic Press.

Richardson, James L. 2001. *Contending Liberalisms in World Politics: Ideology and Power.* Boulder: Lynne Rienner Publishers.

Schlosberg, David. 2007. *Defining Environmental Justice: Theories, Movements and Nature.* Oxford: Oxford University Press.

Sen, Amartya. 1999. *Development as Freedom.* New York: Anchor Books.

Seymour, Frances, and Navroz K. Dubash. 2004. World Bank's Environmental Reform Agenda. In *Green Planet Blues: Environmental Politics from Stockholm to Johannesburg*, ed. Ken Conca and Geoffrey D. Dabelko. Boulder: Westview Press.

US Department of Treasury. 2010. *U.S. Comments on IFC Policy and Performance Standards on Social and Environmental Sustainability and Policy on Disclosure of Information*. Washington, DC: US Department of Treasury.

Wissenburg, Marcel. 2006. Liberalism. In *Political Theory and the Ecological Challenge*, ed. Andrew Dobson and Robyn Eckersely. Cambridge, UK: Cambridge University Press.

World Resources Institute (WRI). 2010. *Review of IFC Performance Standards and Sustainability Policy: Overview of Key Issues*. Washington, DC: World Resources Institute.

Wright, Christopher. 2007. From "Safeguards" to "Sustainability": The Evolution of Environmental Discourse inside the International Finance Corporation. In *The World Bank and Governance: A Decade of Reform and Reaction*, ed. Diane Stone and Christopher Wright. Aldershot, UK: Ashgate.

14

Transparency Revisited

Michael Mason and Aarti Gupta

This book has sought to understand the rise and effects of a "transparency turn" in global environmental governance. Across a range of environmental issue areas, a call for transparency informs actor expectations and institutional rules, expressed in practice by diverse governance forms. The preceding chapters featured a variety of cases of environmental governance in which information disclosure is employed to steer the behavior of selected actors—what, following Gupta, we label *governance by disclosure* (2008).

As is clear from the preceding contributions, our analysis of governance by disclosure takes stock of environmental governance initiatives led by state and nonstate actors, constructed at the international or transnational scale by crossborder regulation or other means of coordinated steering, and facilitated by information and communications technology, including web-based publicity and functionality. This global scaling encompasses vertical and horizontal alignments of decision-making authority, which recasts, rather than displaces, national policy spaces (Andonova and Mitchell 2010).

This bears affinities with wider scholarship on multilayered or multilevel governance (Bache and Finders 2004; Enderlein et al. 2010; Piattoni 2010) in the sense that all the contributors to this book identify complex configurations of transparency practices *across jurisdictional boundaries*. Even part 2 of this book on state-led multilateral transparency initiatives, which might be expected to mirror state-centered tenets of public international law, reveals disclosure modalities with innovative forms of governance—from the public compliance mechanism of the Aarhus Convention to the risk-based information management deployed in global rule making on pesticides and genetically modified organisms (GMOs). These cases illustrate vertical scalings of interstate authority renegotiated according to specific transparency demands from coalitions of state and civil society actors. A common finding, however, is that the resultant disclosure regimes are skewed in operation by market interests: insofar as multilateral disclosure of environmental information targets profit-driven business actors, states are often obliged to defer to powerful corporate constituencies.

The chapters in part 3 encompass examples of horizontal (or "networked") multilevel governance, in which disclosure regimes are mainly coordinated by, and targeted at, nonstate actors, respectively, global sustainability reporting, carbon disclosure, energy governance, environmental certification programs, and private investment projects in developing countries. These cases are emblematic of multilevel governance forms insofar as they feature task-specific, flexible steering with voluntary or contractual lines of accountability. Nevertheless, these analyses diverge as well from the functionalist claims of governance theory by treating information disclosure as more than just a regulatory strategy or means of organizational learning. They share with the other contributions to this book a *critical theoretical* perspective, one that problematizes the transparency turn by examining its differential development within broader political economic and discursive contexts, notably the unstable global dominance of market liberalism.

By embracing a critical take, the authors in this book also collectively acknowledge the unavoidable *normativity* (value-laden structure) and *materiality* of governance by disclosure. As Mol argues in chapter 2, the normative kinship often assumed between transparency and ideas of democracy does not necessarily correspond in practice with the disclosure regimes favored by private and state actors. A number of chapters respond to his thesis that transparency has "lost its innocence" in environmental governance: whether or not the authors accept this claim, there is common empirical interest in uncovering the normative background and content of selected transparency initiatives. Across the chapters, there is also an analytical concern with the materiality of transparency—the ways in which governance by disclosure is shaped by the (potential) environmental harm being governed and its location in wider circuits of material production and consumption. This is most evident in emerging issue areas of environmental rule making, because governance responses crystallize around novel problems and risk profiles. This is illustrated in the efforts to find disclosure settings adequate to the challenges of governing transgenic crops, genetic resources, and forestry-related climate mitigation actions (reducing emissions from deforestation and forest degradation—REDD+) in developing countries. In these examples, what to be made transparent is subject to intense political negotiation, largely because the scope and content of environmental information (and its disclosure) generates uneven costs and benefits.

From these shared points of departure, the contributors to this book address the three research questions outlined in the introduction: Why transparency now? How is transparency being institutionalized? What effects (normative, procedural, and substantive) is it having? They also consider the working hypotheses attached to each question. These include H1—adoption of transparency in global environmental governance is driven by democratization and marketization; H2—institutionalization of transparency decenters state-led regulation and opens up political space for new actors; and H3—transparency is more likely to be effective under contexts resonant with the goals and decision processes of both disclosers and recipients. The response of the contributors to these research questions and hypotheses enables us to offer concluding observations on the transparency turn in global environmental governance in this chapter. What follows is a comparative review of their findings on the uptake, functioning, and effects of transparency as information disclosure.

Embracing Transparency

Throughout this book, there is a methodological sensitivity to the historicity of governance trajectories featuring transparency as information disclosure. Within particular issue areas, governance by disclosure is, of course, influenced by context-dependent conditions and events in which multiple participants, with differential resource endowments and capabilities, move to support, shape, or oppose specific transparency norms and practices. Nevertheless, in corroboration of H1, there is strong evidence from the chapters that democratization and marketization are leading societal drivers of the uptake of transparency in global environmental governance, although the marketization logic, as we subsequently argue, tends to dominate and is often in tension with ideas of democratic accountability.

By itself, the democratization driver is by no means straightforward in scope and content. Given that most chapters acknowledge *close linkages between the transparency turn and democratization,* it is tempting to conclude that information disclosure regimes derive from, or foster, liberal democratic structures of decision making, for example, the rapid diffusion of transparency in the new democracies of Central and Eastern Europe. Yet as Florini and Jairaj show in their context-setting chapter

3, the freedom-of-information laws and regulations of liberal democracies are *not the only* precursors of information disclosure in global environmental governance, because environmental information disclosure has also appeared selectively in closed political systems, notably China. Indeed, they identify transnational learning as an autonomous influence of the crossnational uptake of information disclosure.

In his chapter on the Aarhus Convention, Mason similarly notes that although states and international organizations have played a significant role in spreading liberal democratic framings of transparency, other (social democratic) understandings are evident as well in promoting uptake of transparency. These findings suggest that it is more accurate to identify the transparency turn as a consequence of, and influence on, democratization understood more generally as *discursive or deliberative modes* of social coordination (Dryzek 2010). Shorn of its association with liberal democratic state forms, this shifts methodological attention to the specific engagement of public discourses and their application to those public or private authority holders responsible for producing significant harm or risks (Mason 2005).

Florini and Jairaj also view democratization in such broader institutional terms, noting that information disclosure tends to gain traction in societies and political systems broadly hospitable to the idea of transparency, including where civil society is sufficiently autonomous to call for, and act on, disclosed information. This holds as well for transnational scalings of civil society action. The contributions on multilateral rule-making in part 2 thus identify NGOs and activist coalitions as triggers for information disclosure in global regulation of pesticides and genetic resource flows (although this was *not* the case for GMOs and REDD+, where disclosure is being pushed for by developing and developed countries, respectively). Civil society actors are similarly often the catalysts for information disclosure as a means of enlarging communication (and sometimes participation) on issues of collective concern in the cases of horizontal disclosure-based governance explored in part 3. Salient examples here include the Publish What You Pay campaign (Van Alstine), the Carbon Disclosure Project (Knox-Hayes and Levy), and transparency policies within the International Finance Corporation (Ehresman and Stevis).

Yet this general trend hides important differences in institutional practice. In chapter 12, Auld and Gulbrandsen report that although civil society pressure prompted the adoption of environmental certification schemes, and the Forest Stewardship Council carried through a commitment to open, inclusive deliberation in environmental standard setting, this democratic imperative was displaced in the Marine Steward-ship Council by a technocratic preference for expert-led governance. This is akin to the techno-statist imperative for disclosure in global pesticide governance identified by Jansen and Dubois in chapter 5.

At the same time, many contributors to this book concur that *marketi-zation represents a dominant driver of disclosure regimes within global environmental governance.* By marketization, we refer to market-based mechanisms of resource allocation and attendant ideological discourses justifying market liberalization as the default setting for collective choic-es. Market liberalism, which has globally reasserted itself after the 2008 financial crisis, remains the dominant political doctrine and economic project privileging market-based solutions to environmental challenges.

Across the chapters in this book, there is a striking presence of mar-ket liberal political interests. In the cases of state-mediated governance, market liberalism justifies the exclusion of private businesses from direct information disclosure obligations (Aarhus Convention), the dilution of prior informed consent (PIC) norms (global governance of pesticides and GMOs), and the use of commercial confidentiality to block public access to information (bioprospecting). There are also demands for disclosure issuing from market-based actors, typically in response to perceived costs and benefits arising from the management of environment-related risks (Clapp and Helleiner 2012, 492–493). Thus, marketization tends to favor environmental information disclosure when it assists private investment decisions (Global Reporting Initiative, Carbon Disclosure Project, Inter-national Finance Corporation), reinforces intellectual property rights (en-vironmental certification, genetic resources), and facilitates the commodi-fication of environmental resources (REDD+). The spread of market-led transparency is not of course predetermined; however, there is a high level of consent and acquiescence (hegemony) to political, economic, and dis-cursive forces favoring marketization as a development path.

The tension between democratic and market-based pressures for dis-closure of environmental information reflects wider processes of econom-ic globalization and their socioecological impacts. Global networks of production, trade, and investment create what Dingwerth and Eichinger (chapter 10) label *markets for transparency* to facilitate the commodi-fication of environmental information flows. Yet, at the same time, the transboundary pathways of environmental risk and harm generated by global interdependence drain legitimacy from states unable to protect

326 Michael Mason and Aarti Gupta

their populations: multilateral transparency initiatives thus become one collective response to help address deficits in environmental regulation. This interplay between private and public authority accounts, we argue, for the double-sided character of the transparency turn in global environmental governance. On the one hand, environmental disclosure regimes are embraced as *market facilitating*, correcting for market inefficiencies and creating new markets by valuing previously unrewarded ecosystem resources or services (e.g., genetic resources or forest carbon stocks); on the other hand, they serve *market-forcing* demands for legitimation in the face of perceived accountability deficits (e.g., extractive industries transparency and environmental certification schemes). The contradictory imperatives here reflect an innate tension between the marketization and the democratization of environmental responsibility—one played out in political negotiations and struggles over the appropriate governance role for transparency.

Institutionalizing Transparency

It would be surprising if there were no connection between the broader societal drivers just highlighted and the means by which global transparency and disclosure initiatives have been institutionalized. The information infrastructures detailed in the preceding chapters are, to be sure, diverse and often complex: the operational norms and rules structuring particular transparency practices have their own dynamics—shaping and shaped by immediate contexts of application. Nevertheless, we argue that the contributions to this book reveal structured patterns of disclosure relating to distinctive configurations of actors and institutional practices. More precisely, we find partial validation for our hypothesis (H2) that *institutionalization of transparency decenters state-led regulation and opens up political space for new actors.* However, as we discuss next, we modify this confirmation of H2 to acknowledge the comparative finding that state sovereign powers are not necessarily diluted or weakened by global transparency initiatives.

The contributors to this book examining multilateral disclosure regimes observe ways in which *transparency qualifies state sovereign authority.* In one sense, this is no more than the negotiated pooling of sovereign powers well established in public international law, which creates state entitlements and duties on the basis of the voluntary consent of parties to a treaty. This is evident, for example, from the general access to information provisions in the Aarhus Convention and the more specific disclosure rules on chemicals and genetic resources in, respectively, the Rotterdam Convention and Convention on Biological Diversity. However, a salient trend identified here—one not captured by H2—is a *transition from soft law to hard law institutional practices* and the role of various international organizations (including UN agencies) in selling transparency to state actors. There were voluntary guidelines and codes preceding the establishment of hard law disclosure regimes in all three multilateral environmental agreements just mentioned, although this was *not* the case with information disclosure for trade in GMOs—covered by a different protocol under the Convention on Biological Diversity—in which contentious, protracted negotiations have resulted in very limited mandatory disclosure rules. Van Alstine similarly shows in chapter 11 how the Extractive Industries Transparency Initiative prompted the Ghanaian government to institutionalize mandatory transparency in domestic legislation on the oil industry. These findings corroborate the claim that nonbinding soft law institutions are a favored vehicle for ambitious environmental norms, which, depending on growing internal credibility and/or external political support, are then converted into hard law rules (Skjærseth et al. 2006).

From the chapters, it is evident that the propensity of states to adopt multilateral transparency norms and rules reflects their sensitivity to perceived domestic and external impacts on sovereign authority, constituting what we label a *geopolitics of information disclosure* that reflects power differentials within and between developed and developing countries. A prominent institutional logic is the external promotion by developed countries of transparency norms and rules with high political and policy currency in their domestic contexts. This is reflected, for example, in the uptake of pollutant release and transfer registers under the Aarhus Convention and the diffusion of transparency obligations compatible with market liberal property rights in global regulatory negotiations on genetic resources and GMOs. Beyond multilateral environmental agreements, there is also the US- and European-led instillation of transparency as a good governance norm in global energy governance (chapter 11) and the International Finance Corporation (chapter 13). Both chapters reveal that international organizations can effectively promote information disclosure practices to domestic governments (typically from the global South), though this is less likely if such organizations are perceived by target audiences as lacking governance competence or credibility (Bauhr and Nasiritousi 2012).

By contrast, many developing countries resist information-disclosure obligations that impinge on their sovereign authority over natural resources and on their domestic regulatory space. In their chapter on the measuring, reporting, and verification (MRV) systems under development within the REDD+ provisions of the climate change convention, Gupta and colleagues cite China's opposition, in these terms, to general third-party review and validation of its voluntarily assumed carbon-mitigation activities, and Brazil's opposition to international verification of its REDD+-related claims. Furthermore, poorer developing countries may be unable to renegotiate, contest, or apply multilaterally negotiated stringent MRV standards because of capacity constraints.

Environmental disclosure rules within multilateral treaties sometimes acknowledge these inequalities and, at least in principle, facilitate technological and financial assistance as well as differentiated obligations. Jansen and Dubois highlight this for the Rotterdam Convention, which features a less burdensome notification procedure for developing countries in bringing hazardous imported pesticides under the treaty's PIC procedure. Similarly, developing countries with major genetic resources are favored by the PIC rules of the Nagoya Protocol to the Convention on Biological Diversity—in this case, obliging resource users (typically private corporations from developed countries) to provide information on the agreed legal and commercial terms of their access. Orsini et al. (chapter 7) view the negotiation of such information disclosure as evidence that developing countries are asserting sovereign control over the use of their genetic resources, questioning the premise of H2 that the institutionalization of transparency in global environmental governance necessarily decenters state-led regulation. Nevertheless, the hypothesis still carries explanatory weight, they argue, because key disclosure provisions on the origin of genetic resources are nonbinding.

Contestation over PIC norms and rules is arguably the key flashpoint for the geopolitics of environmental information disclosure, though the alignment of national interests varies with the issue area. For example, the governance-by-disclosure regime for trade in GMOs, negotiated under the Cartagena Protocol to the Convention on Biological Diversity, has pitted leading GMO exporters (including the United States, Canada, Australia, and Argentina) against bulk agricultural commodity importers in developed and developing countries. Here the operative PIC norm of advance informed agreement navigates geopolitically between the two groups, although poorer developing countries are again at a disadvantage relative to the mature transparency and regulatory infrastructure of the

European Union and Japan. Indeed, Gupta concludes in chapter 6 that the minimal disclosure obligations of the Cartagena Protocol benefit least those who might need them the most.

The institutionalization of transparency through PIC norms and rules demonstrates as well how *private authority inflects multilateral disclosure arrangements.* Thus, information disclosure relating to the use of genetic resources is, according to Orsini and colleagues, ultimately about the regulation of private market actors as users, deferring to a market liberal logic protective of their intellectual property rights. A similar truncation of disclosure duties for relevant private actors is evident in the governance of pesticides and transgenic crops: in both cases, the political mobilization of agro-corporate interests has significantly influenced the formulation of mandatory disclosure obligations. To recall the marketization process previously mentioned, the market-facilitating, rather than market-forcing, institutionalization of disclosure is also structurally favored by a global political economy underpinned by market liberal norms, such as nondiscrimination in trade and investment and the caveat emptor (let the buyer beware) dictum. Additional evidence for this in PIC regimes relates to the use of commercial confidentiality opt-outs by market producers to restrict public information to, at best, that which is already available.

For the chapters in part 2 addressing horizontal forms of disclosure in which nonstate actors play a lead role, the marketization process is omnipresent, as we noted previously, in driving the uptake of transparency, with consequences for its institutionalization. Within these governance initiatives, transparency is a means of correcting those informational deficits or asymmetries that lead to environmental goods and services not being accorded a "socially optimal" market valuation. Surveying a variety of governance forms, these contributions document how nonfinancial reporting on environmental and social impacts is being institutionalized, and how it is offsetting significant political pressure for state-led regulation.

Arguably, the dominant institutional logic across these case studies is *the key role of nonstate intermediaries in managing and/or validating information disclosure, confirming H2 on the significant governance role for new actors.* In chapter 13 by Ehresman and Stevis, the intermediary is an intergovernmental organization (the International Finance Corporation) applying transparency to its internal social and environmental standards. These standards feature public disclosure of environmental and social information by private sector clients, including requirements to engage with the affected communities of proposed investment projects. Van Alstine similarly demonstrates the role of NGOs in deepening global transparency about financial transfers in the extractive industries sector. In the cases of voluntary nonfinancial reporting, covered by the Global Reporting Initiative, the Carbon Disclosure Project, and nonstate certification schemes (the Forest Stewardship Council and Marine Stewardship Council), there is ongoing bargaining between nonstate rule makers and corporate disclosers over the quantity and quality of disclosed information. One example is the tension between the information comparability goal of the Global Reporting Initiative and the discretion permitted to companies to incentivize their self-reporting. Similarly, Auld and Gulbrandsen note, in chapter 12, the trade-offs involved in the difficult political steering between buy-in of corporate disclosers and public credibility of the host schemes. The FSC and MSC delegate assurance-accreditation roles to independent auditors, who in turn face self-regarding pressures not to antagonize participating businesses. There is also a trend for nonfinancial reporting to become commodified: the Carbon Disclosure Project and Global Reporting Initiative have, directly or indirectly (via commercial intermediaries), generated paywalls (i.e., barriers to accessing webpage content without payment) behind which enhanced interpretive products are available, weakening their public transparency claims.

The above discussion also highlights the complex configurations of public and private authority structuring the institutionalization of transparency in global environmental governance. Governance by disclosure encompasses public (mandatory) initiatives conditioned by market liberal interests and private (voluntary) disclosure under the shadow of hierarchy, even as both sources of authority are shaped to a greater or lesser degree by civil society actors. This is in line with an important ongoing debate that questions a sharply drawn public-private divide in global environmental governance processes and outcomes (e.g., Pattberg and Stripple 2008).

However, across the cases, greater disclosure of environmental information faces recurring barriers from what is regarded by power holders as the *legitimate, limited scope of transparency* under liberal environmentalism—notably, more openness from state actors than private actors, respect for private property rights, and a deference to commercial confidentiality. These limits are continually challenged by proponents of greater environmental transparency, who claim moral authority from well-established expectations of democratic accountability. Furthermore, despite technological advances in information availability and processing, there are still significant deficits and uncertainties impairing the generation of environmental information. We claim, nevertheless, that the partial transparency evident from the institutionalization of governance by disclosure studied in this book is delimited more by political-economic rather than by technical markers.

Effects of Transparency

In the introduction to this book, we presented as an overarching goal the analysis of the transformative impacts of governance by disclosure. To assess this systematically, we proposed a broad typology of effectiveness in order to capture a range of (potential) effects issuing from transparency as information disclosure—normative, procedural, and substantive. This conception reflects the critical theoretical stance of the book by acknowledging that disclosure practices are arenas of sociopolitical negotiation and are inherently normative, whether or not relevant actors make this explicit. Our selection of H3 as a hypothesis for this book reflected existing scholarship, positing that transparency is more likely to be effective under contexts resonant with the goals and decision processes of both disclosers and recipients (e.g., Fung et al. 2007; Hood and Heald 2006; Mitchell 2011; see also Mol, this book, chapter 2). However, consistent with our critical theoretical approach, we presented a directional version of H3 as well—that *in liberal environmental contexts, transparency, if adopted, will have minimal market-restricting effects*. We highlight in the following section the volume's findings on the transformative potential of transparency, by discussing the normative, procedural and substantive effectiveness of disclosure-based governance.

Normative Effects
As anticipated in our introduction, the most common normative goal underpinning the governance by disclosure initiatives examined in this book is the "right to know," addressed mainly to civil society recipients but also directed at states and corporate actors. For individuals (as citizens or consumers), the moral authority infusing the right to know echoes, as Mol notes in chapter 2, its affiliation with concepts of democracy and participation. Its strongest legal expression in global environmental governance is the access-to-information entitlement under the Aarhus Convention, where it attains the status of a universal human right with a nondiscriminatory application in all convention parties. Although the right to know also features prominently in the other examples of governance by

disclosure examined here, it is restricted to national settings (e.g., domestic right-to-know laws), subsumed within state-endowed treaty entitlements and the policy prescriptions of an international agency, or facilitated in actor- and sector-specific domains by civil society organizations.

Across all these manifestations—including Aarhus rights—the right to know provides a significant asset for political claims by citizens and states, but tends to be restrained or diluted by countervailing moral and legal norms, unsettling its governance legitimacy. The most potent of such norms are those underpinning the private authority of actors in market liberal systems of resource allocation; thus, the cases reveal that right to know is countered by norms of corporate voluntarism (Aarhus Convention, nonfinancial reporting systems), intellectual property rights (pesticides, genetic resources), and the caveat emptor (let the buyer beware) dictum (GMOs). Moreover, although state sovereign norms are sometimes used to challenge market actors to reveal more—for example, the assertion of sovereign natural resource rights by developing countries over genetic resources, as discussed in the ABS chapter—they can also be invoked to oppose environmental disclosure requests, as observed in the chapter on REDD+ MRV systems. In summary, *although right to know serves as a widely accepted normative justification for information disclosure in global environmental governance, its legal application tends to be compromised by the political deployment of market liberal or state sovereign norms.* This comparative finding confirms, for the case studies featured in this book, the directional version of H3 with regard to the normative effects of transparency.

Procedural Effects

When inviting contributors to consider the procedural effects of transparency, we emphasized governance by disclosure as due process—the openness and inclusiveness facilitated by disclosure—with the aim being not only to inform but also to empower. Procedural goals of disclosure include, as we suggested in the introduction, empowering information recipients to perform meaningful governance roles, notably holding disclosers accountable and making choices that are more informed. These two facets are connected, thus the procedural *quality* of information disclosure co-determines intended procedural outcomes. Here we single out the most salient cross-chapter comparative finding: the *limitations to the sustained empowerment of intended information recipients in global environmental governance,* which holds for both civil society and state actors. This means that the symmetry in goals and decision processes between disclosers and recipients assumed by H3 is *not* sustained, resulting in no clear validation of this hypothesis for procedural effectiveness. Although the transparency initiatives studied have delivered procedural openings tailored to particular disclosure contexts, these gains seem not to have led, as we argue subsequently, to significant empowerment gains for information recipients.

For *civil society recipients* of environmental transparency in national regulatory contexts, information is typically seen as a means to realize communicative and accountability gains vis-à-vis particular wielders of power, as chapter 3 by Florini and Jairaj shows. Of course, this linkage between transparency and public accountability is more problematic for global environmental governance, in which state sovereignty and higher information costs present major obstacles to civil society recipients of information seeking to hold foreign actors to account for transboundary environmental harm. Again, the Aarhus Convention has arguably made the greatest legal progress in ensuring transnational public entitlements to environmental information and noncompliance notifications as a way to empower through the conferral of procedural rights. Yet, as argued by Mason, there have been repeated procedural blockages by convention parties to public information requests, and this opposition is often justified in relation to the discretion allowed parties when implementing treaty obligations. The formal procedural rights for the public created by the Aarhus Convention are not mirrored, according to the research featured in this book, in disclosure regimes under the biodiversity and climate conventions facilitating the provision of information on different types of transboundary environmental risk.

Procedural shortcomings concerning access to information by civil society actors are also apparent from the chapters on global disclosure initiatives led by nonstate actors. In their contribution, Ehresman and Stevis identify room for improvement in the engagement of affected communities under the sustainability and disclosure policies of the International Finance Corporation. In the chapters on voluntary nonfinancial reporting and product certification, civil society actors are either a primary or a secondary recipient of information. The shared rhetoric across these regimes that disclosure is at least partly a means of public accountability thus falls short in practice. Across the Global Reporting Initiative, Carbon Disclosure Project, and environmental certification schemes, there are weaknesses in public participation at the systemic governance level and in terms of the usability of information for making accountability claims against disclosers. For example, although procedural openness is lauded in the transparency infrastructure of the Marine Stewardship Council, Auld and Gulbrandsen identify a closed decision-making structure and nontransparent accreditation process: this reduces opportunities for outsiders to hold the rule makers and disclosers to account.

There are good reasons to expect greater procedural effects when *states are environmental information recipients*. These include the formal equality of treatment bestowed on sovereign states by multilateral rule making and the extensive currency of disclosure norms in international environmental law, encompassing obligations on states to exchange information, notify, consult, seek consent, and monitor (Louka 2006, 120–126, see also Mitchell 1998). Rational choice theorists of environmental treaty making posit, in addition, that states have self-interest in fostering information disclosure as an efficient means of distinguishing cheaters from cooperators (Barrett 2003, 269–291). It is thus rational for states with mature governance by disclosure capacity to support capacity building of disclosure systems in poorer countries, thus generating credible data concerning transboundary environmental problems or improvements.

Several chapters in this collection identify such activities, including within the Rotterdam Convention, the Convention on Biological Diversity, and REDD+ MRV discussions within the climate change convention. What is striking, then, is the shared evaluation of authors that there has been little empowerment of poorer developing countries in terms of their capacity to generate and/or receive information flows prescribed by the selected multilateral environmental treaties. This holds for global governance of pesticide flows, GMOs, genetic resources, and forest carbon accounting for REDD+: each case study provides evidence of an unfair onus, placed de facto on poorer developing countries, to establish institutional frameworks for transparency conducive to the efficient implementation of relevant disclosure norms. A common reason for the underattainment of informational equity between states seems to be the disproportionate bargaining power of states (including emerging economies such as China, India, and Brazil) representing producer or extractive interests, and whose actions generate and entrench particular informational asymmetries.

It is noteworthy that developing countries lose out regardless of the category of state soliciting information and regardless of differences in the materiality of the environmental resources concerned. In the GMO case, involving mainly industrialized countries (GMO exporters) disclosing to potential importers largely located within developing countries, the latter—as *recipients*—have not secured requested levels of transparency. In the case of REDD+, certain developing countries struggle to—as *disclosers*—provide required environmental information to industrialized countries in their capacity as donors. Moreover, in access and benefit sharing relating to genetic resources, whereby access calls for disclosure from developing countries and benefit sharing calls for disclosure from developed countries, poorer states have been doubly disadvantaged by the institutionalization of transparency that favors quicker establishment of access versus benefit-sharing infrastructures. Whether developing countries are seeking disclosure or are required to disclose, the geopolitics of transparency reveals unequal structures of power harming their interests.

Substantive Effects
To recall from our introduction, governance by disclosure also includes substantive regulatory goals, such as reduced pollution emissions, risk mitigation, or conservation of biodiversity. The direct substantive effect often attributed by proponents of disclosure is that sharing of information will render producers of environmental damage or risk more responsive to regulatory pressures. For global environmental governance, in which substantive regulatory aims converge on the prevention and mitigation of significant transnational harm that must be appraised according to local vulnerabilities and values, this is a heavy behavioral burden to place on communicative processes. In these circumstances, the absence of substantive environmental standards in the procedure-centered Aarhus Convention is no surprise. Yet, as we also find, multilateral disclosure initiatives aiming to mitigate specific environmental problems also fail to avoid this burden. A revealing finding of this book is *how little evaluation there is within the global disclosure initiatives of their impact on environmental outcomes*. Despite the rhetoric accompanying disclosure initiatives about their potential to improve environmental outcomes or generate other substantive effects, assessing whether this is being achieved is not prioritized and/or little evidence is being generated about substantive impacts within the initiatives themselves.

Multilateral environmental agreements are certainly animated by harm-prevention goals, as outlined in the case analyses of disclosure-based global governance of pesticides, GMOs, genetic resources, and forestry-related climate mitigation activities. Yet there are negligible treaty-based data sources on the environmental effects of the relevant disclosure measures, for reasons that include evaluative uncertainties (genetic resources), measurement difficulties (REDD+), and a preoccupation with trade effects rather than environmental outcomes (pesticides). It is instructive that, in the GMO case, various countries have bypassed the

Cartagena Protocol by opting for unilateral moratoria or bans to achieve environmental and health protection goals.

In the voluntary realm of (non)financial reporting systems, which focus on managerial processes, the evidence on substantive environmental effectiveness is also slight. Dingwerth and Eichinger note the rising number of corporate reports registered under the Global Reporting Initiative, but caution that lack of data specificity and comparability prevents any meaningful assessment of environmental performance patterns. Knox-Hayes and Levy reach the same conclusion in relation to carbon disclosure systems that, they claim, do not appear to be shifting core product or marketing strategies in a low-carbon direction. The revenue transparency initiatives examined by Van Alstine are not directly geared to reducing environmental harm or risk: it is notable, however, that the contract transparency they promote has, so far, not led to voluntary or mandatory disclosure on environmental effects in the oil and gas industries.

Of the various other voluntary disclosure systems studied in this book, nonstate environmental certification schemes provide the most detailed information on the environmental impacts of disclosed corporate practices. Auld and Gulbrandsen label this *outcome transparency,* which in principle captures regulated and unregulated behaviors causing relevant environmental effects, thereby enabling a systematic evaluation of product certification. Their careful study of the Forest Stewardship Council and Marine Stewardship Council shows that, even here, major challenges remain in connecting disclosure with actual improvements in environmental performance—for example, by tracking substantive environmental effects over time. As with mandatory governance by disclosure, the monitoring and analysis of environmental outcomes by voluntary disclosure systems is still in its infancy.

In summary, *there is insufficient evidence from the case studies on this category of effects to confirm H3*—that global transparency initiatives have greater environmental effectiveness when governance contexts are resonant with the goals and decision processes of both disclosers and recipients. That the various governance by disclosure initiatives studied here have so little self-evaluation of their substantive environmental impacts provides prima facie evidence, we argue, that they do not equip those who receive such information to make effective accountability claims against targeted actors causing significant environmental harm. In a global political economy dominated by market liberalism, this seems to offer support to our directional version of H3 *that transparency has minimal market-restricting effects*; substantive market-forcing effects are not apparent from the disclosure examples analyzed here. Instead, transparency in the service of environmental service valuation, commodification or market facilitation, is a more likely scenario, as revealed by the genetic resources, forest carbon and GMO examples. However, this finding would benefit from more extended comparative analysis, with a stronger methodological focus on mapping differentiated environmental effects of specific transparency initiatives.

Conclusion: The (Il)legitimacy of Transparency

The relatively recent embrace of transparency as a governance mechanism in the global environmental realm cautions against too quick a dismissal of its potential to generate substantive environmental improvements. This is also because substantive effectiveness demonstrates regulatory competence and is therefore an important wellspring of political legitimacy. Furthermore, the transformative scope of governance by disclosure goes beyond substantive impacts to include important normative and procedural effects as well. As shown by the contributors to this book, however, these latter effects are being circumscribed in practice by market liberal norms. We conclude by considering here whether transparency-based governance faces a *legitimation deficit*, fed also by the uncertainty and lack of evidence relating to the environmental effectiveness of governance by disclosure.

The global transparency turn derives, in part, from a democratization impetus to governance, creating expectations among domestic and transnational publics that information disclosure will facilitate accountability claims against state and nonstate actors responsible for producing significant environmental harm or risk. This implies that disclosure-based governance is seen as a politically legitimate approach in the global environmental realm. Disclosure also fosters political legitimacy insofar as it enriches public understanding of what is proper in relation to the collective decisions of (potential) harm producers. Here the *critical theoretical* perspective adopted in this book is highly relevant: examining governance by disclosure according to its own terms of reference draws attention away from systemic configurations of political and economic authority shaping informational entitlements and capabilities. In this sense, transparency was never "innocent" of wider structures of political and economic power. If so, making clear the situational contexts of its use is necessary to securing its emancipatory promise in given circumstances.

Critical theoretical analysis thus seeks to explain the restless dynamic between legitimacy and effectiveness associated with governance by disclosure. Neither outcome admits simple methodological access at transnational and global scalings. The inadvertent, indirect harm typically associated with transboundary environmental problems lends many transparency initiatives an air of experimentation concerning their intended substantive effects, and legitimacy becomes less feasible when expected from steering mechanisms coordinating dispersed decision makers and affected publics. Furthermore, as the contributions to this book reveal, there remains a political struggle over the legitimate arenas for disclosure rule making and implementation, across diverse contexts and across hybrid configurations of state and nonstate authority. There are, to be sure, cogent suggestions that increasing transparency in state-led (vertical) and nonstate (horizontal) multilevel governance can increase political legitimacy, if fed into more inclusive, deliberative systems of decision making (Bernstein and Cashore 2007; Dryzek and Stevenson 2011).

However, it may also be that increasing transparency will instead amplify the current legitimation deficits in global environmental governance, by locating the systemic sources of harm production in broader relations of political and economic power (Newell 2008). Alternatively, transparency itself may be rendered ever more illegitimate as a mechanism of governance, if it takes on forms that belie its promise. Yet, if a consequence of this is *resistance and transformative politics*, rather than functional effectiveness within the strictures of market liberalism, then the democratization driver of transparency may well prevail. Whether or not this comes to pass, the metamorphosis of transparency as a central tenet of global environmental governance will continue to command increasing attention in the years to come.

References

Andonova, Liliana B., and Ronald B. Mitchell. 2010. The Rescaling of Global Environmental Politics. *Annual Review of Environment and Resources* 35: 255–282.

Bache, Ian, and Matthew V. Finders, eds. 2004. *Multi-level Governance*. Oxford: Oxford University Press.

Barrett, Scott. 2003. *Environment and Statecraft: The Strategy of Environmental Treaty-making*. Oxford: Oxford University Press.

Bauhr, Monika, and Naghmeh Nasiritousi. 2012. Resisting Transparency: Corruption, Legitimacy, and the Quality of Global Environmental Politics. *Global Environmental Politics* 12 (4): 9–29.

Bernstein, Steven, and Benjamin Cashore. 2007. Can Non-state Global Governance Be Legitimate? An Analytical Framework. *Regulation and Governance* 1 (4): 347–371.

Clapp, Jennifer, and Eric Helleiner. 2012. International Political Economy and the Environment: Back to the Basics? *International Affairs* 88 (3): 485–501.

Dryzek, John S. 2010. *Foundations and Frontiers of Deliberative Governance.* Oxford: Oxford University Press.

Dryzek, John, and Hayley Stevenson. 2011. Global Democracy and Earth System Governance. *Ecological Economics* 70 (11): 1865–1874.

Enderlein, Henrik, Sonja Wälti, and Michael Zürn, eds. 2010. *Handbook on Multi-level Governance.* Cheltenham, UK: Edward Elgar.

Fung, Archon, Mary Graham, and David Weill. 2007. *Full Disclosure: The Perils and Promises of Transparency.* New York: Cambridge University Press.

Gupta, Aarti. 2008. Transparency under Scrutiny: Information Disclosure in Global Environmental Governance. *Global Environmental Politics* 8 (2): 1–7.

Hood, Christopher, and David Heald. 2006. *Transparency: The Key to Better Governance?* Oxford: Oxford University Press.

Louka, Elli. 2006. *International Environmental Law: Fairness, Effectiveness and World Order.* Cambridge, UK: Cambridge University Press.

Mason, Michael. 2005. *The New Accountability: Environmental Responsibility across Borders.* London: Earthscan.

Mitchell, Ronald B. 1998. Sources of Transparency: Information Systems in International Regimes. *International Studies Quarterly* 42: 109–130.

Mitchell, Ronald B. 2011. Transparency for Governance: The Mechanisms and Effectiveness of Disclosure-Based and Education-Based Transparency Policies. *Ecological Economics* 70 (11): 1882–1890.

Newell, Peter. 2008. The Political Economy of Global Environmental Governance. *Review of International Studies* 34 (3): 507–529.

Pattberg, Philipp, and Johannes Stripple. 2008. Beyond the Public and Private Divide: Remapping Transnational Climate Governance in the 21st Century. *International Environmental Agreement: Politics, Law and Economics* 8 (4): 367–388.

Piattoni, Simona. 2010. *The Theory of Multi-level Governance.* Oxford: Oxford Univeristy Press.

Skjærseth, Jon Birger, Olav Scram Stokke, and Jørgen Wettestad. 2006. Soft Law, Hard Law, and Effective Implementation of International Environmental Norms. *Global Environmental Politics* 6 (3): 104–120.

Contributors

Graeme Auld is an associate professor at the School of Public Policy and Administration, Carleton University, Ottawa, Canada.

Klaus Dingwerth is an assistant professor in political theory of global governance at the University of St. Gallen, Switzerland, and a professor at the Institute for Intercultural and International Studies (InIIs) at University of Bremen, Germany.

Milou Dubois holds an LLM in law and politics of international security from the Vrije Universiteit Amsterdam. She is now a trainee project manager at the Province of Friesland in the Netherlands.

Timothy Ehresman is a visiting assistant professor of political science at the University of the South-Sewanee, Tennessee, United States.

Margot Eichinger holds a master's in International Relations from the University of Bremen and Jacobs University Bremen, Germany, and is now working as a project manager for Deutsche Gesellschaft für Internationale Zusammenarbeit (GIZ) GmbH, Eschborn, Germany.

Ann Florini is a professor of public policy at the School of Social Sciences, Singapore Management University, Singapore, and a non-resident senior fellow of the Brookings Institution, Washington, DC, United States.

Lars H. Gulbrandsen is a research professor and director of the Global Environmental Governance Programme at the Fridtjof Nansen Institute, Lysaker, Norway.

Aarti Gupta is an associate professor at the Environmental Policy Group, Department of Social Sciences, Wageningen University, the Netherlands.

Bharath Jairaj is a senior associate at the World Resources Institute, Washington, DC, United States.

Kees Jansen is an associate professor in the Knowledge, Technology and Innovation Group, Department of Social Sciences, Wageningen University, the Netherlands.

Janelle Knox-Hayes is an assistant professor at the School of Public Policy, Georgia Institute of Technology, Atlanta, United States.

David Levy is a professor of management and Associate Dean in the College of Management, University of Massachusetts, Boston.

Michael Mason is an associate professor at the Department of Geography and Environment, the London School of Economics and Political Science, United Kingdom.

Arthur P. J. Mol is a professor in environmental policy, Department of Social Sciences, Wageningen University, the Netherlands, as well as the director of the Wageningen School of Social Sciences, and a professor in environmental policy at Tsinghua University, Beijing, China.

Sebastian Oberthür is a professor and the academic director at the Institute for European Studies at the Vrije Universiteit Brussel, Brussels, Belgium.

Amandine Orsini is a professor of international relations at the Université St Louis, Brussels, Belgium.

Till Pistorius is an assistant professor at the Institute of Forest and Environmental Policy, University of Freiburg, Germany.

Justyna Pożarowska is a researcher at the Institute for European Studies at the Vrije Universiteit Brussel, Brussels, Belgium.

Dimitris Stevis is a professor in the Department of Political Science at Colorado State University in Fort Collins, United States.

Esther Turnhout is an associate professor at the Forest and Nature Conservation Policy Group, Department of Environmental Sciences, Wageningen University, the Netherlands.

James Van Alstine is a lecturer in environmental policy and program manager of the MSc Sustainability (Environmental Politics and Policy) in the Sustainability Research Institute, University of Leeds, United Kingdom.

Marjanneke J. Vijge is a PhD researcher at the Environmental Policy Group, Department of Social Sciences, Wageningen University, the Netherlands.

Index